Abroad in America: Visitors to the New Nation 1776–1914

Illustrations selected by
    ROBERT G. STEWART, *Curator*
    MONROE H. FABIAN, *Associate Curator*

Historian's Staff
    AMY E. HENDERSON, *Assistant Historian*
    JEANETTE M. HUSSEY, *Research Historian*
    CLAUDIA K. JURMAIN, *Researcher*

BEVERLY JONES COX, *Curator of Exhibitions*

JOSEPH MICHAEL CARRIGAN, *Chief of Exhibits Design and Production*

RUSSELL BOURNE, *Editorial Consultant*

MARVIN SADIK, *Director, National Portrait Gallery*

Abroad in America:

Visitors to the New Nation 1776-1914

Edited and with an Introduction by
MARC PACHTER, *Historian, National Portrait Gallery*

Co-edited by
FRANCES WEIN, *Editor, National Portrait Gallery*

Published in association with the
National Portrait Gallery, Smithsonian Institution
by
Addison-Wesley Publishing Company

*Reading, Massachusetts · Menlo Park, California · London ·
Amsterdam · Don Mills, Ontario · Sydney*

LIBRARY OF CONGRESS CATALOGING IN PUBLICATION DATA

Main entry under title:

Abroad in America: Visitors to the New Nation 1776–1914.

Essays written to accompany the exhibition at
the National Portrait Gallery, Smithsonian Institution.
Bibliography: p. 303
Includes index.
1. United States—Description and travel—1783–
1848—Addresses, essays, lectures. 2. United
States—Description and travel—1848–1865—Addresses,
essays, lectures. 3. United States—Description
and travel—1865–1900—Addresses, essays, lectures.
4. Visitors, Foreign—United States—Addresses,
essays, lectures. I. Pachter, Marc. II. Wein,
Frances. III. National Portrait Gallery, Smithsonian Institution.
IV. Smithsonian Institution. Washington, D.C.
E164.A27   917.3′04′0922   75-39542
ISBN 0-201-00031-8

Contents

Foreword

In these pages, the National Portrait Gallery highlights the observations of European, South American, Asian, and African visitors to the United States during the first century-and-a-half of its existence as a nation. The twenty-nine essays written by foreign writers, each discussing a compatriot's journey to the New World, and by American specialists in the cultures of other travelers, trace across time and from many vantage points the emergence of this country. *Abroad in America* is, however, not only about the opinions of earlier observers of this land, but also, ineluctably, a contemporary compendium of international attitudes. This is entirely appropriate because America has ever been a place characterized by almost constant change, a nation which even after two centuries of the most accelerated growth in human history is still in the process of becoming.

After his first visit to America in 1842, Charles Dickens wrote, "I do fear that the heaviest blow ever dealt at liberty will be dealt by this country in the failure of its example to the earth." A quarter of a century later, during his second visit, Dickens withheld such absolute judgments and said instead of the country: "It is a good sign, may be, that it all seems immensely more difficult to understand than it was when I was here before."

Whether America can yet be what the founding fathers intended, and immigrants before and since have dreamed it would be, remains to be seen. However, so long as change is possible, the promise lives. "Hope, the great divinity," John Butler Yeats believed, "is domiciled in America."

MARVIN SADIK, *Director*
National Portrait Gallery
Smithsonian Institution

Acknowledgments

In preparing *Abroad in America: Visitors to the New Nation 1776–1914*, the National Portrait Gallery worked with museums from more countries around the world than ever before. Gallery Librarian William B. Walker with his assistants, Mrs. Katharine Ratzenberger and Mrs. Alison Abelson, Mrs. Doris Rauch of the Curator's Office, and Mrs. Carol Cutler, Public Affairs Officer, were all most helpful in establishing contact and translating incoming and outgoing correspondence with many of these museums. Miss Wendy Wick, Assistant Curator for Prints, located many prints throughout the country. Mr. Eugene Mantie of the photographic laboratory performed heroic work in providing photographs—in many cases improving immeasurably on the originals. And finally, Mrs. Eloise Harvey, Secretary to the Historian, dealt magnificently with the barrage of languages, telegrams, and manuscript drafts which went into the final preparation of this book.

Many other people have assisted in the collection of the material for this book and exhibition, and should be mentioned here: MR. CLIFFORD S. ACKLEY, *Assistant Curator, Department of Prints and Drawings, Museum of Fine Arts, Boston;* DR. KARL JOHN RICHARD ARNDT, *Clark University, Worcester, Massachusetts;* A. K. BARAGWANATH, *Senior Curator, Museum of the City of New York;* MRS. HÉLÈNE BALTRUSAITIS, *Fine Arts Consultant, Services Américains d'Information et de Relations Culturelles, Paris;* THE RIGHT REVEREND BISHOP ZOLTAN BEKY *and* MR. LASZLO ESZENYI, *the Hungarian Reformed Federation of America;* SWAMI BHASHYANANDA, *Vivekananda Vedanta Society, Chicago;* DR. FELIX BORNEMANN, *Charles Sealsfield Society, Stuttgart, Germany;* PROFESSOR DAVID BRANDENBURG, *American University, Washington, D.C.;* MILLICENT H. BRANDENBURG, *Washington, D.C.;* JOHN BULLARD, *Director, New Orleans Museum of Art;* MRS. GEORGIA B. BUMGARDNER, *Curator of Prints, American Antiquarian Society, Worcester, Massachusetts;* DR. ALFRED KAIMING CH'IU, *Rare Books Division, Yenching Library, Harvard University;* MISS WINIFRED COLLINS, *Assistant Librarian, Massachusetts Historical Society;* B. DAHLBACK, *Superintendent,* and M. ROSSHOLM, *Svenska Portrattarkivet, National Museum, Stockholm;* MRS. ALFRED W. DATER, JR., *Stamford Historical Society, Stamford, Connecticut;* HENRY W. DEARBORN; MS. SANNA DEUTSCH, *Registrar, Honolulu Academy of Arts;* DR. RICHARD W. DOWNAR, *Vice President, American Council of Learned Societies;* MR. ANDRIES EKKER, *Press and Cultural Counselor, Netherlands Embassy;* SANDRA EMERSON, *Department of Paintings, Museum of Fine Arts, Boston;* DR. ZLATICA FIALOVA, *Ministry of Culture, Prague;* THURMAN O. FOX, *Chief Curator, State Historical Society of Wisconsin;* MR. IRA GLACKENS, *Washington,*

D.C.; MR. JAN HARASZTHY, *Buena Vista Winery, Inc., Sonoma, California;* ROBERT HARLEY, *The Old Print Shop, New York;* DR. EINAR HAUGEN, *Professor, Program in Scandinavian, Germanic Languages and Literatures, Harvard University;* MITSUHIKO HAZUMI, *Counselor, Embassy of Japan, Washington, D.C.;* MARY HENDERSON, *Museum of the City of New York;* LA COMTESSE D'HÉROUVILLE, *daughter of the late Comte de Tocqueville;* MRS. CHANG SU HOUCHINS, *for her assistance in corresponding with our Japanese lenders;* DR. TSU-WANG HU, *son of Hu Shih;* PROFESSOR PHILIP HUANG, *University of California at Los Angeles;* MISS KATHLEEN JACKLIN, *Archivist, and* MISS BARBARA SHEPHERD, *Cornell University Libraries;* JAMES L. JACKMAN, *member of the Vedanta Society of Northern California;* EMIL L. JORDAN; NATHAN M. KAGANOFF, *Librarian-Editor, American Jewish Historical Society;* MADOKA KANAI, *Historiographical Institute, University of Tokyo;* PROFESSOR KAO CHII-HSUN, *Committee on the Hu Shih Memorial, Academia Sinica, Taipei, Taiwan;* JERRY KERNS, *Library of Congress;* JOHN KERSLAKE, RICHARD ORMOND, *and* SARAH WIMBUSH, *National Portrait Gallery, London;* MORITA KIYOSHI, *Yokosuka, Japan;* JOHN KORDEK, *United States Information Agency, Washington, D.C.;* ANDREW Y. KURODA, *Japanese Section, Orientalia Division, Library of Congress;* CHARLOTTE LA RUE, *Museum of the City of New York;* MR. KAI-HSIEN LIU, *Head of Chinese Cataloging Division, Yenching Library, Harvard University;* MR. ROGER LORT, *Vice President-Treasurer, Salzburg Seminar in American Studies;* CHARLES R. MEYER, *Cultural Attaché, American Embassy, Buenos Aires;* MRS. PERRY MILLER, *Cambridge, Massachusetts;* MR. WANG MING, *for his assistance with Chinese calligraphy;* EMIKO MOFFITT, *Curator, East Asian Collection, Hoover Institute, Stanford University;* AUGUST J. MOLNAR, *Executive Director, American Hungarian Foundation;* FRANCIS MOORE, *Baldwin, New York;* STEPHANIE MUNSING *and* BERNARD REILLY, *Library Company of Philadelphia;* MURAGAKI JIRO, *Tokyo;* N. FREDERICK NASH, *Librarian, Rare Book Room, University of Illinois, Urbana-Champaign, Illinois;* DR. ADA NISBET, *Professor Emeritus, University of California at Los Angeles;* JAIME E. OVIEDO, *Audiovisual Materials Coordinator, and* CHARLES L. HEADEN, *Photographic Librarian, Organization of American States;* MRS. JOHN DEWITT PELTZ; THE REV. JOHN L. PHARR, *Pastor, Fifteenth Street Presbyterian Church, Washington D.C.;* SWAMI PRABUDDHANANDA, *Vedanta Society of Northern California;* MRS. LOIS B. PRICE, *Portage Free Library, Portage, Wisconsin;* MRS. SUE W. REED, *Department of Prints and Drawings, Museum of Fine Arts, Boston;* DR. ALFRED A. REISCH, *Library of Congress;* LUIS MARIA RICCHERI, *Embassy of the Argentine Republic, Washington, D.C.;* MRS. MONAWEE RICHARDS, *Department of Drawings, Museum of Modern Art;* HAROLD RIEGELMANN, *Former Director, Hu Shih Memorial Scholarship Fund;* MICHAEL AARON ROCKLAND, *Associate Professor and Chairman, American Studies Department, Douglass College, Rutgers University;* HENRY B. RYAN, *Cultural Attaché, American Embassy, Oslo;* NADA SAPORITI, *Photographic Services, Metropolitan Museum of Art;* H. D. SCHEPELERN, *Curator, Nationalhistoriske Museum, Frederiksborg, Denmark;* MR. MICHAEL S. SHAPIRO, *Director, American Swedish Historical Museum;* G. V. SMIRNOV, *Curator of 19th Century Paintings, State Museum of Leningrad;* ROBERT C. SMITH, *Department of Art History, University of Pennsylvania;* SHANTI TAYAL, PH.D., *Executive Secretary, The Vedanta Society of Greater Washington, Inc.;* MISS GERDA TELGENHOF, *NRC Handelsblad, Rotterdam, Holland;* STEPHEN M. TIBER, *Hirshhorn Museum, Smithsonian Institution;*

Niels Toft, *Cultural Counsel, Embassy of Denmark;* Mrs. V. O. Ugbodaga, *Director's Office, Nigerian Museum, Lagos, Nigeria;* Fartein Valen-Sendstad and Jakob E. Ågotnes, *Aulestad, Bjørnstjerne Bjørnson's home, now a museum, Follebue, Norway;* Reverend Edmund Vasvari, *Washington, D.C.;* Swami Vidyatmananda, *Centre Védantique Ramakrichna, Gretz, France;* Cornelius C. Walsh, *U.S. Embassy, Warsaw, Poland;* Dr. Wilcomb E. Washburn, *Director of American Studies, Smithsonian Institution;* Mrs. Julia Westerberg, *Chicago Historical Society;* Dr. Walter Wieser, *Director, Bild-Archiv und Porträt-Sammlung, Austrian National Library, Vienna;* Miss Marjorie G. Wynn, *Research Librarian, Beinecke Rare Book and Manuscript Library, Yale University;* and Senator Michael Yeats, *Dublin, Ireland.*

Introduction

AMERICA was the China of the nineteenth century—described, analyzed, promoted, and attacked in virtually every nation struggling to come to terms with new social and political forces. Sure of her destiny, she commanded international attention. The Declaration of Independence appealed to the conscience of the world, the Revolution enlisted international support, and the Constitution thrust an unknown political personality into the society of nations. What had been a somewhat obscure, occasionally romanticized backwater of colonial exploitation became, virtually overnight, a phenomenon to be investigated, a political and moral experiment to be judged. Throughout the following century thousands of foreign visitors—reporters, social critics, and artists among them—took up the challenge.

What most of these travelers felt in common was a sense of intense curiosity about the future and about America as the country of the future. From its establishment as a liberal republic in the late eighteenth century through its development into what Gertrude Stein would call "the oldest country in the twentieth century," the United States has served the world as a lightning rod for opinion and confusion about the furious changes in modern life. Although republicanism and democracy clearly did not begin here, nor did the Industrial Revolution, this was the first arena given over entirely to new social ideas and to technological innovation, and often the first to show the benefits and to suffer the shocks of change. The history of foreign observation of the United States is therefore the history not only of our society, and of international reaction to it, but of the dilemma of modernism itself.

Passions ran high about this country in its first century because, more than the direction, the very definition of civilization seemed at issue. If human achievement was best expressed by prosperity rather than by great art, by equality rather than by elegance, by know-how rather than by sophistication, then the United States stood in the forefront of progress. If the reverse were true, then she was a backward culture and, more than that, a dangerous one because she challenged the traditional structure of civilization. In the literature of American travel, this battle of ideals was fought by unevenly matched forces. Although the conservatives did have an impact and even, for a time, seemed to dominate the field, the nineteenth century was primarily a liberal age, with most travelers committed to the American experiment. Yet America had a way of disconcerting even her friends, of befuddling their expectations. Progress, it turned out, could be ugly, and equality suffocating. The momentum of the society carried it far beyond the orderly bounds of the Ideal Republic, into uncharted regions. In the end, it was the liberals who began to wonder if civilization were at stake in America.

Our review of foreign observation begins in the late eighteenth century, when the attitude toward the future inaugurated by the United States was all optimism. We are no longer accustomed to thinking of ourselves as the hope of the world but, in the afterglow of the Revolution, we were exactly that. America offered a new beginning, a chance to create a rational society unburdened by obstructive traditions. Conditions were ideal—endless resources, a hard-working population with the habits of free men, and an enlightened leadership. It was that last advantage, remarkable in a society on the edge of the civilized world, which most appealed to the cautious liberalism of the Marquis de Chastellux, member of the *Académie Française* and officer with Rochambeau's French Expeditionary Forces in revolutionary America. Under the balanced leadership of George Washington—whom Chastellux's travel diary elevates to near sainthood—the new nation seemed in reach of public happiness.

Still, there were dangers. What would happen when a political community tossed out the old social restraints, removed the props from the human pyramid, and offered in their place the good will of a population "created equal?" In fact, as the eighteenth century saw it, citizens were unequal in property and talent, and therefore American prospects for success rested on maintaining a balance between the will of the people and the good sense of the leadership. Chastellux saw lurking behind the radiant figure of General Washington the uncomfortable presence of Samuel Adams, a radical democrat who could unleash forces no less dangerous to the rule of reason than the old arbitrary governments.

The United States turned into just the kind of rambunctious paradise of the average man that Chastellux had warned against. By the late 1820s, the Virginia and New England lines of aristocratic Presidents had yielded to the log-cabin administration of Andrew Jackson. The result, however, had not been chaos. Civilization, defined as order, had held. Alexis de Tocqueville, a young French aristocrat in Jacksonian America, uncovered the roots of this stability. It was a society in which everyone had a stake. The aggressive merchant, the "as-good-as-you-are" servant, the democratic bore at dinner parties all hung their sense of self-worth on the common ideals of popular sovereignty, equality, and enterprise. Individual aggrandizement had not come at the expense of the community because the Americans had shown a remarkable gift for organization—in town government, in business, and, most of all, in the myriad associations they put together for the prevention of this and the advancement of that. As a final bond, there was religion, which the Americans took very seriously. If equality was indeed the wave of the future—which Tocqueville did not doubt—then the United States had shown that order could coexist with jostling, leveling democracy.

But was this really civilization? A long line of British travelers in the early nineteenth century made their reputations by arguing that the United States, crude and bellowing, was a pariah among nations. Mrs. Frances Trollope was not the most sophisticated of these visitors, but she earned her preeminence by pouring the resentments which came of a three-year American residence into a lively and malicious account of American manners. What she had observed in Cincinnati, Ohio, then on the edge of the frontier, was human nature uncorseted, a shapeless mass of impulses. That the tooth-picking, tobacco-chewing Yankee and his sour-faced wife —who offset her husband's grossness by presenting a caricature of propriety—presumed to step onto the world stage ahead of polished Europeans seemed to her and to thousands of her English readers grotesque. Mrs. Trollope was not afraid to say so; she detested the idea of equality and the hypocrite who had spread it, Thomas Jefferson.

The Tory barbs hit their mark. Outraged American pride spawned a literature of self-defense, which included James Fenimore Cooper's heavy-handed *Notions of the Americans,* presented as the travel account of an *objective* Englishman, James Kirke Paulding's parody version of an English travel diary, *John Bull in America or the New Münchausen*, and a play in which Mrs. Trollope reappeared as the ridiculous Mrs. Wollope. By the time Charles Dickens wrote his *American Notes* in 1843, the shouting match between Great Britain and the United States had settled into ritual. Dickens, though no Tory, nevertheless felt compelled to remind his countrymen that America—always excepting Boston—was no fit place for an Englishman. His American critics found his comments a fresh occasion for resentment, and were unimpressed by the novelist's many favorable remarks about their country. In the end, all that was proven conclusively was that the Americans and the English could make each other very uncomfortable.

Americans were unable to hear, across the language barrier, other, friendlier voices. For every book by a condescending British visitor, there was another, written in German or in Spanish, in Polish or in Norwegian, which spiritually embraced the New Man. Mrs. Trollope's report on American vulgarity was not disputed by the enthusiasts, only her sense of its significance. The average Yankee was no exquisite, but he could read, he could vote, and he could stare down a prince. It was easy enough to call his social clumsiness barbaric, but for true barbarism one had to look to the blind obedience of the Argentinian gaucho, to the superstitious ignorance of the Russian *muzhik* (peasant), or to the drunken stupor of the Norwegian cotter. From the vantage point of societies with uneven distribution of wealth and little freedom, a community created for the benefit of the many, not the few, had set the right priorities.

The idealist visiting this country in the middle of the nineteenth century embarked on the moral equivalent of a Grand Tour. His itinerary was likely to include Philadelphia, as an example of rational city planning and Quaker benevolence; the factory towns of Massachusetts, and particularly Lowell with its working population of healthy young women totally unlike the factory drudges of Europe; Cincinnati, among the miracle cities of the West, which had suddenly emerged out of the wilderness; and at least one of the country's Utopian communities, perhaps Oneida in New York, or Robert Owen's New Harmony settlement in Indiana. Radically innovative public institutions encouraged happy speculation: orphan asylums free of the Dickensian pallor; free schools and libraries; insane asylums which preserved the dignity of the inmates; and a prison system, developed in the Auburn Penitentiary of New York, which imposed absolute silence as a new and, it was believed, humane means of prisoner control and rehabilitation. There was an air of achievement about the country, of inventiveness and well-being, which was intoxicating.

Still, it was surprisingly easy to grow weary of America. "They enjoy here," an irritated Tocqueville wrote home, "the most insipid happiness." The intensity and diversity of older societies had evaporated, in the attainment of universal prosperity, into middle-class blandness. For its celebrants, though, America's lack of fulsomeness, its monotony, was no more than a passing disappointment; but there was a darker side to the matter which many sensed and Tocqueville most fully appreciated. In an egalitarian society, there was as much flatness to the spiritual as to the social landscape, for only certain principles were tolerated, only certain ideas given expression. The pressure of community opinion squeezed the individuality out of a society of individualists. Democracy, then, had its price. Tocqueville's insight has come to seem more important now than in his own time. Modern social analysts see in him the prophet who anticipated the coming of the organization man, but to many of his contemporaries, for whom the very achievement of democracy was still miraculous, America's egalitarian uniformity was a luxury problem—like gout, a disease of the fortunate which the poor man would gladly risk.

There was, however, no down-playing one egregious failing of American life, the institution of slavery. It was the serpent in the garden, and each traveler approached it warily. The Austrian Charles Sealsfield, who noticed on his first trip the contrast between the neat prosperity of free Ohio and the moral and physical slovenliness of neighboring slave states, nonetheless learned, after he had purchased a Louisiana plantation, to live with the American contradiction. Few others were able to reach such a *modus vivendi* with the abomination; yet the Argentinian Domingo Faustino Sarmiento, for one, stressed that it was, after all, Europe which had implanted the poison, and that America was therefore trapped by her heritage. Harriet Martineau allowed no such excuses for the survival of slavery. A strong-willed English writer who belied the American impression that all travelers from the mother country were hostile to democracy, she held the New Man accountable to his own ideals and gave her support to the uncompromising Boston abolitionists. The most personal reaction, and the most poignant, was Fanny Kemble's. Married to the master of a Georgia plantation, the liberal English actress was trapped by her complicity in an institution she loathed, and vented her frustration in the writing of a journal of her own plague year.

Pro-American travelers were able to protect their democratic faith by treating slavery as a vile aberration. At the same time it was clear that this "peculiar institution" was undermining the stability of the republic. North and South were at each other's throats and, as Miss Martineau discovered when she was threatened with lynching for her abolitionist sympathies, at the throats of visitors who entered into the fray. Most foreign observers preferred to stay above the battle, discouraged as much by the ferocity of the abolitionists as by the brutality of the system they sought to eradicate.

Although few welcomed the outbreak of hostilities between the North and the South in 1860, there was a certain relief in seeing the issues finally resolved. Put in its best light, the war was a last chance for renewal. William Russell, war correspondent for the *Times* of London, saw in it the possibility of "purification" for the North's dollar-chasing society "which required a little humbling." Incensed Northerners dismissed Russell—"Bull Run

Russell" they called him after his detailed and, some said, malicious account of the Northern defeat at Bull Run, Virginia—as just another Englishman come now to gloat over the misery of the republic. He was run out of the country. Other travelers, more predictably, fastened their hope for the moral rededication of the Union on the blotting out of the slave power. As liberals viewed it, the war and its political aftermath, the reconstruction of the defeated South, amounted to what a young French reporter here in the late 1860s, Georges Clemenceau, called "a second revolution."

The rejoicing over America's rebirth survived even the collapse, in the 1870s, of all attempts to extend civil rights to freedmen. International opinion accommodated itself quite easily to the abject condition of America's blacks once it was no longer defined as slavery. Unnoticed behind the injustices of the brutal institution had been a flaw in American democracy which remained long after the Civil War: its principle of exclusion. The circle of privilege had been drawn more widely than in Europe, but it stopped at the barrier of race. From across that line, Edward Wilmot Blyden, a Liberian writer and statesman who traveled here throughout the late nineteenth century, judged the situation hopeless and urged his fellow blacks to abandon their American exile and return to Africa. Other travelers indulged in only casual speculation about the problem, one expecting that it would be resolved by black migration to Texas and Mexico, another placidly suggesting that the black population of the South would "slowly die out," as had that other inconvenient race, the American Indian.

Such callousness was not willful but automatic in an age which had, from our vantage point, several blind spots. These allowed an advanced society to ignore the political rights not only of blacks but of women. While it had become a convention among travelers to congratulate the New World woman on her social freedom, and on the consideration afforded her by chivalrous males, Harriet Martineau saw a similarity between the indulgences of females and the subjugation of blacks in their common exclusion from the political community. This point was lost, however, in the century's great preoccupation with the problem of class. *That* was the barrier reformers wanted to bridge, and America had led the way.

The United States, in the post-Civil War period, presented the world with a moral and material spectacle. Energies which had gone into decades of political and military hostilities were channeled into an industrial boom. The country operated now on a large scale and at a phenomenally accelerated pace. Where the steamboat had once been America's principal wonder, the late-nineteenth-century visitor was witness to an incredible array of inventions—gadgets and world-changing marvels both—which poured out of the Patent Office. Where Tocqueville had noted enthusiastically that only some thirty years had gone into the creation of Cincinnati, the Polish writer Henryk Sienkiewicz reported that Chicago had rebuilt itself, after its great fire, in two, and the English novelist H.G. Wells, when he heard of the San Francisco earthquake in 1906, expected the city to rise anew overnight. The vitality of the place, the sense that anything was possible here exerted a fascination which went beyond the usual theorizing. To John Butler Yeats, Irish painter and talker, American life was "a gigantic fair"; the Cuban poet José Martí found his symbol for America in Coney Island, and meant it as a compliment. There were those prepared to argue that all this was an accident of good fortune, the inevitable result of great natural resources and a fresh start, but to the converted, American prosperity and energy were clearly benefits of the national ideals.

During this period, for which Mark Twain coined the phrase "the Gilded Age," the United States reached a high point of political corruption and economic turmoil, but visitors could retain their sense of awe because their primary concern always lay with the failings of their own societies. America's very real limitations amounted to, at most, distractions from its central function as the fortunate opposite of a stagnant Holland, or a caste-bound India. The antipathy to Old World ways and conditions at the heart of pro-Americanism encompassed America's immigrant communities. Travelers were impatient to see "human slag," as one of them put it, reconstituted into New Men. The Russian-Jewish writer Sholom Aleichem was one of the few to see the immigrants from their own worried perspective. Others drew invidious comparisons between their transplanted compatriots and the radiant Yankees, and wondered how long it would take to instill in them the habits of prosperity.

Through the First World War, America would continue to stand for the triumph over age-old injustice, yet early signs of unease appeared in the travel accounts of the 1880s and 1890s. It was not the country's failings, but the implications of its successes which began to trouble the confidence of modernists. Corruption was an old sin in human experience which America could be expected to overcome. Where she sinned originally, however, was in the extravagance of her energy, in the relentlessness of her material development. What was attractive was also alarming. Chicago, as inevitable a stop for travelers now as Cincinnati had been some forty years before, stood as the principal case in point. At once a stunning achievement and a merciless environment, the city was all motion, without direction and beyond control. A great distance had been traveled from Philadelphia's planned society as emblem of the New World. The rational republic presided over by Washington had become Theodore Roosevelt's land of "the strenuous go." Growth, change, and material acquisition were pursued for their own sakes. That the future, however securely based in liberal ideals, could be aimless was, for foreigners, the unwelcome surprise of the American experiment. America had emerged as a modern society in ways hitherto unimagined, not as an Ideal Republic, but as a dynamo of impersonal social forces.

Over a century after the marquis de Chastellux's investigations into an enlightened New World, H. G. Wells, in 1906, expressed his own cautious hope for the future in America. Wells detected the stirrings of spiritual renewal, a harnessing again of energy to ideals in "the birth strength of a splendid civilization." His optimism was genuine but, like Chastellux, he wrestled with the suspicion that America might be swallowed up in the forces it had unleashed. The *philosophe* and the socialist both sensed that the country of the future gave little thought to anything but the present, living on its momentum alone. As the twentieth century progressed, liberals in increasing numbers turned away from America toward newer experiments which satisfied their need for structure and ideology. When, in 1919, a traveler announced that he had "seen the future and it works," he was, significantly, an American, the journalist Lincoln Steffens, abroad in the

Soviet Union. Yet if America has lost her appeal for visionaries, she has nonetheless come to dominate the modern age. It is unnecessary now to travel to the United States to witness the effects of technology, of uncontrolled growth, and of mass-based prosperity. We are no longer seen as the hope of the world; we have become its reality.

MARC PACHTER, *Historian*
National Portrait Gallery
Smithsonian Institution

Abroad in America: Visitors to the New Nation 1776–1914

Marquis de Chastellux, attributed to Mme Marie Louise Elisabeth Vigée-Le Brun,
oil on canvas, 1789. Le Comte Louis de Chastellux.

Chastellux's appointment as a major general in the French Expeditionary Forces in Revolutionary America gave him an opportunity to travel through the young country, and the satisfaction of seeing his political ideals come to life. This portrait, attributed to Mme Marie Louise Elisabeth Vigée-Le Brun, a favorite painter of Queen Marie Antoinette, was supposedly painted from memory in 1789, the year following Chastellux's death.

1
François-Jean Marquis de Chastellux
1734-1788

by Alan Charles Kors

In establishing among themselves a purely democratic government, had the Americans a real love of democracy? And if they have wished all men to be equal, is this not solely because, from the very nature of things, they were in fact equal, or nearly so? . . . Now such is the present happiness of America that she has no poor, that every man there enjoys a certain ease and independence, and that if some individuals have been able to obtain a smaller portion than others, they are so surrounded by resources that their future status is considered more important than their present situation. . . . Now, Sir, suppose that the increase of population reduces your artisans to the status they have in France and England—do you then believe that your principles are democratic enough so that the landholders and the opulent would still continue to regard them as their equals?

—Travels in North America

ALAN CHARLES KORS is currently an Associate Professor of History at the University of Pennsylvania. He is the author of *D'Holbach's Coterie: An Enlightenment in Paris,* a study of a circle of French *philosophes* which included the Marquis de Chastellux.

FRANÇOIS-JEAN MARQUIS DE CHASTELLUX was a military hero, Enlightenment philosopher, man of letters, historian, and pamphleteer, whose life and work captured the attention and admiration of his contemporaries. He was the author of two works, in particular, which secured his fame: *De la félicité publique* (1770; *An Essay on Public Happiness*), which Voltaire termed superior to Montesquieu's *De l'espirit des lois* (*Spirit of Laws*); and *Voyages de M. le Marquis de Chastellux dans l'Amérique Septentrionale* (1786; *Travels in North America*), which caught the public fancy with its eye-witness descriptions of the new republic.

Chastellux was born in Paris to one of the most prestigious families of the French nobility of the sword, and his mother was herself the daughter of the Chancellor of France. With such a pedigree, the young nobleman enjoyed a name and status which opened wide for him the prospects of a military career in the France of the *Ancien Régime*. Entering the service in his teens, he earned a series of rapid promotions, and by 1769 he held the rank of brigadier. Gradually, during peacetime, he severed his ties with the army, but when France decided to intervene in the American Revolution, Chastellux petitioned to return to active service.

By that time, he was a leading figure in the world of French thought and letters, one of the forty "immortals" of the *Académie Française,* and an active partisan of the camp of the Enlightenment. Chastellux enjoyed great success with his works on philosophy, aesthetics, and history, and he participated in all of the great causes of his day, writing pamphlets and treatises in support of inoculation, freedom of trade, religious toleration, and freedom of the press. The first nobleman (if not the first person) in France to be inoculated, in a conscious effort to demonstrate its safety to his countrymen, Chastellux was not without his courage and his sense of *noblesse oblige,* and he could not resist the opportunity to fight at the Americans' side.

He served in the United States from July 1780 until January 1783, one of three *maréchaux de camp* (major generals) directly under Rochambeau, who commanded the French expeditionary force. Although he did on occasion exercise direct military command in combat situations, most notably at the siege of Yorktown, Chastellux served primarily as liaison officer between the American and French commands, a natural function given his ease and fluency in English. In this capacity, he frequently traveled throughout the new nation, exchanging information and views with American military and political leaders. In the course of these journeys, he kept a diary. In 1786, upset by the appearance of inaccurate, pirated versions of these journals (which originally had been printed privately for his friends), Chastellux authorized the official publication in France of his *Voyages*. This work, his correspondence, and a *Discours sur les avantages ou les désavantages qui resultent, pour l'Europe, de la découverte de l'Amérique* (1787; which may be translated as "Discourse on the advantages and disadvantages which result for Europe from the discovery of America"), provide us with a French *philosophe's* first-hand observations on the nature, promise, and perils of the new United States.

Chastellux focused a remarkable mind and eye on the emerging republic. Ever curious, perpetually fascinated by the differences between America and France, and, as befitted a philosopher and historian, always eager to

Washington and his Generals at Yorktown, attributed to Charles Willson Peale,
oil on canvas, circa 1786. The Maryland Historical Society, Baltimore.

Chastellux, who appears here as the second figure from Washington's left, assisted Rochambeau (standing between them) at the conference in the spring of 1781, to plan the Yorktown
campaign. Although he was second in command of the French forces under Rochambeau, his
exact duties at Yorktown are unclear. One camp wag joked that "a certain general" had been
too involved in composing philosophical treatises to prepare for a surprise enemy attack.
Chastellux's military achievement was not brilliant, but he was an important intermediary and
earned a reputation as "the diplomat of Rochambeau's army."

find in the details of life in the United States the mores, customs, and
spirit of a unique people and civilization, Chastellux reflected upon far
more than military strategy and the political prospects of the revolution.
Impressed by American agricultural achievement, especially the rapid
clearing of new land, he described a nation in the act of mastering nature
by hard work and neighborly cooperation. Viewing the French countryside
as hopelessly bound to tradition and rote, he marveled at the ability of the
American farmer to learn from direct experience, to adapt behavior and
thinking to new needs, and to create ingenious solutions to problems that
others might find insurmountable. The United States was, for Chastellux,
"the country where hope springs eternal," and the creative settling of the
wilderness exhilarated him. After describing the process whereby forests
were converted into inhabited, prosperous centers of farming, he commented: "Such are the means by which North America, which one hundred
years ago was nothing but a vast forest, has been peopled with three
million inhabitants. . . . Four years ago one might have traveled ten miles
in the woods I traversed [between Hartford and Litchfield] without seeing a
single habitation." The rapidity of the construction of a "handsome wooden

A Design . . . of an American Settlement or Farm, by.James Peake after a drawing by Thomas Pownall, engraving, in *Scenografica Americana,* 1768. Library of Congress.

In his travels, Chastellux had occasion to observe more than military strategy. He was intrigued by America's phenomenal growth. Where there was once wilderness, small farms now dotted the countryside. The rapid settling of new land exemplified a people's spirit of cooperation.''

house,'' which he found superior to the dwellings of rural France, amazed Chastellux, but he understood the element of mutual assistance involved:

> *I shall be asked, perhaps, how one man or one family can be so quickly lodged? I reply that in America a man is never alone, never an isolated being. The neighbors, for they are everywhere to be found, make it a point of hospitality to aid the newcomer. A cask of cider drunk in common, and with gaiety, or a gallon of rum, are the only recompense for these services.*

Countless Americans, including the relatively humble, opened their doors to Chastellux, and he was fascinated by his hosts and, indeed, by the American family. He appreciated the open and direct communication of these free citizens, noting that, even among relative strangers, "all American conversation must end with politics." He did not, however, find American mores uniformly attractive. It took him some time to become accustomed to the American habit of drinking coffee with any and all meals; and, as a Frenchman, he did not enjoy the uses of etiquette in this country:

> *I have often had occasion to observe that there are more ceremonies than compliments in America. All their politeness is mere form, such as drinking healths to the company, observing ranks, giving up the right of way, etc. But all this comes only from what they have been taught, none of it arises from feeling; in a word, politeness here is like religion in Italy, all in practice and nothing from principle.*

Unmarried women, Chastellux observed, were allowed to be high-spirited and even publicly affectionate towards men; but married women were expected to be plain, dowdy, and domestic. This disturbed him: "American women are very little accustomed to give themselves trouble, either of mind or body; the care of their children, that of making tea, and seeing the house kept clean, constitute the whole of their domestic province." The rarity of children remaining, once married, in their parents' houses also struck Chastellux as a contrast with his native France, although, as a good theorist, he related this to the need for new settlements: "It is very rare for young people to live with their parents, when they are once settled in the world. In a nation which is in a permanent state of growth, everything favors this general tendency, everything divides and multiplies."

One particular aspect of the American character which seemed to affect Chastellux deeply was its generosity and lack of ferocity in war. A veteran of several cruel European campaigns, he found these traits of the rebel soldiers to be dramatic virtues. Commenting on the treatment of Burgoyne and his defeated army by the Americans, he added:

> I confess that when I was conducted to the spot where the English laid down their arms . . . I shared the triumph of the Americans, and at the same time admired their nobility and magnanimity; for the soldiers and officers beheld their presumptuous and sanguinary enemies pass, without offering the smallest insult, without suffering an insulting smile or gesture to escape them. This majestic silence offered a striking refutation of the vain declamations of the English general, and bore witness to all the rights of our allies to the victory.

An unabashed admirer of the spirit of the people whom he met on his travels, Chastellux nonetheless was cautious in his assessment of the

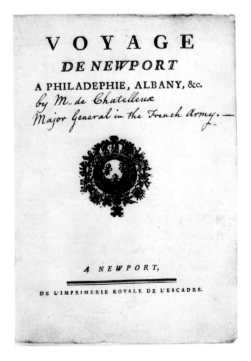

Title page of *Voyage de Newport a Philadephie, Albany, &c.,* 1781. Princeton University Library.

Part I of Chastellux's travel account, the *Voyage de Newport a Philadephie, Albany, &c.,* was printed by a Newport-based French fleet press in an edition of twenty-four copies. When Chastellux returned to Paris in early 1783, he circulated this three-volume manuscript among close friends, but publishers outside France soon began to print pirated versions of it, and he was eventually forced to consent to publish the entire work. A two-volume edition was issued in the spring of 1786.

Scene in a Quaker meeting house, by an unidentified artist,
oil on canvas, circa 1790. Museum of Fine Arts, Boston.

Chastellux found Philadelphia difficult to comprehend. It was a product of Quaker rule, and "these sectarians consider every species of private or public amusement as a transgression of their law and as a 'pomp of Satan.'" For Chastellux, the Quakers, with their planned parks, regular streets, and penitent approach to religion, had rendered Philadelphia too stark a city for comfort: "What a gloomy silence reigns in all your towns on Sunday! One would imagine that some violent epidemic, or plague, had obliged everyone to shut himself up at home."

future that awaited the American nation. He stressed the need for realistic expectations on the part of the citizens of the United States, fearing that their legislation would be too theoretical, that they would ignore what he believed to be the need of constitutions to reflect the "particular complexion . . . [and] temperament" of nations. His brief encounters with life in New England, the Middle Atlantic States, and Virginia had been enough to convince him that the regional differences in the United States were of vital significance. Europeans "would indeed be greatly mistaken were they to believe that all the thirteen states of America had invariably been animated by the same spirit, and imbued with the same feelings. They would commit a still greater error were they to imagine that these people all resemble each other in their forms of government, their manners, and opinions." Consequently, no uniform legislation or political system could succeed in providing stability for America.

New England, in Chastellux's analysis, had been peopled by colonists seeking religious freedom, and so had revolted out of principle against despotism. New York and New Jersey, by contrast, had been settled by individuals concerned with economic well-being, and had revolted only out of necessity, because of the restrictions imposed by the British. Virginia, which had been settled by soldiers and gentlemen, had preserved its "prejudices of nobility" and had revolted out of pride. Such differences were reinforced by climate, soil, size of landholdings, the place of trade in the economy, and other factors. As a result, legislators could not simply create a new society; they could only modify what history and conditions had bequeathed. The laws of Virginia, in the midst of the revolution, might be democratic, but "the very spirit of the government will always be aristocratic." New England, on the other hand, imposing on its citizens a barren soil necessitating constant labor, was by its geography and heritage more prone to equality. Pennsylvania, settled by diverse peoples with diverse traditions, and governed patriarchally by propertied wealth in a spirit of "the greatest tolerance and the most complete liberty," never had resolved its identity, contained too many contradictions, and, as a consequence, was "more attached to individual than to public liberty, more inclined to anarchy than to democracy." In fifty years, Chastellux predicted, the spirit and traces of these original characteristics still would be operative.

His conviction that laws and constitutions must be adapted to the particular structure of a society led Chastellux to fear the effect of any imbalance between socio-economic power and political power, a condition which he believed would produce constant discord. He saw that, during the Revolution, the constitution of each state tended toward full political equality, and he agreed that this was necessary for as long as the war with Britain lasted. Furthermore, each American might still realistically aspire to a near-equality with his fellow countrymen, because new land was available

M.ʳ SAMUEL ADAMS.

Samuel Adams, by Samuel Okey after John Singleton Copley, mezzotint, 1775. Massachusetts Historical Society.

To Samuel Adams, popular Revolutionary firebrand and a man he admired for the "energy and scope of his thought," Chastellux insisted that democracy in its pure form opened a veritable Pandora's box. All was well for the moment, "but the success of trade . . . [would] produce inequality of fortunes and of property." It was important, then, for power to reflect this inequality of condition. Adams reassured Chastellux that the Senate would serve as the repository of property, and would moderate, without destroying, the authority of the people. The Frenchman pronounced himself satisfied that Adams had ceased to be "an extravagant partisan of democracy."

on the frontier. As he warned Samuel Adams, however, in a discussion of
pure democracy:

> All this is very well for the present moment, because every citizen is about
> equally well-off, or can become so in a short time; but the success of trade,
> and even of agriculture, will introduce riches among you, and riches will
> produce inequality of fortunes and of property. Now, whenever this in-
> equality exists, the real force will invariably be on the side of property;
> so that if the influence in government be not proportioned to that of property,
> there will always be a contradiction, a struggle between the form of govern-
> ment and its natural tendency; the right will be on one side, and the power on
> the other; hence, the balance can only exist between the two equally dan-
> gerous extremes of aristocracy and anarchy.

For the record, Samuel Adams attempted to reassure him, explaining
that while the people might vote for their representatives in Massachusetts,
a moderating Senate of men of property, elected by men of property, would
always temper, without destroying, the authority of the people. Chastellux
expressed himself relieved to discover that Samuel Adams was no longer
"an extravagant partisan of democracy."

In Chastellux's view, the American people had an unparalleled opportunity to chart a course removed from the tragic and phantasmagoric
history of mankind. In his *De la félicité publique,* Chastellux had depicted
the masses of mankind as forever exploited by their masters, as forever
forced to sacrifice their own happiness upon the altars of war and superstition in order to serve the selfish interests and the selfish pride of the
hereditary or self-appointed rulers of mankind. Pessimistic about the ability
of the people to analyze the causes of their misery, and fearful of the
motives of demagogues, Chastellux saw only one hope for humanity: the
recognition, by the elites of the world, that working for the happiness of
the greatest number was the noblest and most rewarding life for a leader of
men. Such altruism constituted "enlightenment" for Chastellux; and in
America, the enlightened were the leaders of the new state. Therein lay
the great promise of the United States. Chastellux's enthusiasm for the
leaders of the American Revolution was almost unbounded. He met many
of them personally, and his impressions were strong. Washington was
"brave without temerity, laborious without ambition, generous without
prodigality, noble without pride, virtuous without severity," a man of
"perfect harmony." Franklin had "acted like Solon" in Pennsylvania,
giving that state "the best [laws] of which the country was susceptible."
Jefferson was "a Philosopher," a man who "loves the world only insofar
as he can feel that he is useful," who "had placed his mind, like his house,
on a lofty height, whence he might contemplate the whole universe."

For Chastellux, although the citizens of the diverse states were not
united in their experience, there was a common vision among the leaders
who emerged from those states. It was at that level alone that the nation was
unified, its activity concerted, and its ideals given substance and consequence. The political vision that Chastellux had articulated in France—of
enlightened rulers enjoying the confidence of the citizens—had been
realized in North America. It was the first Continental Congress, he learned,
that had awakened all Americans to the importance of the principle at stake
in the Bostonians' resistance: that one must not submit to a tax to which one

has not consented. In short, the people had been "brought to a decision . . . by the confidence they [had] placed in their leaders." The most enlightened Americans had *led* the people from indolence to useful activity, from indifference to foresight.

In contrast with Europe, whose reform was threatened by corruption, superstition, and endless war, America had proven a great success. The *philosophe* in Chastellux wondered, however, if this could be durable:

> *Can we then conclude that some virtue capable of restraining man's injustice really does exist; or are glory and happiness too recently established in America, for Envy to have deigned to cross the seas?*

Chastellux profoundly hoped that the American nation would pay sufficient honor to its useful leaders so that they might be satisfied with the rewards of such public service, and not seek their private happiness in abusive and arbitrary power.

The one profound shadow over the United States in all of Chastellux's accounts was the enslavement of blacks. Although he abhorred slavery, and saw it as inimical to everything that he admired in the American experience, Chastellux did not believe that it would or could disappear rapidly. His analysis of slavery centered on its function of providing higher status to poorer whites in essentially aristocratic regions of the United States, and he believed that this created a powerful community of interest in favor of its preservation. Eventually, he wrote, it would fall beneath the weight of reason and humanity, as education progressed and the contradiction of slavery to the American ethos of political equality became insufferable. His calm analysis of this institution offended many other progressive thinkers in France, and he excused himself by commenting that "I have always thought that eloquence can only influence the resolutions of the moment, and that everything which is not accomplished by time can only be accomplished by reason." He saw little immediate hope for remedying the situation of the blacks, free or enslaved, in the South, and seemed to hope ultimately that eventual miscegenation would render the problem moot, or that the progress of the trade relative to agriculture would eliminate the economic conditions which served as the utilitarian justification for the institution.

For Chastellux, his three years in America had opened his eyes to the promises and dangers of a great experiment in the life of mankind. Describing Samuel Adams, Chastellux had focused on his simplicity, his energy, the scope of his thoughts, and the potential danger of his illusions about the nature of man. Such a description came very close to Chastellux's own view of America as well.

Pavel Petrovich Svin'in, by D. Koch after an unlocated portrait by
Wassilij Andrejewitch Tropinin, engraving, reproduced in *Sketches of Moscow,* 1839. Library of
Congress.

Svin'in's portrait was painted some years after his return to Russia in 1813, from a two-year
assignment as secretary to the Russian Consul General in Philadelphia. During his stay, he
found ample time to produce the sketches and writings which became his *Picturesque Voyage
through North America.*

2

Pavel Svin'in

1787-1839

by Abbott Gleason

You should not look for profound philosophers and celebrated professors in America; but you will be astonished at the correct understanding of the humblest citizen respecting the most abstract matters. The son of a banker goes to the same school with the son of the poorest day laborer. Everyone studies the geography of his country, knows the rudiments of arithmetic and has a general idea about other sciences. That is why every peasant [muzhik] here not only would not be surprised by an eclipse of the moon or the appearance of a comet, but could discuss these phenomena with a fair degree of intelligence.

—A Picturesque Voyage through North America

ABBOTT GLEASON is Associate Professor of History at Brown University, and an associate of the Russian Research Center at Harvard. He is the author of *Emperor and Muscovite: Ivan Kireevsky and the Origins of Slavophilism* and is now working on a study of the beginnings of the revolutionary movement in Russia.

THE RUSSIAN–AMERICAN comparison was one to which nineteenth-century Europeans were strikingly prone. These two nations, with their uncertain relation to the European heartland, were coming to be regarded as heirs apparent. Alexis de Tocqueville's conclusion to the first volume of *Democracy in America* has come to be recognized as one of his most inspired prophecies. "Their starting point is different" he wrote, "and their courses are not the same, yet each of them seems marked out by the will of heaven to sway the destinies of half the globe."

The writings and watercolors of Pavel Svin'in, secretary to the Russian Consul General in Philadelphia (1811–1813), allow us to see what one Russian thought of America in the early nineteenth century. Believing that "no two countries bear a more striking resemblance than Russia and the United States," he set out to describe the new country with energy, curiosity, and a painter's eye. Svin'in did not often generalize about the United States; his descriptive powers with both pen and brush were greater than his analytical talents. The water-colors and drawings he produced were particularly valuable, because few American artists of the time thought it appropriate or worthwhile to record the scenes of everyday life which Svin'in found so interesting. As late as "the eve of the Civil War," Neil Harris has noted, "many critics insisted that an American genre painter was an impossibility. No one had lived long enough in any one spot to develop the appropriate local habits. There was no American low life and no American high life." Of the former, at any rate, Svin'in provided abundant evidence, and he makes us realize how idiosyncratic was the judgment of the American critics.

Svin'in was, on the whole, a sympathetic observer of the United States. Insofar as he had a formulated view, it was that of a Russian liberal of the Alexandrine age (the first quarter of the nineteenth century). He stands at the divide between Enlightenment and Romantic attitudes—without, perhaps, being very deeply touched by either. If he did not, like Catherine the Great, proclaim his "republican soul," he was prepared to appreciate many aspects of the republican form of government. His writings on America reveal a thoroughly eighteenth-century belief in progress which he combined with an intense curiosity about picturesque, non-European peoples and their customs, and a romantic love of scenery—particularly of the grand and impressive variety.

Pavel Svin'in was born into a well-to-do gentry family on June 7, 1787. About his family background we know almost nothing, but he received the best and most humanistic education available in the Russia of his day at the Boarding School for the Nobility (*Blagorodnyi pansion*) attached to the University of Moscow. In those days, the scions of "good families" did not attend Russian universities, which were the preserve of the sons of the lower gentry and the offspring of priests and lawyers preparing for a career in the bureaucracy. Svin'in's interest in the visual arts was sufficiently developed so that, after graduating with honors from his fashionable preparatory school, he spent some time at the Academy of Fine Arts in St. Petersburg.

No later than the summer of 1806, however, Svin'in was already embarked on his career as a diplomat. Over the next fourteen months, he was attached to the staff of a Russian admiral and participated in the rather desultory campaign against the Turks in the Adriatic. He also discovered in himself a voracious appetite for sightseeing. Wherever he went, he immersed himself delightedly in the customs, language, and history of the region. He enjoyed meeting people and appears to have met them easily. After the Treaty of Tilsit, between Napoleon and the Russian Emperor Alexander I, Svin'in left the fleet at Lisbon and traveled back to Russia in a leisurely way. The pronounced Anglophilia which he had imbibed at the Boarding School for the Nobility led him to visit Fielding's grave in Lisbon; and he spent some time in Portugal, Spain, France, and Germany (whose stolid and phlegmatic citizens rather put him off), arriving in St. Petersburg at the end of 1807. Between 1808 and the fall of 1811, Svin'in seems to have devoted himself more to drawing and painting than to diplomacy. On September 13, 1811, two days before he sailed for America, he was elected to the Academy of Fine Arts which he had previously attended as a student.

Svin'in spent about twenty months in America, from October 1811 until June 1813. Diplomatic relations between Russia and the United States had been in existence for only a little more than three years when Svin'in arrived to take up his post as secretary to the Russian Consul General in Philadelphia. As had been the case during his previous tour of duty in the Near East, he did not let his duties interfere with his devotion to sightseeing and exploration. He ranged the East Coast, from Virginia to Maine, recording, with both pen and brush, all that took his fancy.

Svin'in's first effort to compare Russian and American development is found in a volume entitled *Sketches of Moscow and St. Petersburg. Ornamented with Nine Coloured Engravings taken from Nature. By Paul Svenin.* It was published by Thomas Dobson in Philadelphia in 1813, and included a brief (and rather fanciful) essay on the Cossacks, as well as a drawing of a Don Cossack "in his Military Dress" and a sketch of the Emperor Alexander. Svin'in's purpose in publishing this small volume was to substitute serious historical information about Russia for the "ridiculous wonders and strange falsehoods" which were the sum of what the American public seemed to know about his country. In doing so, he developed several points of comparison between Russia and the United States. In the first place, he was struck by the rapid development, in both countries, of impressive cities—St. Petersburg, Philadelphia, New York—where, little more than a century ago, there had been nothing but "impenetrable forests and marshes, inhabited by bears and wolves." His second point of comparison, while plausible enough in 1813, cannot be broadly endorsed by historians of Russia today. Both nations, wrote Svin'in, were places where "the unfortunate and the persecuted find an asylum and a home." Svin'in was most agreeably struck by the religious toleration in America and found the situation similar in Russia. But, on the Russian side, the toleration of which Svin'in spoke was grounded in nothing more substantial than the mystical yearnings of the Emperor, and did not survive the early 1820s.

Svin'in's major work on the United States seems to have been written up from notes after his return to Russia. It appeared in St. Petersburg in 1815 under the title of *Opyt zhivopisnago puteshestviia po severnoi*

A View of the Summer Garden in St. Petersburgh, by William Kneass after a drawing by Pavel
Petrovich Svin'in, engraving, in *Sketches of Moscow and St. Petersburg,* 1813. The Library
Company of Philadelphia.

In Philadelphia in 1813, Svin'in published his *Sketches of Moscow and St. Petersburg,* which
included this *View of the Summer Garden in St. Petersburgh.* Attempting to counter American
myths about Russia, and believing that "no two countries bear a more striking resemblance
than Russia and the United States," he stressed their common capacity for growth. Indeed, it
had been "little more than a century since, from the bosom of impenetrable forests and
marshes, inhabited by bears and wolves, rose the superb cities of St. Petersburg, Philadelphia,
and New York."

Amerike (which may be translated as "A Picturesque Voyage Through
North America"). Although the American struggle for independence
had been of interest to Russians, and had been the occasion for several
descriptive pamphlets, Svin'in's brief book was the first which could
be called a real traveler's account of the United States by a Russian.

Svin'in found at the heart of the national character a passion for
"mercantile enterprises." The commercial spirit of Americans did not
altogether please him. "Money," he observed, "is the American's deity;
only his piety and the wealth of the country have until now sustained his
morals." Nevertheless, Svin'in hoped to stimulate the growth of commerce
between Russia and America, while advancing his own fortunes in a variety
of ways. Attempting to play a major role in the production and development
of steamboats for Russia, Svin'in set forth the conditions for his cooperation
in a letter to the American inventor Robert Fulton: "1st—That your company honor me with the title of Superintendent of the Steamboats of Russia.
2nd—That it will grant me on my arrival in Russia an annual salary as will
seem most just." But Svin'in's efforts to become Superintendent came to
nothing; nor did Fulton avail himself of the concession granted to him
by the Russian government.

The Russian diplomat warned his readers that they "should not
look for profound philosophers and celebrated professors" in America,
but he was impressed by "the correct understanding of the humblest

Deck Life on the Paragon, by Pavel Petrovich Svin'in, watercolor, circa 1812.
The Metropolitan Museum of Art, Rogers Fund, 1942.

"Conceive of a vessel having the appearance of a flat-bottomed frigate," wrote Svin'in in a
Russian journal, "imagine it to be unafraid of storms, independent of wind, careless of foul
weather, to move with amazing speed and security, and to run on schedule time." Svin'in
looked forward to a time when the steamboat would replace the barge in Russia: "How many
thousands of brawny hands will be restored to the fields . . . . The peasants, who at barge-
towing met exhaustion and sometimes death, will find behind the plow true riches and health."

Frenzied Negro Methodists Holding a Religious Meeting in a Philadelphia Alley, by Pavel Petrovich
Svin'in, watercolor, circa 1812. The Metropolitan Museum of Art, Rogers Fund, 1942.

Svin'in's sense of the picturesque in American life is vividly conveyed in his treatment of the
more extreme Protestant sects. He was fascinated by the physical expression of belief in re-
vivalist worship, where the congregation would jump up in agony, writhing and whirling like
dervishes to expel all satanic elements from their bodies.

citizen about the most abstract matters and things." American orphanages, hospitals, and prisons called forth his admiration. He found their order and cleanliness "astonishing." He particularly admired the prisons, which he reported "are more like factories. In them, humanity is not tortured—but merely punished; it is not degraded—merely deprived of liberty, the first good."

Above all, Svin'in was fascinated by the customs and practices of religions and cultures which excited his love of the "picturesque": the Indians, blacks, and Protestant sects like the Quakers, Shakers, and Anabaptists. He devoted a considerable section of his short book to Indian dances. With reference to the Protestant sects, he remarked condescendingly that "their numbers, oddities and contrasts would present an entertaining and most striking picture of the passions and confusions of the human mind." (One would never guess, to read his account of sectarian extremism in the United States, that far more "picturesque" sects were flourishing in Russia at the same time.) Svin'in's detailed account of a Black Methodist Church service in Philadelphia is so vivid that it deserves to be rendered at length:

> In a fluent, hoarse voice, the preacher began his sermon, setting forth in bombastic style, the terrors of Hell and the Wrath of God. At first, everything went along peacefully enough, but little by little the preacher got excited and fired the imagination of the congregation with terrible pictures and gestures. Then from all sides were heard the groans of the penitent, the cries and exclamations of the possessed. At the end, when in a strong, powerful voice he pronounced the destruction of the universe, pointed to the black cloud, pregnant with the all-destroying thunders, and described the tortures and sufferings awaiting the sinners—then the foundations of the edifice were shaken and the vaults trembled at their terrible bellowing. I confess that at the moment I myself feared the destruction, if not of the universe, then at least of the gallery.

His concluding remarks were most disparaging; he compared the Methodist minister to a Jacobin agitator haranguing a revolutionary crowd ("foaming at the mouth") and his congregation to the Eumenides. A far cry, he concluded rather smugly, from the beauties of the Orthodox service to which he was accustomed.

Svin'in was particularly fascinated by the physical excitement often generated at the religious gatherings of the more extreme Protestant sects. After a knowledgeable, if rather dutiful, description of the Quakers and their charitable activities, his account suddenly quickens:

> The Quakers gather every Sunday and observe a profound silence until someone (man or woman) feels himself inspired, stands up and says whatever may come into his head. The Quakers always begin to speak in a quiet, drawling, trembling voice; but little by little the preacher becomes so inflamed that one can scarcely make out his words. To cool himself off, he frequently removed his hat, then his long coat, and finally his camisole. Not infrequently their meetings end in general silence. On one occasion . . . I happened to see a woman rise from her seat, after a particularly long silence, and pronounced these words: the sun's rays make the flowers bloom. . . Having said this she fell silent. Everyone devoted himself to his meditations and soon the meeting broke up.

The Pennsylvania Hospital, by Pavel Petrovich Svin'in, watercolor, circa 1812.
The Metropolitan Museum of Art, Rogers Fund, 1942.

The eighteenth-century vision of America as the arena for testing enlightened ideas about man and institutions was realized in the humane hospitals, orphanages, and prisons Svin'in found in Philadelphia. He thought the Pennsylvania Hospital "astonishing" in its order and cleanliness. The emphasis Americans placed on healing and rehabilitation, whether physiological or social, marked striking progress in man's moral development.

Svin'in's drawings and watercolors may be of even more interest to the student of American history than his writings. When he sailed from the United States to join the Russian forces in Europe in June 1813, he brought with him a portfolio of fifty-two watercolors. Ostentatiously alleging patriotism as the reason, he passed up the opportunity to publish his sketches in England in 1815, and after they were published in Russia in that same year, the portfolio dropped out of sight for more than a hundred years. Following World War I, it was purchased in Russia by a member of the American Red Cross mission, and it subsequently came into the possession of Mr. R. T. H. Halsey who, together with Avrahm Yarmolinsky, later produced the fine volume containing all fifty-two watercolors and Yarmolinsky's biographical essay and summary of the "picturesque voyage."

Sad to say, the latter phases of Svin'in's career do not present a very edifying spectacle, although for a time he seemed a success. In 1818, he founded a journal, the *Otechestvennye zapiski* (translated "Annals of the Fatherland"), which he edited for twelve years, publishing a great many ethnographic, historical, and travel essays. One of them, "Nabliudeniya russkago Amerike" (translated "The observations of a Russian in America"), was an unpublished excerpt from his *Picturesque Voyage* dealing with the fine arts in the United States.

Almost alone among early visitors to this country, Svin'in believed that the Americans had "by nature a great gift for the Arts," and partic-

John Bill Ricketts, by Gilbert Stuart, oil on canvas, circa 1793–1799.
National Gallery of Art.

During Svin'in's stay in Philadelphia, Gilbert Stuart, who painted this unfinished study of
the equestrian and circus entrepreneur John Bill Ricketts, was one of the most popular of
American portrait painters. Svin'in reported that, even as an old man, Stuart's "flaming,
penetrating eyes" could grasp "not only the appearance, but the very innermost essence of a
man, and paint a portrait after having seen a person twice." Bored with painting backgrounds,
Stuart had playfully transformed the dark area of this portrait into a horsehead frame for
Ricketts's head. The work was left unfinished when the circus owner drowned with his horses
on a voyage to England.

ularly for portrait painting—an art highly developed, he explained, because of their vanity. Gilbert Stuart, whom he met as "an old man, haunched, gouty, but with flaming, penetrating eyes, such as I have never beheld in anyone," was the best of the portraitists, although his canvases were "more like excellent sketches than like completed paintings. Those . . . to which he tries to give a more careful finish lose their vividness and technical excellence entirely and even cease to be good likenesses." Still, the wealthy citizens clamored "to have their portraits painted by Stuart, and pay a hundred dollars for it, no matter what the quality of the work may be. Hence it is usual to speak of these portraits as 'Stuart's hundred dollar notes.'" Profitable, too, was his production of George Washington portraits, which Americans revered as Russians did their icons: "The country is glutted with bust portraits of Washington from the brush of this master. It is noteworthy that every American considers it his sacred duty to have a likeness of Washington in his home, just as we have images of God's saints."

Svin'in's aesthetic judgment may well be questioned. Of the Peale brothers, including Rembrandt Peale, he commented, "they are all painters and very wretched ones." But one of Rembrandt Peale's works was an exception: "Truly, both in composition and execution it would not shame the greatest of the European masters." The work, "the Roman Daughter," was, as Avrahm Yarmolinsky has pointed out, the cause of an embarrassing confrontation between the two men, which did nothing to help Svin'in's flagging credibility. He charged that the painting was a copy of an original he had seen in Paris, but Peale, whose reputation was at stake, posted a challenge to Svin'in's claim in a Philadelphia newspaper, the *American Daily Advertiser,* and forced the Russian to admit that he had been mistaken.

At the time of the publication of his essay on the fine arts in America, Svin'in's character was again under attack. Perhaps under pressures which his journal imposed, his intellectual integrity and scholarly competence seem to have suffered. He developed a reputation among his fellow writers for, on the one hand, not checking the accuracy of his facts and on the other, for inventing or appropriating descriptions of faraway places and passing them off as his own. To Alexander Pushkin and other noted writers of the 1820s, he seems to have become primarily a figure of fun. His bad reputation was increased by what might charitably be termed his political flexibility. The Emperor Alexander became more conservative toward the end of his reign, and so did Svin'in. He even wrote a sycophantic poem to Count Alexis Arakcheev, the most influential of Alexander's advisers, and the most hated man in Russia during the Emperor's last years.

When all is said and done, it is a pity that Svin'in's energy, enterprise, and desire to be of service were not complemented by greater strength of character, scholarly integrity, and literary discernment. Nevertheless, Svin'in's *Picturesque Voyage* remains a valuable view of the new republic, and at this point in time would appear to be his most considerable and durable achievement.

Charles Sealsfield, by C. Rust, photograph, 1864. Sealsfield-Sammlungkresse, Charles Sealsfield Gesellschaft, Stuttgart.

Changing his name from Karl Postl, Charles Sealsfield escaped from the Austrian Empire to
the New World. His first work, *The United States as They Are* (published anonymously in 1827),
was followed by a series of novels, in German, about frontier life. This is the only known
photograph of him, taken in Switzerland in the year of his death.

National Portrait Gallery

Supplement to *Abroad in America: Visitors to the New Nation 1776–1914*

The following items, not in the Checklist, have been included in the exhibition:

Giacomo Costantino Beltrami, 1779–1855

ENRICO SCURI, 1805–1884

Oil on canvas, date unknown
87 × 59

Accademia Carrara di Belle Arti

H. G. Wells, 1866–1946

SIR WILLIAM ROTHENSTEIN, 1872–1945

Black chalk on paper, 1912
15⁷/₈ × 12¹/₄

National Portrait Gallery, London

The First State Election in Detroit, Michigan

THOMAS MICKELL BURNHAM, 1818–1866

Oil on canvas, 1837
24¹/₂ × 30³/₄

The Detroit Institute of Arts, Gift of Mrs. Samuel T. Carson

Mrs. Anthony Wayne Rollins [Sarah (Sallie) Harris Rodes]

GEORGE CALEB BINGHAM, 1811–1879

Oil on panel, 1834
28 × 23

Mrs. Ellsworth A. MacLeod

Battle of the Little Big Horn

Unidentified Indian artist

Pictograph, natural dye on cotton
69 × 87

Mrs. Andrew Wyeth

Poster, Adler Thomashefsky National Theatre, September 26, 1913 for play by Abraham Goldfaden

Printer: Lipshitz Press, New York
44 × 27

American Jewish Historical Society, Waltham, Massachusetts

European Notions of American Manners and Customs

FREDERICK BURR OPPER, 1857–1937

Chromolithograph, in *Puck*, November 16, 1881

Enoch Pratt Free Library, Baltimore, Maryland

The Playfair Papers, or: Brother Jonathan, the Smartest Nation in all Creation

Hugo Playfair, London, 1841, 2 vols.
Princeton University Library, Richard Waln Meirs Collection of Cruikshankia

Including: "Liberty Hall Dining Parlor," aquatint by Robert Cruikshank, 1789–1856, and "House of Representatives During a High Debate on Denouncing the Anti Slavery Petitions," etching by Robert Cruikshank

Checklist entries 32, 107, 110, 112, 113, and 121 were not included in the exhibition.

3

Charles Sealsfield (Karl Postl)
1793-1864

by Christian F. Feest

As soon as one of the members of Congress opens his mouth, you may tell to what part of the Union he belongs. The more literate Yankee borrows from Shakspeare [sic] and Byron, blundering through both these and other authors, in order to embellish the offspring of his genius. . . . The poor Ohian [sic] tells us, "that he came from the very lowest orders of society," and giving us a specimen of lamentation, leaves uncertain whether he is not attempting to raise a subscription for himself. The proud Georgian speaks of violated rights and civil war because he is not permitted to drive the Indians into the wildernesses of Oregan [sic]. The Carolinian declares that he is going to live and to die with his slaves, while the Pennsylvanian, quietly seated on his bench, seems to be perfectly astounded and perplexed by the wisdom, energy, good sense, learning, and elegance of his honourable brethren.

—The United States of North America As They Are

CHRISTIAN FEEST is the Curator of the North and Middle American Indian collections, Museum für Völkerkunde, Vienna. His most recent book is *Das rote Amerika* (which may be translated as "The America of the Indians"), and he has published articles in American journals. In 1972, he was a Smithsonian Post-Doctoral Fellow.

Kreuzherren Monastery, Prague, by an unidentified photographer, date unknown.
Charles Sealsfield-Gesellschaft.

In the Kreuzherren Monastery, which housed the Knights of the Cross of Prague, Karl Postl
lived for nine years. Oppressed by the bleak environment, he fled to Vienna and, ultimately,
to the United States.

ON MAY 11, 1823, thirty-year-old Karl Postl secretly deserted the Order
of the Knights of the Cross of Prague, whose member he had been for nine
years. Fleeing the choking coercion of his congregation's hierarchy, which
he had been feeling for some time, the young priest forsook a possible
ecclesiastical career that had already made him the youngest secretary of
his congregation in history. What Postl was aiming at was a secular position in the bureaucracy of Vienna, the capital of the absolutist Austrian
Empire. But his move was timed badly; his prospective patrons in Vienna
were of little help; and when the secret police began to investigate the case
of the runaway priest, Postl's only realistic option was to leave the country.

After it had become apparent that he had indeed left Austria, the
police closed its files on Postl. Having severed himself from his order and
his country, the young man now severed himself from the rest of his past
life. In Switzerland, he was furnished with new personal documents and
soon left for the United States, the best place to start a new life. Since neither
his family, his friends, nor his former superiors ever heard of him again,
he was universally believed to be dead after a few years had passed. There
is an irony in this story: it was his affiliation with the religious order he had
come to detest which made possible his future career in the United States.
Only through the order could the gifted son of Moravian peasants have

gained higher education and access to aristocratic society. It was, moreover, only his disenchantment with the order which led him to risk an illegal escape across the Atlantic at a time when even legal emigration was almost impossible.

Perhaps under the name of Charles Sidons, he arrived in New Orleans in the late summer of 1823 and stayed in Louisiana for five months. Here he could make use of his knowledge of French while picking up some English. For the next twenty months, he settled in western Pennsylvania, afterwards returning to Louisiana by the way of Ohio, Kentucky, Indiana, Illinois, Missouri, Tennessee, Arkansas Territory, and Mississippi. When he returned to Europe in August 1826, he carried a passport identifying the bearer as "Charles Sealsfield, Citizen of the United States, clergyman, native of Pennsylvania."

The transformation of Karl Postl into Charles Sealsfield may be best understood as an attempt to start afresh. At first, Sealsfield probably knew very little about America. Austrian censorship prevented the dissemination of balanced information on its politics and life. Books both promoting emigration and warning against it, and journals dealing with American affairs were being published in Germany; but it is doubtful whether these had a significant circulation during Metternich's time. The romantic fascination with America, so prominent in Germany during the next decades and visually epitomized in the work of the Swiss artist Carl Bodmer, had barely started to grow. Sealsfield, depending more on his personal experience, never was part of this particular tradition.

"Every European is blind about America for seven years," Sealsfield wrote after his first three years in the United States. He specifically blamed German immigrants for being unfit for America due to their slavish upbringings, lack of independence, and lack of good judgment. Much as he tried to bridge the gap between the old world of Karl Postl and the new

John Quincy Adams, by Horatio Greenough, marble, 1828 or 1829. Museum of Fine Arts, Boston.

Relishing his new freedom, Sealsfield spoke out fervently against John Quincy Adams, Andrew Jackson's opponent during the 1824 presidential campaign. He characterized Adams as a treacherous monarchist with the capacity to become, in the New World, what Prince Metternich was in the Austrian Empire: "His pride or rather arrogance, is a family failing . . . . In private life he seems anxious to conceal this passion under the mask of republican carelessness, and a certain *nonchalance.* His countenance betrays a cold ambitious mind, his dark eye exhibits the heartless diplomatist."

Political—A German Speech by Samuel Frey, by Lewis Miller, watercolor and ink, circa 1847. The Historical Society of York County.

The self-imposed linguistic isolation of Pennsylvania German settlements, suggested in this naïve portrayal of a garbled political speech, greatly disheartened Sealsfield. "Passive under a kind of self-satisfied ignorance which never consents to learn more than their forefathers, and adhering to their axiom never to become Irish (thus they designate the Anglo-Americans who take their revenge by nicknaming them the Dutch), they are contented with their own German idiom."

world of Charles Sealsfield, his first book, *The United States of North America as They Are* (1828; first published as *Die Vereinigten Staaten von Nordamerika* in 1827), indicates that he himself had also been blinded by the sudden transition from absolutist Austria to democratic America.

Sealsfield witnessed the presidential campaign in 1824 and its aftermath in Jackson country (the Deep South and western Pennsylvania), and he probably believed most of what had been said in the fever of pre- and post-election days. In Austria, little was publicly spoken about politics—and this little was not to be trusted. In the United States, politics was everybody's main concern—and much of what was said seemed to be true. For the most part, Sealsfield's work is a partisan account of American politics in the 1820s. Andrew Jackson—although some of his shortcomings are noted—is cast as the people's true champion, a savior who alone would be able to lead America back to a path of democratic virtue. John Quincy Adams is pictured as a treacherous monarchist eager to subvert democratic principles:

> *His pride or rather arrogance, is a family failing. . . . In private life he seems anxious to conceal this passion under the mask of republican carelessness, and a certain* nonchalance. *His countenance betrays a cold ambitious mind, his dark eye exhibits the heartless diplomatist. . . . If taken upon the whole, he may be considered a most dangerous man to the freedom of the Union, and if he had been sent by Metternich himself, he could not pursue more closely the principles of the Holy Alliance.*

Sealsfield's second book, *Austria as It Is,* was published anonymously in London in 1828. Though not concerned with America, it complements his American travel book. In this stinging attack on his forsaken country, Austria and the United States were never explicitly compared, but the two books taken together testify vividly to the contrasting impressions the author must have received. He predicted the downfall of the Austrian Empire, and the rise of the United States and Russia as the superpowers of the future. He expected Russia to expand her sphere of influence over much of Europe, and consequently "before two centuries have elapsed, the Genius of Europe, to avoid Scythian fetters, will have alighted on the banks of the mighty Mississippi."

After living in London for a few years, Sealsfield returned to the United States. This second visit lasted from July 1827 to November 1830, perhaps interrupted by a brief trip to Mexico. After an unsuccessful attempt to earn a living as an American correspondent for a German publishing house and an equally frustrating attempt to operate a farm in Louisiana, Sealsfield worked as a political journalist in New York, particularly for the Bonapartist *Courrier des Etats-Unis.* Besides journalism, the emigrant also tried his hand at fiction. His first novel, *Tokeah or The White Rose,* and some short stories dealing mainly with American topics, were published in 1829. He returned to London, perhaps as Joseph Bonaparte's agent, but continued to publish English fiction until he moved to Paris. In 1832, he finally settled in Switzerland, where he remained for most of the rest of his life.

Between 1833 and 1843, Sealsfield published, in German, seven novels, five of which deal primarily with American history and life (the remaining two focus on Mexico). His descriptions of Indian–white relations during the War of 1812, of French and American life in Louisiana, of the colonization of Texas, of the world of big money, and of the great monetary speculation of 1836 (which caused the author's return to the United States for four months in 1837) brought him instant fame in Germany.

The fact that his works appeared anonymously served to heighten the interest of the reading public, whose appetite for American topics had been whetted by James Fenimore Cooper. Facts about the author emerged from a mist of conjectures: his name was Seatsfield or Sealsfield; he was either an American living in Europe or a native speaker of German who had spent most of his life in the United States. Some even claimed that the alleged author was in fact the murderer of the real Sealsfield whose manuscripts he was now publishing as his own; or that the novels had been written by different German authors dispersed all over the world. After 1842, when the first translations appeared in the United States, similar questions were being asked. Was this man really an American, and if so, should he not be considered as "the Greatest American Author?"

Although writing in German, Sealsfield looked upon himself as an American author trying to give his readers an account of his country. Cleverly blending fact and fiction, he succeeded in helping to shape a more realistic German image of the United States. His novelistic portrayal of America was much less romantic than that of other continental writers, and lacked the strong German bias of his colleagues, whose heroes were mostly German emigrants or adventurers. If German characters appeared at all in Sealsfield's novels, they were somewhat deformed by the political realities of their country of origin, and they had a hard time trying to understand what the United States was all about.

In his fiction, as well as in his political philosophy, Sealsfield's true hero is the American people; individual experiences are seen as relevant only insofar as they reflect the social, material, political, and religious circum-

The Olivier Plantation, Alexandria, Louisiana, by Marie Adrian Persac, watercolor and collage, 1861. Louisiana State Museum.

In the Louisiana countryside, Sealsfield was charmed by the sight of plantations lining the Mississippi River banks. Here was the wealthy planter's "airy mansion . . . surrounded with orange, banana, lime, and fig trees" in a climate nearly tropical. He purchased a plantation on the Red River and came to justify slaveholding.

stances of the community. Regardless of their different characters, the Yankee merchant, the Southern planter, and the rough frontiersman are all seen as equally respectable (if not always equally likable) and useful members of society. At the heart of Sealsfield's transatlantic patriotism was a studied admiration for American democracy.

Sealsfield had been brought up in a strongly hierarchical society and, by rising from peasants' son to respected clergyman, had come to accept it. So for him, democracy was not love at first sight, "because it levels all differences." But his American experience had taught him that, in the United States, democracy was "a necessary condition for the prosperity of the country, because it unifies the population into a homogenetic whole working for the public good." Even the insatiable hunger for profits—by itself a rather abominable inclination—was ennobled by being put to work for the public good. Within fifty years, the most avaricious Yankees (a variety of the *homo americanus* particularly contrary to Sealsfield's Southern taste) had created a civilization out of Ohio's wilderness "which surpasses some European kingdoms in extent and wealth, and most of them in civility and enlightenment." Since every American had an equal opportunity to receive an adequate education, any farmer, even in the remote regions of the West, was easily superior to the European peasant.

Trying to reconcile his respect for European hierarchy with his endorsement of American democracy, Sealsfield proposed that Europe should have a centralization of power because of its high density of population, whereas in the sparsely populated New World individual initiative was essential. In Europe, where the need for society was greatest, for example among the French, "the individual submits more easily to the limitations necessary for . . . the centralization of social powers." Thus the French—and this included the Louisiana French—were not very well suited for democracy. In America, on the other hand, society strengthened the self-reliance and independence of its men and women. The enormous feat of opening up "this most beautiful continent for civilization" could only be accomplished through the encouragement of individualism, which led to a "millionfold increase of free agencies." Sealsfield found confirmation for his hypothesis in the cities of the East Coast, for there the increasing population and the decreasing importance of the agrarian base had brought about a new aristocracy based on wealth, and even a taste for European styles.

Sealsfield's theory of democracy also proved to him that it was only suitable for Americans. Republicanism in Europe always had to be artificial: it was not a garment worn from early childhood, and did not fit Europeans,

Justice's Court in the Backwoods, by Tompkins Harrison Matteson, oil on canvas, 1850. New York State Historical Association.

In his wide-ranging comments on American society, Sealsfield inclined to generosity, but some things he found incomprehensible. To a European, even a disillusioned European, the ease with which one could escape punishment was appalling. He blamed America's plague of lawyers: "A murderer was committed to a gaol, and . . . was discharged by the aid of five hundred dollars paid to three lawyers for undertaking his defence. In this manner were three murders acquitted in the space of three weeks. I am far from maintaining that the people of the United States are a lawless or a bloodthirsty race of savages. They yield in point of morality to no other people in the world; but should they in future have less moral feeling, it will be justly attributable to the lawyers."

being too loose in some places, too tight in others. Sealsfield, therefore, had no problem praising American democracy while at the same time supporting the Bonapartist cause. He did not believe that the American model could usefully be transplanted to Europe. He merely wanted Europeans to understand the United States as a country of the future: a nascent world power using self-interest as a means to accomplish rapid growth.

With his Southern bias, Sealsfield found it easy to accept and defend slavery. His descriptions of blacks, in terms of all the stereotypes racial discrimination could muster, must have left his readers with the impression that it was indeed an act of humanity to own slaves. But these views, and the fact that he himself owned slaves on a Red River plantation in Louisiana, caused him the loss of some sympathy in Europe. He was not blind to the basic contradiction posed by slavery in a democratic society, but he saw no solution. The strict enforcement of democratic principles in the "federalist-aristocratic" society of the South would, he felt, "necessarily lead to anarchy, and finally to monarchy." Sealsfield did share his European readers' sympathy for the Indians; he deplored the unjust treatment they were receiving. But he believed that, because of their unwillingness to conform to the white man's culture, they stood in the way of civilization.

The authorship of Sealsfield's novels was officially disclosed in 1844, primarily because German laws protected the copyright of anonymous works for only fifteen years. His collected works continued to be published, and he began work on his next novel. Its publication was delayed, however, and finally the revolution of 1848 put an end to Sealsfield's popularity. German fiction on America was taking a romantic turn away from his solid realism. Disappointed with his publisher's reluctance to print any new book by a far from best-selling author, and increasingly impeded in his writing by failing eyesight, Sealsfield concerned himself more and more with investing his capital in European and American stocks.

To be better able to take care of his property in the United States, he left Europe in October 1853 for his fourth and longest visit. Spending the winters on his Red River plantation and traveling the rest of the time, he found the United States changed very much for the worse. During his brief visit in 1837, he had already noted that the country "had relapsed rather than progressed in its political life during the past seven years." This had made him realize that his earlier conviction that Jackson's leadership would cure all problems had been wrong; and he had come to blame the former President for the apparent decay. Now, sixteen years later, things looked even more disturbing to the man whose image of the United States had been formed when was a fugitive from totalitarian Austria. "The excess of freedom has degenerated into a mobocracy which threatens to undermine all social, legal, and political conditions. . . . Never before has the political and religious disunion been greater and more dangerous."

In 1858, Charles Sealsfield returned to Europe to live a secluded life in Switzerland. Physically ailing, he had no illusions about his further career as a writer; but still, in spite of all he had seen, he felt strongly for the United States. His eccentricity, which had always been noticeable, came even more clearly to the fore with old age. From his desk he followed the sad news about the Civil War. He viewed the war as a necessary purification for the country, whatever the final outcome of the struggle might be. Democracy, which he had known, understood, and loved, had to give way to another system of government. It was a thing of the past, having "fully served its purpose." It had been the agent of civilization, however imperfect the result was; but with the loss of the equalizing conditions of the frontier, needed to prevent the rise of a new aristocracy, it could no longer function as before. The former Jacksonian Democrat in Sealsfield may have been disappointed; the conservative in him was certainly not surprised.

After his death on May 26, 1864, his will was found to contain an indirect acknowledgement of his past as Karl Postl by making his astounded Austrian relatives heirs to his estate. But it closed with a confession to his later life. It is signed: "Charles Sealsfield, Citizen of the United States."

Frances Milton Trollope, by Auguste Hervieu, oil on canvas, circa 1832.
National Portrait Gallery, London.

Mrs. Trollope's entourage, which included Auguste Hervieu, a French exile who taught drawing to her children and would later illustrate her books, arrived in Cincinnati in early 1828.
In difficult financial straits, Mrs. Trollope sought her fortune in the United States and found
it, after numerous failed business ventures, in writing her outrageous *Domestic Manners of
the Americans.*

4
Frances Trollope
1780-1863

by Marcus Cunliffe

I do not like them. I do not like their principles, I do not like their manners, I do not like their opinions.

> —*Domestic Manners of the Americans*

MARCUS CUNLIFFE is Professor of American Studies at the University of Sussex, England. His books include *The Literature of the United States* and *Soldiers and Civilians: The Martial Spirit in America, 1775–1865*. His Jefferson Memorial Lectures, to be given at Berkeley in 1976, will deal with the idea of private property in American history.

FRANCES TROLLOPE had just reached her fifty-second birthday when her first book, *Domestic Manners of the Americans*, was published in London in March 1832. She was to produce a spate of novels and other travel books during the next couple of decades. Two of her five children, Thomas Adolphus and Anthony, would become established authors. At her death in 1863, Mrs. Trollope could look back on a richly busy life which had also been financially rewarding.

Before the publication of *Domestic Manners*, however, things had been very different. She was married to a querulous lawyer with a dwindling practice. The Trollopes lived beyond their means, in the illusory hope of inheriting a fortune from a rich uncle. Mrs. Trollope's journey to the United States at the end of 1827, with three children and a manservant, looked like yet another stage on the family road to disaster. (Her husband remained in England for a time to look after the education of their two older sons.) She traveled in company with Frances Wright, a wealthy young radical who had persuaded her to spend some time at the new community of Nashoba, which Miss Wright had established near Memphis. Nashoba proved to be a wretched chaos. Mrs. Trollope's second scheme was to continue upriver to Cincinnati, which she had heard was a flourishing new city, and open an emporium, to be called the Bazaar, where she would tap the flow of dollars by selling European novelties. This venture was a dismal failure. She managed to survive in Cincinnati for two years, supported by the efforts of a young French artist-protégé Auguste Hervieu.

In poor health and with ailing children, she headed eastward, wintered in the vicinity of Washington, D. C., visited the Middle Atlantic States, and sailed for home in the summer of 1831. Her one hope was to make a book out of her experiences. Even to the strong-willed woman the prospects could not have seemed bright. She had never appeared in print. Her education was haphazard—a governessy smattering of poetry, French and Italian, botany, and general romanticism. She had spent only a few days in New Orleans on arrival; she had merely passed through Baltimore and Philadelphia; and New England remained unknown to her. A recent English account, Captain Basil Hall's *Travels in North America in the Years 1827 and 1828*, which may have stimulated her to try her own hand, was also discouragingly—in her eyes—knowledgeable, ambitious, and complete. She regarded Captain Hall as a deep thinker; her own narrative, she confessed, amounted to "gossiping."

To her surprise and delight, the manuscript of *Domestic Manners* was accepted by a London publisher—largely on the recommendation of Captain Hall. The two volumes of the first edition included twenty-four lithographs by Hervieu, who was to illustrate several more of her books. To her still greater delight, *Domestic Manners* brought her some cash, some fame, and a good deal of notoriety. She followed up immediately with a novel, *The Refugee in America* (1832). Things continued to go wrong within her family—she was not able to ward off bankruptcy for her wretched husband, and then he and two of her children died—but at least, after a half-century of scrabbling frustration, Frances Trollope could enjoy the solace of success. She wrote three more novels about America: *The Life and Adventures of Jonathan Jefferson Whitlaw; or Scenes on the Mississippi* (1836),

Cincinnati: The Public Landing, by John Casper Wild, gouache, 1835.
The Cincinnati Historical Society.

Cincinnati, which called itself the "Queen City" of the West, was a flourishing town of about twenty thousand people when Mrs. Trollope arrived in 1828. Brought to life by the Ohio River, Cincinnati had burgeoned into a major entrepôt, exporting such western produce as flour, whiskey, and pork. The city took pride in its social and moral refinements, boasting a medical college, a hospital, a theatre, libraries, churches, schools, and an Academy of Fine Arts. But Mrs. Trollope found the city an "uninteresting mass of buildings" without domes, steeples, or towers. And she was horrified by such "amenities" as garbage dumped into the middle of the city streets.

The Bazaar, by an unidentified artist, lithograph, circa 1881. The Cincinnati Historical Society.

Mrs. Trollope's "Bazaar" was to be a glittering emporium where provincial Cincinnati could buy dry goods from London and Paris. Soon christened "Trollope's Folly," the Bazaar was a combination of Moorish, Greek, and Gothic architecture: its most prominent exterior feature was an Egyptian colonnade of four massive columns, three stories high, crowned by a fourth-story entablature. The interior contained a grand circular staircase, a long hallway, rows of Doric columns, a grand ballroom, and galleries for music and art. Hervieu's paintings and mosaics covered walls, ceilings, and floors. Whatever Mrs. Trollope had in imagination, she lacked in business acumen; and, according to one observer, "every brick in her Babel cost her three prices." When the Bazaar finally opened, the $10,000 worth of goods sent by her husband were confiscated by the sheriff to help pay construction costs; he then seized all her household effects. In March 1830, Frances Trollope got on board the *Lady Franklin* steamboat and left Cincinnati forever.

The Barnabys in America (1843), and *The Old World and the New: a Novel* (1849).

Americans took offense at *Domestic Manners*; and it cannot be denied that the "old woman" Trollope gave cause. The Americans, she announced, exhibited a "total and universal want of manners, both in males and females." They were inquisitive, boring, uncultivated, uncouth, humorless, and self-satisfied. Public behavior was appalling. She saw a woman suckling a baby at the theater. Men sat on the edge of boxes, their backs to the audience, or sprawled with their feet propped up. American women, when young, were "the handsomest in the world," and yet "the least attractive"; they held themselves badly and had scrawny figures. The males were similarly unappealing: "I never saw an American man walk or stand well . . . they are nearly all hollow chested and round shouldered." Table manners were particularly repugnant:

> *The total want of all the usual courtesies of the table . . . the loathsome spitting, from the contamination of which it was absolutely impossible to protect our dresses; the frightful manner of feeding with their knives, till the whole blade seemed to enter into the mouth; and the still more frightful manner of cleaning the teeth afterwards with a pocket knife, soon forced us to feel that . . . the dinner hour was to be any thing rather than an hour of enjoyment.*

Except for Negroes, Americans had no ear for music: "I scarcely ever heard a white American . . . go through an air without being out of tune before the end of it." She was shocked by the casual treatment accorded to President Andrew Jackson when he came to Cincinnati in 1829:

I was at his elbow when a greasy fellow accosted him thus: "General Jackson, I guess?"

The General bowed assent.

"Why they told me you was dead."

"No! Providence has hitherto preserved my life."

"And is your wife alive too?"

The General, apparently much hurt, signified the contrary, upon which the courtier concluded his harangue, by saying, "Aye, I thought it was one or the t'other of ye."

In spite of her avowed emphasis on mundane detail—what she called in her preface "the daily aspect of ordinary life"—Mrs. Trollope did not hesitate to generalize. She noted the contempt for law: "Trespass, assault, robbery, nay, even murder, are often committed without the slightest attempt at legal interference." She commented on American indifference to the rights of slaves and Indians:

You will see them with one hand hoisting the cap of liberty, and with the other flogging their slaves. You will see them one hour lecturing their mob on the indefeasible rights of man, and the next driving from their homes the children of the soil, whom they have bound themselves to protect by the most solemn treaties.

Cupid at a rout at Cincinnati, by Auguste Hervieu, watercolor, circa 1830. Cincinnati Art Museum, gift of Mrs. George H. Warrington.

In Cincinnati, Mrs. Trollope observed, the very arrangement of gatherings, the strict separation of men and women, paralyzed conversation: "The women invariably herd together at one part of the room, and the men at the other . . . . The ladies look at each other's dresses till they know every pin by heart; talk of Parson Somebody's last sermon on the day of judgment, on Dr. T'otherbody's new pills for dyspepsia, till the 'tea' is announced, when they all console themselves together for whatever they may have suffered in keeping awake, by taking tea, coffee, hot cake and custard . . . . After this meal is over, they return to the drawing-room, and it always appeared to me that they remained together as long as they could bear it, and then they rise *en masse,* cloak, bonnet, shawl, and exit."

She singled out Thomas Jefferson for particular criticism. He was responsible for the foolish and dangerous proposition that all men were created equal—and yet he kept slaves. With typical American hypocrisy, "Mr. Jefferson is said to have been the father of children by almost all his numerous gang of female slaves." She pictured America as "a vast continent, by far the greater part of which is still in the state in which nature left it, and a busy, bustling, industrious population, hacking and hewing their way through it"—with scant regard for natural beauty. "This country," she asserted, "may be said to spread rather than to rise."

In her final chapter, Mrs. Trollope declared that apart from a "small patrician band" of well-bred and congenial people, the American population was dull, brutal, and arrogant. By the test of prosperity, the principles of equality and the system of government no doubt suited the Americans. But the result was distressing for a European. "A single word indicative of doubt, that any thing, or every thing, in that country is not the very best in the world, produces an effect which must be seen and felt to be understood." How could a person of sensibility, especially a foreigner, be happy in such an environment? If Americans should ever mend their ways, "if refinement once creeps in among them, if they once learn to cling to the graces, the honours, the chivalry of life, then we shall say farewell to American equality, and welcome to European fellowship one of the finest countries in the world." But Mrs. Trollope did not seem to feel this was a likely change. In her portrayal Americans, endowed with a fine country, were destroying it, and wrecking themselves morally in the process.

There are two obvious and opposite ways of interpreting Mrs. Trollope's book and the impact it had in the United States. The first reaction, which was the commonest one in the 1830s, is to dismiss *Domestic Manners* as a potboiler, written by an ill-informed woman who, having done badly in America, resorted to supercilious Toryism. This view is supported by the various passages in her book (and in her later novels about America) in which she appears to be upset not so much by bad manners as by the absence of social deference. She is shocked by the brusque behavior of household help, or by the discovery that men in public life are often not "gentlemen." Her preface, rather different in tone from her first-draft version, warns England against the "jarring tumult and universal degradation which invariably follow the wild scheme of placing all the power of the state in the hands of the populace." As the Whig *Edinburgh Review* observed in 1832, *Domestic Manners* was "an express advertisement against the Reform Bill." The book was published while Britain was locked in argument over electoral reform, which Tory sentiment opposed. The United States was cited as a dreadful warning of what might happen if "the mob" gained political power. Basil Hall had recommended Mrs. Trollope's manuscript because it bolstered his own more cautious analysis of the weaknesses of American democracy. Mrs. Trollope's revised preface and her final chapter may well have been composed on her return to England with the Reform Bill controversy directly in mind. Along the same lines, *Domestic Manners* may be seen as a standard English reaction of the time to the humiliations of the War of Independence and the War of 1812. In these decades, and indeed to the end of the century, Americans felt they detected a jealous, disdainful resentment on the part of the mother country. So it

The Trollope Family, by Childs and Inman, lithograph, 1832.
The Cincinnati Historical Society.

After the appearance of *Domestic Manners of the Americans,* Mrs. Trollope was ridiculed with
a vituperativeness which threatened to escalate into an international incident. This caricature
was published depicting Mrs. Trollope, her daughters, and Auguste Hervieu—painting his
heroic *Landing of Lafayette in Cincinnati,* with a cartoon bumpkin for a model. What made
Frances Trollope the best known and "worst hated" author in America was her suggestion that
the country's greatest weakness, its "total and universal want of manners," stemmed from its
obsession with equality.

could be said that *Domestic Manners* ministered to a British willingness to believe that in achieving independence the United States had gone astray. On their side, Americans would naturally resist a rendering of themselves so impressionistically prejudiced.

The alternative possibility is that Frances Trollope angered Americans not by propagandizing but by telling the truth. There is some evidence in favor of this theory. After all, American contemporaries such as James Fenimore Cooper sometimes offered similar criticisms—and made themselves unpopular by doing so. Foreign visitors were expected to pay compliments. The young nation was touchy in the extreme. Americans derided the author of *Domestic Manners*. But perhaps the shout of "Trollope!" at a man with his feet up in a theater was admission that there was in fact room for improvement in such matters. With the passage of time, at any rate, certain Americans were prepared to admit that Mrs. Trollope's testimony had in previous decades not been altogether inaccurate. In the suppressed passages of *Life on the Mississippi*, Mark Twain said that "poor candid Mrs. Trollope . . . lived three years in this civilization of ours; in the body of it—not on the surface of it, as was the case with most of the foreign tourists of her day. She knew her subject well, and she set it forth fairly and squarely, without any weak ifs and ands and buts. She deserved gratitude—but it is an error to suppose she got it." In 1908, John Graham Brooks's dispassionate study *As Others See Us* cited Frances Trollope as one of the foreign visitors whose criticisms had had a salutary effect.

The America of Twain and Brooks was a maturer, worldlier place than the America of Mrs. Trollope. When the sting had long departed from her words, it was possible to consider objectively that she had actually lived in middle America. She had not arrived by the front door, armed with letters of introduction to the polite society of the seaboard. Though she showed only a cursory acquaintance with American literature, there was, except for James Fenimore Cooper, not much of it to discuss in 1830. The glories of American art and architecture likewise lay in the future. To her credit, she did express a warm admiration for the young sculptor Hiram Powers, and

Box at the Theatre, by John B. Pendleton after Auguste Hervieu, lithograph, in *Domestic Manners of the Americans,* 1832. Harvard University Library.

"It was not the fashionable season for the theatres, which I presume must account for the appearance of the company in the boxes, which was any thing but elegant; nor was there more decorum of demeanour than I had observed elsewhere; I saw one man in the lower tier of boxes deliberately take off his coat that he might enjoy the refreshing coolness of shirt sleeves; all the gentlemen wore their hats, and the spitting was unceasing." Outraged as the American public was by Mrs. Trollope's condescension, some found merit in her criticism and awarded her an odd immortality. To commit a "Trollope" became synonymous in the American vocabulary with gross social impropriety.

subsequently found an English purchaser for his "Greek Slave" statue.

Some Americans, contemplating the Bicentennial celebration with a measure of skepticism, may thus be inclined to raise Mrs. Trollope's reputation still higher, as one who was not afraid to draw attention to the less rosy features of American life. Ralph Waldo Emerson praised England as the land of plain speaking, whose creed was: "Let us know the truth. Draw a straight line, hit whom and where it will."

What was Mrs. Trollope, a Tory snob, garrulous and sometimes spiteful, or a lively indomitable woman who had both the wit and the courage to say what she thought? Neither explanation of her and her book is entirely tenable. In the first place, probably without realizing so, she was a contributor to a dispute over the New World which, as Antonello Gerbi has shown, had already been in train for over three centuries. The issue was whether the American continent marked an advance on Europe or was a backward hemisphere. Most Europeans, other than potential emigrants, were conditioned almost from birth to believe in American degradation, and to demand proofs to the contrary. Most Americans of course upheld the opposite view, and were correspondingly prejudiced against Europe. In perspective, *Domestic Manners* falls into place as yet another exhibit in a very long line.

The relations between the United States and Britain were especially complex. As Emerson remarked in *English Traits,* "English believes in English." Most of the people Mrs. Trollope liked in America seemed to be English by birth. There is something in the tone of the book that might well have irked Americans and led them to question her credentials. Her style has been called "clever." It is apt, however, to be clever mainly in being "smart." She scores points off people in dialogues that she recounts. She is breezy rather than funny. Her persona is that of the well-bred Englishwoman confronted with vulgarities and absurdities. She operates from within a fortress of assumed impregnability. She is almost always sure of her opinions, and intimates that—since they are based upon a superior upbringing—no appeal is possible from her judgments. She disclaims expert knowledge or profundity, but implies that her own grounding in common sense is thoroughly adequate. Such Englishry, also noticeable in her son Anthony Trollope's *North America*, does not amount to blatant prejudice. But it can be annoying because it confuses candor and condescension.

The American response to this tinge of proprietary disapproval tended to be sharp. The mother country was attacked as moribund and aristocratic. From Tom Paine's ridiculing of George III in *Common Sense*, American reactions to the mother country had a sort of myth-destroying element. It was psychologically necessary to deny the parental bond. At any rate, it is tempting to speculate on the forms of abuse that greeted Mrs. Trollope in the America of the 1830s. Why, for example, was there so much exaggeration of the ugliness and elderliness of "Dame Trollope?" In squibs of the day she was the "old woman"; in waxwork effigy she was caricatured as an ancient crone. True, in *Domestic Manners* she tells of being referred to as "old woman" by unceremonious neighbors. But the taunt may have seemed particularly fitting for American contemporaries who wished to deny the legitimacy of any criticism emanating from England.

On the other hand, her book is not wholly defined by the Anglo-American context. It is liberally sprinkled with allusions to French and Italian literature and music. Her faithful friend and companion during her entire American stay was the Frenchman Auguste Hervieu. She treasured a meeting with Lafayette in Paris in 1824. There was a romantic radicalism in her makeup, of a Continental European variety, that we miss if we write her off as an English Tory. Indeed, how could she have been a friend of Frances Wright if her views had simply been those of the London *Quarterly Review*—the only British periodical which wrote appreciatively of *Domestic Manners*? The creditors drove her to live in Belgium. Her own choice of domicile, when she was able to indulge her fancy, was Florence in Italy. Some of her sharpest comments on America, to the effect that it was boring and materialistic, are remarkably close to the conclusions of certain French intellectuals. Victor Jacquemont, a young French naturalist who had visited the United States in 1827, read *Domestic Manners* in India in 1832 and gleefully discovered that it confirmed his own observations. Jacquemont's friend the writer Stendhal, who also read Mrs. Trollope in 1832, thought too that she was right about the heaviness of American life.

Domestic Manners of the Americans is not a subtle book, nor a dazzlingly original one. Perhaps it is best understood as a fairly artless mixture of several books, written by a woman of uncommon energy and aspiration, yearning for an existence that had so far eluded her. At any given point, her attitudes are sincere, and usually transparent. They do not make a perfect fit. The desperate, impoverished matron with an ineffectual husband coexists with the creature who would like to read soul-stirring literature on a mountain top; and with a third lady who would love to be a *grande dame* instead of Dame Trollope. Undoubtedly there is too a Tory presence in the offing. Stendhal described her well as *"un sot ultra avec de l'esprit,"* which might be rendered as "a fool with spirit." An irony which offers a further insight is that for Stendhal the English somewhat resembled the Americans. In castigating the Americans for being solemn, materialistic, and graceless, the English were unconsciously convicting themselves.

The unevenness, the innocent multiplicity of the book helps to explain why it was so peculiarly exasperating for American readers of the 1830s. Frances Trollope was not really ensconced within a fortress. She was herself a vulnerable commentator. The Canadian humorist Stephen Leacock once wrote that "half truths, like half bricks, go further in argument." That may be the best summary of *Domestic Manners*. Its author, not quite knowing who she was, did not quite know what she meant to say. It was a half brick of a book, with a half unintended wallop.

5

Sándor Farkas Bölöni
1795-1842

and

Ágoston Mokcsai Haraszthy
1812-1869

by Anna Katona

The clergy and the army, the police and the judges, the scholars and the bankers, these are common equal citizens. And how inconceivable it is to the stranger on top of all this, that none of the forty-eight religions is dominant, all have equal rights, that the clergy has no status, there is no standing army! There are no privileges, no nobility! no titles, no estates, no guilds, no secret police! How important all these issues are to the stranger!

—A Journey to North America, 1838

There is one single point to which all are driving, and this is 'wealth.'
—A Journey to North America, 1844

ANNA KATONA is now Visiting Professor at the College of Charleston, South Carolina, and was formerly Chairman of the English Department at Debrecen University in Hungary. She is the author of a Hungarian monograph on George Eliot, co-author of a Hungarian history of English literature, and has also written on Anglo–Hungarian and American–Hungarian cultural relations.

Sándor Farkas Bölöni, by an unidentified artist, engraving, in his *West European Diary,* 1943.
Alfred A. Reisch.

Called by his biographer the ''Columbus of Democracy,'' Sándor Farkas Bölöni came to
America in 1831. His travel account, *A Journey to North America,* contributed to Hungary's
national awakening during the first half of the nineteenth century.

Ágoston Mokcsai Haraszthy, by an unidentified photographer, date unknown.
Portage Free Library.

A practical man, Ágoston Mokcsai Haraszthy flourished as an entrepreneur in America. His
account, which tallied up the material advantages of American life, was no ode to the glories
of democracy but a guidebook for the enterprising.

45   *Bölöni and Haraszthy*

Travelogues on America became important as a political tool in Hungary during the first half of the nineteenth century. The country was suffering from colonial status under the Hapsburgs and from almost medieval conditions in all fields of life. During the 1830s, a period of national awakening, there emerged an interest in the young American republic which had gained independence from colonial status, had established a democratic political regime, and had achieved remarkable economic progress. Since there was no middle class in Hungary at that time, it was the radical part of the nobility who had the money and occasionally the opportunity to go abroad and see for themselves. Two leading figures of the Age of Reform, Ferenc Wesselényi and Count István Széchenyi, both wished to visit the United States but were prevented from doing so by the Austrian Minister Metternich.

Others, however, did succeed in getting permission to cross the Atlantic. Before 1848, two travelogues on the United States appeared in Hungary: *Utazás Észak Amerikában* (translated as "A Journey to North America") in 1838, preceding Tocqueville's *Democracy in America* by a year and, in 1844, *Utazás Ejszakamerikában* (also translated "A Journey to North America"). Both writers, Sándor Farkas Bölöni, who traveled in this country from September 1831 to November 1832, and Ágoston Mokcsai Haraszthy, in America from March 1840 through December 1841, came from a similar background, the middle stratum of nobility. However, they differed considerably in character and career. Bölöni was a political idealist, a Transylvanian by birth, belonging to the Unitarian church and therefore handicapped in a Roman Catholic country. His enthusiastic book about the United States made him suspect, and he died, a disappointed man, in 1842. Haraszthy was an enterprising individual who bought some land and made some money on his visit to the United States, and in 1848 returned for good. Bölöni, called by his biographer "the Columbus of Democracy," went in search of the country of political liberty and freedom. Haraszthy went with a view toward establishing trade links between the two countries. Bölöni's book reads like a poem in praise of the young republic. He described a visit to Mount Vernon lyrically: "Had I not been withheld by cool considerations of reason, I should have fallen on my knees." Haraszthy, writing in a dry, matter-of-fact style, simply enumerated the Washington relics to be found in Alexandria. Bölöni quoted the Declaration of Independence; Haraszthy overloaded his book with statistics about all fields of American life.

In spite of their entirely different approaches, they both saw the American republic as a model for Hungary. Struck by the otherness of America, "the new country of humanity," Bölöni emphasized the newness of the society. Haraszthy was impressed by the potential of an ambitious population on a huge continent. Bölöni's political essay had the greater impact. In spite of the danger of strong censorship, he expressed his admiration for the Constitution and the Declaration of Independence, which he called "the political Bibles of the Americans"—with the obvious wish that they might provide political guidance for his own country. In those days, this was a revolutionary gesture. Together with the Hungarian translation of Tocqueville's book by Gábor Fábián in 1841, it became a textbook on democracy for progressive minds and was eagerly quoted in parliamentary arguments.

In Count Széchenyi's opinion, no one had ever honored Hungary "with a more useful and more beautiful present."

Bölöni saw a basic distinction between European charters and the American Declaration of Independence. While the charters contained some grants by the king to the community, in the Declaration of Independence, rights had "been transferred by the people to the officebearers." Outraged by the excesses of Kings—"placed above us like heaven's messengers"— and local tyrants like the official who had his friend Király-King sentenced to a beating of twenty-five lashes, Bölöni agreed that the American Constitution had profited from Europe's failures, based as it was on two happy ideas: the abolition of state religion, of a standing army, and of hereditary offices, and the separation of the legislative, judicial, and executive powers. Haraszthy found in the American system relief from what he considered the damned Hungarian complacency, the reactionary *"extra Hungaria non est vita"* attitude.

The liberty and equality of the citizens struck both travelers as basic elements of democracy. And yet their conclusions were different. For Bölöni, freedom meant the mature and responsible behavior of an independent nation. In America, government intervention was on a minor scale; the people thought for themselves. Such immense enterprises as the Erie Canal convinced him that a free people did behave responsibly. The liberty of any citizen to set up a printing press seemed to him the main safeguard of freedom:

> *The population of the two Hungarian countries [meaning Transylvania and Hungary proper] almost equals that of the United States, and in the two Hungarian countries only 10 newspapers and magazines . . . drag on miserably —while 1015 are published in the United States. The village of Peekskill has had a paper for a considerable time, but in Marosvásárhely and Debrecen, and in most of our Hungarian cities, the Hungarian citizen still considers the newspaper to be a mendacious letter.*

Tomb of Washington, Mount Vernon, by George Lehman from a drawing by J. R. Smith, lithograph, 1832. The Mount Vernon Ladies' Association of the Union.

Wishing to pay homage to America's revolutionary heritage, Bölöni visited Mount Vernon and was moved by the sight of Washington's tomb modestly set in the woods. "Had I not been withheld by cool considerations of reason," he later wrote, "I should have fallen on my knees."

View of the Water Works on Schuylkill, seen from the top of Fair Mount, by Thomas Doughty, oil on canvas, 1826. Private collection.

Celebrating the Americans' inventiveness, both Bölöni and Haraszthy pointed to public improvements—waterworks, roads, and canals—as grand examples of the ways in which American enterprise tamed the continent.

An Indian family on the hunt probably near Utica, New York, by the Baroness Hyde de Neuville, watercolor, 1807. The New-York Historical Society.

"Poor Indians! You are already strangers in your own land," wrote Bölöni, "and those enemies who had massacred your ancestors already consider you strangers." He saw some hope in the Removal Act of 1830, which moved all Indians west of the Mississippi. Haraszthy, who had lived for a time with Indians in the West, was less sanguine, believing that contact between the two cultures was fatal to Indian society.

As a Unitarian in Roman Catholic Hungary, he was pleased to see in America the variety of religious sects. Even extreme experiments, such as the many Utopian religious communities, only strengthened his respect for a political system which could tolerate all sorts of behavior without seeing any threat to the stability of the country.

Haraszthy fully shared Bölöni's admiration for American liberty, but for him the most important aspect was freedom of enterprise. He saw industry, self-reliance, and endurance as the characteristics of a practical country. In his view, the driving force in American life was the quest for private wealth; thus he attributed the underdevelopment of Washington, D.C., to its lack of private industry. Liberty meant to him limited government interference with private enterprise. Bölöni and Haraszthy both recommended emigration to America, but for very different reasons. Haraszthy felt that self-reliant, resourceful people could take advantage of America's unlimited economic opportunity. Bölöni was convinced that America had something more important to offer than material welfare: the magic appeal of its democratic institutions. Each traveler responded to one strain in the American character: Bölöni to its passionate idealism, Haraszthy to its aggressive materialism (he bought land, made money, and founded a settlement, Széplak, in Wisconsin; and as a later immigrant, he was one of the pioneers in California's wine industry). Bölöni also admired American prosperity, although he felt that much of the public wealth came from saving the money spent in Europe on monarchy, armies, government officers, and police.

American equality was achieved, in Bölöni's view, through the system of public education, because the Americans "know that where the knowledge of sciences and law is limited to a certain class or to the few, the more learned can easily rule over the less learned." He also saw an ideal of equality expressed in the American's lack of humility before authority. He expressed his enthusiasm in a lyrical passage: "In vain does the stranger look for people of high rank, for powerful superiors, pompous officials, all are but common citizens." Haraszthy noticed the phenomenon as well. "The rich man here," he wrote, "is not ashamed of poor relatives."

Both travelers were interested in the two humane features of America's prison system: it provided the convicts, during their internment, with useful work and sought to restore them to respectability afterwards. Bölöni particularly applauded the assumption of America's legal system that "each man was born equal and honest." Americans did not, for example, bother with passports and customs. All this seemed wonderful to citizens of a country with very strict class distinctions, where political power was in the hands of the few.

The wilderness had a special appeal for both men. Of course, Bölöni saw much less of it. He preceded Haraszthy by nine years, and that amounted to much in the period of Manifest Destiny when America was continually expanding. Bölöni went only as far as Ohio. "Traveling in the American inner states," he wrote, "is similar to those fairy tales where through some magic force you tumble in the midst of deserted forests on bright cities, or else you wander in the region of great waters and find hotels similar to splendid castles." All this gave the country an aspect of youthfulness.

Haraszthy ventured far into the Midwest and undertook a dangerous trip in what then was truly Indian territory. He described the lonesome life on the trading frontier, and the immense effort, as well as the rich reward, that went into clearing the forest and breaking the virgin soil. Haraszthy was delighted to see how hard everyone worked, in contrast to Hungary, where the leisure class, the "so-called lords," took pride in their idleness, and the poor were often dependent upon charity. In the frontier states, as he explained to his Hungarian readers, there were no charity institutions; the industrious Americans were richly rewarded for their labor in the West, and no idle person dared venture into the new territory. Taken aback by the tempo of growth, he wrote: "Everything is as quick as lightning in the hands and brain of the American. He conceives his plans immediately and carries them out in spite of all obstacles with a firm determination, quickly and mercilessly." Bölöni, too, was impressed by American inventiveness: he admired the macadam road in Philadelphia, went into raptures about the "steam-carriage" (as he called it), and admired the fine architecture of the bridges in Pittsburgh. Haraszthy singled out the Patent Office, the steam-ferry, and the water-conduits in New York and Philadelphia. He foresaw a future when America would overtake and surpass Britain in trade and industry.

Measured against reality, the American dream did reveal some unmistakable flaws. The New Adam, like the Old, was not late in spoiling his "Paradise" (as Haraszthy called Wisconsin). Bölöni, encountering America's "moneyed aristocracy" in Albany and in Boston, was dismayed by their display of luxuries "incompatible with republican simplicity." Yet, he allowed, wealth was a "rightful benefit of Liberty, of Industry and Ambition." Haraszthy was even more lenient, wondering what else rich Americans could be expected to do with their money. On the subject of emigration, Bölöni was willing to accept its hardships as inevitable. Haraszthy was more compassionate. He saw the misery of emigrants on the ship, the disappointment of those who hoped for easily available mountains of gold, and the menace of crime among recent arrivals.

The plight of the Indians troubled both of them. "Poor Indians! You are already strangers in your own land," Bölöni wrote, "and those enemies who had massacred your ancestors already consider you strangers." All means of cheating and terror were used against them by white people. Yet Bölöni saw hope in the efforts of the American government to pay off the tribes willing to withdraw beyond the Mississippi. Both he and Haraszthy recognized the human qualities of the savages. Haraszthy, who lived among them for a time, held the white men responsible for the misfortunes of a whole race whose rightful land they had invaded and occupied and whose natures they had corrupted with alcohol.

If the Indian cast a shadow over the New Eden, so much more did the Negro slave. When Bölöni noticed, in Maryland, an advertisement for the sale of a Negro, he felt "as if an icy hand had clutched my heart." Obsessed as he was with his image of a perfect democracy in the States, he tried to shift the blame to the English for having introduced the institution of slavery. He described the attempt to send the Negroes back to a free African state as "a glorious step." Haraszthy, always practical, devoted more space to providing exact data on the slave populations of individual states than to theorizing about the issue. He discussed the climate of the South and

Buena Vista Ranche, Sonoma County, California: Residence of A. Haraszthy, by an unidentified artist, wood engraving, in *Grape Culture, Wines, and Wine-making*, 1862.

Following his own advice, Haraszthy returned to America and embarked on a variety of business ventures. In 1852, he imported the first European grapevines to California. His house, built in the Sonoma Valley, was a monument to his prosperity.

concluded that only those Europeans who could afford to pay the high price of healthy slaves should settle there.

In Bölöni's poem in prose, America emerged as a Paradise of Democracy and, in Haraszthy's matter-of-fact description, as the Paradise of Possibility for smart people. For both, it was a foil to backward conditions in the home country. Haraszthy saw America as "a glorious country which [would] shortly surpass in power all other countries of the world." Bölöni's farewell message to the United States reflected the hope of a better life, of which America was a symbol to millions in Europe in general, and to the political leaders of the Hungarian nation in the Age of Reform in particular: "Farewell once more, glorious country. Be thou the eternal protector and shelter of the rights of humanity! Be thou an eternal frightening landmark to tyrants! Be thou an eternal stimulating example to all oppressed!" Those, like Ferenc Wesselényi, who were prevented from seeing America for themselves, went into raptures over the reading of Bölöni's travelogue: "Yours is a beautiful fate. You have been able to see with your own eyes the young giant of human rights and freedom; your tears were able to fall on Washington's grave, and you could rest on the mounds of which, from the sacred blood of the fighters, arose the new era of common sense; you could embrace the unspoiled sons of that happy continent and breathe the air of freedom that God breathes and could not be tainted by either priviliges or despotism."

Alexis de Tocqueville, by Théodore Chassériau, oil on canvas, 1850.
Musée National du Château de Versailles.

A student of Ingres, Théodore Chassériau completed this portrait, one of his best, in 1850.
Nearly twenty years before, Tocqueville, then a minor government official, undertook his
travels in the New World which resulted in the classic study, *Democracy in America.*

6

Alexis de Tocqueville

1805-1859

by Patrice Higonnet

I know of no people who have established schools so numerous and efficacious, places of public worship better suited to the wants of the inhabitants, or roads kept in better repair. Uniformity or permanence of design, the minute arrangement of details, and the perfections of administrative system, must not be sought for in the United States: what we find there is the presence of a power which, if it is somewhat wild, is at least robust, and an existence checkered with accidents, indeed, but full of animation and effort.

—Democracy in America

PATRICE HIGONNET was born in Paris and educated in France, Britain, and the United States. He has written *Pont de Montvert* and some articles on aspects of French History from the eighteenth to the twentieth century. He teaches at Harvard University.

SOME MONTHS after the July revolution of 1830—on April 2, 1831, to be precise—two aristocratic young French administrators, rather disgusted by the turn of affairs in their own country, set off for the New World on the American packet *Havre*. The official purpose of Alexis de Tocqueville (a grandnephew of Malesherbes, the lawyer of Louis XVI in his trial of 1793) and of Gustave de Beaumont (soon to be grandson-in-law of Lafayette) was to study the American penal system. But their true goal was to withdraw from administrative careers now become distasteful to them, and to write a definitive and "scientific" book that would be based on a detailed examination of the mechanisms of American life. Thirty-eight days later, when they disembarked at Newport, they started at once on a very wide sweep which would take them from Boston to New Orleans and from Macon to Michigan, then on the very edge of civilized settlement. The impressions garnered on this ten-month journey were put to good use: Beaumont, a rather dull and prudish fellow who would later bowdlerize Tocqueville's correspondence, produced a study of the penal system and a novel entitled *Marie: or Slavery in the United States*. Tocqueville, for his part, published in 1835 the first volume of *Democracy in America*, which was followed in 1840 by a second more pessimistic and more theoretical tome.

In the mind of its author, the purpose of *Democracy in America* went far beyond America itself. Primarily, the United States was of interest because, there, the future could be studied in the present. To understand America in 1830, Tocqueville assumed, would be to understand, also, the future in Europe of both individualism and liberty; and the book would enable him to develop his views on the prospects of civil liberty and institutional pluralism in a mass society.

In addition, America was a curiosity in its own right; and no less than twelve hundred Frenchmen had already written something on the subject. Tocqueville was obviously fascinated by the day-to-day business of American life, and nothing escaped his attention: we are presented, for example, with reflections on American girls who are serious and independent—as one might suppose they would be, since in that rough country one "can hardly expect a girl to show . . . virgin innocence . . . and . . . naïve and artless graces." Also considered are architecture, literature, social manners, manners of speech, the theater, equality between the sexes, wages, and the conditions of officers in democratic armies. Tocqueville was particularly interested in the development of communications in America; there are long pages on the delivery of the mails and on river traffic. One of the steamboats on which he traveled sank during the voyage, and another ran up on a Mississippi sandbank: "Water journeys," he remarked, "do not agree with us." Conditions of travel were very rough: stagecoaches were "infernal." But Tocqueville noted with admiration "the tranquility of Americans"—decidedly a race of pioneers—"over all of these inconveniences. They seem to bear them as necessary evils."

There is, however, a persistent leitmotif to Tocqueville's observations, and it lies in his aristocratic perspective of America as an egalitarian society. He finds in America little concern for those fine points of sartorial elegance which in Europe reflect social hierarchy and, for the aristocracy, the daily social schedule. Tocqueville also sees, with some regret, that American women dress at eight o'clock in the morning "for the whole day." American lack of style is particularly evident at dinner parties: even in New York, where one should expect better, "vegetables and fish are served before the meat, the oysters for dessert. In a word, complete barbarism." Americans, he notes, have no sense for any of the finer arts of life that are born of aristocratic leisure. Moreover, they have no feeling for their language, and their orators are ridiculously pompous. Even their cities are dull: New York, for example, is "bizarre," monotonous, and "not very agreeable. . . . One sees neither domes, nor bell towers, nor great edifices, with the result that one has the constant impression of being in a suburb."

Like American cities, American life is flat, and so, for that matter, is American society. There is no indigenous aristocracy, and wealth is everything; it is "the only social distinction" in a country where "the desire for property is universal and where there is no profession at which a man works except for pay." Hence the conformity and *ennui* of American life: since money is "at the heart of everything the Americans do," there is "a family likeness to all their passions." It is true that there are no excesses, no war and pestilence; but neither is there art, literature, or eloquence: "They enjoy here the most insipid happiness which can be imagined. . . . Society is less brilliant and more prosperous." How different, then, from France: "We are in another world here" which, though interesting to visit, is best considered from afar. And it is worth noticing that although America made Tocqueville famous, he never found time to return to it.

Americans are, in a sense, hardly civilized, which is only to be expected, since there is in America no aristocracy and, for that matter, no class distinction of any sort: "The whole of society seems to have melted into a middle class." Indeed, Tocqueville feels, the very idea of a stable class structure is unthinkable in a country which is in constant flux and where "feverish activity" prevails. The poor of today may be the rich of tomorrow; and

Gustave de Beaumont de la Bonnière, by an unidentified artist, drawing, 1837. From an unlocated original. Photograph courtesy of G. W. Pierson.

Gustave de Beaumont was from an aristocratic family which Tocqueville fondly described as "calm of imagination, and tranquil of heart." The two travel-companions had planned to publish a joint study of American customs and political institutions but, on a trip through the Mohawk Valley, Beaumont's interest shifted. They had come in search of the Indians romanticized by Cooper and Chateaubriand; what they found along the Finger Lake trails was a scattered group of women, clothed in rags and begging for whiskey. This experience led Beaumont to take up the question of the American Indian. His *Marie,* a fictional treatment of the condition of Indians and slaves, was published in 1835, the same year as the first volume of Tocqueville's *Democracy in America.*

View of the prison at Auburn from the roof of the American Hotel, by Gustave de Beaumont, drawing, 1831. From the lost sketchbook, photograph courtesy of Beinecke Rare Book and Manuscript Library, Yale University.

Auburn Prison was a remarkable example of the new American penitentiaries Tocqueville and Beaumont had come to study. Under warden Elam Lynds, who later supervised the construction of Sing Sing, the Auburn "congregate" system allowed convicts to work unfettered and under only light guard in open quarries above the prison. Discipline was imposed by silence, and if there were no walls, neither were there any revolts.

he notes that "I never met a citizen too poor to cast a glance of hope and envy towards the pleasures of the rich, or whose imagination did not snatch in anticipation things which fate had obstinately refused to him." Thus, the concept of class does not apply in America; and neither, for that matter, does the concept of family which, "if one takes the word in its Roman or aristocratic sense, no longer exists there." In America, he writes, "the authority of the father is reduced almost to nothing . . . there is less of rule and authority." Bonds of affection do survive, to be sure, since relations between fathers and sons become "more intimate and gentle" when "mores and laws become more democratic"; but the fact remains that individualism in America prevails over family ties.

Flux and rampant individualism are a law of life in this country, where everyone moves feverishly up and down the social scale and exercises, in rapid succession, a bewildering variety of trades or professions. "The American," Tocqueville writes, "has no time to tie himself to anything. He grows accustomed only to change, regarding it as the natural state of man. He feels the need of it, more, he loves it; for instability, instead of meaning disaster for him, seems to give birth only to miracles all about him." Nor is this surprising: in America social conditions depend on wealth, and wealth is constantly being created.

In this respect, it is incidentally symptomatic of Tocqueville's seriousness that he should have devoted such time and energy to visiting the frontier, where individualism and change thrived in a pure state. His uncle, Chateaubriand, had also gone West, drawn as he was by the exoticism of

Niagara Falls and of bears, drunk with honey, idling on the banks of the Mississippi. But what Tocqueville seeks in Green Bay and Detroit are the archetypal forms of American social life. He is fascinated by the growth of western cities and the ever-receding frontier which provide, in the mind's eye, the material precondition of classlessness, democratization, and triumphant individualism. Whereas Mrs. Trollope, for example, had found little grace in Cincinnati, Tocqueville is truly impressed by this city "which seems to want to rise too quickly for people to have any system or plan about it." His companion, Gustave de Beaumont, concurs as always: "I don't believe that there exists anywhere on earth a town which has had a growth so prodigious. . . . Thirty years ago, the banks of the Ohio were a wilderness. Now there are 30,000 inhabitants."

In short, America is for Tocqueville a laboratory for the future, where the prospects of liberty in the world can best be gauged, because it is in America that individualism is hyper-developed. At worst, this force is merely a new form of egoism; at best, it can be defined as enlightened self-interest, "suited to the needs of our time." But it is always a force that must be reckoned with, since it is of "democratic origin" and "threatens to grow as conditions become more equal." In France, which is always in the back of Tocqueville's mind, individualism exists only in its worst guise. In the

Saginaw Woods, by Gustave de Beaumont, ink and wash drawing, 1831. From the lost sketchbook, photograph courtesy of Beinecke Rare Book and Manuscript Library, Yale University.

"Man accustoms himself to everything," wrote Tocqueville (shown below, with Beaumont and their guide) of their expedition into the northern woods of Michigan. They were determined to experience frontier life, but even in the 1830s, it was "more difficult than one thinks to find the wilderness." With extraordinary speed, "the forests fall, the swamps dry up . . . . The wildernesses become villages; the villages, towns. A daily witness of all these marvels, the American sees nothing astonishing in them. This unbelievable destruction, this still more surprising growth seem to him the usual procedure of the events of this world."

Hibernia Fire Engine Company No. 1 of Philadelphia, by Peter S. Duval, lithograph, 1857. INA Corporation.

In Tocqueville's view, the quality which most evoked the nation's spirit was its genius for forming associations. It was the Americans' propensity continually to group together—"to give entertainments, to found seminaries, to build inns, to construct churches, to distribute books, to send missionaries to the antipodes"—which made them so unlike the French villagers, who were "as inert as their huts."

name of egalitarianism, all social, financial, and cultural distinctions are erased, and the society degenerates into selfish atomism. The theme of *Democracy in America* develops against this background: given that the French have failed to secure both equality and liberty, is this failure everywhere inevitable? It is in this respect that America is for Tocqueville an experimental model which encourages his qualified optimism. "In democracies," he writes, "ignorance as much as equality will increase the concentration of power and the subjection of the individual"—and this despite the fact that "hatred of being ruled by one's neighbor . . . is a general and permanent sentiment in democracies." But America has the best chance of reconciling individualism in society and liberalism in politics.

The fundamental reason for this is that, although Americans are just as selfish as the next man and far more greedy, they are at the same time moved by a genuine concern for the liberty of others and the well-being of their community. This is a constant theme of *Democracy in America,* where Tocqueville repeatedly and sententiously reminds his French readers that, in the United States, he has "often seen Americans make real sacrifices for the common good. . . . I have noticed a hundred cases in which, when help was needed, they hardly ever failed to give each other trusty support." Where individualism makes allowances for the rights of others, liberty may triumph: in America, this has been done: in France, however, this will prove far more difficult, and perhaps even impossible (as Tocqueville implied in his *Ancien Regime,* a study of France before the Revolution of 1789, published in 1856 after the failure of the liberal Revolution of 1848).

Instinctively, therefore, Tocqueville, in his description of America, turns time and again to those aspects of social life which do not exist in France, but which, in America, reconcile the individual to society. Americans, to begin with, are not an ideological people: "In America, personalities are everything, principles are insignificant"—and therefore the citizens are not divided by ideological quarrels. In the United States, new political ideas and constitutional tenets "naturally and constantly balance and correct each other."

Moreover, Americans are, for historical and practical reasons, a deeply religious people. Within a month of his arrival in New York, Tocqueville already reflects that he has "never . . . been so conscious of the influence of religion on the morals and the social and political state of a nation." Americans, he feels, are genuinely pious, especially in the Western states, where people turn in relief from excessive materialism to religion; and, everywhere in America, "Sunday is rigorously observed." All of this is of fundamental importance: "In France," he muses, "I had almost always seen the spirit of religion and the spirit of freedom marching in opposite directions. But in America, I found that they were intimately united." To be sure, Americans are a law-abiding people and their lawyers are the natural aristocracy of the land; but the law in itself is no restraint: it allows Americans to do as they please, and it is "religion which forbids them to commit what is rash or unjust."

Finally and most importantly, in America, public good and private good are easily reconcilable, because the citizens have a genius for forming associations. As Tocqueville discovered:

Election Day at the State House, by John Lewis Krimmel, India ink and watercolor, 1816. The Historical Society of Pennsylvania.

The "confused clamor" of American society captivated Tocqueville. He respected America as a busy, moral, and prosperous society well suited for democratic institutions, but he was somewhat alarmed "at the inadequate securities which one finds there against tyranny." Where did an individual apply for redress of wrongs? "If to public opinion, public opinion constitutes the majority; if to the legislature, it represents the majority, and implicitly obeys it; if to the executive power, it is appointed by the majority, and serves as a passive tool in its hands . . . . However iniquitous or absurd the measure of which you complain, you must submit to it as well as you can."

> *Americans of all ages, all conditions, and all dispositions constantly form associations. . . . They have not only commercial and manufacturing companies, in which all take part, but associations of a thousand other kinds religious, moral, serious, futile, general or restricted, enormous or diminutive. Americans make associations to give entertainments, to found seminaries, to build inns, to construct churches, to distribute books, to send missionaries to the antipodes; in this manner they found hospitals, prisons, and schools.*

How far removed, indeed, from a French village which is "a congeries of mere huts and peasants as inert as their huts." More than anything else, it is the principal of association which, in America, reconciles the individual to the whole, socially and politically. There are, in *Democracy in America,* long and rather tedious pages on the Constitution, state governments, the presidency, Congress, and the courts. But clearly it is the town meeting which fascinates Tocqueville; and in both the first and second volume of his book, he dwells at length on those "local liberties" which have "induced a great number of citizens to value the affection of their kindred and neighbors [and which] bring men constantly into contact, despite the instincts which separate them, and force them to help one another."

There are some serious flaws in Tocqueville's work. It can, for example, be argued that he ignores the force of industrialism, that he misunderstands the nature of class, and that, generally speaking, he fails completely to explain *why* America is the way that it is. His emphasis on what he holds to be salient traits of American society is often more a reflection of his own concerns than of the reality of American life. For similar reasons, Tocqueville is very hard put to understand Jacksonian democracy as a struggle against aristocratic privilege, since he sees America as a society "where privileges of birth [have] never existed." On balance, it is not unjust to conclude that *Democracy in America* is not really a very good guide to the social and political structure of the United States in the early nineteenth century, or indeed in the nineteenth century generally. But it is a remarkable essay in cultural anthropology. It does not explain American society, but it describes life in America with brilliance and, oddly enough —given Tocqueville's character—with some charm. Therein is the strength of the book; and since it is a perspicacious description of a country which *was* the future, *Democracy in America* still has a contemporary tone and still speaks to the problems that face modern mass societies. Clearly, Tocqueville is a first-rate critic and moralist. His talent there may well outweigh his deficiency as a social scientist; and although he did not really understand the structure of American society, both foreigners and Americans themselves have had reason to interpret the new nation more through the prism of his work than through that of any other writer.

Harriet Martineau, by Charles Osgood, oil on canvas, 1836.
Essex Institute.

Seeking a respite from her hectic literary life in London, Harriet Martineau sailed for America in 1834 determined not to write a book about her experiences. She spent two years observing a people "possessed with an idea" and, in the end, wrote three. This portrait was completed as she was ending her journey with a final summer month in New England. Before sailing home from New York in August 1836, she had stopped to visit friends in Salem, Massachusetts, and her host commissioned a local artist, Charles Osgood, to do this painting.

7

Harriet Martineau
1802-1877

by Marghanita Laski

I regard the American people as a great embryo poet: now moody, now wild, but bringing out results of absolute good sense: restless and wayward in action, but with deep peace at his heart: exulting that he had caught the true aspect of things past, and at the depth of futurity which lies before him, wherein to create something so magnificent as the world has scarcely begun to dream of. There is the strongest hope of a nation that is capable of being possessed with an idea; and this kind of possession has been the peculiarity of the Americans from their first day of national existence til now. —Society in America

MARGHANITA LASKI, a novelist, critic, and journalist, lives in Hampstead Heath, London. Among her works are *Domestic Life in Edwardian England* and, most recently, *George Eliot and her World.*

On August 9, 1834, the packet *United States* left the Mersey estuary for New York. Among the passengers she landed there on September 19 was Miss Harriet Martineau, aged thirty-two, totally deaf, almost totally devoid of the senses of smell and taste, yet already famous on both sides of the Atlantic.

This fame was of recent and mushroom-rapid growth. Until 1830, Harriet had barely emerged from her childhood unhappiness as the handicapped and, she believed, unloved child of a large family of professional and mercantile origins, members of a devout Unitarian community in the East Anglian town of Norwich. In the economic disaster of 1825, the family had lost its financial security. "I have no fear for any of my daughters, except poor Harriet," said Mrs. Martineau in 1829, when her husband had died and the factory on which the family depended had finally gone bankrupt. "The others can work, but with her deafness, I do not know *how* she can ever earn her own bread."

By fancy work, a recourse that she was to enjoy till the very day of her death, Harriet could earn a little, but not enough. She had been writing, anonymously and for tiny returns, for some time, but it was not until 1831, when under three different names she won three separate prizes offered by the Unitarian Association for tracts addressed to the Mohammedans, the Catholics, and the Jews, that it became apparent that the handicapped young woman in Norwich was a well-educated writer of cogent polemical force. Her eruption into international fame arose from a brilliantly original notion of her own, that of writing a series of simple tales to illustrate the principles of political economy: the first of these was published in 1831. Harriet Martineau was at last able to set up in London as a professional author, and there she was lionized as, perhaps, no English woman writer had been since Maria Edgeworth.

By 1834, when Harriet crossed the Atlantic, she was well known in America, not only as the author of the political economy tales, but, by now, of many other stories and articles on the issues of the day. She was known, by her story *Demerara,* to hold strongly hostile views on slavery. Abolitionists with eagerness, anti-abolitionists with apprehension, awaited the formation of her impressions. The New York newspapers thrown on the deck by the pilot at Sandy Hook had been warning Americans how to treat her: at the least, they should not chew tobacco or praise themselves in her presence.

Miss Martineau declared all such precautions unnecessary. She had not come with any intention of writing a book, but only, on the advice of her friend Lord Henley, for two years' rest and self-improvement (later, in a different mood, she declared that she had come "to rough it"). With no preformed views, she intended to see as much as she could of the United States, and to talk freely with people of all conditions. Her deafness would prove no impediment. Not only had she two kinds of ear trumpet: she had also her companion, Louisa Jeffrey, a pleasant young woman who could confirm and supplement her own observations. It was sometimes said that Miss Martineau obtained only partial pictures through her inability to assimilate general conversation, but she had her prodigious background reading to refer to. A more serious disadvantage was her enormous self-satisfaction, her certainty of her own exceptional powers of observation and of her

FIFTH ANNIVERSARY
OF THE
MASSACHUSETTS ANTI-SLAVERY SOCIETY,
WEDNESDAY, JANUARY 25, 1837.

[☞ The public meetings, during the day, will be held in the SPACIOUS LOFT, OVER THE STABLE OF THE MARLBOROUGH HOTEL, and in the evening, in the REPRESENTATIVES' HALL.]

HOURS OF THE MEETINGS.
Meeting for Delegates at 9 o'clock in the morning, at 46, Washington-Street.
First public meeting at 10 o'clock A. M., in the LOFT OVER THE STABLE OF THE MARLBOROUGH HOTEL.
Second public meeting at 1-2 past 2 o'clock, P. M. same place.
Evening meeting at 1-2 past 6 o'clock, in the REPRESENTATIVES' HALL.

☞ The Committee of Arrangements respectfully inform the ladies that ample accommodations have been prepared for them. The loft is spacious, clean, well warmed, and will accommodate, with ease and perfect safety, at least 1000 persons.

☞ AMOS DRESSER, a citizen of this State, who was 'Lynched' at Nashville, for the crime of being an Abolitionist, will be present, and during the meetings in the afternoon and evening, will give a history of that affair.

By virtue of special compact, Shylock demanded a pound of flesh, cut nearest to the heart. Those who sell mothers separately from their children, likewise claim a legal right to human flesh; and they too cut it nearest to the *heart*.—*L. M. Child*.

On, woman! from thy happy hearth
Extend thy gentle hand to save
The poor and perishing of earth—
The chained and stricken slave!
Oh, plead for all the suffering of thy kind—
For the crushed body and the darkened mind.   *J. G. Whittier.*

Meeting Announcement of the Massachusetts Anti-Slavery Society, broadside, 1837.
Sophia Smith Collection.

Harriet Martineau arrived in Boston on the very day William Lloyd Garrison was mobbed, dragged through the streets, and only narrowly saved from being tarred and feathered. Shortly thereafter, she attended her first abolitionist meeting with friends and decided to speak out: "I consider slavery as inconsistent with the law of God . . . . and I now declare that in your *principles* I fully agree." While not a rousing call to arms, it was an endorsement, and it signalled the beginning of Harriet Martineau's lifelong public commitment to the abolitionist cause.

moral and physical courage. Add to this her immense garrulity (Sydney Smith, the editor of the *Edinburgh Review,* dreamed he "was chained to a rock and being talked to death by Harriet Martineau and Macaulay"), and it will be clear that open-mindedness was unlikely to be her chief virtue.

In two years, and with £400 "in credits," Harriet Martineau virtually quartered the then more accessible America. From New York she went up the Hudson to Albany and, of course, to Niagara. She stopped at Northumberland, to which Dr. Priestley, the great English Unitarian, had emigrated; and then she went on to Philadelphia, where it is revealing that she, on rational grounds, found the system of solitary confinement at the Penitentiary to be admirable, while Dickens, who brought his heart to the matter, knew it to be abominable. After visiting Baltimore, Washington, and the University of Virginia (whose first English visitor she claimed to be), she traveled south through the Carolinas and to New Orleans. The steamboat *Henry Clay* took her up the Mississippi to Cincinnati; she went by boat back to Virginia and, in July 1835, back to New York. Autumn was spent in New England. The money was running out and Miss Jeffrey had to go home, but Harriet managed another trip West. After touring the Rappite settlement at Economy, Ohio, a German communal experiment, she went back to New York and left for England on August 1, 1836, her return fare paid by an anonymous American well-wisher.

Almost everywhere she went she was, enthusiastically or cautiously, welcomed and feted—"Lafayetted," she maintained, was the American word for it. The only exception—and this she may have taken too seriously —was a threat received on her last trip to lynch her if she visited Louisville; she changed her route. Earlier in the slaveholding states she had been courteously received, though all she saw deepened her belief that slavery was degrading to master and slave alike. But inevitably she tended to be most at ease with people of similar background to her own—the New England Unitarians, the Boston abolitionists—and it was at the instance of these last that she made the gesture that was to be, for her, the most permanent influence of her American visit. Asked to say a few words at an abolitionist meeting, she hesitated, believing that non-involvement was appropriate in a visitor, and then decided that integrity demanded her voice and stood up to bear witness for the cause.

But though some of the Boston intellectuals were already distrustful of, as they saw it, her too-ready enthusiasms and prejudices, too often founded on credulously accepted gossip, Miss Martineau left the United States with, on the whole, as good a reputation as when she came. Most people found her likable, and some, enchanting. She had proved an ungrumbling traveler, a guest eager to be pleased, and an especial success with children. She had consistently declared that she had no intention of writing about her experiences, but few believed her, and, in the end, not one but three

Margaret Fuller, by Henry Bryan Hall, Senior, engraving, date unknown.
National Portrait Gallery, Smithsonian Institution.

Harriet Martineau's acquaintance with Margaret Fuller, a leader of Boston's intellectual society, began inauspiciously, with Miss Fuller declaring the issue of slavery too low and disagreeable a topic for polite conversation. The difference between them, Miss Martineau later wrote in her *Autobiography,* was that Margaret Fuller lived and moved in an ideal world, "talking in private and discoursing in public about the most fanciful and shallow conceits," which the Transcendentalists mistook for philosophy—while she herself was committed to moral action.

books emerged directly from her American visit. These were: in 1837, *Society in America,* and in 1838, *How to Observe* and *Retrospect of Western Travel.*

How to Observe was a commissioned contribution to an educational series, and was roughed out on the voyage to America. It is of interest in our present context, because what Miss Martineau was teaching her readers to observe and assess were societies other than their own. And not only were many of her illustrations drawn, when she came to complete the book, from the American visit, but we are entitled to assume that the plan, drawn up before the visit, was the one on which she intended to act.

It was, as we should expect, an entirely rational plan, demanding observation of Things before People and People before Institutions. Moral Outlook might be judged from Epitaphs, from Popular Idols and—Miss Martineau can always surprise us—from Popular Songs. We should observe Religion (the Clergy, Superstitions, Suicides) and Ideas of Liberty and Progress. There was no allowance—how could there be?—for culture shock, and it says much for Miss Martineau and for the Americans that from this remorselessly rational assessment they emerged, on the whole, very well: "The people of the United States have come the nearest to being characterized by lofty spiritual qualities."

The most delightful of the three books is the *Retrospect.* In her response to natural beauty and to ordinary domestic life, Miss Martineau most nearly escaped self-consciousness; and it is in these regions that we find her most sympathetic responses to America. She had slipped into the first book; now, in *Retrospect,* she could enthusiastically expand, writing, for example, about her voyage up the Mississippi, or about the Christmas party she attended at Hingham, Massachusetts, with what must have been one of the first Christmas trees outside Germany.

It was, however, the first book and the dullest that was the most important. She had wished to call it not *Society in America* but *Theory and Practice of Society in America,* and this, though the publisher wouldn't allow it, more fairly expressed her intention, which was to measure the society against the ideals of the Founding Fathers as expressed in the Declaration of Independence. Could any American, she asked, wish to be judged by any lesser test than that "furnished by the great principles propounded in the State House at Philadelphia?" Could he quarrel with results thereby fairly brought out, "whether they inspire him with shame or complacency?" It was to appear that he could.

Yet in Miss Martineau's judgment of America, there *was* much material for complacency. She looked on most of the evils she found as only temporary stumbling-blocks on the road to that social perfection to which, in her contemporary world, America came nearest:

> *The striking effect upon a stranger of witnessing, for the first time, the absence of poverty, of gross ignorance, of all servility, of all insolence of manner, cannot be exaggerated in description. I had seen every man in the towns an independent citizen; every man in the country a land-owner. I had seen that the villages had their newspapers, the factory girls their libraries. I had witnessed the controversies between candidates for office on some difficult subjects, of which the people were to be the judges.*

The Sportsman's Last Visit, by William Sidney Mount, oil on canvas, 1835.
The Museums at Stony Brook, Gift of Mr. and Mrs. Ward Melville, 1958.

Nineteenth-century travelers' accounts conventionally stressed the independence of the American woman and the unique position assigned her by a chivalrous society. But Harriet Martineau's angle of vision was rarely in plumb with accepted convention, and most certainly not in the area of women's rights: "While woman's intellect is confined, her morals crushed, her health ruined, her weaknesses encouraged, and her strength punished, she is told that her lot is cast in the paradise of women . . . . That is to say,—she has the best place in the stage-coaches: when there are not chairs enough for everybody, the gentlemen stand: she hears oratorical flourishes on public occasions about wives and home, and apostrophes to women: her husband's hair stands on end at the idea of her working, and he toils to indulge her with money: she has liberty to get her brain turned by religious excitements, that her attention may be diverted from morals, politics, and philosophy: and, especially, her morals are guarded by the strictest observance of propriety in her presence. In short, indulgence is given her as a substitute for justice."

And later, "America was meant to be everything." Set against such praise, how could Americans reasonably resent criticisms, intended only to point the way to correction? They would surely wish to know that Miss Martineau had found the health of Americans generally poor; their rooms overheated and their baths too few; their chief faults too great a terror of opinion coupled with a continual demand for flattery, whether from strangers or from their own clergy and politicians; the Indians' condition pitiable, and that of women atrocious.

How, she wondered, could the voteless condition of women in America be reconciled with the principle that government derives its just powers from the consent of the governed? "That woman has power to represent her own interests, no one can deny till she can be tried." But in America as much as in Europe, "female education . . . is training women to consider marriage as the sole object of life, and to pretend that they do not think so." Apart from the splendid factory girls of New England, with their libraries and lyceums, the opportunities for women's employment are no better than in the Old World. "The morals of women are crushed": "The whole apparatus of opinion is brought to bear offensively upon individuals among women who exercise freedom of mind." And "in my progress through the country I met with a greater variety of extent of female pedantry than the experience of a lifetime in Europe would afford. . . . Where intellect had a fair chance, there is no pedantry."

On slavery, Miss Martineau did not fall into the coarse error of supposing the oppressed ennobled by suffering; and she found that slavery degraded the master no less than the slave. The ruling class was corrupted by its belief that labor was disgraceful—a "vicious fundamental principle of morals." The wives of slaveholders were, as they themselves declared, "as much slaves as their negroes. If they will not have everything go to rack and ruin around them they must superintend every household operation, from the cellar to the garret: for there is nothing that slaves can do well." That there were social virtues in the slave state Miss Martineau was glad to grant: patience, mercy, indulgence—but "indulgence can never atone for injury . . . the extremest pampering, for a lifetime, is no equivalent for rights withheld, no reparation for irreparable injustice."

In England, *Society in America* was much admired. Miss Martineau professed to have expected, and not to have resented, its nearly universal condemnation in America. But this had the almost inevitable result of reinforcing her emotional links only with those who approved of her there: with Dr. William Ellery Channing, with William Lloyd Garrison, who evoked her perfervid admiration, and, above all, with the singleminded Maria Weston Chapman, a Boston abolitionist. Mrs. Chapman came to love Harriet Martineau a long way that side of idolatry, and it was she whom Harriet asked to edit the *Autobiography* she wrote in 1855, on one of the several occasions when she enjoyed finding it necessary bravely to face imminent death. In fact she lived till 1877 (and she did then face death bravely), and it was not until then that the *Autobiography* was published, though Mrs. Chapman's editing proved less than adequate. But the book is interesting in that, when Harriet returned in it to her American journey, she felt posthumously free to comment uninhibitedly on those Americans who had not responded to her as Mrs. Chapman did.

United States Senate Chamber, by Thomas Doney after James A. Whitehorne, engraving, probably 1846. National Portrait Gallery, Smithsonian Institution.

Although she had freely lambasted such obvious flaws as slavery and the inferior status of women, Harriet Martineau was exhilarated by the spectacle of America's democratic institutions. ''The American Senate is a most imposing assemblage. When I first entered it, I thought I never saw a finer set of heads than the forty-six before my eyes. . . . Mr. Calhoun's countenance first fixed my attention; the splendid eye, the straight forehead, surmounted by a load of stiff, upright, dark hair; the stern brow; the inflexible mouth;—it is one of the most remarkable heads in the country. Next to him sat his colleague, Mr. Preston, in singular contrast,—stout in person, with a round, ruddy, good-humoured face, large blue eyes, and wig, orange to-day, brown yesterday, and golden to-morrow. Near them sat Colonel Benton, a temporary people's man, remarkable chiefly for his pomposity. He sat swelling amidst his piles of papers and books, looking like a being designed by nature to be a good-humored barber or innkeeper, but forced by fate to make himself into a mock-heroic senator. Opposite sat the transcendant Webster, with his square forehead and cavernous eyes: and behind him the homely Clay, with the face and figure of a farmer, but something of the air of a divine, from his hair being combed straight back from his temples. Near them sat Southard and Porter; the former astute and rapid in countenance and gesture; the latter strangely mingling a boyish fun and lightness of manner and glance with the sobriety suitable to the Judge and the Senator. His keen eye takes in every thing that passes; his extraordinary mouth, with its overhanging upper lip, has but to unfold into a smile to win laughter from the sourest official or demagogue. Then there was the bright *bon-hommie* of Ewing of Ohio, the most primitive-looking of senators; and the benign, religious gravity of Frelinghuysen; the gentlemanly air of Buchanan; the shrewdness of Poindexter; the somewhat melancholy simplicity of Silsbee. . . . I have seen no assembly of chosen men . . . half so imposing to the imagination as this collection of stout-souled, full grown, original men, brought together on the ground of their supposed sufficiency, to work out the will of their diverse constituencies.''

The bitchiness with which she does so surely reveals a sense of hurt rejection hitherto carefully concealed. She attacked the strange management of children proposed by "the extraordinary self-styled philosopher" Mr. Bronson Alcott of Concord; the insensate ambition, insincerity, double-dealing of such politicians as Webster, Clay, Calhoun; and the obliviousness of the Transcendentalist writer Margaret Fuller to the anti-slavery movement: "While Margaret Fuller and her adult pupils sat 'gorgeously dressed,' talking about Mars and Venus, Plato and Göthe [*sic*], and fancying themselves the elect of the earth in intellect and refinement, the liberties of the republic were running out as fast as they could go."

Mrs. Chapman and the abolitionists had offered Miss Martineau the chance to write for their paper, the *Anti-Slavery Standard,* at the start of the Civil War. In her articles, she expressed outrage at Northern insistence that abolitionism was not the prime cause of the war. The Americans resented dogmatic lectures from what the *Boston Transcript* described as "this excessively conceited and peevish old spinster" whose only visit to America had been nearly thirty years before. The articles were suspended, but Miss Martineau did not desert the United States in its trial. She took on herself the duty of interpreting America to England; and in her regular outlet, the *Daily News,* and elsewhere, she felt able to assure her readers in 1861 that the South, rotted by slavery, beset by mutinous soldiers and starving workers, would collapse at the first blow. And when it did not, she sent to the *Atlantic Monthly* a series of articles on Military Hygiene, prepared with the help of her friend Florence Nightingale. But no more than most could she look on the aftermath of the war with hopefulness, whereas thirty years earlier, she could not *but* be hopeful about America. Temperamentally and by self-education she had had no alternative, in 1834, to seeing the future in America and finding that it worked, despite blotches that would surely be remedied. Harriet Martineau's America of 1834, as all other aspects of the world she wrote about, was made in her own image, and Douglas Jerrold's quip on an atheistic book of hers, "There is no God and Harriet is His prophet" is a fair comment on any of her multitudinous enthusiasms and disapprobations. It was perhaps a change in Harriet Martineau as much as in the America she had loved, respected, admonished, and, sometimes, almost felt she owned, that her last recorded comment on America was "I am, like many others, almost in despair for the great Republic."

Frances Anne Kemble, by Thomas Sully, oil on canvas, 1833.
Pennsylvania Academy of the Fine Arts.

A famous beauty, the English actress Fanny Kemble, here portrayed in the role of "Beatrice"
(*Much Ado About Nothing*), was painted thirteen times by Thomas Sully. Two years after arriving in the United States, she married a Georgia plantation owner and came to experience
slavery, already offensive to her liberal beliefs, as a personal nightmare.

8
Fanny Kemble
1809-1893

by Duncan J. MacLeod

*I was summoned . . . to receive the petition of certain poor women
in the family-way to have their work lightened . . . . They said they
had already begged "massa," and he had refused, and they thought,
perhaps, if "missis" begged "massa" for them, he would lighten their
task. Poor "missis," poor "massa," poor woman, that I am to have
such prayers addressed to me! I had to tell them that, if they had already
spoken to their master, I was afraid my doing so would be of no use,
but that when he came back I would try; so, choking with crying, I
turned away from them, and re-entered the house, to the chorus of
"Oh, thank you, missis! God bless you, missis!"*

—Journal of Residence on a Georgian Plantation

DUNCAN MACLEOD did his graduate studies at Churchill College Cambridge, Princeton University, and the University of Chicago. Now at Oxford University, he is University Lecturer in American History and a Fellow of St. Catherine's College. He is the author of *Slavery, Race and The American Revolution.*

FANNY KEMBLE was born into a famous acting family and, although she always affected to despise the profession, it was as an actress that she first visited the United States. Successful in her career, she had early won for herself a degree of financial independence not then common among women, and there was a persistent feminist streak in her behavior and attitudes which was to influence her view of America. Her English background was upper-class but, in English terms, liberal; in American terms, it was also genteel. In 1834, two years after arriving in the United States, Fanny Kemble married Pierce Butler, the absentee owner of two Georgian plantations and several hundred slaves. The marriage was a disaster; it was a serious mismatch not only of personality but of ideology. Fanny Kemble was an outspoken opponent of slavery. She was later to claim that at the time of the marriage she had no notion of the source of Butler's wealth. The unhappy marriage was also to influence her reaction to America as a whole. It took her to Georgia, thus prompting the work for which she is now best known (*Journal of Residence on a Georgian Plantation*); it gave her, also, in the person of her husband, a model of the slaveholder which was greatly to shape her conception of slavery.

Out of the thirteen or more years that she lived in or visited the United States, Fanny Kemble actually spent only a few months in Georgia (from December 1838 to April 1839). Most of her time was spent in or around Philadelphia and in Massachusetts. She had written another journal, of her first two years' experiences in America, even before she married Butler. What is most striking about her observations in both journals, and in her letters and later writings, is the degree of consistency she maintained in her views of America. Her reactions to American society and customs always reflected her liberal upper-class background.

Fanny Kemble began to form her opinions of America during a decade of great activity. The rapid territorial growth of the 1830s combined with the development of transportation, commerce, and manufacturing to suggest a vital nation on the move. It was a decade, moreover, in which factionalism was, on the one hand, giving way to a more coherent system of party politics and, on the other, was finding reinforcement from a plethora of reform movements. The most dramatic of these, antislavery, was to mold many of her opinions and was to plague her personal life. The fluidity of American life and its comparative lack of sophistication would produce in Fanny Kemble a certain ambivalence. She applauded the range of opportunities which promised to emancipate the working classes and at the same time deplored the lack of services to which she was accustomed. Not only were traveling conveyances, for instance, uncomfortable, but the inns at which she was forced to stay lacked many basic amenities. Worst of all, perhaps, the courtesy and deference accorded to one of her social standing in England were conspicuous in the United States by their absence. Fanny Kemble may have been an English liberal who disliked the idea of stratified society, but she was no democrat. Her intellect and sensibilities found much in the United States which she did not admire, and it is no accident that she was most comfortable in the high society of New England.

To the high society of the South, Fanny Kemble reacted with a mixture of awe and distaste. While she saw the planter class as bold, chivalrous, and romantic—in the whole of the United States, it was only in Charleston that she detected a willingness to break ranks with the prevailing pressures for conformity—she was never taken in by the Southern legend. She never succumbed to the fabled charm of the Southern aristocracy, because she found it anything but charming. It was barbarously feudal, cruel, and over-bearing. With "their furious feuds and slaughterous combats," she wrote, "their stabbings and pistolings, their gross sensuality, brutal ignorance, and despotic cruelty, [they] resemble the chivalry of France before the horrors of the Jacquerie admonished them that there was a limit even to the endurance of slaves." In part, no doubt, her opinions reflected her relations with her husband. Despite his great sophistication, Pierce Butler was never prepared to discuss his affairs with her and sought often to end their many violent quarrels by retreating into a cold aristocratic calm.

But her dislike of the planter class went beyond her aversion to Butler. She recognized the paternalistic nature of most slaveholders but found it offensively condescending. "I had several . . . favourite slaves presented to me," she wrote, "and one or two little negro children, who their masters assured me were quite pets." Such condescension was dehumanizing both for the blacks and for the poorer whites who were also its victims. Fanny Kemble noted that in some respects those slaves who most benefited from the kindnesses of their masters also suffered the most. Domestic servants lived in conditions no better than those of the field hands; they were con-stantly on call and thus had little freedom to relax in their own company; and contiguity with the white master class made them acutely conscious of the indignity of their position. Fanny Kemble could not reconcile herself to a view of the master class as constituting a civilized, natural aristocracy; on the contrary, it was a peculiarly savage aristocracy which wore its obligations upon its sleeve as obviously as it did its culture. She found

Pierce Butler, photograph from a lost da-guerreotype, date unknown.
The Historical Society of Pennsylvania.

In her husband, Fanny Kemble saw the characteristics of his class—"haughty, overbearing irritability, effeminate indo-lence, reckless extravagance, and a union of profligacy and cruelty." Pierce Butler's indifference to the treatment suffered by his slaves made communication between husband and wife impossible and led to their estrangement.

The Butlers' house on the Sea Isle plantation, by an unidentified photographer,
in *Fanny, the American Kemble,* 1972.

The Georgia plantation, where Fanny Kemble lived briefly as Mrs. Butler, was very plain. In
her journal she described the house as altogether "a mere wooden out-house"; its floors were
earthen, and the walls unpainted. "Such being our abode, I think you will allow there is little
danger of my being dazzled by the luxurious splendors of a Southern slave residence."

especially obnoxious the origin of the domineering spirit which defined
the planters: slavery promoted it in white children at a very early age. Her
own child was to be afflicted. Her daughter was not yet four years old
when the slaves sang of her as:

> *Little Missis Sally,*
> *That's a ruling lady.*

When Fanny Kemble heard talk of the natural stupidity and laziness
of blacks, she was amazed. Indeed, she commented more than once on the
pride blacks took in their jobs. She was especially impressed by the black
"mammies," by the strength and willingness of the boatmen who rowed
her between the island plantations and the shore, by the refusal of slaves to
permit others to do the jobs they considered their own. She perceived,
moreover, that although they had to depend on their master, they recognized that they were being exploited. It was obvious to them that their
labor with the hoe was a cheap substitute for the mule and plow. By
observing slavery from class rather than from racial or traditional perspectives, Fanny Kemble detected, too, the potentiality of an alliance planters
feared everywhere, between white and black labor.

Fanny Kemble was not herself free from condescension. She constantly
lamented that her husband's slaves were not her own "people" to educate
and emancipate. She remarked that there was "one almost admirable
circumstance in this slavery; you are absolute on your own plantation."
That absolutism was responsible for the defects she detected in the planter

class; but it also might have permitted a form of benevolent despotism within which the interests of the slave could be made paramount. On her husband's plantation, however, this was impossible. She was horrified at the dirty conditions of the slave quarters, at the poverty of their clothes, and at the filth and squalor of the plantation hospital:

> In the enormous chimney glimmered the powerless embers of a few sticks of wood, round which, however, as many of the sick women as could approach were cowering, some on wooden settles, most of them on the ground, excluding those who were too ill to rise; and these last poor wretches lay prostrate on the floor, without bed, mattress, or pillow, buried in tattered and filthy blankets, which, huddled round them as they lay strewed about, left hardly space to move upon the floor.

Slaves Escaping Through the Swamp, by Thomas Moran, oil on canvas, 1863. Philbrook Art Center, Tulsa, Oklahoma.

In her long walks around the plantation, Fanny Kemble was both awed by the natural beauty and repulsed by the pervasive atmosphere of slavery. She found the grounds enchanting, strung with a "thicket of glittering evergreens, over which hung, in every direction, streaming garlands of these fragrant golden cups, fit for Oberon's banqueting service." But the sense of entrapment was overpowering. Here was "a scene of material beauty and moral degradation, where the beauty itself is of an appropriate character to the human existence it surrounds: above all, loveliness, brightness, and fragrance; but below! it gives one a melusina feeling of horror—all swamp and poisonous stagnation, which the heat will presently make alive with venomous reptiles."

A Planter's Lady, by Auguste Hervieu, engraving, in *The Life and Adventures of Jonathan Jefferson Whitlaw or Scenes on the Mississippi*, 1836.

"Oh, if you could imagine how this title 'Missis,' addressed to me and to my children, shocks all my feelings!" Fanny Kemble wrote to her New England friend Elizabeth Sedgwick. "Several times I have exclaimed, 'For God's sake do not call me that!'" She sought to cope by setting an example: "Yet it can not be but, from my words and actions, some revelations should reach these poor people; and going in and out among them perpetually, I shall teach, and they learn involuntarily a thousand things of deepest import . . . but oh! my heart is full almost to bursting as I walk among these most poor creatures."

Slavery was for its victims a dead end; there was no hope of self-improvement or achievement. This lack of future combined with the direct brutality of masters and overseers, in Fanny Kemble's view, to brutalize the slaves. It accounted for their incessant insolence to each other and for their failure to engage in any leisure pursuits other than fighting and dozing. Blaming the system for the poverty of the blacks, both material and cultural, Fanny Kemble was always inclined to compare the slaves favorably with the white lower class. Thus she thought Irish laborers stupid and lazy; and she noted that on Sundays blacks scrubbed themselves clean and wore an assorted finery which clearly distinguished them from the grubby poor whites, whom she described as "filthy, lazy, ignorant, brutal, proud, penniless savages, without one of the nobler attributes which have been found occasionally allied to the vice of savage nature."

Slavery, she noted, was especially hard on women. She had nothing but praise for the black "mammy," but she deplored the impact of slavery upon black motherhood. Slave women lacked even those inadequate securities enjoyed by women elsewhere—the comforts and protection of fathers and husbands. They were forced to seek satisfaction in the enjoyment of motherhood alone. But that role was distorted: their infants were left in the somewhat dubious care of older children while they labored elsewhere, and the consequences were sometimes fatal. Moreover, sex and motherhood were too closely related to the needs and desires of the planters. Fanny Kemble was disturbed to hear slave men singing that "Twenty-six black girls not make mulatto yellow girl." She was even more disturbed at their unhealthy pride in childbirth, which emphasized it as a benefit to the master. "This was perfectly evident to me," she wrote, "from the meritorious air with which the women always made haste to inform me of the number of children they had borne . . . 'for you and massa.'" Nowhere, it seemed, was slavery more dehumanizing than in the strains it imposed upon slave women.

Fanny Kemble's journal was written in the form of letters to her New England friend Elizabeth Sedgwick. Her close friendship with the Sedgwick family dated from her first years in the United States when she met Catherine Sedgwick, who later introduced her to her sister-in-law Elizabeth. The Sedgwicks were a distinguished family of strict Federalist descent, centered in the Berkshire Hills of Massachusetts. Calvinists turned Unitarians, they embodied both what was splendid in New England society and its exclusiveness. Catherine Sedgwick was a noted authoress, and her home in Lenox became a meeting place for some of New England's intellectual elite and for such European travelers as Alexis de Tocqueville and

Woodcutter's Cabin on the Mississippi, by Endicott and Swett after Auguste Hervieu, lithograph, in *Domestic Manners of the Americans,* 1832.

On a drive through the scrub lands of Georgia—a wilderness she found "wearisome"—Fanny Kemble observed the "pine-landers," rural whites whom she saw as casualties of slavery: "They will not work, for that, as they conceive would reduce them to an equality with the abhorred negroes; they squat, and steal, and starve . . . and their countenances bear witness to the squalor of their condition and the utter degradation of their natures."

Harriet Martineau. It was there, indeed, from such people as the renowned Unitarian clergyman, Dr. Ellery Channing, and Dr. Charles Follen, Professor of German at Harvard, that Fanny Kemble imbibed much of her antislavery attitudes.

Fanny Kemble, then, viewed America from three rather special vantage points: the upper-class, genteel, English background; the peculiar position of an antislavery plantation mistress; and the plateau of New England high society. When she was on an acting tour in Baltimore and found herself in competition with a rival theatre company, it was remarked that she attracted the "aristocratic" elements of Baltimore's society and her rival the "democratic." She found the fact more comforting than chastening, and it enhanced her contempt for the crudeness of American life and many of its people. Yet, in spite of her aloof attitudes, she was enamored of America's republican meaning. When she traveled in Italy, she could not help but contrast the lamentable state of the Italian peasantry with that of their American counterparts. Her reaction to American politics, therefore, was somewhat ambivalent: she was hostile both to Andrew Jackson as a radical democrat and to his opponent Henry Clay as a "leader of the aristocratic party."

Fanny Kemble reacted adversely to the crass materialism of American life as she perceived it. In the decade before the Civil War, she regarded dubiously the enormous bustle of business, the rapidity with which the country was growing in wealth, the fierce invective of politics: taken together they added up to a self-indulgence which offended her sensibilities. It did not help that the future of her children was threatened by the speculative mania of the age. Her ex-husband, Pierce Butler, lost over half a million dollars in the fifties, a sum he was able to recoup only by the sale of about half his slaves. While she might not always like the manifestations of American freedom, Fanny Kemble continued to respect it, and she remained unreservedly loyal to the Union cause despite the criticism of much of her social circle in England. Having lived in the South, however, she was inclined to be less optimistic than her New England associates about its outcome. She recognized the complexity of the social problems which would follow emancipation.

Fanny Kemble's visits to the United States took place over a forty-year period. She was no ordinary visitor: her marriage to an American, and the similar marriages of her children, established a closer connection than most. America was so much a second home to her that she once expressed a wish to be buried in the Sedgwick family cemetery at Lenox. She was never able to stand back and view the scene around her with complete objectivity. Nor was it compatible with her temperament that she should. A passionate woman, she reacted impulsively to people and places. Her domestic embarrassments colored her attitudes and her behavior. That behavior, moreover, was sometimes unwise. Thus, when she was in Georgia, she undertook to teach some slaves to read, notwithstanding the state law to the contrary. More significantly, she talked openly to the slaves about their freedom. In themselves, such actions were admirable, perhaps, but they were not calculated to advance either the interests or the long-term happiness of the slaves. Despite all these factors, Fanny Kemble was one of America's more perceptive visitors. Especially in her Georgia *Journal,* she revealed an acute sensitivity to the social situation seen as a whole. She was consequently able to write about slavery passionately and with judgment, while remaining free from mere sentimentality. When in the United States, she was inclined to be critical of its customs and its society; when in England, she defended it against all aspersions—the issue of slavery aside. It was, then, no coincidence that Henry James frequently sought her company during his self-imposed exile; Fanny Kemble was herself something of an expatriate both in America and in England.

Charles Dickens, by Francis Alexander, oil on canvas, 1842.
Museum of Fine Arts, Boston.

As Dickens rode from Tremont House to Francis Alexander's studio to sit for his portrait, crowds would line the streets to see him. The studio also served as a salon, and there the author met the elite of Boston. False rumor had it that Alexander had clandestinely met Dickens on his ship, while it was quarantined in Boston Harbor, to obtain exclusive rights to paint him—leading the local press to characterize Alexander as an "art jockey" and Longfellow to use the word "Alexandered" to mean badgered.

9

Charles Dickens

1812-1870

by Philip Collins

"And how do you like our country, sir?" asked Mrs. Hominy.

"Very much indeed," said Martin, half asleep. "At least—that is —pretty well, ma'am."

"Most strangers—and partick'larly Britishers—are much surprised by what they see in the U-nited States," remarked Mrs. Hominy.

"They have excellent reason to be, ma'am," said Martin. "I never was so much surprised in my life."

—Martin Chuzzlewit

PHILIP COLLINS is Head of the Department of English at Leicester University, England. He is the author of *Dickens and Crime* and many other studies and editions of Dickens: most recently, the Clarendon edition of his *Public Readings*. He has held visiting professorships at Berkeley and Columbia.

CHARLES DICKENS visited America in 1842, entirely expecting to like it, and determined not to be prejudiced. As he often said afterwards, his "young enthusiasm" was "anything but prepared" for the disillusion he later experienced; "no stranger could have set foot upon those shores with a feeling of livelier interest in the country, and stronger faith in it." Before he left home, he read the English travel books about America but resisted the "preparation" they offered him. As he lectured one such author,

> I think you are rather hard on the Americans and that your dedication like Mrs. Trolloppe's [sic] preface seems to denote a foregone conclusion . . . . My notion is that in going to a New World one must for the time utterly forget, and put out of sight the Old one and bring none of its customs or observances into the comparison.

He landed at Boston on January 22, 1842, with hopes high. As Boston publisher J. T. Fields, later a close friend, recalled, "He seemed all on fire with curiosity, and alive as I never saw mortal before. From top to toe every fibre of his body was unrestrained and alert. . . . He seemed like the Emperor of Cheerfulness on a cruise of pleasure." But it was not meant to be just a pleasure cruise. Certainly Dickens wanted a change and some diversion, however hectic, after writing five novels in five years—that brilliant debut which made him an international celebrity in his twenties. (He had his thirtieth birthday in America.) From 1837 onwards, his letters mention his ardent desire to visit the United States, whose "soil I have trodden in my day-dreams many times, and whose sons (and daughters) I yearn to know and to be among." He was contracted to write "an account of my trip" (an intention he cagily hid from his American friends, until safe home), but this was less the reason for his going than an obvious way to finance his and his wife's holiday. He wanted to meet Washington Irving, William Cullen Bryant, and other writers he admired: and he may be forgiven for wanting to savor the adulation he was promised ("Washington Irving writes me that if I went, it would be such a triumph from one end of the states to the other, as was never known in any Nation"). But most of all, he wanted to see this exciting young nation. As a strong critic of British political and social shortcomings, he shared the general Radical belief that "westward, look, the land is bright."

Even before he arrived as "The Literary Guest of the Nation" (the title under which he was to be toasted at dinners), enthusiasm for him ran high. "Nothing talked of but Dickens' arrival," R. H. Dana, Jr., author of *Two Years Before the Mast*, noted in his diary. "The town is mad." Within days, William Wetmore Story was writing: "People *eat* him here! never was there such a revolution; Lafayette was nothing to it." Dickens was welcomed, not only as a great entertainer, but also as a kindred spirit, one of Nature's Americans, through his sympathy for the poor, his attacks on pride of place, his concern over social evils. His novels were regarded, his literary friend John Forster remarked, "as a kind of embodied protest against what was believed to be worst in the institutions of England." Clearly, with such intoxicatingly high hopes on both sides, the scene was set for a triumph. "How can I give you the faintest notion of my reception here," he wrote home, a week after landing; and two days later, "There never was a King or Emperor upon earth, so cheered, and followed by crowds." But just as clearly, a love affair of such ardency, with each party more enamored than

State Street, Boston, by S. Lacey after a drawing by William H. Bartlett, engraving, in *American Scenery,* 1840. The Bostonian Society.

Boston, English in spirit, was the only American city Dickens found entirely agreeable: "The golden calf they worship at Boston is a pigmy compared with the giant effigies set up in other parts of that vast counting-house which lies beyond the Atlantic; and the almighty dollar sinks into something comparatively insignificant, amidst a whole pantheon of better gods."

fully aware of the other, could easily crash, amid mutual recriminations. And this, in a way, is what happened.

In the short run, Dickens jumped to favorable conclusions. In a conversation, soon after his arrival, he said that Englishmen who had lately written about America had shamefully treated it. On February 4, he wrote home: "The American poor, the American factories, the institutions of all kinds—I have a book already," (and he continues, enthusiastically, about the absence of hunger, beggars, and illiteracy). From Boston, he wrote that Americans "are as delicate, as considerate, as careful of giving the least offence, as the best Englishmen I ever saw.—I like their behaviour to Ladies better than that on my own countrymen; and their Institutions I reverence, love, and honor." And though he later found some Americans less delicate and considerate, he stayed faithful to these judgments, and to Boston: "I sincerely believe," he wrote in his account of his journey, *American Notes* (1842), that its "public institutions and charities . . . are as nearly perfect, as the most considerate wisdom, benevolence, and humanity, can make them." In this book and in his letters, he praises many other American institutions, and (for instance) the model factory-town of Lowell, though he also criticized, temperately and intelligently, various jails, hospitals, and workhouses, which he thought ill-administered or ill-conceived. (His criticism of the Penitentiary in Philadelphia, internationally regarded as a model, started a controversy which continued for decades.)

"Boston is what I would have the whole United States to be," he wrote two years later. Boston indeed misled him about America—partly because he saw it with eyes yet unjaundiced, partly because it had real merits which were less conspicuous elsewhere, but perhaps most because (though he didn't realize it) Boston was more anglicized, easier to take, than other parts. Dickens proved to be more rootedly English than he had realized, or ever acknowledged. An interesting minor sign of this appears in his delighted description of New England towns and villages: but they "would have been the better for an old church; better still for some old graves." He delighted too in the literary and intellectual circles of Boston. This remarkable gathering of talent provided him with a more uniformly distinguished society than he was used to frequenting in London, and he warmed to it immensely. Generalizing about the American character in the "concluding remarks" of *American Notes,* he says:

> They are, by nature, frank, brave, cordial, hospitable, and affectionate. Cultivation and refinement seem but to enhance their warmth of heart and ardent enthusiasm; and it is the possession of these latter qualities in a most remarkable degree, which renders an educated American one of the most endearing and most generous of friends. I never was so won upon, as by this class; never yielded up my full confidence and esteem so readily and pleasurably, as to them; never can make again, in half-a-year, so many friends for whom I seem to entertain the regard of half a life.

He meant Boston. Where else could "Boz" (his pseudonym) be imagined becoming immediately and lastingly a bosom friend of a Professor of Greek?—Cornelius C. Felton, later to be President of Harvard. The professors at Harvard were "noble fellows," he reported, and in *American Notes* he praised the college highly, and implied its superiority in intellectual and social spirit to Oxford and Cambridge.

He soon encountered, however, Americans who were far from "noble fellows." The trouble began over international copyright. The United States had declined to make a reciprocal agreement with Great Britain, so Dickens's American readers, while giving him love and homage, provided him with no income. He spoke out on this issue, and many newspapers—very interested parties—hit back hard. By February 22, he was writing: "I have never in my life been so shocked and disgusted, or made so sick and sore at heart, as I have been by the treatment I have received . . . in reference to the International Copyright question . . . [with] scores of your newspapers . . . attacking me in such terms of vagabond scurrility as they would denounce no murderer with." Further irritations followed: newspapers wrote about his and his wife's dress and physique with offensive intrusiveness, or invented biographical details. Those Emperor-size crowds began to pall, especially when they lined up to shake his hand or peered in through the window while he and Catherine were dressing. One newspaper warned of revenge: "One could not but pity Boz with a full heart . . . and if any of the thousands who have run and jumped, screamed and halloed to see Boz should find themselves in print [in a novel] . . . why they must nor complain." And indeed, Dickens did later write a novel, *Martin*

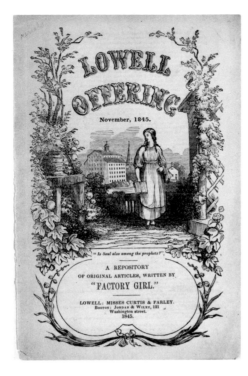

Title page of *Lowell Offering* for November 1845. Massachusetts Historical Society.

Arriving in the model factory-town of Lowell, Massachusetts, just after the mid-day meal, Dickens observed the factory girls returning to work. He thought them well-dressed, clean, and healthy, unlike Europe's "degraded brutes of burden." That these workers were also literary would, Dickens felt certain, startle his English readers. The *Lowell Offering* compared "advantageously with a great many English annuals. . . . A strong feeling for the beauties of nature . . . breathes through its pages like wholesome village air."

Chuzzlewit (1843–1844), in which the hero, who visited America, was treated with "no . . . remorse, or delicacy, or consideration."

Martin's arrival in America provides a quick anthology of what Dickens disliked there. Significantly, he arrives at New York, a city Dickens found much less congenial than Boston: this is typical of the novel's almost total concentration on the vices and ridiculous aspects of American life. Chuzzlewit's first experience of America, like Dickens's, was the invasion of his ship by newsboys. The episode is handled fiercely:

"Here's this morning's New York Sewer!" *cried one. "Here's this morning's* New York Stabber! *Here's the* New York Family Spy! *Here's the* New York Private Listener! *Here's the* New York Peeper! *Here's the* New York Plunderer! *Here's the* New York Keyhole Reporter! *Here's the* New York Rowdy Journal! *Here's all the New York papers! Here's full particulars of the patriotic loco-foco movement yesterday, in which the whigs was so chawed up; and the last Alabama gouging case; and the interesting Arkansas dooel with Bowie knives; and all the Political, Commercial, and Fashionable News. Here they are! Here they are! Here's the papers, here's the papers!"* . . .

"It is in such enlightened means," said a voice almost in Martin's ear, "that the bubbling passions of my country find a vent."

The American press, between Dickens and which a mutual loathing had developed (with exceptions on both sides), played a predominant role in his relationship with America. There is much in the novel about news-papers' filth, blackmail, and use of forged letters. Independence ("we do as we like") is the excuse for libel and tyranny. Party feeling, erupting violence, and political immorality, corruption, and trickery are vividly

New York, Park and Worth Streets called "Five Points," by an unidentified
artist, lithograph, 1827, in *Valentine's Manual*, 1855.
National Portrait Gallery, Smithsonian Institution.

After Boston, New York proved raucous and unpredictable. Dickens found his symbol for the
disorder of the city in its street population of pigs: "They are the city scavengers, these pigs . . .
never attended upon, or fed, or driven, or caught." He noticed a "solitary swine lounging
homeward. . . . his small eye twinkling on a slaughtered friend, whose carcase garnishes a
butcher's door-post . . . he grunts out 'Such is life: all flesh is pork!' buries his nose in the
mire again, and waddles down the gutter."

presented. In commercial and public life, too, swindling is tolerated in the
national worship of "smartness" ("We are a smart people here, and can
appreciate smartness").

Private and domestic life, manners, and customs, are similarly presented, in *Martin Chuzzlewit*, in their ludicrous aspects. Tobacco-chewing
and spitting—that constant theme of *American Notes* and other travel books
by Englishmen—quickly make their first appearance. So do picking one's
teeth in public, men's wearing their hats indoors (and wearing dirty linen),
and everyone's bolting their food in a hideous race of voracity. The bad
manners, lack of amenity, and indifference to the arts and the graces of life
are automatically defended by the slogan "We are a busy people, sir, and
have no time for that." Americans have queer customs—stressing the
wrong words, using expressions unfamiliar to Englishmen, giving every
man a military, or other, title. Pseudo-distinction is so widespread that, in
a single chapter, Martin three times hears that he is meeting "one of the
most remarkable men in our country": but this is just another example of
American excitability and overstatement (America "always *is* depressed,
and always *is* stagnated, and always *is* at an alarming crisis"). Their houses
are too hot, and their city streets full of pigs. The people are "strangely
devoid of individual traits of character" (except the sizeable minority who
are "the most remarkable people in the country")—this partly because of
the national spiritual emptiness, partly because of the pressure of public
opinion. All these points are made in the first American chapter (Chapter

16). The only targets introduced later are the American belief that they have monopoly of "a moral sense," the snobbery of pseudo-enlightened Americans, the reckless dangerousness of their trains, the hideous indignity of levées, the fraudulence (and implicit skepticism about expansion westwards) represented by Eden, and the lampoon of Transcendentalism given in the sublime vacuity of the Literary Ladies.

"I am a Lover of Freedom, disappointed—That's all," Dickens wrote in 1842. "This is not the Republic I came to see. This is not the Republic of my imagination." And elsewhere: "I tremble for a radical coming here, unless he is a radical on principle, by reason and reflection, and from the sense of right. I fear that if he were anything else, he would return home a tory. . . . I do fear that the heaviest blow ever dealt at liberty will be dealt by this country, in the failure of its example to the earth." Reflecting Dickens's bitterness, Martin Chuzzlewit observes that the Stars and Stripes, "a gay flag in the distance," when viewed more closely, is only "sorry fustian!" As their ship sails away, Martin and his companion Mark Tapley redesign the American Eagle:

The thriving city of Eden as it appeared on paper. The thriving city of Eden as it appeared in fact, engraving after Hablot Knight Browne, in *Life and Adventures of Martin Chuzzlewit,* 1910. Library of Congress.

In his novel, *Martin Chuzzlewit,* Dickens took his vengeance on America's fast-talking, profit-oriented society. Martin becomes an unwitting partner in the Eden Land Corporation, a shady group which has enticed him with a giant plan depicting the flourishing city of Eden, replete with banks, churches, markets, theatres, and a daily journal, the Eden Stinger. The real Eden (modeled on Cairo, Illinois) turns out to be a miserable slough: "There were not above a score of cabins in the whole; half of these appeared untenanted; all were rotten and decayed." For one of them, Martin's companion "brought forth a great placard . . . bearing the inscription, CHUZZLEWIT & CO., ARCHITECTS AND SURVEYORS, which he displayed upon the most conspicuous part of the premises, with as much gravity as if the thriving city of Eden had a real existence."

THE THRIVING CITY OF EDEN, AS IT APPEARED ON PAPER.

THE THRIVING CITY OF EDEN, AS IT APPEARED IN FACT.

"I should want to draw it [*says Mark*] *like a Bat, for its short-sighted-*
ness; like a Bantam, for its bragging; like a Magpie, for its honesty; like a
Peacock, for its vanity; like an Ostrich, for its putting its head in the mud,
and thinking nobody sees it—"

"And like a Phoenix, for its power of springing from the ashes of its
faults and vices, and soaring up anew into the sky!" said Martin. "Well,
Mark. Let us hope so."

Dickens's New York friend, the eminent Philip Hone, a diarist who had
written, after the unfavorable reception of *American Notes* ("a very fair and
impartial book"), that no writer had been "more unfairly treated by my
countrymen," felt let down by *Chuzzlewit* and called it an indefensible,
ungrateful, and "exceedingly foolish libel." Other critics, both British and
American, were just as uncomplimentary. Their attacks rankled with
Dickens. As over none of his other writings, he remained very defensive,
taking several opportunities to say "I told you so," when events in America
seemed to prove his criticisms right. "I very often dream I am in America
again," he told Felton in 1843; "I am always endeavouring to get home again
in disguise, and have a dreary sense of the distance."

Dickens maintained warm friendships with Felton, Longfellow, and
other American friends: one, whom he met later, Captain Morgan of the
American merchant service, became, in Captain Jorgan of *A Message from
the Sea,* the only genial American figure in his fiction. He continued to like
and warmly praise the American character, in its private manifestations,
but he remained skeptical, or scathing, about American public life and
national pretensions. When the Civil War broke out, he felt little sympathy
for either side. "Heaven speed you in that distracted land of troubled vaga-
bonds!" was his Godspeed to a friend, Frederick Lehmann, who traveled
there in July 1862; and when Lehmann returned in May 1863, Dickens
treated his belief that the North would win as "a harmless hallucination."

However, soon after the war, Dickens did return to America, for a foray
into its profitable lecture market. He was very worried lest Americans had
not forgiven him for his offenses (and, remembering the anti-British
"Astor Place Riots" which had driven his actor friend Macready out of
New York in 1849, he knew that the mob could be dangerous). His stay
lasted from November 1867 to April 1868. He took every precaution against
offending American susceptibilities: neither he nor his staff nor his weekly
magazine would make any statements about America, and before leaving
England he gave a mollifying and much-publicized speech about "the
astonishing change and progress of a quarter of a century over there." He
inserted some tactful phrases into the Preface to a new edition of *Chuzzlewit.*

He need not have feared. "It is a great pleasure to see Dickens again
after so many years," wrote Longfellow soon after his arrival. "The enthusiasm for him and for his Readings is immense. One can hardly take in the
whole truth about it, and feel the universality of his fame." Giving seventy-
five performances, he took nearly a quarter of a million dollars. With a tight
work-schedule, and increasingly poor health, he had little opportunity for
hobnobbing, sightseeing, and visiting institutions, though he managed a
little of these, and rejoiced to meet his friends again in "my native Boston."
His letters home show preoccupation with his work and his health, and he
had decided to publish nothing about this trip. Three points recur in his

remarks on the changes in America after twenty-five years. Firstly, on its expansion: "New York has grown out of my knowledge, and is enormous. Everything in it looks as if the order of nature were reversed, and everything grew newer every day, instead of older." Secondly, "I see *great changes* for the better, socially. Politically, no. . . . The change in manners is remarkable. There is much greater politeness and forbearance in all ways." There was even improvement in the newspapers—"a much more responsible and respectable tone than prevailed formerly." Thirdly, there is a much less compassionate note in his references to Negroes. Emancipation was right, but "their enfranchisement is a mere party trick to get votes."

He declined public and private invitations but eventually had to accept a farewell dinner. His hosts were the New York press—ironically, in view of the earlier antagonism; but suitably agreeable sentiments were expressed all around, the author George William Curtis making a felicitous reference to Dickens's earlier "offense": "Fidelity through his own observations is all we can ask of any reporter. . . . He was obliged to . . . report many things that were not pleasant or flattering. It is the fate of all reporters." Dickens paid tribute to "the amazing changes" he had observed—"Nor am I, believe me, so arrogant as to suppose that in five-and-twenty years there have been no changes in me, and that I have nothing to learn and no extreme impressions to correct from when I was here first." This was no mere bow to etiquette. Dickens confessed his new humility before the extraordinary and unfathomable fact of America in a private letter from Boston:

> *Again; there are two apparently irreconcilable contrasts here. Down below in this hotel every night are the bar loungers, dram drinkers, drunkards, swaggerers, loafers, that one might find in a Boucicault play. Within half an hour is Cambridge, where a delightful domestic life—simple, self-respectful, cordial, and affectionate—is seen in an admirable aspect. All New England is primitive and puritanical. All about and around it is a puddle of mixed human mud, with no such quality in it. Perhaps I may in time sift out some tolerably intelligible whole, but I certainly have not done so yet. It is a good sign, may be, that it all seems immensely more difficult to understand than it was when I was here before.*

The British Lion in America, by an unidentified artist, woodcut, 1868, in *Dickens in Cartoon and Caricature,* 1924.

Twenty-five years after his first visit, Dickens returned to America on a lecture tour which, between November 1867 and April 1868, earned him a quarter of a million dollars. This time, he took great care not to offend American sensibilities. The "British Lion in America" talked of "the astonishing change and progress of a quarter of a century," and issued a new edition of *Martin Chuzzlewit* incorporating a tactful new introduction.

Manjirō, by an unidentified Japanese artist, wood block print, in *Hyo Yo Sadan*, 1853.
Hiroshi Nakahama.

A shipwrecked Japanese fisherman rescued by a New England captain who brought him home
to Fairhaven, Massachusetts, John Manjirō became legendary in Japan for his "discovery of
America." Here he is portrayed, after his return to his country in 1851, wearing the uniform
of an American seaman.

10
John Manjirō
1827-1898

by Lee Houchins

The residences of American rulers are built on flat ground, and not one of them is constructed like a daimyō's *castle in Japan. When the ruler retires, he receives a pension and spends the rest of his life without want or worry. [Their] officials do not flaunt their authority in public.*

—Manjirō's commentary given during interrogation, following his return to Japan in 1851

LEE HOUCHINS is currently a Research Associate at the Smithsonian Institution. He has frequently lectured in Japan and has taught the history of American-East Asian relations at Georgetown University.

WHEN Captain William H. Whitfield's *John Howland* entered New Bedford harbor on May 7, 1843, after a highly successful whaling voyage of three years and seven months to the central and northwest Pacific whaling grounds, she carried more than 2,500 barrels of sperm oil. On board the ship was Manjirō, a bright and spirited young Japanese, known affectionately to the crew as "John Mung"—a name that Whitfield had devised by combining the name of his ship and his rendering of the boy's name. Manjirō was to spend the next seven years in New England, first attending school in the town of Fairhaven, Massachusetts, and then becoming increasingly competent as a seaman and officer on American whalers, before he returned to Japan in 1851.

Manjirō was born in 1827 on the Pacific coast of the Japanese main island of Shikoku. His home village, Nakanohama, was situated within a few days' walk of Kōchi, Tosa *han,* one of the fifty-odd feudal domains of mid-nineteenth-century Japan. His father died when he was nine years of age, and it was necessary for him and his four brothers to seek casual employment with fishermen operating out of the distant harbor of Usaura. In such humble circumstances, it was not possible for Manjirō to receive any sort of formal education.

Early in the new year of 1841, Manjirō joined his friends, Denzō, Toraemon, Jūsuke, and Goemon, in what was expected to be a brief excursion in a twenty-four-foot boat off the Tosa coast. They made a good catch, but were caught by a severe storm before they could retrieve their nets and return to port. The storm damaged their steering oar and blew them far out to sea. They drifted for seven days in the open Pacific, until they were swept close to Torishima, a small, uninhabited island more than two hundred and fifty miles from any land. Manjirō and his companions lost their boat while making the landing and were marooned for almost six months, living in a cave and barely subsisting on rainwater, albatross, roots, shellfish, and seaweed. Their situation steadily worsened until late in June, when the *John Howland* hauled into view and, after a full morning of being suspensefully observed by the castaways, lowered two boats for a look around the island for turtles—as a supplement to the monotonous fare on board the whaling ship. Frightened as they were by the appearance of the bearded, rough-looking American whaling men, two of whom were black-skinned, the Japanese were nevertheless anxious to get aboard the ship, hoping to find there food, warmth, and water.

Captain Whitfield gave the castaways a most humane reception. He ordered hot food for them and provided them with warm clothing. The next day, the *John Howland* sailed off in search of whales. In their five months at sea before arriving at Honolulu, the Japanese recovered their health and learned to perform the basic work of whaling men. Manjirō, who stood out as the brightest of the five, was invited by Whitfield to accompany him home. After consulting with his companions from Tosa, Manjirō made the decision to sail in the *John Howland* to America, where he could gain an education and learn a trade. Denzō, Toraemon, Jūsuke, and Goemon remained in Honolulu, where, through Captain Whitfield's good offices, they were placed in the care of American missionaries.

Manjirō had often heard the *John Howland* crewmen talk about their home towns, especially New Bedford, which was then a bustling whaling

Stern of the John Howland, by Kawada Shōryō, wood block print diptych, in *Hyo Sen Kiryaku,* circa 1851. Hiroshi Nakahama.

After half a year as a castaway on a small island, Manjirō saw a ship looming in the distance. The *John Howland* was easy to spot: a large whaler sailing out of New Bedford, it had three tall masts hoisting over ten sails and jibs, and carried a crew of more than thirty men. Captain William H. Whitfield saw Manjirō and his four companions frantically waving, and invited them aboard.

port of more than twenty thousand population, and the much smaller and quieter harbor suburb of Fairhaven, across the wide mouth of the Acushnet River. But, as the *John Howland* stood into Buzzards Bay and entered New Bedford harbor, Manjirō was nearly overwhelmed with the strange sights and sounds. The Japanese youth, now sixteen, was taken directly to the Oxford Street home of James Akin, an old shipmate of Whitfield's, who was to provide room and board while the captain, a widower, went to New York on business. Whitfield also arranged for the young man's admission to Miss Jane Allen's nearby Oxford School, a typical one-room schoolhouse that accommodated about thirty pupils. Throughout that fall and winter, Manjirō studied English, penmanship, arithmetic, and other subjects.

When Captain Whitfield returned from New York, he brought his new bride, Albertina, and settled on a modest farm four miles to the east of Fairhaven. Manjirō joined them there at the end of August. On the Whitfield farm, he took particular delight in riding about the fields on horseback. Had he remained in Tosa, he could hardly have dreamed of such an opportunity because, in Japan, horsemanship was a martial art practiced only by *samurai* and their lords. In February 1844, he entered Mr. and Mrs. Lewis Bartlett's Academy, a rather special kind of middle school, where he was able to study somewhat more advanced mathematics, surveying techniques, astronomy, and navigation, in addition to ordinary subjects. Manjirō spent well over two years there. It was during this period that he purchased a copy of Nathaniel Bowditch's *The New American Practical Navigator,* the standard American work on piloting and navigation.

Manjirō was quick to grasp the first opportunity to extend his experience at sea. In mid-May, 1846, he sailed as an ordinary seaman in the New Bedford whaling bark, *Franklin*, Ira Davis, master. During this voyage, which took him around the Cape of Good Hope and across the Indian Ocean into the Pacific, he established himself as a highly effective seaman and navigator. When the captain was put ashore at Manila because of his deepening insanity, Manjirō was promoted to second-in-command. He must have realized that, in Japan, his humble status would have prevented him from aspiring to much beyond the ownership of a small fishing boat; yet he must also have begun to formulate the hope that, upon his eventual return to his family, his newly acquired knowledge, experience, and status as the first mate of an American whaler would somehow be appreciated by Japanese authorities, with the result that his personal and family fortunes would greatly improve.

When Manjirō left Fairhaven for the second time in October 1849, he was determined to return to Japan and his family. He and a young friend shipped as seamen in a lumber schooner bound for San Francisco, via Cape Horn. Within three days of their arrival in San Francisco, they went up the Sacramento River toward the gold fields on a sidewheeler steamer. In just over two months, Manjirō earned one-hundred-eighty silver dollars working in an established mine, and more than four hundred additional dollars and a small quantity of gold dust and nuggets after striking out on his own. Returning to San Francisco, he booked a twenty-five-dollar passage for Honolulu in the steamship *Elisha*.

In Honolulu, Manjirō tried to find a way back to Japan. He sought out Captain Whitmore, the master of the *Sarah Boyd,* an American merchantman

Boston Harbor and Old North Church, by Kawada Shōryō, wood block print, in *Hyo Sen Kiryaku*, circa 1851. Hiroshi Nakahama.

Manjirō's first impressions of New England are suggested in this drawing of Boston made from his sketch by Kawada Shōryō, a talented Japanese artist who would later be his patron. In this port scene, the Old North Church and surrounding buildings take on an oriental aspect; a stripes-and-stripes version of the American flag is visible; and a sampan-like day sailer is just putting out of the harbor.

in the China tea trade, who was preparing to sail for Shanghai. Recognizing that his great circle route would take his ship close to the Ryūkyū islands, the captain agreed to carry Manjirō, his friends, Denzō and Goemon, and a small boat. They hurriedly purchased a second-hand whaleboat, rigged her as a sloop, and named her *Adventurer,* which name was proudly painted on her stern. Manjirō procured provisions and sundries; most of the latter, along with the gold nuggets from California, were intended as presents for his mother. He also stowed his most treasured possessions: his Fairhaven schoolbooks and later acquisitions, including Bowditch's *Practical Navigator*, mathematics texts, a dictionary, the *Farmers' Almanac*, and a biography of George Washington. An additional item, which would prove to be a mixed blessing, was a group passport, issued by the American consul. It was an impressive document which, in effect, presented Manjirō as an American agent intent upon opening Japanese ports to American ships.

The *Sarah Boyd* cleared Honolulu in December 1850, and, after a tedious passage of nearly fifty days, approached the southern tip of Okinawa. Captain Whitmore eased the *Sarah Boyd* in as close to a beach as prudence would allow, and dropped her sails. The *Adventurer* was lowered into the choppy seas in strong winds and under heavy rain and hail. Manjirō manned the oars, bringing the sloop into the lee of the land, while the *Sarah Boyd* disappeared over the near horizon. The following morning, February 3, 1851, they landed and made their way to a cluster of houses visible beyond the beach. It was ten years and one month since they had sailed Denzō's small fishing craft out of Usaura harbor.

Even if Manjirō had been blessed with the diarist's urge, he could not have maintained a record of his experience abroad, simply because his lack of a formal Japanese education left him unable to read and write Japanese. In any case, we have no diaries of his American sojourn, and his notebooks, written in English, seem not to have survived. Except for a few sketches, some of which were transformed into charming book illustrations by professional artists and copyists after his return to Japan, the only comprehensive record of his impressions and perceptions is found in the transcripts of the intense and prolonged interrogations to which he was subjected through the first year following his return to Japanese sovereignty. Manjirō and his companions spent six months under detention where they had landed. A thorough examination of their belongings and a relatively gentle interrogation were conducted by both local officials and representatives of Shimazu Nariakira, the feudal lord of the Ryūkyū islands. Manjirō and his friends were eventually moved to Kagoshima, the main castle town of Satsuma *han*, where they were questioned by Nariakira himself, who seemed particularly impressed with Manjirō's strong assertions that, unlike the Japanese, Americans judged a man by his competence and ability, rather than background or social status. In this exchange, Manjirō's views reflect his own personal resentments toward the late-feudal Japanese social system.

After forty-eight days of questioning, the three returnees were transferred to Nagasaki for investigation by the representative of the Tokugawa shogunate, Japan's late-feudal, military-bureaucratic government.

Processing a whale on board the John Howland, by Kawada Shōryō, wood block print diptych, in *Hyo Kyaku Danki,* circa 1851. Hiroshi Nakahama.

After three years in New Bedford, Manjirō took a long whaling voyage around the Cape of Good Hope and across the Indian Ocean to the Pacific, and established himself as an expert seaman. One day, as his ship headed for new whaling grounds near British Guiana, a giant turtle was spotted, and it was Manjirō's harpoon which found the mark. The ten-foot monster struggled violently; Manjirō jumped into the sea, got astride the turtle, and plunged a dagger into its neck. His bravery won the crew's admiration and led to Manjirō's appointment as first mate.

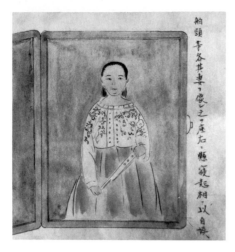

Crew Keep their wives portraits, by an un-identified artist, wood block print, in *Hyo Yo Sadan*, circa 1853. Hiroshi Nakahama.

One of the things which fascinated Manjirō about Americans, particularly his mates on whaling expeditions, was their custom of carrying a pocket-sized image of someone they loved. Manjirō's perception of a da-guerreotype, then unknown in Japan, is shown here in a Japanese sketch based on his description.

Manjirō and his companions were subjected to eighteen intensive in-terrogation sessions, the transcripts of which were transmitted to the shogunal headquarters in Edo (modern Tokyo). It is from these and similar documents that we have most of Manjirō's impressions of America.

In the course of the interrogations, Manjirō was pressed to give an ac-count of his adventures and a detailed description of all the places he visited. He had adopted the values and religious attitudes of the typical mid-nineteenth-century New Englander, but he was fully aware of the tra-ditional Japanese hostility toward Christianity, and toward Catholicism in particular. He purposely left his personal copy of the Bible behind in Fair-haven, and none of the books or other objects which he brought back with him could be considered as religious. Nonetheless, Japanese officials prodded him with questions regarding American religious practices. Manjirō replied:

> the kurishitan [*Catholic*] *religion hardly exists in America. There are a few* kurishitan *temples with sacred images inside, so the* kurishitan *religion is not actually prohibited, but people don't become* kurishitans *because they are very practical and can't be bothered with something as strange as that. The ordinary structures are very large and have a clock tower two or three hundred* shaku [*one* shaku *being nearly one foot*] *high. There are no Buddha-like figures inside. I hear that they worship the one who made this world on each seventh day. This ceremony is called the* shandei shabasu [*Sunday service*], *and it is also conducted aboard ship. There are many seats inside the temple. All those attending the* Shandei shabasu *bring their [prayer] books. The one who presides stands on a high place hold-ing his book. He asks them to open their books to certain places; then they all read together; then they listen to his explanation; and then they all leave together.*
>
> *Their funeral ceremony is generally the same as ours. The corpse is put in a casket and buried in the ground. Sometimes something like Buddhist sutras are read by the priest, but this man is different from a Buddhist priest, since he has a wife and children. They erect tombstones and occasionally go there to weed [around the grave], but there is no ancestor worship in Amer-ica, and no special mourning costumes.*

Manjirō's responses frequently led from religious ceremony to broader perceptions of American society. Regarding marriage, for example, he observed:

When girls reach thirteen, fourteen, or fifteen [thirteen to seventeen, western style] years of age, they look for husbands by associating with several people. Young men and women exchange correspondence [directly], and there are no go-betweens [a reference to the Japanese custom of arranged marriages]. When they decide to get married, they tell their parents and the rest of their immediate families. Sometimes there are difficulties involved in this pursuit. Occasionally, a young man or woman marries without family consent; when this happens, they are sometimes disowned by their parents.

Even the terribly wealthy have only one wife.

When questioned on hairstyles, he stated:

Both men and women don't change their hairstyles very much from youth to old age. The men usually wear theirs curled [and] covered with a hat. The women wear theirs straight down, so as to hide their ears, then swept back and tied in a [bun]. Women use warm water to smooth their hair.

About music in America, he said:

They have musical instruments called the piana, seruko *[cello] and a sort of* samisen, *called a* banchō *[banjo]. They have popular songs, one of which goes "When I see you coming over yonder hill, I cry . . ." and another, "For whom I adorn myself in the morning and evening . . ."*

Manjirō judged the American system of criminal justice to be eminently fair. His comments reflect the intensifying resentment he must have felt at the way he was treated during the interrogation. He and his companions were kept under strict confinement in prison cells which were hardly better than cages. He said that American criminals were not manacled, but were free to move about in a large area of confinement. They were taught new skills and produced useful items; many were engaged in the manufacture of textiles. American criminals were sentenced to different periods of imprisonment according to the seriousness of their crimes, and were often pardoned after serving only a portion of their sentences.

Manjirō did not always understand everything that he saw or heard about in America. His description of the telegraph is the most naïve:

Wires are hung above the roads. Probably something like a magnet is used to stick to the steel wires, and a letter can be attached to this to be dispatched automatically from one station to another without the services of an express messenger. How the system manages to avoid likely possibilities of confusion, I do not know.

As for railroads and their steam engines, Manjirō reported the following to the Japanese government councils: "Their steam engine car is called a *reirō* [phonetic for railroad], and twenty or thirty people ride this so as to travel without exerting themselves."

While on the topic of arithmetic, Manjirō described, for his investigators, the small blackboard slate used in American schools:

Their counting system is the same as ours, but the abacus that they use is definitely different. [Theirs] is made of thin, amethyst-colored stone and framed in wood about one shaku *square. Something that resembles a nail is used to inscribe letters for counting. If, after counting, one wipes the stone with his fingers, all the letters that have been inscribed disappear.*

During these months of interrogation, the same ground was gone over repeatedly and the questions were frequently naïve, or simply foolish. Manjirō's patience sometimes wore thin. In one exchange, he was asked, "What do the Americans call *hibashi* (fire tongs)? A *teppin* (iron kettle)?," and so forth. Manjirō replied, "The same: *hibashi, teppin* . . ." When Katsu Rintarō, who was present on this particular occasion, protested that he was not being very helpful, Manjirō finally gave a serious answer: "As for Americans, the ones who occupy high positions are men of lofty ideas, their leaders are thus wiser and more intelligent than the ones we have in Japan. On this point, the difference between Japan and America is like the difference between heaven and earth." Katsu Rintarō, well known as a formidable personality, accepted Manjirō's response without comment.

Even after the castaways were returned to Tosa in the middle of 1852, they were retained for several more months of questioning before being cleared for visits to their homes. It was during this period that Manjirō came under the patronage of the talented and enlightened artist, Kawada Shōryō, who transformed some of Manjirō's maps and sketches into attractive, if sometimes fanciful, illustrations for widely published—and frequently copied—accounts of Manjirō's adventures abroad. The Tosa *daimyō* became both interested in and proud of Manjirō and awarded him a minor retainer's rank, with the privilege of wearing a single sword. After a pitifully short visit with his mother at Nakanohama, Manjirō was assigned as a teacher in a school sponsored by the Tosa *daimyō*.

Despite his knowledge and general brightness, Manjirō's obvious pride, highly developed sense of personal worth, and seemingly unrestrained enthusiasm for Americans and their country brought him dangerously close to imprisonment—and worse—as an American spy. It was, ironically, the arrival of Commodore Perry in July 1853 that drew Manjirō, as an authority on the Americans, closer to the center of Japanese politics —although, because of the suspicion toward him of conservative political forces, he was not allowed to play a direct part in the negotiations with Perry, nor in the 1856–1859 negotiations with Townsend Harris toward a treaty of commerce between the United States and Japan. Even after his appointment as a *bakufu* bureaucrat, with the right to wear two swords, a modest annual stipend of rice, and permission to assume a family name— Nakahama—Manjirō constantly felt the effect of the extreme social disadvantage of his humble birth. However, he rose to be the personal secretary of Egawa Toraemon, one of the most progressive and imaginative teachers in Japan, who was also an influential *bakufu* official. Unfortunately for Manjirō, however, Egawa died in 1855.

Manjirō's contributions to Japan's transition from feudalism to the modern world were thus restricted to other important spheres: naval science, navigation, shipbuilding, whaling enterprises, and the teaching of English. Even so, the recounting of his long experience amongst the Americans was an important influence on some of the major figures of the Meiji restoration movement.

In 1860, the first Japanese Mission to America departed for San Francisco on the *Kanrin Maru,* and Manjirō was aboard. He was so closely watched by *ometsuke* (*bakufu* censors, or spies) that he could not risk writing to Captain Whitfield until he reached Honolulu on the return voyage.

Later in the same year, Manjirō made an unauthorized visit to one of the first American ships to enter a Japanese port under the Harris treaty. For this indiscretion, he lost his valued assignment as an instructor in the Japanese government naval school in Edo. He never fully recovered from the disgrace, although he did continue in the service of the central government and individual *daimyō*.

In 1870, Manjirō was sent by the new Japanese government as an interpreter on an official mission to Europe. When he reached New York, he was given permission to make an overnight visit to Fairhaven, where he stayed up most of the night in conversation with his old friend Captain Whitfield. A few months later, he fell ill in London and returned to Tokyo and his post as teacher of English. In his later life, he reminisced about his happy years in America where, although he did not then fully understand the notions of freedom and equality, he felt free and good and took courage from the realization that the same blue sky under which he rode through the Fairhaven fields extended to Japan and Tosa.

Manjirō, by an unidentified American photographer in Japan, photograph heightened with watercolor, 1875. Hiroshi Nakahama.

In 1870, Manjirō, on his way to Europe, stopped in Massachusetts to see his old friend. Captain Whitfield wrote: "John Mungero has made me a visit. He remembers [those who] befriended him when he was poor. It is wonderful to see the workings of Providence or of God, to bring about his ends."

Domingo Faustino Sarmiento, by Franklin Rawson, oil on canvas, 1845. Muséo Historico Sarmiento. Photograph by Michael A. Rockland.

Convinced that an ordered society was dependent on an enlightened citizenry, Sarmiento became an outspoken teacher and newspaper publisher, and was forced to flee to Chile, where this portrait was painted. Sarmiento's search for a rational society ultimately brought him to the United States.

11

Domingo Faustino Sarmiento
1811-1888

by Irving A. Leonard

The American is a man with a home or the certainty of having one, a man beyond the clutch of hunger or desperation, a man with hopes for the future as bright as the imagination can invent, a man with political sentiments and needs. He is, in short, master of himself, with a spirit elevated by education and a sense of his own dignity. It is said that man is a rational being to the extent that he is able to acquire and exercise reasoning powers. From this point of view there is no country on earth which has more rational beings than the United States.

—*Travels: "The United States"*

IRVING A. LEONARD is the Domingo F. Sarmiento University Professor of Spanish American History and Literature, Emeritus, at the University of Michigan. As the Assistant Director of Humanities for the Rockefeller Foundation from 1927 to 1940, he traveled extensively in Latin America. He is the author of *Baroque Times in Old Mexico*.

"FAREWELL to the United States! I carry them away with me as a happy memory and as a model . . . the Republic as an institution and as a promise of the world's future! Farewell! Farewell!" With these parting words, the Argentine Minister Plenipotentiary, Domingo Faustino Sarmiento, sailed from New York in the summer of 1868 to assume the presidency of his country. Probably no other foreign visitor of distinction came to the shores of the American republic more favorably inclined to admire it, and few departed with a more exalted conviction of its greatness. Sarmiento, later called the great "Teacher-President" of Argentina, was a statesman who waged a lifelong battle, against appalling odds, to transform his country's government from an arbitrary authoritarianism into a viable democracy; he was a national teacher with a mystical faith in the redemptive power of popular education; and he was a gifted writer whose works, preeminent among them the classic *Facundo* (1845; English title is *Life in the Argentine Republic in the days of the Tyrants*), served as weapons in his battles for reform. This South American deserves a niche in the pantheon of nation-builders of the Western Hemisphere along with Benjamin Franklin, Thomas Jefferson, Andrew Jackson, and Abraham Lincoln, for he possessed something of the genius of these great figures.

Born into a humble family in the closed society of San Juan, a small interior city of Argentina near the foothills of the Andes, Sarmiento—like his contemporary, Abraham Lincoln—read whatever books fell within his grasp. One of the first works to inspire his lifelong admiration for the United States was the *Autobiography of Benjamin Franklin*. Later, in his own book, *Hometown Recollections*, Sarmiento wrote:

No other book has done me more good than this one. Franklin's life was to me what Plutarch's Lives *were to him . . . . I felt myself Franklin. And why not? I was very poor like him, studious like him and, by being shrewd and following his footsteps, I might one day come to be like him. . . . I might even receive an honorary doctorate like him and make a place for myself in [South] American literature and politics.*

Sarmiento believed that a book on Franklin's life belonged in every primary school, and he cherished an unfulfilled hope of preparing a text for elementary classes. Nowhere else, he believed, was there such a practical model and so human a type to point the way to the finest aspirations of the land. "A poor and humble youth like Franklin," Sarmiento continued, "who, with only his own wit . . . makes his name famous, serves his country by helping it to break away from its oppressors, and one day presents the whole of mankind with a single instrument to control the lightning and can thus boast of saving millions of lives . . . that man should surely be on the altars of mankind . . . and be called 'the People's Saint.'"

At a young age, Sarmiento was forced to flee from the dictatorship of his own country into Chile; there, self-educated, he became, in time, an important educator. In 1845, the Chilean government sent him to Europe to study foreign institutions, and he became profoundly disillusioned by the glaring discrepancies between the teachings of the French philosophers and the actual living conditions of the masses. He described Europe as a "sad mixture of greatness and abjection, of wisdom and brutalization, sublime and filthy receptacle of all that both elevates and degrades man." In England, in 1848, Sarmiento came across a copy of

A nineteenth-century Argentine gaucho, by an unidentified photographer, in *Recuerdos del Peru,* 1868. Library of Congress.

In 1845, Sarmiento published his greatest work, *Facundo,* which argued that civilization as represented by education, permanent settlement, and cities, continually struggled with the barbarism inherent in the gaucho's nomadic life. Unlike the horseman of the Argentine pampas, the independent North American frontiersman was, for Sarmiento, a hero involved in an epochal attempt to win a continent for civilization.

Horace Mann, attributed to William Rimmer, marble, circa 1866. Muséo Historico Sarmiento. Photograph by Michael A. Rockland.

Meeting Horace Mann, America's great spokesman for public education, was the principal object of Sarmiento's first trip. Some years later, he had marble busts sculpted of Mann and Lincoln, "the two men I love the most." Mary Mann, who arranged the commission, wrote to Sarmiento that the sculptor, William Rimmer, "would be most happy to cut the heads for you. He thinks with you that they are eminently representative American heads and he had longed to do them both."

Horace Mann's *Report of an Educational Tour in Germany, France, Holland and Parts of Great Britain and Ireland* and promptly decided to visit the United States in order to meet the great educational reformer. Horace Mann has been described as a "human cyclone, the tall, humorless man in the long frock-coat, so exacting, so dogmatic, with the will of a battering ram"—and this description fits almost exactly his South American counterpart save, perhaps, for the lack of humor. These two men met in Mann's West Newton home. Their excited exchange of ideas—facilitated by Mrs. Mann, one of the celebrated Peabody sisters, who acted as interpreter—marked the beginning of Sarmiento's lifelong veneration of this couple.

His visit to the United States lasted scarcely two months. Traveling first to New York, the Niagara Falls, Montreal, and Boston, he then proceeded to Washington by way of Philadelphia and Baltimore, and later swung west to Pittsburgh and Cincinnati, and then down the Mississippi to New Orleans, where he embarked for South America. Sarmiento was essentially a tourist with a discerning eye, and his record of impressions, in the form of letters, has a freshness and mild humor. The United States then was essentially an agrarian society, still largely pre-industrial and pre-capitalist; and its relatively uniform prosperity, widespread public school system, and general spirit of equality greatly excited him. Unlike the European, "a minor under the protective guardianship of the state," the Yankee, Sarmiento found,

> is his own keeper, and if he wants to kill himself, no one will interfere. If he is running after a moving train and dares to jump and hang from a railing, barely missing the wheels, he has a perfect right to do so. . . . That is the way the character of a people is formed and how it benefits by personal freedom.

Sarmiento marveled also at the freedom of unmarried women to travel about unescorted. To a traveler of Latin American origin, accustomed to the almost Moorish seclusion of women, this comparative freedom of North American females to conduct their own lives was astounding; but he thoroughly approved. As he observed:

The unmarried woman, until the moment of entering the domestic cocoon to fulfill her social obligations in marriage, is as free as a butterfly. . . . After two or three years of flirting—that's the American word for it—of dancing, taking walks, and courting . . . the upshot of the matter is a formal engagement of which the parents are not notified until the very eve, though they already knew about it from the neighborhood gossip.

He continues to describe these mating habits of our ancestors with especial delight: "When the marriage takes place, the bride and groom depart forthwith in the train and display their happiness in all the parks, towns, and cities, and hotels. In the railroad coaches one perpetually sees these charming twenty year old couples in one another's arms. . . .Matrimonial propaganda could hardly be offered in more alluring form." The American river boats, which filled Sarmiento with wonder, made luxurious provision for the newlyweds: "There's a holy of holies . . . called the Bridal Chamber" in which "pink lamps glow at night . . . and there is the perfume of flowers and scented water." But soon the bride had to face the "sanctified tedium" of married life:

Henceforth, the shut-in walls of her domicile are her perpetual prison: henceforth, Roast Beef her eternal accuser; a swarm of fair and chubby children her constant burden; and a rude though good natured husband her lord by day and loud snorer by night, her accomplice and her shadow.

The curious liberties that North Americans took with each other were another aspect of life that profoundly impressed and slightly shocked Sarmiento's Latin reserve and decorum, although he accepted them, on the whole, as a concomitant of democratic ways. He was amused to see his Chilean traveling companion, Santiago Arcos, adopt the Yankee manner:

It was in Cincinnati where Arcos, on seeing a peaceful Yankee seated at the door of his shop reading a Bible, stopped in front of him, withdrew from the pious reader's mouth the cigar that he was smoking, lit his own with it, and then returned it and continued on his way without the good fellow even raising his glance from his book, or making any movement other than opening his mouth to receive back the borrowed cigar.

The easy familiarity, the extreme informality of North Americans was expressed in the undignified postures they assumed in public:

Four individuals seated around a marble table will infallibly have their eight feet upon it unless they can procure a chair upholstered in velvet, which, in the matter of softness, the Yankees favor over marble. In the Tremont Hotel in Boston I have seen seven Yankee dandies in amicable discussion seated as follows: two with their feet on the table, one with feet on the cushion of an adjacent chair; another with his leg passed over the arm of his own chair; another with both heels supported on the edge of the cushion of his own chair so as to rest his chin between both knees; another embracing or, rather, wrapping his legs around the back of his chair.

Sarmiento was careful not to exaggerate the importance of these rude customs in his evaluation of American society. Delicate manners were not,

St. Charles Exchange Hotel, by S. W. Thayer and Co., lithograph, 1845. Louisiana State Museum.

Traveling by steamboat down the Mississippi to New Orleans, Sarmiento sighted, as he neared the city, a dome which "brought to mind the dome of Saint Peter's in Rome which you can see from all positions of the compass as if it were the only thing there. . . . At last I was going to see in the United States a basilica designed along classic lines and on a scale dignified enough for religion. Someone asked us if we had hotel arrangements and suggested the Saint Charles as the best appointed. . . . The Saint Charles, which lifted its proud head above the surrounding hills and woods, the Saint Charles, which had called up my memory of Saint Peter's in Rome, was no more than a hotel!

"Here is the sovereign people who build palaces to shelter their heads for a night! Here is the religion which is dedicated to man as man, and here the marvels of art are lavished on the glorification of the masses."

for him, the essence of human progress. In the struggle against the barbarism of poverty, ignorance, and degradation, only the rule of reason, expressed through the widespread diffusion of knowledge and of wealth, made the crucial difference. By that standard, Europe was barbaric and South America more so. "I have come to the conclusion," he wrote, "that the Americans are the only really cultured people that exist on this earth and the last word in modern civilization." The general happiness and prosperity, the flexibility and inventiveness, the dynamic growth of the new society, which had turned to advantage resources that South America had left untouched, confirmed him in his conviction that man could indeed progress to a higher state.

But, with all his optimism, Sarmiento was not blind to the perilous blemish on the body politic of the great North American republic. Negro slavery filled him with immense foreboding, soon to be realized in a bloody civil war:

Ah, human slavery! That deep seated ulcer and incurable fistula which threatens with gangrene the vigorous body of the Union! . . . By what ill fate is it that the United States which, in practice, has brought about the greatest progress in the feeling of equality and charity, is doomed to wage the final battle against the ancient injustice of man to man already won all over the rest of the earth?

Eighteen years later, in 1865, Domingo Sarmiento returned to the United States, as the Minister Plenipotentiary of Argentina, for "the three happiest years of my life." Mrs. Horace Mann, now a widow, became his most enthusiastic advocate because of his espousal of her late husband's theories (she often referred to him affectionately as "Mr. Sarmy"). With her great influence, she made it possible for Sarmiento to meet such distinguished Americans as Ralph Waldo Emerson, and Henry Wadsworth Longfellow (whose spoken Spanish Sarmiento considered excellent), and George Tichnor, the historian of Castilian literature. Likewise, through her mediation, Sarmiento made the acquaintance of many government figures and educational leaders. President Erastus Otis Haven of the University of Michigan, one of Sarmiento's earliest acquaintances while Minister Plenipotentiary, bestowed upon him a long-desired honorary Doctor of Laws

Reading Room, Astor House, by Nicolino V. Calyo, watercolor, circa 1840. Museum of the City of New York.

Because he measured civilization by the rule of reason instead of by delicate manners, Sarmiento believed that Americans were "the only really cultured people that exist on this earth." But he was amused by their lack of dignity: "While conversing with you, the Yankee of careful breeding lifts one foot knee high, takes off his shoe in order to caress the foot and listens to the complaints that his overworked toes make. Four individuals seated around a marble table will infallibly have their eight feet upon it."

degree, in Ann Arbor on June 24, 1868. In a letter to Senator Charles Sumner of Massachusetts, Mary Mann declared: "I think Mr. Sarmiento one of the most remarkable men that ever lived—he may be called the 'Horace Mann of South America' with ten thousand more difficulties than we ever had to contend with." Later, during the stormy years of his presidency, Mrs. Mann was to continue to support his educational endeavors by correspondence, and more effectively by selecting and sending young American women to Argentina to staff the lower and secondary schools as well as the normal schools (for the training of local teachers), which Sarmiento was establishing all over his country—America's first peace corps.

Although New England impressed the Argentine visitor most, in its dedication to education and generalized culture, he made frequent visits to the Middle West. He inspected schools at all levels, attended conferences of educators of all degrees, presented papers at these gatherings, and prepared a report for his own government entitled *Las Escuelas: Base de la Prosperidad y de la Republica en los Estados Unidos* (1866; translated "Schools, the Basis of the Prosperity of the United States"). These experiences, in a sense, provided his graduate training in education and political science, and the honorary degree granted by the University of Michigan on the eve of his departure was his diploma. After three years, he sailed homeward, full of plans to bring to his native land the blessings he had witnessed. For the remainder of his life, he kept near him, as his "household divinities," marble busts of Horace Mann and Abraham Lincoln.

There is no doubt that Sarmiento came to the United States, on both occasions, well prepared to admire the country and its people, and there is reason to believe that what he witnessed exceeded his expectations. Commenting, in the account of his first trip, on the remarkable ability of settlers of distant Oregon to organize themselves into a political community, Sarmiento wrote:

> If you want to understand fully the road this people has followed, get together a group of Englishmen, Frenchmen, Chileans, or Argentines, not common people but all from the cultivated classes, and ask them without warning to constitute themselves an association. They will not know what you are talking about, and will not be able . . . to establish with any precision the foundations upon which the government of a new society must rest.

Despite some flaws that he did not fail to note—as a Latin American, he was particularly critical of American expansionism in the war against Mexico—the United States remained, for him, an example of what he wished for his own country. He believed that Argentina, with its temperate climate and broad fertile pampas, could also become a united and prosperous people if it encouraged European immigration and a universal school system.

During his administration, Sarmiento faced numerous obstacles. A ruinous war with Paraguay diverted him from his primary objectives at the outset. He also had to deal with recurring epidemics, economic depressions, and civil strife in the interior provinces—and all this against a backdrop of the entrenched traditionalism of his countrymen, the resistance of the owning classes to educating the illiterate masses, the resentment felt by many toward his North American innovations, the mockery and derision of *"el*

Doctor de Michigan," as his enemies jeeringly called him, and the powerful political opposition stirred by his fiery speeches and passionate battling for reforms. Nevertheless, Sarmiento wrought fundamental changes in Argentina and laid the foundation for the best primary educational system in South America and, to a degree, one of the best in the world.

Deafness presently slowed down his activities, increasing his irascibility. The lusty battles to which he had given his vast energy had finally weakened his physique and severely taxed his heart, bringing death to the great "Teacher-President" of Argentina on September 11, 1888. Shortly before the end, he had written to a friend: "I feel my strength is waning. I know that my body is frail and that I must soon start upon one last journey. But I am ready because so little luggage is required for that journey; and I carry with me the only acceptable passport, because it is written in every language. It reads: Serve Humanity!"

In his declining years, Sarmiento had liked to reminisce about his travels in the great North American republic. To a friend he had written: "My journey, then, was like that of Marco Polo. I discovered a new world, and I never renounced it."

The Argentine Legation to the United States in 1865, by an unidentified photographer. Muséo Historico Sarmiento.

In 1865, Sarmiento returned to the United States as the Argentinian Minister Plenipotentiary for "the three happiest years of my life." Pictured here (seated at the left) with the Argentine Legation, Sarmiento in fact spent little time on his ministerial duties; he preferred to tour the country, lecturing on education and meeting with some of America's most prominent intellectuals. The University of Michigan awarded him an honorary Doctor of Laws degree in 1868. Later that year, he returned to Argentina as President.

Fredrika Bremer, by Olof Johan Södermark, oil on canvas, 1843. Östermalms Gymnasium, Stockholm. Photograph courtesy of Svenska Portrattärkivet, National Museum, Stockholm.

This portrait of Fredrika Bremer by Södermark, who had studied under Winterhalter in Paris, was painted six years before the Swedish novelist set out on her "voyage of destiny" to America. There she observed home and family life and the status of women in a democracy.

12
Fredrika Bremer
1801-1865

by Signe Alice Rooth

America is the land of experiment. . . . One of its sons drew the lightning from the clouds; another created wings out of steam for all the people of the earth, so that they might fly round the world; a third has, oh the happy man! discovered the means of mitigating life's bitter enemy, bodily suffering, and of extending the wings of the angel of sleep over the unfortunate one in the hour of his agony! And all this has been done in the early morning of the country's life. . . . What will not this people accomplish during the day?

—The Homes of the New World

SIGNE ALICE ROOTH, a linguist of Swedish ancestry, was born in New York. She is senior editor in the Division of General Assembly Affairs, United Nations, and author of *Seeress of the Northland: Fredrika Bremer's American Journey, 1849–1851*.

FREDRIKA BREMER was born in Finland, then part of the kingdom of Sweden, on August 17, 1801, but grew up in Stockholm and at her family's nearby estate in Årsta. She did not have to earn her living but early showed an aptitude for writing and published her first book in 1828. Just as she was launched on a literary career, Fredrika received an offer of marriage from her dear friend and teacher Per Böklin. After much soul-searching, she declined, saying, "In another way than the usual one I want to try to fulfill my womanly calling: that of being an alleviating and animating power in life." Fredrika Bremer felt she had a mission to help the distressed and to further women's rights, and she continued to write her domestic novels which marked the beginning of the realistic novel in Sweden.

Miss Bremer kept abreast of books by distinguished European travelers to the New World. She was greatly influenced by Tocqueville's classic work *De la démocratie en Amérique,* which she called "an epoch-making book in my life because of the perspectives it opens, the thoughts it lets me think, the results it helps me to arrive at. It has enabled me to live a great deal." In the 1840s, allusions to the young and dynamic land became more frequent in Fredrika Bremer's correspondence. She wished to see for herself what effect American democratic institutions had upon the individual; she wanted, above all, to study the home, the family, and the position of women, as well as the influence of the social structure on the development and happiness of the individual. Her projected journey to the land of promise was based on "a need to embrace, to comprehend a larger world." She told a Danish theologian: "I am going to America to see the human being in the new home, in the free state, and from this point to cast a glance at the future and what we can hope from it, all we people who are going in the same direction as the American people have gone and are going."

On September 22, 1849, at the age of forty-eight, Fredrika Bremer set out from Liverpool on the S. S. *Canada* for the journey that, she felt, was written in her book of destiny. The courageous Swedish lady approached the West with eager expectations and a thousand questions in her soul. Unlike many of her less fortunate compatriots emigrating to America, she traveled first class. She was the only Swede among some sixty passengers, and one of a dozen women. On the thirteen-day crossing, she read Longfellows's *Evangeline.* Delayed by a storm at sea, the Cunard steamship entered New York harbor on October 4.

At the Astor House, the renowned novelist was besieged by callers— she shook hands with almost eighty people the second day of her visit— and was deluged with invitations, letters, and requests for autographs. The *New York Semi-Weekly Express* of October 9 stated on page one: "MISS BREMER has already become the lioness of the town, from her gentleness and great good sense, and is in all respects worthy of the attention she is receiving at the hands of our countrymen." The American press reported her activities throughout her stay. At literary soirées in her honor, the author of *The Neighbors* and *The Home* soon met important American authors of the time, including George Bancroft, William Cullen Bryant, Washington Irving, and Bayard Taylor. In a poem dedicated to her, John Greenleaf Whittier welcomed the

> Seeress of the misty Norlånd,
> Daughter of the Vikings bold.

Fredrika Bremer, being somewhat frail, found life in America over-powering. She was unprepared to be a visiting literary celebrity; soon after landing, when she heard a tap at the door, she exclaimed: "O! I wish I was a little dog that I could creep under the table and hide myself." She was assailed with questions as to how she liked the country, how long she planned to stay, where she would travel, and so forth. Later she would enjoy American hospitality, but her first banquet was an ordeal: "Is there in this world any thing more wearisome, more dismal, more intolerable, more indigestible, more stupefying, more unbearable, any thing more calculated to kill both soul and body, than a great dinner at New York?" In the city proper, Fredrika wrote, "people crowd as if for dear life, and the most detestable fumes poison the air." She felt in such a "state of combat" and so fatigued that she had to seek refuge in Brooklyn. Later, when she was dragged off to a party at midnight, she declared: "It was too much! And that is the way they kill strangers in this country."

The Swedish author did not, however, let public adulation or transitory annoyances cloud her judgment; she was determined to be open-minded. Unlike Charles Dickens, she saw the positive side of the newly forming society; her innate good will and kindness prevailed. She commented: "As some travelers see and make a noise about their [the Americans'] failings, it is very well that there should be somebody who, before any thing else, becomes acquainted with their virtues. America's best judges and censors of manners are Americans themselves."

Fredrika Bremer spent three months in New England. She established rapport with the great figures of the American literary renaissance and was fascinated by the intellectual atmosphere. She was a guest of Ralph Waldo Emerson, Henry Wadsworth Longfellow, and James Russell Lowell, and made sketches of them in her album. About Emerson, the "sphinx of Concord," she wrote: "He is a very peculiar character, but too cold and hyper-

Fredrika Bremer, attributed to Mathew Brady, photograph, circa 1849. National Archives and Records Service, Washington, D.C.

By the time Fredrika Bremer arrived in America in the fall of 1849, her "domestic novels" had already earned an enthusiastic audience there. She soon became the sensation of the social season, barraged with invitations to receptions, dinners, and great soirées. This photograph by Mathew Brady, then in his twenties but already one of the best-known photographers in the world, was probably taken at his Broadway studio during Miss Bremer's hectic first encounter with New York.

Escaping New York, Fredrika Bremer spent three months in New England, where she met Ralph Waldo Emerson. She was intrigued with the "sphinx of Concord," finding him "a very peculiar character, but too cold and hypercritical" to please her entirely. Her sketch portrays a character dominated by "a strong, clear eye, always looking out for an ideal, which he never finds realized on earth; discovering wants, shortcomings, imperfections."

critical to please me entirely; a strong, clear eye, always looking out for an ideal, which he never finds realized on earth; discovering wants, short-comings, imperfections; and too strong and healthy himself to understand other people's weaknesses and sufferings, for he even despises suffering as a weakness unworthy of higher natures. This singularity of character leads one to suppose that he has never been ill." Miss Bremer admired the Transcendentalist philosopher's idealism but, as a devout Christian, she confessed to a secret antagonism towards him as the "Himalaya of heathenism." She recognized his genius and later translated passages from his essays and poems for Swedish readers (she was the first person to translate Emerson into a foreign language).

Fredrika Bremer's ambivalence towards Emerson carried over to the whole Transcendentalist movement. She participated in a few of Amos Bronson Alcott's "Conversations" and concurred with some of his ideas on education, eugenic marriage, and women's rights. She did not, however, share his belief that sin could be driven out by diet. "The man is incorrigible. He drinks too much water, and brings forth merely hazy and cloudy shapes. He should drink wine and eat meat, or at least fish, so that there might be marrow and substance in his ideas." To her, Alcott was a dreamer, as were all but one of the Transcendentalists: "a kind of people . . . found principally in . . . New England, and who seem to me like its White Mountains or Alps, that is to say they aim at being so. But as far as I have yet heard and seen, I recognize only one actual Alp, and that is Waldo Emerson."

In New England, Miss Bremer associated with many people prominent in the antislavery cause, among them the orators William Lloyd Garrison, Wendell Phillips, and Senator Charles Sumner, and Julia Ward Howe, who would later write "The Battle Hymn of the Republic." As a "thinking Christian," Miss Bremer condemned the system of slavery but waited to pass judgment on slaveholders in America until she could observe conditions at first hand. She was suspicious of party spirit and its blindness; her motto was "Justice and moderation before every thing!" She spoke with Garrison and, though warmly sympathizing with his moral fervor, told him that she thought the extravagance of the abolitionists, the violent tone of their attacks, could not benefit but rather must damage their cause.

The Swedish visitor wanted to be generous to the South but, when she arrived in Charleston, South Carolina, late in March 1850, some Southerners, knowing of her abolitionist views, were suspicious of her. She affirmed: "I am come hither to see and to learn, not as a spy." After visiting the plantation of Joel Roberts Poinsett, former American Minister to Mexico, Fredrika concluded that she would rather live on bread and water than live as a slave. She considered the institution "a great lie in the life of human freedom, and especially in the New World." But, for all that, she had not come to preach rebellion among the slaves.

In Washington, D.C., that July, Senators Stephen A. Douglas and James Shields from Illinois took the Swedish author for a drive along the banks of the Potomac; and as they viewed the hamlets, churches, villas, and cottages amid their garden-grounds, General James Shields exclaimed: "This is America!" She agreed: "And so it is. The true life of the New World is not to be seen in the great cities, with great palaces and dirty alleys, but in the abundance of its small communities, of its beautiful private dwellings, with their encircling fields and groves, in the bosom of grand scenery, by the sides of vigorous rivers, with mountains and forests, and all appliances for a vigorous and affluent life."

Southern Vegetation, by Fredrika Bremer, ink on paper, circa 1850. Carolina Rediviva Library, Universitetsbiblioteket, Uppsala.

Tiring of the bleak winter and severe morality of New England, Fredrika Bremer headed for the milder climate of the South in February 1850, arriving in Charleston, South Carolina, in mid-March. Her travels through South Carolina, Georgia, and Florida left her in awe of the South's extravagance. Possessed of a "wild, luxuriant beauty defying the power of man," the sensuous southern landscape was "unspeakably interesting" to her.

Julia Ward Howe, by Fredrika Bremer, ink on paper, circa 1849. Fredrika-Bremer-Association. Photograph courtesy of Svenska Portrattärkivet, National Museum, Stockholm.

At the time of her first acquaintance with Fredrika Bremer, Julia Ward Howe was just beginning to engage actively in abolitionist activities. Fredrika Bremer believed that the American woman had only to increase her sense of social responsibility before she would "stand forward as the earth's most beautiful and most perfect woman." Even the problem of slavery could be resolved "if the women would but awake."

Mrs. Julia Ward Howe

Fredrika Bremer turned her attention to other aspects of America. After admiring the "goddess" Niagara Falls, she traveled west alone, across the Great Lakes, following in the footsteps of Scandinavian emigrants. One of them, Gustaf Unonius, had called on her when she landed in New York and asked her to warn Swedes against emigration and its sufferings. But Fredrika wanted to see for herself. She met Swedish settlers in Chicago and Milwaukee and visited some prospering Norwegian settlements near Madison. One Sunday was spent among the Swedes at Pine Lake, Wisconsin, where the beautiful scenery reminded her of home. She partook of her countrymen's hospitality, led the dancing with the blacksmith, sang Scandinavian songs, and slept in a log cabin. One Swedish pioneer widow, old before her time, said that she did not regret having come to America "because, as regarded her children and their future, she saw a new world opened to them, richer and happier than that which the mother country could have offered them, and she would have been glad to have purchased this future for them at the sacrifice of her own life." Despite the hardships the emigrants endured, Fredrika Bremer took a long-term view and prophesied a millennium. Her glowing accounts were no doubt a contributing factor to the subsequent wave of Swedish emigration: "But this Minnesota is a glorious country, and just the country for Northern emigrants—just the country for a new Scandinavia."

From St. Paul—"one of the youngest infants of the Great West"—the author sailed down the Mississippi to New Orleans and later to Havana, where she had a brief visit with a compatriot, Jenny Lind. After three months, she returned to the southern states, this time visiting Florida with Dorothea Dix: "What an empire, what a world is North America, embracing all climates, natural scenery, and products. It is indeed an empire for all the nations of the earth." She found the climate of America "terribly exciting to the nerves," and when she was asked what similarity there was between the climate of Sweden and that of America, her standing reply was: "That between a staid married man and a changeable lover."

In her travels by steamboat, train, stagecoach, and covered wagon in twenty-seven of the thirty-one states then in the Union, Fredrika Bremer had seen the vast diversity of the new nation. Responding to the main currents of American thought of the day, she had studied public institutions; religious sects like the Quakers, Shakers, and Mormons; and some Utopian communities. In Philadelphia, she had visited Independence Hall and had laid a wreath on Benjamin Franklin's grave. She had spent the Fourth of July at Mount Vernon; and in Washington she had seen Millard Fillmore sworn in as the thirteenth President of the United States. She had also seen "Bloomer ladies" (feminists of the time) at a ball, consulted a homeopathic physician in Boston, met a phrenologist in Cincinnati, and heard "spiritual rappings" in Rochester.

After farewell visits with her good friends, Andrew Jackson Downing, and Marcus and Rebecca Spring, in New York City, Fredrika Bremer sailed for Liverpool on September 13, 1851. Grateful, she thanked God for all that she had seen. She spent several weeks in England, meeting the writers George Eliot and Charles Kingsley, among others, and then returned to Sweden. She considered writing a novel about the United States with her American friends as its heroes and heroines, but instead decided to publish the letters she had sent to her recently deceased sister Agathe, to her old teacher Böklin, and to Danish friends. While editing the voluminous and candid letters, she felt "magnetized by the genius of the Western world and spellbound by its power." The English author, Mary Howitt, undertook the English translation, although her knowledge of Swedish was far from perfect and the manuscript pages of *Hemmen i den nya verlden* (1853–1854) were hard to decipher. *The Homes of the New World: Impressions of America* (1853) was published by Harper & Brothers in New York in two volumes, each containing approximately 650 pages. Five printings were exhausted within a month, and the book was translated into Danish, Dutch, French, and German.

Fredrika Bremer's perception is best represented in her approach to a question close to her heart—women's rights. "Emancipated ladies" such as Dorothea Dix, Lucretia Mott, and Lucy Stone, and writers such as Catharine M. Sedgwick and Lydia H. Sigourney, influenced her profoundly. She welcomed the widened horizons for her sex. In American schools, girls studied Latin, Greek, mathematics, and the natural sciences, subjects then considered in Sweden to be difficult for the female intellect. Fredrika spoke with women workers in the mills at Lowell, Massachusetts, and was impressed by their good character. However, she believed, the "citizeness" was not as yet fully awakened to her role. If only her public spirit would increase, she would then "stand forward as the earth's most beautiful and most perfect woman." Fredrika Bremer remarked that solving the problem of slavery would not be difficult "if the women would but awake." She commended Harriet Beecher Stowe for *Uncle Tom's Cabin:* "Honor and blessing be hers! What will not that people become who can produce such daughters!"

On the subject of marriage, the author noted that money frequently had a great influence in the selection of a spouse. The American marriages not

The Sailor's Wedding, by Richard Caton Woodville, oil on canvas, 1852.
The Walters Art Gallery.

Accepting life as an unpredictable proposition, the Americans, Fredrika Bremer observed, "hung along its path, dispensing with all needless forms and fashions." Five minutes was a sufficient time in which to be married. Moreover, there was always the alternative of divorce. Having less patience than others with imperfection, the Americans preferred "to cut the Gordian knot asunder rather than labor through a course of years in unloosening it. 'Life is short!' they say."

entered into for the sake of money were, she felt, the only happy ones (she compared Americans who were arrogant about their wealth to Laplanders, who valued a man according to the number of his reindeer). And she noticed something else. A wedding she attended, at which the bride was already in her travel costume, elicited the comment: "This marriage ceremony seemed to me characteristic of that haste and precipitation for which I have often heard the Americans reproached. Life is short, say they, and therefore they hurry along its path, dispensing with all needless forms and fashions which might impede the necessary business of life, and perform even this as rapidly as possible, making five minutes suffice to be married in." Moreover, she found that "the frequency of divorce here may . . . be caused by the circumstance of the Americans having less patience than other people with imperfection, and preferring to cut the Gordian knot asunder rather than labor through a course of years in unloosening it."

In Sweden, Fredrika Bremer devoted herself to social reform and welfare work and played an active role in the women's rights movement, putting into practice many of the ideas she had formed in America. She maintained contact with American friends and, in 1858, met Nathaniel Hawthorne and his wife Sophia in Rome. Afterwards he wrote: "There is no better heart than hers, and not many sounder heads; and a little touch of sentiment comes delightfully in, mixed up with a quick and delicate humor and the most perfect simplicity. . . . She is a most amiable little woman, worthy to be the maiden aunt of the whole human race."

During the Civil War, Fredrika Bremer felt anxious for her friends in both North and South. She had faith that America would still fulfill its destiny as the promised land of humanity. In May 1864, she wrote in an appendix on the Civil War for the second edition of *Hemmen i nya verlden:* "My heart bleeds when I think of those flourishing cities, those beautiful homes, where I enjoyed beyond words the hospitality of the people and the characteristic beauty of nature in the South,—when I see them laid waste, their owners fugitive or exposed to all manner of want, to all kinds of sacrifices." She concluded with a prayer for peace and reconciliation. Fredrika Bremer lived to rejoice in the end of the tragic war but died soon after in Sweden on December 31, 1865.

Louis Kossuth, by Walter G. Gould, oil on canvas, 1851. The Hungarian Reformed Federation of America on extended loan from The Historical Society of Pennsylvania.

In exile after his term as governor of the short-lived Hungarian Republic, Kossuth met the expatriate American artist Walter Gould, a pupil of Sully, in Kutalia, Asia Minor. Five months later, in December 1851, Kossuth began a triumphant tour of the United States to gain support for his cause.

13
Louis Kossuth
1802-1894

by Elemer Bako

Yes, Gentlemen, either America will regenerate the condition of the old world, or it will be degenerated by the condition of the old world.

— *Speech delivered in*
Concord, Massachusetts, May 11, 1852

ELEMER BAKO, born in Hungary, is the Finno–Ugrian Area Specialist at the Library of Congress. A linguist, bibliographer, and cultural historian, Dr. Bako has taught at the universities of Debrecen (Hungary), Munich, and at Columbia University.

IN A SERMON preached on Thanksgiving Day, November 27, 1851, the Reverend Joseph P. Thompson, Pastor of the Broadway Tabernacle Church in New York, issued this greeting:

> *Thou Noble Magyar!*
> *We welcome thee for thine own sake and thy country's. . . . We know the*
> *heroism that for years bore up in thy far banishment, the cause of Hungary*
> *before the world and God. We welcome thee to a dominion over free hearts*
> *that honor virtue, truth and liberty. . . . In thy own tongue we bid thee wel-*
> *come. Éljen! Isten Hozta! Kossuth!*

The person thus addressed was not present; owing to stormy weather, his ship was still out on the ocean. But his fame had preceded him: the newspapers were already filled with accounts of his heroic efforts to preserve Hungary's first constitutional government against the overwhelming military power of the Austrian and Russian Empires. The bloodbath that had followed the imperial victory earned worldwide contempt for the two emperors. Concerted efforts were made by the United States, England, and France, directed by Secretary of State Daniel Webster and his British counterpart Lord Palmerston, to rescue Louis Kossuth and his compatriots who had taken refuge in Turkey. Deeply grateful, Kossuth, throughout his life, urged the "two Anglo-Saxon nations" to liquidate their historical differences and to join forces against despotism everywhere in the world.

Louis Kossuth (in Hungarian, Kossuth Lajos), a Protestant, was born in 1802 in the northern part of Hungary, to a prominent family. The generation of young reformers who emerged in Hungary in the beginning of the nineteenth century, under the influence of Count István Széchenyi, founder of the Hungarian Academy of Sciences in 1825, soon accepted Louis Kossuth as their leader. After the gross betrayal of Hungary on the part of Metternich's Austria, he rose to national prominence. When others began to hesitate, Kossuth did not, and was soon elected by the embattled representatives of the nation as a "Governor-President" after the House of Hapsburg was dethroned on April 14, 1849.

Kossuth tried to direct the government of his nation toward the American model. His love for America had its roots in his youth. Among his most important guides to American life, history, and institutions were two works: the Hungarian translation of Alexis de Tocqueville's *La démocratie en Amérique,* which followed the publication of the original by just a few years, and an enthusiastic account of a journey to the United States in 1831 and 1832 by Sándor Bölöni Farkas. After Kossuth became President, the United States Government, and particularly Secretary of State Daniel Webster, enthusiastically took up the cause of the "American model at the Lower Danube." A young Transylvanian, Count Samuel Wass, Kossuth's personal emissary, was tacitly permitted to set up "Committees for Hungary" in the summer of 1849 throughout the United States; at one of these meetings, in Springfield, Illinois, a resolution was passed, upon Abraham Lincoln's recommendation, to recognize Hungarian independence.

After the struggle had been lost, Kossuth was finally able to visit the country which had fostered his ideal and then had rescued him from his exile in Turkey. Upon disembarking at Staten Island from the Mississippi frigate which the American government had dispatched to Istanbul, Kossuth expressed his gratitude to his hosts:

Kossuth Attended by the Spirits of Freedom and History and the Guardian Genius of Hungary, with his Own Good Angel Calmly Bearing him through Space to America, by an unidentified artist, wood engraving, from *Gleason's Pictorial Drawing Room Companion,* December 27, 1851. The Hungarian Reformed Federation of America.

In December 1851, Kossuth sailed into the New York harbor a hero. Americans, feeling a kinship with the Hungarians in their effort to win freedom and constitutional liberty, hoped to see, in the words of Daniel Webster, an "American model at the Lower Danube."

> *The United States of America . . . declared by this unparalleled act their resolve to become the protectors of human rights. . . . Others spoke, you acted, and I was free! . . . At this act of yours tyrants trembled, humanity shouted with joy, the Magyar nation, crushed but not broken, raised its head with resolution and with hope, and the brilliancy of your stars was greeted by Europe's oppressed millions as the morning star of liberty.*

Kossuth had his official welcome two days later when he was escorted by a deputation of prominent New Yorkers aboard the steamer *Vanderbilt,* amidst the salvos of the nearby forts and the cheers of the throngs on nearby ships. Castle Garden was filled with thousands of people, waiting for the procession which formed at the Battery. As the procession moved up Broadway, Kossuth, standing up in an open carriage, his feathered Hungarian hat (soon very fashionable wear for many thousands of liberal Americans, and called a "Kossuth hat") in his right hand, escorted by some of his Hun-

KOSSUTH'S ENTRANCE ON THE BATTERY FROM CASTLE GARDEN.

Kossuth's Entrance on the Battery from Castle Garden, by Edward B. Purcell, wood engraving, in *Gleason's Pictorial Drawing Room Companion,* December 27, 1851. The Hungarian Reformed Federation of America.

Kossuth was welcomed by a group of prominent New Yorkers on the steamboat *Vanderbilt,* to the salute of cannon and the cheers of thousands aboard ships filling the harbor. Later, accompanied by his Hungarian Hussar officers on horseback, he led a procession up Broadway, standing in an open carriage and waving his befeathered hat. It was a military spectacle reputed to be "the finest ever seen in the city."

garian Hussar officers on horseback, created a lasting impression. "The military display," it was later reported, "was undoubtedly the finest ever seen in our city. . . . Taken all in all, New York never before gave such a generous ovation to either fellow-countryman or stranger."

Kossuth's response to this generous welcome was given in several major addresses, beginning with the one delivered at the "Corporation Dinner" at Irving House on December 11, in which he pleaded for American intervention in European affairs: "People of the United States, humanity expects that your glorious republic will prove to the world, that republics are founded on virtue,—it expects to see you the guardians of the laws of humanity."

In a country whose independence had been secured by the intervention of another country (France), Kossuth's plea was irresistible. "There is," he insisted, "a striking resemblance between your course and that of my country." Kossuth's request for American support stemmed from his belief in the universal applicability of the American principle:

that all races are capable of a noble development under noble institutions.
Give freedom to the Celt, the Slavon, or the Italian, or whatever other peo-
ple, give them freedom and independence, establish among them the great
principle of local self-government and . . . they will in due time ripen into
all the excellence and all the dignity of humanity.

After making a number of other speeches and receiving some thirty
delegations over several weeks, he left New York on December 23, and
went on to Philadelphia and Baltimore, where he reiterated his plea for
American help in the restoration of Hungarian liberty in preparation for
his bid for official support in Washington. There he would face the powerful
lobbies of the embassies of Austria, Russia, and Prussia, who formed a
veritable alliance against him.

Arriving in Washington on the 30th, Kossuth was first greeted by President Fillmore at a state dinner on January 3. He was received by both the
Senate and by the House of Representatives, an honor which had been previously granted only to Lafayette. After a dinner given for him by Congress
on January 7, Kossuth addressed the company; and contrary to custom, "a
large number of ladies, anxious to hear the speech of the distinguished
Magyar . . . were admitted" (as reported by the Recording Officer of the
House). Kossuth emphasized, again, the importance of recent United States
actions on behalf of his person and his country. Secretary of State Webster
underscored Kossuth's message:

We shall rejoice to see our American model upon the Lower Danube, and on
the mountains of Hungary. But that is not the first step. . . . I do not profess
to understand the social relations and connections of races, and twenty other
things that may affect the political institutions of Hungary. All I say is, that
Hungary can regulate these matters for herself infinitely better than they can
be regulated for her by Austria, [applause] and therefore I limit my aspira-
tions for Hungary, for the present, to that single and simple point—Hun-
garian independence. [Mr. Seward: Hungarian independence!—Applause.]
Hungarian self-government; Hungarian control of Hungarian destinies.
[Renewed applause.] These are the aspirations which I entertain, and I give
them to you, therefore, Gentlemen, as a toast.

The evening was also significant for some who had not been invited.
Opponents of Hungary's cause moved into action. The most zealous among
them was a very unhappy diplomat, Mr. Hülsemann, the Austrian chargé
d'affaires who— as reported by the British ambassador—regarded Mr.
Webster's toast and sentiment "a distinct manifestation of hostility and
disrespect to the Austrian government." In an informal communication,
undated, President Fillmore tried to smooth the feelings of Hülsemann by
stating his own "sincere desire to maintain cordial and friendly relations
with the government of Austria." As he put it, he understood that "Mr.
Webster's speech is to be revised," and therefore he, the President, had not
"read it" and could "express no opinion upon it." But he did want to say
that "Mr. Webster's speech . . . must be regarded as his individual, un-
official opinion, and not as the sentiments of my administration." When
Prince Schwarzenberg, the Austrian Foreign Minister, continued to press
Hülsemann for the removal of Webster as the only "acceptable satisfaction,"
the unhappy diplomat took off to the Southern states for some exploration
of the American domestic situation on his own.

Kossuth's further itinerary covered the Northeast and the Midwest, where he met with continuing success. According to the January 14 issue of the *New York Herald*, Kossuth's proposal for "intervention for non-intervention" had been, by that time, submitted for consideration in the assemblies of the states of New York, Massachusetts, Maine, Pennsylvania, Maryland, Ohio, Kentucky, Indiana, Tennessee, and Alabama. Notes on this tour were taken by the talented, Viennese-educated wife of Francis Pulszky, Kossuth's indefatigable right hand in the organization of his American visit. Therese Pulszky's entry for February 6 was typical:

Feb. 6th—On the 4th, we set out from Cleveland in a railway-car gaily adorned, as usually, on our journey. It was fully crowded, so much that I was surprised to read in the paper that it was a special car for us. But the committees that accompanied us were numerous; their wives, children, and relatives liked to participate in the festive trip. . . . We stopped at Beria, Grafton, Lagrange (so called in honour of the country seat of Lafayette in France), at Wellington and New-London. All these embryos of future towns consist of scattered plank-houses, and sketches of streets, paved as yet only with mud. The scenery offered no attraction; the woods around are all young. A tree two centuries old is very rare; they were burnt in the Indian border-warfare, to frighten away the deer, and with them the hunters. . . .

I had an interesting conversation with a German resident of Cleveland, who . . . remarked that sooner or later all the Germans coming to the United

One-dollar bond, Hungarian Fund.
The Hungarian Reformed Federation of America.

As Kossuth swept across the Middle West, the South, and up the East Coast, financial support appeared in the form of "Kossuth Fund dollars." That his American visit had turned into a triumphal procession was reflected in the popularity of the bonds, which were issued for the procurement of ships, armaments, and ammunition in 1, 5, 10, 20, and 100-dollar denominations.

"*Governor Kossuth Welcome to Massachusetts,*" by an unidentified artist, wood engraving, from *Gleason's Pictorial Drawing Room Companion,* May 15, 1852. The Hungarian Reformed Federation of America.

The enthusiasm which greeted Louis Kossuth during his three-week New England tour was dazzling. "Wherever we go," wrote Therese Pulszky, "bells are ringing, guns roar their salvos, the streets are decked in festive colors, banners flutter, and the population throngs in the streets."

> *States lose their nationality. I told him that I thought that it was because their language and turn of mind are too metaphysical, that they must yield to a practical people. Power has always rested with force and action, not with thought and reasoning.*
>
> *We dined at Shelby. It was one of those public meals where hundreds of curious eyes devour every one of our glances and our movements, and our appetites into the burguin. The dishes on the table were choice,—a mixture of English, French and German fare; but, as generally in America, they were not cleanly prepared, and therefore not savory. Our party had hardly left the seats, when the public rushed to the table, seized upon the dainties, and made them disappear in an instant.*

That same evening, they arrived at Columbus, and there Kossuth delivered his great address, "Democracy, the Spirit of Our Age," to the Ohio Legislature. In it he said:

Almost every century has had one predominant idea which imparted a common direction to the activity of nations. This predominant idea is the spirit of the age, invisible yet omnipresent, impregnable, all-pervading, scorned, abused, opposed and yet omnipotent. The spirit of our age is Democracy. All for the people and all by the people. Nothing about the people without the people.

As Governor Wood requested, the manuscript of this address was left in the care of the State Archives of Ohio.

Kossuth went on to Cincinnati and addressed a banquet honoring Washington's birthday. During his stay there, he was received as a member of the Free and Accepted Masons. His application gives the following description of his residence and profession:

Being an exile for liberty's sake, he has no place of fixed residence; is now staying at Cincinnati; his age is 49 and a half years, his occupation is to restore his native land, Hungary to its national independence and to achieve by community of action with other nations civil and religious liberty in Europe.

[signed] Louis Kossuth.

From February 26 through March 2, the party of the Hungarian leader went to Indianapolis, Indiana, and to Madison, Ohio. At the State House in Indianapolis, Kossuth spoke on the differences between the political systems in Europe and America:

How different the condition of America! It is not men who rule, but the law. And the law is obeyed, because people are respecting the general will by respecting the law. Public office is a place of honor, because it is the field of patriotic devotion. Governments have not the arrogant pretention to be the masters of the people, but have the proud glory to be its faithful servants. A public officer does not cease to be a citizen.

He then traveled South—to St. Louis, where he delivered a splendid address on the fourth anniversary of the bloodless revolution of the Hungarian youth on March 15, 1848 and then on to Mississippi, Louisiana, Alabama, Georgia, South Carolina, North Carolina, and back to Washington, D. C., on April 13. Visiting Washington's grave at Mount Vernon, Kossuth remarked on the neglected state of "these hallowed grounds" and moved some Protestant clergymen to make it their duty to maintain it.

In late April, Kossuth went to New Jersey and then to New England, the climax of his stay in America. The enthusiasm in Massachusetts, Therese Pulszky wrote, was beyond anything they had yet experienced: "Kossuth's tour resembles a triumphal march. Wherever we go, bells are ringing, guns roar their salvos, the streets are decked in festive colors, banners flutter, and the population throngs in the streets." He delivered three addresses in Boston, and said to an overflowing audience at Faneuil Hall: "It is . . . in the question of foreign policy, that the heart of the immediate future throbs. Security and danger, prosperity and stagnation, peace and war, tranquility and embarrassment, yes, life and death will be weighed in the scale of foreign policy."

In Cambridge, Kossuth met some of the greatest men of America, among them the dean of the local clergy, Charles Lowell, whose son, the poet James Russell Lowell, wrote in a poem honoring him:

> *Thou hast succeeded, thou hast won*
> *the deathly travail's amplest worth,*
> *A nation's duty thou has done,*
> *Giving a hero to our earth.*

Leaving Massachusetts, Kossuth then toured New York state and then, on July 14, he sailed back to England on the steamer *Europe,* in the company of his wife and a few friends.

Many regarded him as defeated in his purpose to secure military and financial assistance for his troops at the Lower Danube, who were waiting to launch an attack for the liberation of Hungary. Washington Irving, for one, foresaw inevitable failure in Kossuth's attempt to move the politicians in their "smoke-filled rooms" to a grand act on behalf of his tortured fatherland. Nevertheless, Kossuth had an impressive number of distinguished supporters, and was given more than mere encouragement. Prominent citizens gave him detailed advice and pledges regarding the procurement of ships, armaments, and ammunition, and financial support in the form of "Kossuth Fund dollars" in denominations of 1, 5, 10, 20, and 100. While traveling through New Haven, on his way to New England, Kossuth had been invited to inspect the plant of the Whitney Arms Manufacturing Company, where he was shown a long row of stands stacked with firearms bearing the inscription "Material Aid for Hungary." Others joined forces with Hungarian officers to set up a munitions plant in New Jersey. In 1860, when there was again hope of Hungarian independence, Colonel Alexander Asboth, Kossuth's former aide-de-camp, and soon a Major General in Abraham Lincoln's army, was able to report "with humble regard for His Excellency, the Governor of Hungary," Louis Kossuth, that he had rifles and ammunition for the leader's planned military actions.

Kossuth, however, was destined to remain in exile for the rest of his life. While he may have become bitter toward some European heads of state, who betrayed him, after having used the Hungarian issue for their own advantage, his sentiments towards the United States, and especially towards the American people never changed. In the preface of his multivolume recollections, entitled *Emlékeim az emigrációból* (1882; translated "Memories of my Exile"), he recalled his American sojourn as the most cherished, most warmly felt period of his *émigrée* life. Future generations, in both America and Hungary, have regarded Kossuth as the most powerful link between the two nations, a link so powerful and so shining that it has survived every adverse act and turn in history.

The Japanese Ambassadors at the Washington Navy Yard, attributed to Mathew Brady, photograph, 1860. National Archives and Records Service, Washington, D.C.

The First Japanese Mission to the United States marked the culmination of American diplomatic overtures begun seven years before by Commodore Perry. Brought to America on the U.S.S. *Powhatan,* the Japanese company consisted of three envoys, seventeen officials, fifty-one clerks and servants, and six cooks.

14

The First Japanese Mission to the United States

1860

by Tadashi Aruga

One day, on a sudden thought, I asked a gentleman where the descendents of George Washington might be. . . . His answer was so casual and indifferent that it shocked me. Of course, I knew that America was a republic with a new president every four years . . . but I could not help feeling that the family of Washington would be revered above all other families.
> —*The Autobiography of Yukichi Fukuzawa*

TADASHI ARUGA, who has studied at the University of Tokyo, Princeton University, and the University of Wisconsin, is Professor of Diplomatic History and American Studies at Seikei University, Tokyo. He has published *Amerika Seijishi* (which may be translated "A Political History of the United States") and several articles on American–Japanese relations.

In 1860, the Shogunate government of Japan sent an embassy to the United States. With the exception of a few castaways such as John Manjirō Naka-hama and Joseph Hikozo, these official visitors were the first Japanese to step on American soil.

The traditional "closed door" policy of the Tokugawa Shogunate had been shaken in 1853 by the arrival of Commodore Perry. Confronted with Perry's formidable fleet, the Shogunate reluctantly agreed, in the Treaty of 1854, to admit American ships into two Japanese ports. Japan's closed door was opened a little, but the American objective of obtaining a treaty of commerce remained to be accomplished. The task was assigned to Townsend Harris, the first resident representative of the United States, who arrived in Japan in 1856.

Although the Japanese officials persistently tried to delay the negotiations, the American diplomat strove for the goal with great tact and zeal. Eloquently, Harris pleaded for the wisdom of concluding a treaty of commerce with America on better terms than those which the European nations would provide. He also argued earnestly that opening Japan for foreign intercourse would bring progress and prosperity to the nation.

Elder (Minister) Masamutsu Hotta, Bicchū-no-kami, a leading cabinet member of the Shogunate in charge of foreign affairs, agreed with Harris. He began to think that opening the country was not merely a passive response to foreign pressures but a positive policy for national progress. Other cabinet members liked to preserve, if possible, the traditional policy, but they were aware that China's resistance had led to her humiliation by Western arms. Therefore they wished to avoid a similar disgrace by agreeing to open the country to foreign commerce.

Many feudal lords, however, remained unconvinced of the wisdom of this open door policy; the policy itself seemed to be a disgrace. The Shogunate, aware that its authority was in decline, attempted to enlist the support of the Imperial Court in Kyoto, the hitherto nominal ruler of the nation. The Court, ignorant of the current international situation and enjoying the sense of its new political importance, refused to give its approval to the treaty pending with the United States. The Court was now becoming a key element in the political turbulence which resulted in the Meiji Restoration.

Again the Shogunate government asked Harris to wait. But Harris strongly advised Shogunate officials to act immediately. He emphasized the importance, for Japan, of securing America's friendship, warning that the British and French fleets, victorious in China, might soon come to Japan. This warning was effective. Naosuke Ii, Kamon-no-kami, who assumed the post of the Grand Elder in June 1858, was forced to make a hard decision. On July 29, the Treaty of Amity and Commerce was signed without the Emperor's approval. This action angered the Imperial Court and gave impetus to an anti-Shogunate movement, although the Court later approved the treaty as a temporary measure.

The authority of the Shogunate was weakened further by a factional conflict over the choice of an heir to the childless Shogun. Ii began to remove the rival faction from the government and pursue a harsh repressive policy towards those whom he regarded as subversive activists. Progressive officials in the Office of Foreign Affairs, as well as the enlightened Elder

Hotta, happened to belong to his rival faction. One by one, they lost their positions in the government.

Eager to obtain a first-hand knowledge of the advanced country, the progressive officials, of whom Tadanari Iwase, Higo-no-kami, was the most ambitious and resourceful, conceived the signing of the treaty as an opportunity to tour in the United States. Harris was of course delighted with this idea. Thus the treaty specified Washington as the place to exchange ratifications. Because of the political shakeup in the Shogunate, however, these progressive officials could not travel officially as ambassadors.

The post of the Chief Ambassador was assigned to Masaoki Shimmi, Buzen-no-kami, a new Foreign Affairs Commissioner. Having served as Shogun's chamberlain for years, Shimmi was a refined gentleman, and this was his major credential for ambassadorship. The post of the Vice Ambassador went to Norimasa Muragaki, Awaji-no-kami, another Foreign Affairs Commissioner. With his experience in various posts in the Shogunate bureaucracy, Muragaki was a competent if not innovative official. The third member of the embassy was Censor (Counselor) Tadamasa Oguri, Bungo-no-kami, of the Censor's Office, who had a reputation for brightness. "Among the three envoys," a famous journalist recalled later, "Oguri was the only one with outstanding ability." The three envoys were accompanied by seventeen officials, fifty-one clerks and servants, and six cooks.

Since Japan lacked a suitable vessel to convoy the embassy, the United States dispatched a man-of-war, the U.S.S. *Powhatan*, for this purpose. As an official gesture, the Shogunate decided to send an escort ship, the *Kanrin Maru*, a small schooner purchased from Holland. Admiral Yoshitake Kimura, Settsu-no-kami, and Captain Rintarō Katsu, and other *Kanrin Maru* officers were the core of the infant Shogunate navy. Among civilian members aboard the vessel were Yukichi Fukuzawa and John Manjirō Nakahama.

The *Powhatan* sailed from Edo (now Tokyo) on February 9, 1860, and departed from Yokohama four days later. The *Kanrin Maru* sailed from Uraga on February 10. With the help of Lieutenant John M. Brooke and several American crew members, the inexperienced Japanese officers and crew managed to navigate the small vessel across the rough ocean, arriving in San Francisco on March 17, twelve days earlier than the arrival of the *Powhatan*, which stayed two weeks in Honolulu. The *Kanrin Maru* group did not travel to the eastern part of the United States. But they had ample time to see San Francisco and its vicinity while the vessel was under repair. The ship departed from San Francisco on May 8 and returned to Edo by way of Hawaii on June 23.

Meanwhile the embassy, again aboard the *Powhatan*, left San Francisco for Panama on April 7. After a train ride across the isthmus, the embassy embarked on the U.S.S. *Roanoke,* which took them to Hampton Roads, Virginia. On May 14, the embassy arrived in Washington amid a large crowd of curious Washingtonians. During their twenty-five-day stay in the federal city, the embassy officials had audiences with President James Buchanan, exchanged the ratification documents, attended the President's reception and banquet, visited the Capitol, held a reception in their own hotel, and visited various places of interest.

On June 8, the embassy left Washington. After an overnight stop in Baltimore, they traveled to Philadelphia. There they settled the exchange

America's first ruler, George Washington, by an unidentified artist, wood block in nineteenth-century Japanese history book. Lee Houchins.

In the middle of the nineteenth century, the Japanese looked upon America's evolution as an international power with curiosity and respect. This heroic figure of George Washington, standing for his nation's revolutionary heritage, appeared in a popular series of pamphlets on world figures.

rate of the currencies after observing the assaying at the Philadelphia Mint. One week later, they went to New York, where they spent two weeks before their departure for Japan.

Everywhere the Japanese embassy was treated with utmost hospitality. Not only the Federal Government but also local officials and citizens welcomed the Oriental visitors warmly. The fact that Japan had sent her first embassy to the United States, not to a European nation, greatly pleased Americans. "We ought to remember," a congressman remarked, "that this embassy is sent to us in preference over all other nations who have solicited the Japanese to send embassies to them. We cannot do it too much honor." The Americans saw themselves as a civilizing influence. "It is fortunate," a Philadelphia newspaper commented, "that the Japanese have selected this Republic as the medium through which they propose to seek acquaintance and intercourse with the nations of Christiandom." Americans were of course interested in expanding commerce with Japan and hoped that the arrival of the embassy would be the first step towards trade expansion. These sentiments and considerations contributed to the Americans' warm hospitality.

The exotic *samurai* procession of the embassy was certainly a tremendous show in an age of few entertainments. Everywhere they were greeted by a huge curious crowd. But the procession of the embassy was something more than an exotic show for Americans. It excited them because it gave them a vivid sense of the American horizon spreading beyond the cultural, as well as geographical, distance of the Pacific. For a people troubled by grave internal dissension, it was certainly a pleasant diversion. Walt Whitman, a witness of this pageantry, expressed the sense of excitement:

"Over sea, hither from Niphon, Courteous the Princes of Asia. . . . This day they ride through Manhattan."

While many newspaper accounts convey American impressions of the Japanese visitors, the Japanese impressions of America can be found in a number of diaries, of which Muragaki's is the most famous. These diaries testified to American hospitality. Because of cultural differences, however, the visitors could not fully enjoy social events held in their honor. Most of the dishes served at sumptuous dinners did not suit their taste. Dancing after a dinner was a strange custom to them. Although some of the younger, lesser *samurai* learned to enjoy it, Muragaki could never accept the "extraordinary sight of men and women hopping about the floor, arm in arm." To him, it was tantamount to rudeness for the American host to allow such a thing at a party held in their honor. Equating unfamiliar customs with impoliteness, Muragaki often felt that Americans were "a people with no etiquette"; and he observed, "We had not entirely been wrong in calling them Western barbarians." But their goodwill was unmistakable. "I would forgive their impoliteness," he wrote, "because of their friendliness."

Kanrin Maru, by an unidentified artist, medium unknown, in *Ma'en Gannen Kenbei Shisetsu Zuroku,* circa 1860. Keio University.

On board the *Kanrin Maru* was the core of the infant Shogunate navy. This small schooner escorted the U.S.S. *Powhatan,* a man-of-war provided by the United States government to convey the Japanese officials. The *Kanrin Maru* crew, although inexperienced, successfully crossed the Pacific and arrived in San Francisco twelve days before the *Powhatan.*

Presentation of an American Lady to the Japanese Ambassadors at Willard's, Washington, by "M.N.," wood engraving, in *Harper's Weekly,* May 26, 1860. National Portrait Gallery, Smithsonian Institution.

The active role American women played in public life disconcerted the Japanese emissaries; in their own country, women had no such function in diplomatic or ceremonial occasions. The captain of the *Kanrin Maru* thought American women "arrogant"—a characteristic which would be considered intolerable in traditional Japanese culture—but in time the delegation grew to accept and even to enjoy the presence of women on formal occasions.

Other diarists were more enthusiastic. "In general, the people of this country were very generous, honest and faithful," observed one diarist. "They never show contempt for foreigners. They show utmost sincerity even to strangers." "They have no fictitious and suspicious nature," remarked another. "Most of the embassy officials and their followers had distrusted Americans before our journey," confessed a young clerk of the Censor. "But we all realized that we had been entirely wrong when we became acquainted with them."

The embassy members were surprised to learn that the President of the United States dressed and behaved like ordinary people and lived in a mansion which did not much differ from an ordinary house. Compared with the highly stratified, etiquette-ridden Japanese society, the republican nation was strikingly informal and devoid of class and status distinctions. To the conservative Muragaki, these American characteristics were distasteful. Some *samurai* of lower status, however, viewed the same characteristics with favor. For example, one of Muragaki's clerks wrote: "In this country, even the President does not surround himself with an overly elaborate system of decorum. He behaves in a practical manner." In a similar vein, another *samurai* observed: "Even high ranking officials do not show contempt towards men of lower classes. Neither do they act in a domineering manner. Therefore the ordinary people need not flatter high officials. Thus the nation prospers and the people feel secure."

The social role and status of American women attracted the curiosity of the Japanese. Most diarists noted that women were treated by men with great courtesy. The presence of ladies on ceremonial and social occasions surprised the Japanese at first. But they apparently enjoyed the ladies. Harriet Lane, President Buchanan's niece, who served as the hostess of the White House, was especially admired by the Japanese guests, and inspired Chief Ambassador Shimmi to write a poem:

It was a pleasure I had never dreamed of
to be escorted to such a dinner table
and sit next to a flowering beauty.

The Japanese visitors saw the black people in cities and heard about their low status. But they were not exposed to the reality of slavery and did not realize that it was the critical issue dividing the nation. Although they gained some knowledge of the American political system, the Japanese visitors were not aware of the high political tension prevailing in the country. It was difficult for them to imagine that a country whose ruler could

The Japanese Embassy reviewing the New York Volunteer Troops in Union Square, near the Statue of Washington, on the day of their reception in New York, June 16, 1860, wood engraving in an unidentified American newspaper, 1860. Reproduced from *The First Japanese Embassy in America,* 1920. Library of Congress.

The exotic appearance of the Japanese delegation in a procession up Broadway drew thousands of New Yorkers. Witnessing the spectacle, Walt Whitman wrote:

Sultry with perfume, with ample and flowing garments.
With sunburnt visage, with intense soul and glittering eyes,
The race of Brahma comes.

Ball given by the City of New York to the Japanese Embassy at the Metropolitan Hotel, June 25, 1860, by an unidentified artist, wood engraving, in *Harper's Weekly*, June 30, 1860. National Portrait Gallery, Smithsonian Institution.

At the many balls given in their honor, the Japanese were presented with the "extraordinary sight of men and women hopping about." As Kiyoyuki Monta, Treasurer of the mission, related in his diary: "Having thus made pairs, they started dancing to music. At first, they turned around slowly. Then they speeded up their motion. They turned around and around so swiftly that we spectators felt dizzy. All pairs continued until they were almost out of breath. Noisiness was beyond expression. I would say that the dancing was not obscene at all. But we could not bear seeing this strange sight."

live in a mansion with no fortifications or military guards was on the verge of civil war. Probably only one interpreter was able to read English with competence. With this drawback, it was almost impossible for the embassy to gather information about America's political condition. In fact, the embassy was not interested in such a task.

   With vivid impressions of American friendliness, the embassy members bade farewell to the United States on June 30, 1860. Sailing from New York aboard the U.S.S. *Niagara*, they reached Edo, by way of the Indian Ocean, on November 9. During their absence, Japan's political turmoil had deepened. After the assassination of Grand Elder Ii in March, the Shogunate had been left with weak leadership. Clamoring "Respect the Emperor and Expel the Aliens," the anti-Shogunate movement had gained momentum. Terrorism had become rampant. The Shogunate government was pursuing an ambivalent policy, trying to keep foreign intercourse to a minimum, while assuring the Imperial Court that the traditional policy would eventually be restored. Therefore, the Shogunate gave the returning embassy a cool reception. Significantly, no salute was fired to greet the arrival of the *Niagara*. Thus the warm hospitality with which the Americans had treated the embassy did not have any immediate effect upon Japanese diplomacy. Meanwhile, America's East Asian policy became inactive because of the Civil War.

It took four more years to create a national consensus for seeking friendly relations with the Western nations. Military retaliations by Britain and other western powers against Satsuma and Chōshū, two major antiforeign provinces, were necessary to convince all the Japanese of the futility of attempting to expel the Westerners. In the last years of the Shogunate rule, Tadamasa Oguri, the third envoy of the embassy of 1860, emerged as an energetic promoter of modernization in the Shogunate officialdom. Many of his innovative ideas, like the construction of a navy yard and the formation of commercial companies, had their origin in his observations of America. If the Shogunate had been able to transform itself into a modern government, Oguri might have become a leader of modern Japan. But the Shogunate was destined to fall, and Oguri was assassinated in the turmoil of 1868.

In spite of the fall of the Shogunate, however, the historical significance of the embassy of 1860 should not be underestimated, for its effects survived the change of the regime. The embassy succeeded in creating in Americans the favorable impression that the Japanese were courteous and intelligent. This image persisted until Japan fell under the control of militarists. American friendliness and advanced technology, reported by the embassy, were not overlooked by the Meiji government. The first overseas mission of the Meiji government visited the United States in 1872 before going to Europe. Many students were sent to America in the same year.

The *Kanrin Maru* voyage, a by-product of the embassy, had its own impact upon the development of modern Japan. Several *Kanrin Maru* officers, including Captain Rintarō Katsu, who became later Count Yoshiyasu Katsu, played an important role in building the Japanese navy in the Meiji Era. In spite of his background as the Shogun's vassal, Katsu was invited to enter the Meiji government and became a prominent statesman in Meiji Japan.

The *Kanrin Maru* group also produced a foremost educator, journalist, and champion of enlightenment in Meiji Japan—Yukichi Fukuzawa. As a young student of western languages and science, Fukuzawa had volunteered to serve as a clerk of Admiral Kimura in order to see America. Because of his knowledge, he was not surprised by scientific and industrial devices he saw there. But he experienced a series of shocks in "matters of life and social custom and ways of thinking." Although he was able to visit only California, that was enough to make him aware of the blessings of a progressive, democratic society. His later trips to America and Europe reinforced his conviction. He opened a school named Keiō Gijuku (which later became a university), wrote many enlightening books, and founded a newspaper. Paraphrasing a passage of the American Declaration of Independence, Fukuzawa began his widely read series of essays, *An Encouragement of Learning*, with this message: "It is said that heaven did not create one man above or below another man." He never entered the bureaucracy of the Meiji government, cherishing his liberty as an independent citizen. "Proud and independent" was the motto he gave to his students. Among the Japanese visitors of 1860, it was Fukuzawa who had learned most from American democracy.

Yukichi Fukuzawa with an American girl in San Francisco, by an unidentified photographer, 1860. From an unlocated original, reproduced in *The Autobiography of Yukichi Fukuzawa,* 1966.

"It was as we sailed away from Hawaii that I caused a little stir among the young men of our crew," wrote Yukichi Fukuzawa, a member of the *Kanrin Maru* company who would later become a great enlightenment figure in Meiji Japan. "'You all talk a lot about your affairs,' I said, chiding the surprised seamen. 'But how many of you have brought back a picture of yourselves with a young lady as a souvenir of San Francisco? Without any evidence, what good is it to boast of your affairs now?' The girl was really the daughter of the photographer. . . . I said suddenly, 'Let us have our picture taken together,' She immediately said, 'All right,' being an American girl and thinking nothing of it."

15

William Howard Russell
1820-1907

and

Edward Dicey
1832-1911

by Esmond Wright

There is indeed I believe much of good in this war to the American people for it will purify the air, divert them from a universal hunt after place and contracts and dollars and elevate the whole moral senti-ment of the great race which has such a glorious land of generous impulses, but which pardon me for saying it required a little humbling —as much as ever John Bull did—and that is saying a good deal.
—Letter written from Chicago,
September 25, 1861

According to the popular English view, the whole country is in a state of revolution, trade is bankrupt, and the entire progress of the nation stopped for years to come, yet here, in the West, in the very heat of the war, there was a great country growing into existence by rapid strides. The great march of civilisation was still, as ever, tending westward, building railroads, clearing forests, reclaiming wild lands, raising cities, and making the wilderness into a fertile country. This progress westward across the prairie is the great fact of American history; and those who want to understand the real character of the present civil war, must remember that this progress is still going on without ceasing.
—Six Months in the Federal States

ESMOND WRIGHT is Director of the Institute of United States Studies at the University of London. Among his books are *A Tug of Loyalties,* which he edited, and *Fabric of Freedom.* He has been visiting professor at a number of American universities.

William Howard Russell, by an unidentified artist after a drawing by Theodore Russell Davis, wood engraving, in *Harper's Weekly,* June 22, 1861. National Portrait Gallery, Smithsonian Institution.

Having made his name as the London *Times* correspondent during the Crimean War, William Russell, here portrayed by an American newspaper illustrator, arrived in the United States on the eve of the Civil War. His controversial dispatches were later collected and published in book form both in the United States and in Great Britain.

By 1860, commentaries on the United States by visiting British journalists had become a major industry. The correspondents were drawn to the New World by such things as its inventions, its people and customs, its democracy, and its slavery problem. But by 1861, they had a new and, to them, more exotic reason for visiting: the outbreak of the Civil War. In February 1862, the London *Morning Post*, generally regarded as the mouthpiece of Prime Minister Henry Palmerston, wrote about the secession of the Southern states: "If the Government of the United States should succeed in reannexing them . . . who can doubt that Democracy will be more arrogant, more aggressive, more levelling and vulgarising, if that be possible, than it ever had been before?" And John Lothrop Motley, the American historian and diplomat, reported home:

> Nothing can exceed the virulence with which the extreme conservative party regard us, nor the delight with which they look forward to our extinction as a nation. They consider such a consummation of our civil war as the most triumphant answer which could be made to their own reform party. The hatred of the English radicals is the secret of the ferocity and brutality with which the Times, the Saturday Review, and other tory organs of the press have poured out their insults upon America ever since the war began.

It is against this background that the visit of William Howard Russell to the United States in 1861 has to be seen. He came as special correspondent of that thunderer, the London *Times*, whose editor liked to think that he could make and unmake governments. When Russell met President Lincoln —within two weeks of his arrival—the President greeted him with the remark "Mr. Russell, I am very glad to make your acquaintance, and to see you in this country—The London *Times* is one of the greatest powers in the world—in fact, I don't know anything which has much more power,— except perhaps the Mississippi. I am glad to know you as its minister." Russell had a right of entry to all in government and could treat them as equal—or as inferior. On his second day in Washington, he was invited to dine at the White House—the only newspaperman in a company of judges, diplomats, and statesmen.

Russell was in his own way as eminent a figure as Charles Dickens. He was a great war correspondent, and can perhaps be described as the first of that profession. He had remarkable qualities of observation, and an easy and graphic style. He was energetic and unhesitant. Not English but Irish, he was brought up as a Catholic and educated at (though not a graduate of) that Trinity College, Dublin, which owed its origin to the support of Queen Elizabeth I. In 1854, he was sent to report the Crimean War for *The Times*, and made his name in doing so. The phrase "the thin red line," to describe the British infantry at Balaclava, was his.

Russell was in the United States from March 1861, just after Lincoln's inauguration and before the secession of Virginia, to April 1862, just after the first Battle of Bull Run. His dispatches to *The Times* were published in various forms, and finally as *My Diary North and South* (London, 1863). The dates of his stay are important. He saw all who counted in New York and Washington when they were still numbed by the secession of the wayward South, when half the press were for the South, when few believed that the North had any right or power to coerce. The North was not yet in a warlike mood—Sumter fell as Russell was on his way to Charleston, and he thought the Federal system was not going to be able to survive "the internal convulsion."

At that time, Secretary of State William Henry Seward, not Lincoln, was deemed the strong man of the Union cause. Russell described Seward:

a subtle, quick man, rejoicing in power, given to perorate and to oracular utterances, fond of badinage, bursting with the importance of state mysteries, and with the dignity of directing the foreign policy of the greatest country— as all Americans think—in the world.

Russell was not greatly impressed by Lincoln or his Secretary of State. It was the oddity of the President's appearance and his lack of style that hit Russell, though his respect for Lincoln's "capacity, honesty and plain dealing" was to grow.

After a month, he set off for the South, by steamer to Norfolk, Virginia, then still part of the Union, and then by train to Charleston, which he found in a euphoric mood after Sumter. He saw something of the plantations of South Carolina, and moved from Charleston to Savannah, to Montgomery (still the Confederate capital), and to Mobile, and thence along the coast to Fort Dickens, still in Union hands. He was afraid that if the blockade were tightened he would not be able to get his dispatches out, and so he moved, through a western Kentucky that was about to erupt into war, and by a truce boat to Cairo, Illinois, where with baggage and notebook he was readmitted to Northern lines. He saw a Midwest untouched by war and found a Washington where, now, political confusion was compounded by military chaos and near-panic. He was back in time to accompany the army that moved out to Bull Run in July, and to describe vividly the chaos of the battle and be an eyewitness of the rout that followed.

All the roads from Centreville for miles presented such a sight as can only be witnessed in the track of the runaways of an utterly demoralized army. Drivers flogged, lashed, spurred, and beat their horses, or leaped down and abandoned their teams, and ran by the side of the road; mounted men, servants, and men in uniform, vehicles of all sorts, commissariat wagons, thronged the narrow ways. At every shot a convulsion, as it were, seized upon the morbid mass of bones, sinew, wood, and iron, and thrilled through it, giving new energy and action to its desperate efforts to get free from itself.

It was the famous long report on this—he was to be ever afterwards, as the *New York Times* called him, "Bull Run Russell"—that led to his loss of favor with Lincoln and the new Secretary of War Edwin Stanton, whom he described as "excessively vain . . . a rude, rough, vigorous Oliver Cromwell sort of man." His report was in sharp contrast with Northern press comment. The *Chicago Tribune* said: "We do not know and do not care what he saw, or says he saw, of the fight and the flight, before we found him; but from the errors and misstatements in . . . his narrative . . . we should be justified in believing that he was not at the battle at all. . . . We saw nothing of the flogging, lashing, spurring, beating, and abandoning that he so graphically describes." He was denied a pass to accompany George McClellan in that General's slow opening moves to the Peninsula, and this led him to decide to return to London, without allowing his editor time to dissuade him. He always believed that the coolness was "because I told the truth about Bull Run and would not bend the knee to the degraded creatures who have made the very name of a free press odious to honourable men." He

Blenker's Brigade Covering the Retreat near Centerville, by an unidentified artist, wood engraving, circa 1862, in *Harper's Pictorial History of the Civil War.* Library of Congress.

Russell earned the nickname "Bull Run Russell" for his account of the first Battle of Bull Run, in which he described the panic displayed by green troops: "I . . . asked an 'officer,' who was passing by, a pale young man, who looked exhausted to death . . . where the men were coming from. 'Where from? Well, sir, I guess we're all coming out of Virginny as far as we can, and pretty well whipped too. . . . I know I'm going home. I've had enough of fighting to last my lifetime.'"

sailed for London in April. His judgment was that the republic was "tumbling to pieces" and that the only settlement possible would require the concession to the South of some "qualified independence."

Russell's impressions of the South during his two months' stay there had not been favorable, primarily because of slavery. He was disgusted by the slave auction he witnessed in Montgomery, on his way to the Confederate Congress. If his newspaper's editorials were pro-Southern, the responsibility did not lie with Russell. In addition to the "peculiar institution," he disliked Southern poverty and the braggart politicians he met. Nor did he like the South's traditions: the special notion of honor, the "reckless and violent condition of society," the dueling, the quick temper, "the swashbuckler bravado, gallant-swaggering air of the Southern men." Life in the South did, however, have its compensations:

My chattel Joe, adscriptus mihi domino, awoke me to a bath of Mississippi water with huge lumps of ice in it, to which he recommended a mint-julep as an adjunct. It was not here that I was first exposed to an ordeal of mint julep, for in the early morning a stranger in a Southern planter's house may expect

The first Flag of Independence raised in the South by the Citizens of Savannah, Ga. November 8th 1860. Dedicated to the Morning News, by R. H. Howell after a drawing by Henry Cleenewerck, lithograph, 1860. Library of Congress.

Russell arrived in the South just after the firing on Fort Sumter: "Here was the true revolutionary furor in full sway. The men hectored, swore, cheered, and slapped each other on the backs; the women in their best, waved handkerchiefs, and flung down garlands from the windows. All was noise, dust and patriotism."

the offer of a glassful of brandy, sugar, and peppermint beneath an island of ice—an obligatory panacea for all the evils of climate. After it has been disposed of, Pompey may come up again with glass number two: "Massa say fever very bad this morning—much dew." On one occasion before breakfast the Negro brought up mint julep number three, the acceptance of which he enforced by the emphatic declaration, "Massa says, sir, you had better take this, because it'll be the last he make before breakfast."

In spite of his general lack of sympathy for the South, Russell did recognize that the Southerners were passionately moved by their cause:

At Goldsborough, which is the first place of importance on the line, the wave of the Secession tide struck us in full career. The station, the hotels, the street through which the rail ran was filled with an excited mob . . . flushed faces, wild eyes, screaming mouths, hurrahing for "Jeff Davis" and "the Southern Confederacy". . . . All was noise, dust and patriotism. . . . Secession is the fashion here. Young ladies sing for it; old ladies pray for it; young men are dying to fight for it; old men are ready to demonstrate it. The founder of the school was St. Calhoun. Here his pupils carry out their teaching in thunder and fire. . . . The utter contempt and loathing for the venerated Stars and Stripes . . . on the part of these people cannot be conceived by anyone who has not seen them. I am more satisfied than ever that the Union can never be restored as it was, and that it has gone to pieces, never to be put together again, in the old shape, at all events, by any power on earth.

Russell deplored any permanent severance of the Union, but his thesis was that the war would purify the air and divert Americans from "the universal hunt after place and contracts and dollars": "I am persuaded this prick in the great Northern balloon will let out a quantity of poisonous gas and rouse the people to a sense of the nature of the conflict on which they have entered." He believed that the North, "if properly handled and directed," would in the end win the war. "But what would come then—not a Union such as existed before, but an armed confederation holding a portion of its territory by a military occupation."

Russell did not fully understand that the North brought to the fight against the South a countervailing faith: a zealous hatred of slavery. He reported its uncertainty, not its passion. Nor did he fully take account of the North's superiority in numbers or of its technical and economic resources. In general, he was scornful of the competence of its officers. He did not "spot" Ulysses S. Grant, although he did note the quality of William Tecumseh Sherman. Nor was he especially prescient in judging the quality of the Northern troops. Perhaps it was too early to do so; perhaps after the Charge of the Light Brigade it all looked amateur, hesitant, and disorderly, as indeed it was. The South, with its military academies and cavalry training, had certainly the initial advantage.

Russell won that enconium that greets all objective observers—he was unpopular with both sides. He noted the South's recurring expression of faith that because Cotton was King, Britain would be so hurt by its absence that it must ultimately aid the Confederacy. He noted it but did not share it. In Mississippi, he reported:

Jefferson Davis, by Mathew Brady, photograph, circa 1861.
Library of Congress.

After a visit to Charleston, Russell toured a Carolina plantation and then traveled to Montgomery, Alabama, where he met Jefferson Davis. "He is certainly a very different looking man from Mr. Lincoln. He is like a gentleman—has a slight, light figure, little exceeding middle height, and holds himself erect and straight. . . . Wonderful to relate, he does not chew, and is neat and clean-looking, with hair trimmed and boots brushed. The expression of his face is anxious, he has a very haggard, careworn and pain-drawn look, though no trace of anything but the utmost confidence and greatest decision could be detected in his conversation."

The Governor conversed on the aspect of affairs, and evinced that wonderful confidence in his own people which, whether it arises from ignorance of the power of the North, or a conviction of greater resources, is to me so remarkable. "Well, sir," said he, dropping a portentous plug of tobacco just outside the spittoon, with the air of a man who wished to show he could have hit the centre if he liked, "England is no doubt a great country, and has got fleets and the like of that, and may have a good deal to do in Eu-rope; but the sovereign State of Mississippi can do a great deal better without England than England can do without her."

And in the vigor of his reporting of the rout after Bull Run, Russell was certainly objective, but tactless. In the North, those who read his account were not, like the readers of his Crimean or Indian dispatches, reading of events thousands of miles away. Their own future was at issue, and reports of Northern incompetence on this scale endangered it. So they did not like what they read, and they made it plain.

Russell worked for *The Times* only occasionally after 1863. He was back in the United States in 1881, with the Duke of Sutherland's party, and spent most of his time in the Far West. About this he wrote *Hesperothen: Notes from The West, A record of a ramble in the U.S. and Canada in spring and summer, 1881*, a work of no special merit. He seemed to have grown even more caustic, emphasizing the immorality, corruption, violence, and crime that he held typified American life. Russell was knighted in 1895, and died in 1907 at the age of eighty-six.

Abraham Lincoln, by Alexander Gardiner, photograph, 1861.
Library of Congress.

"This poor President!" Russell wrote about Lincoln. "He is to be pitied . . . trying with all his might to understand strategy, naval warfare, big guns, the movements of troops, military maps. . . . He runs from one house to another, armed with plans, papers, reports, recommendations, sometimes good-humoured, never angry, occasionally dejected, and always a little fussy." Russell's colleague Edward Dicey, on the other hand, found Lincoln impressive, with an "air of strength, physical as well as moral, and a strange look of dignity coupled with all this grotesqueness."

Edward Dicey, by Désiré-François Laugée, from an unlocated drawing, date unknown, reproduced on a carte-de-visite. The Mansell Collection.

A Northern sympathizer, Dicey came to the United States from England in 1862 as special correspondent for *The Spectator* and *Macmillan's Magazine.* His experiences during the war were more restricted than Russell's—he saw little of the battlefield and never traveled South—but he provided an effective counterweight to England's bias toward the Confederacy.

EDWARD DICEY, a Cambridge graduate, was thirty when he visited the United States. The articles he wrote during his six months' stay as the special correspondent of *The Spectator* and *Macmillan's Magazine* were published in London in 1863 as *Six Months in the Federal States.* He was by taste and education a scholar, an academic, and a Liberal. He dedicated his book, with permission, to John Stuart Mill, and some of it—it ran to two volumes —was academic comment on state constitutions and on the Federal Constitution, rather than direct observation of the country at the time. He had not Russell's experience. He lacked his contacts and saw little of the war, as indeed he was prompt to admit, "except some few incidentals."

Dicey never visited the South at all. It was, by the time he came, clearly in rebellion. He called it Slavedom, and his views reflected those of his friends in New England, abolitionists and reformers. Whereas Russell had all but ignored Senator Charles Sumner, Dicey's picture of the abolitionist was lyrical:

> He is a man you would notice amongst other men, and whom, not knowing, you would turn round to look at as he passed by you. . . . You can read in that worn face of his—old before its time—the traces of a lifelong struggle, of disappointment and hope deferred, of ceaseless obloquy and cruel wrong. . . . There are wrongs which the best of men forgive without forgetting, and, since Brook's brutal assault upon him, those who know him best say they can mark a change in Charles Sumner. He is more bitter in denunciation, less tolerant in opposition, just rather than merciful. Be it so. It is not with soft words or gentle answers that men fight as Sumner has fought against cruelty and wrong.

Dicey's bias was clear, but so was his courage. At a time when there was a distinct chance that Britain might help the Confederacy with arms and men as well as with recognition, Dicey made plain where he stood. "In the interests of humanity, in the interests of America and in the interest of England, the success of the North is a thing we ought to hope and wish for." Unlike Russell, with whom his stay overlapped in time, he saw the energing power of the North:

> You had to go far away from Washington to leave the war behind you. If you went up to any high point in the city whence you could look over the surrounding country, every hillside seemed covered with camps. The white tents caught your eye on all sides; and across the river, where the dense brushwood obscured the prospect, the great army of the Potomac stretched miles away, right up to the advanced posts of the Confederates, south of the far-famed Manassas. The numbers were so vast that it was hard to realize them. During one week fifty thousand men were embarked from Washington, and yet the town and neighbourhood still swarmed with troops and camps, as it seemed, undiminished in number.

Also he understood, as Russell did not, the reasons for Northern hesitation:

> The popular instinct, more acute and intelligent than we can conceive in Europe, taught the people that any outspoken decision on slavery would have alienated the loyal Slave States, and would have thus retarded, if not destroyed, the prospect of restoring the Union. Again, any vigorous action as to slavery was inconsistent with the Constitution; while the whole strength of the North, at the first outburst of the war, lay in the fact that it was upholding the Constitution.

Abraham Lincoln made a strong impression on Dicey. American majesty, he noted, had "no externals to be stripped off, and you see her public men always *en déshabille*."

> If you take the stock English caricature of the typical Yankee, you have the likeness of the President. To say that he is ugly is nothing, to add that his figure is grotesque is to convey no adequate impression. Fancy a man six-foot, and thin out of proportion, with long bony arms and legs, which, somehow, seem to be always in the way. . . . Clothe this figure, then, in a long, tight, badly-fitting suit of black, creased, soiled, and puckered up at every salient point of the figure—and every point of this figure is salient . . . add to all this an air of strength, physical as well as moral, and a strange look of dignity coupled with all this grotesqueness, and you will have the impression left upon me by Abraham Lincoln. You would never say he was a gentleman; you would still less say he was not one.

Although Dicey stayed only six months, he traveled widely. If his roots were in New England—an area Russell ignored—he did visit the West, notably Kentucky, Tennessee, West Virginia, Missouri, and Illinois, and saw something of life on the Mississippi. To this he brought considerable literary gifts and great shrewdness. There are fascinating details in Dicey's account. He found one in ten of all the shops in St. Louis to be liquor stores. He thought that Washington looked as if it had been run up in a night "like the cardboard cities that Potemkin erected to gratify the eyes of his imperial mistress on her tours through Russia; and it is impossible to remove the impression that when Congress is over the whole place is taken down and

Federal encampment on the Pamunkey River, Virginia, May 1862, by J.F. Gibson, photograph. Library of Congress.

Dicey vividly described a society at war: "You had to go far away from Washington to leave the war behind you. If you went up to any high point in the city whence you could look over the surrounding country, every hillside seemed covered with camps. The white tents caught your eye on all sides; and across the river, where the dense brushwood obscured the prospect, the great army of the Potomac stretched miles away, right up to the advance posts of the Confederates, south of the far-famed Manassas."

packed up again till wanted. Everybody is a bird of passage in Washington." He liked Boston most of all, but had kind words to say for Chicago, for Cincinnati, which he regarded as the queen city of the West, and above all for New York, "a sort of Venice without canals," and its harbor:

> *The fairy pilot-boats, with their snow-white sails, darted across our path; vessels bearing the flag of every nation under the sun were dropping down with the flood; English, French, and American men-of-war lay anchored in the bay, where all the navies of the world might ride at pleasure; and the quaint Yankee river steamboats which look as though, in an excess of seasickness, they had thrown their cabins inside out, and turned their engines upside down, glided around us in every direction.*

Dicey's book made much less impact in Britain than did Russell's, and was not even published in the United States. But it was honest, accurate, moralistic and, as it proved, prophetic in its expectation of a Northern victory. But Dicey could get the future story wrong:

The probability seems to me that, in the event of Abolition, the fate of the American Negroes, will not be unlike that of the Indian. A portion will move gradually further south, till they reach a climate where white labor cannot compete successfully with their own. Those left in the existing Slave States will slowly die out, by a diminution of their prolific powers, and will disappear with more or less of suffering. It seems as though, by some inscrutable law of Nature, the white man and the black cannot live and work together, on equal terms, on the same soil.

Dicey returned to England permanently affected by his American experiences. Like Russell, he was called to the Bar and, like him, he did not practice law but stayed in journalism. He played a full part in shaping opinion in London as editor of the *Observer* from 1870 to 1889. On the occasion of Lincoln's death he wrote, for *Macmillan's*, a touching tribute:

I do not believe the late President was a man of genius. His record is grand and noble enough without our need to attribute to him qualities which he did not possess. A purer Nelson, a wiser Garibaldi, his name will, if I mistake not, be cherished by the American people much as the memory of the two heroes I have mentioned is honored in their own countries. History, I think, will say that our own days produced a yet nobler representative of . . . courage, and honesty, and self-sacrifice, in the person of Abraham Lincoln.

Washington, D. C., in April 1865, by an unidentified photographer. Library of Congress.

For Dicey, Washington had an ephemeral, almost stage-like ambience: "The whole place looks run up in a night, like the cardboard cities which Potemkin erected to gratify the eyes of his imperial mistress on her tour through Russia; and it is impossible to remove the impression that, when Congress is over, the whole place is taken down, and packed up again till wanted. Everything has such an unfinished 'here for the day only' air about it. Everybody is a bird of passage in Washington."

16
Edward Wilmot Blyden
1832-1912

by Henry S. Wilson

Though Congress has acknowledged Liberian Independence, I, as a citizen of Liberia, was not allowed to enter the House of Representatives, during the session because I was a black man; and before I could leave that distinguished city, I was obliged to get a white man *to vouch that I was a* free man. *Is this not extraordinary for a country making such pretensions? In the city of Philadelphia no coloured person is allowed to ride in the public conveyances; so that delicate females of education and refinement, simply because they are guilty of a coloured skin are obliged to* walk *immense distances in all weathers—and this too in the city of Quakers. Does not the existence of such barbarism in a Christian community seem incredible in this age of the world?*

The whole national conscience, my dear Sir, is demoralized: and the people need just the baptism of blood through which they are passing to purify them.

—Letter to William Ewart Gladstone, June 1862

HENRY S. WILSON is senior lecturer in the Department of History and Centre of Southern African Studies, University of York. He was the editor of *Origins of West African Nationalism* and is the author of the forthcoming book, *The Imperial Experience in Africa.*

Edward Wilmot Blyden, by Rufus Anson, daguerreotype, circa 1852.
Library of Congress.

Soon after he arrived in the United States from St. Thomas Island, Blyden was photographed in
New York by Rufus Anson, a competitor of Mathew Brady. The seventeen-year-old Blyden
hoped to study for the ministry at Rutgers College, but his application was rejected, and he
was forced to endure the "deep seated prejudice against my race."

ON MAY 17, 1850, Edward Blyden, aged seventeen and star pupil of the Dutch Reform Church Bible Class in Charlotte Amalie, St. Thomas Island, sailed for the United States to complete his studies for the ministry. It was his first step towards a future in which he would become the premier African nationalist. Slavery had been abolished in the Danish West Indies (later the Virgin Islands) only in 1848, but Blyden's parents, of wholly African ancestry, were free blacks. With Romeo Blyden working as a tailor and his wife Judith teaching school, they had carved out a respectable niche in Virgin Islands society. Both were devout members of a Dutch Reform congregation with "nearly equal numbers of white and colored persons sitting promiscuously in the different pews and at the communion table no distinction being made."

In 1845, an American Presbyterian minister, the Reverend John P. Knox, became pastor of the church. Young Blyden soon singled himself out by treating each sermon as a guide for his own behavior. Knox responded by providing private tuition and access to his library. Five years later, he decided that his pupil should enter his old theological college, Rutgers, in New Jersey. Edward was to work his passage to New York as a servant to one Mr. Lee. Knox packed him off with some secondhand clothes, six dollars, and a certificate recommending him "to the kind feelings and Christian fellowship of those Christians among whom his lot may be cast." Buoyed up by the hope of following in Knox's footsteps, Edward left his small happy world of Charlotte Amalie for the United States.

America was to prove cruelly disenchanting. Blyden's application was turned down by Rutgers, out of the "deep seated prejudice against my race." Two other theological colleges also shut their doors against him. A decade later, Blyden, in his first pamphlet to appear in America, publicly exposed the illogicality of the Rutgers staff:

> *The faculty had failed to realize their expectations in one or two colored persons whom they had educated. This inductive reasoning here employed was, of course, most conclusive.* Some *colored persons abuse their education, therefore* all *colored persons should be excluded from institutions of learning. . . . Excellent logic!*

Further affronts followed. Denied the protection of a college community, Blyden had to come to terms with American society alone. He scaled down his educational aspirations, enrolled in a night school, and became a servant to support himself. He found no easy camaraderie among fellow blacks. He was an islander living within a racial minority which, like the white society, gave mulattoes precedence. As a callow youth of "ebon hue," he was forced to subordinate himself, in the rooming-house pecking order, to the sophisticated "colored men" of New York. He yearned to return to being "Eddie Blyden," star of his Bible class and a person of status from a respected family in St. Thomas.

Mrs. Knox, spending the summer in New Jersey, intervened to restore Blyden's flagging morale. She urged him to give up his plan of returning home and to accept instead a passage to Liberia from the New York Colonization Society. At the Alexander High School in Monrovia, he might still prepare himself for the ministry and find a new vocation in service to Africa. It took some time for him to respond positively to such a radical revision of his expectations; but when he did, he wholly endorsed the Society's

Mansion-House of President Roberts, Monrovia, Liberia, by August Hoen, lithograph, 1847.
Library of Congress.

Blyden became exasperated with American blacks who failed to acknowledge the hopelessness of their situation, preferring "to sit all the days of their life in the 'basement.' " He urged them to return to Africa where, in Liberia, they could see "colored men rising to the most dignified stations that white men can fill in this country."

view that whites would never, or at least not for a very long time, allow Afro-Americans equality. His fellow boarders, however, did not agree, and he castigated what he called their "strange infatuation":

> *They see that in this country which they call* their own, *the mass of them are degraded, and that the most intelligent of them can never hold any prominent place in the nation, but that in most cases they are "hewers of wood and drawers of water." They see also a remedy. They see in Liberia colored men rising to the most dignified stations that white men can fill in this country. They see them protecting and governing themselves by wise and prudent laws—acknowledged as a Republic by some of the most potent and enlightened nations of Europe; yet they "prefer to fight it out here," to sit all the days of their life in the "basement."*

Baltimore was to be Blyden's port of embarkation. He traveled first to Philadelphia, where the Secretary of the Pennsylvania Colonization Society, twenty-two-year-old William Coppinger, met him and escorted him to Baltimore to board the *Liberia Packet.* For both young men the occasion was deeply moving, creating a lasting bond.

It was to be a full decade before Blyden returned to the United States. Meanwhile, he quickly made his mark in Liberia. In 1853, when only twenty-one, he was called on to deliver the National Independence Day Oration. In 1854, he became a tutor at Alexander High School and frequently acted as principal. In addition to the Liberian newspapers, he had a ready outlet for his writing in the colonization journals in America. In 1853, Gerrit Smith, a wealthy New York landowner and future state congressman, denounced Liberia as a "frightful graveyard." Blyden's spirited reply contrasted the mere "physical freedom" sought by the abolitionists with the full political liberties enjoyed by Afro-Americans in Liberia. Abolitionists who attacked the African republic damaged the prospects of the race in America, because Liberia "was a silent influence for good in behalf of the colored race in foreign lands."

In July 1856, Blyden, now twenty-three, returned in much more radical temper to the controversy over abolition. In a pamphlet, *A Voice From Bleeding Africa,* he ranged Liberians alongside black Americans in a transatlantic plebiscite against slavery. He evoked the symbolic force of the ancestral homeland in advocating racial solidarity: "Africa! there is no heart beating under a covering of sable hue which does not throb with emotion at the sound of this word." But to rejoice fully in such patriotism, Africans and Afro-Americans had to come to terms with their history. In a passage strikingly foreshadowing today's Third World ideology, Blyden characterized Columbus's planting of the first European colony in the Western Hemisphere as "the forerunner of unspeakable blessings to the Europeans" but "the precursor of bloodshed, torture and extermination to the Indian, and suffering, degradation and misery to the African." Herein lay the roots of Africa's contemporary backwardness. Blyden's attitude to the United States has to be seen in the context of his primary aim: the preservation of the integrity of African civilization. In later years, Blyden would contrast "America" (along with "Anglo-Saxon" culture and "Europe") with Africa," not as geographical entities but as logical antitheses. He attacked American and Anglo-Saxon civilization in order to make Americo-Liberians in Monrovia, or Sierra Leone Colony Creoles in Freetown, align themselves with the mass of Africans living in the hinterland.

Pass for a Free Black Man, 1853. David W. Hazel.

The free man's pass, in this case issued to Benjamin Hasell of North Carolina, was an integral part of America's institutionalized subjugation of its black people. When Blyden returned to the United States in 1862, commissioned by the Liberian government to promote black repatriation, he found that, in spite of his official status, he was "obliged to get a *white man* to vouch that I was a *free man*"—and this in "'the land of the free and the home of the brave!'"

Shoemaking class at the Tuskegee Institute, by Frances Benjamin Johnston, photograph, circa 1898. Library of Congress.

During his visit to the South in 1889 to 1890, Blyden met Booker T. Washington, the President of Tuskegee Institute. He later expressed his admiration for Washington's philosophy of vocational education: "When the Negro has attained to that industrial status which will enable him to realize to their utmost his great material possibilities he will not only . . . command the respect of the white man, but he will come nearer to God."

Blyden's career as writer, statesman, politician, ambassador, professor, and university administrator took him to the United States seven times throughout the second half of the century. In all but the last, he tried to encourage black repatriation to Liberia. He inevitably was embroiled in controversy, because he believed that mulattoes should be treated as a separate race, neither "Negro" nor "Anglo-Saxon," and that only true blacks—"the Negro pure and simple"—should qualify for repatriation. His ability as a writer and speaker brought invitations from both black and white communities in the United States. He came to know most of the prominent black leaders, such as the editor and statesman Frederick Douglass, Bishop Henry McNeil Turner of the African Methodist Episcopal Church, and Booker T. Washington, head of Tuskegee Institute.

On the first of Blyden's visits, in the summer of 1861, he preached in New York at the Presbyterian Church on Seventh Avenue, and he was appointed Professor of Classics at Liberia College, Monrovia, then being established by philanthropists from Boston and New York. Next year he was back in the United States, commissioned by the Liberian government

Old Potter Palmer Mansion, living room, showing paintings, by an unidentified photographer, circa 1895. The Art Institute of Chicago Library.

By the time of Blyden's final journey to America in 1895, he had become aware of a growing materialism. Everywhere wealth flaunted itself with peacock feathers and gilt. To his friend, Francis J. Grimké, pastor of a leading black congregation in Washington, Blyden confided his distaste for this ostentation: "Everything seems intended for show—to reproduce—and often spoil in the reproduction—what they see in Europe."

to promote black repatriation. But the Civil War halted such projects, and he found Washington uncongenial. Although many of the public buildings were "gorgeous and impressive," it seemed to him "like a large country town . . . a very disagreeable place, socially and physically." Before leaving, he had to obtain a "certificate of freedom" from the Provost Marshal: "he gave a written 'permishun'—as he spelt the word"—and this in "'the Land of the free and the home of the brave!'"

Later visits took Blyden to black educational centers such as Howard and Lincoln Universities and the Hampton Institute, and to the Presbyterian Church Assembly in Madison, Wisconsin, where he renewed his friendship with his original sponsor, Knox. During a long stay from July 1882 to May 1883, Blyden suffered badly from the New York summer heat, unrelieved by those "tempering breezes" which made Liberia's summers mild. The winter in Atlanta and Washington was equally trying for the itinerant lecturer. Hoarse and rheumatic, he was forced to travel "with other Negroes and dogs and chickens in a damp pent up [railroad] car poorly heated and with no seats but boxes and bundles." Furthermore, "the coloured people have poor accommodation from cold weather and I am not able to get accommodation among the whites." This plight was strikingly different from his experiences in London as Ambassador to the Court of St. James and member of the Athenaeum Club. Yet, as Blyden pointed out, the contrast could mislead:

> There is no room for comparison. The Negro as a class is unknown in Europe. If there were six millions of Negroes in England they would be treated much as they are here. I do not regard the reception I met with there as indicative of the general feeling towards my race. I went to England as the accredited Minister of the Republic of Liberia, and no social barriers were opposed to me.

He added, "The two races should never amalgamate. I say to the American Negroes: 'Come and join us in Liberia, where we have a country of our own.' My people are in exile here."

His most celebrated tour, from August 1889 to March 1890, epitomizes his mature ideas of the relationship between America and Africa. It was at this time that the American Colonization Society was seeking to capitalize on the distress and restlessness of many blacks in the wake of the Federal Government's retreat from Reconstruction. The Society enlisted Blyden to publicize Liberia. His major work, *Christianity, Islam and the Negro Race,* had been published in 1887, and the Society correctly surmised that Americans would welcome the famous author. American newspapers, from Chicago to the Deep South, celebrated Blyden's scholarship and prowess as an orator. This visit was not only one of his longest but, in its sweep from the Middle West to South Carolina and Florida, his most extensive.

In his search for converts to the colonization cause, Blyden concentrated on Charleston with its large black population and important newspaper, the *News and Courier,* whose editors were sympathetic. Many in Charleston sought from Blyden news of the South Carolinians who had emigrated a dozen years before. He was enthusiastically welcomed; he even had twin babies named after him, Edwin and Edwina Wilmot Blyden, during his stay. Randall D. George, reputedly the richest black man in South Carolina and, Blyden was pleased to note, "a genuine negro," was especially hospitable, placing his private carriage at Blyden's disposal. This allowed him to travel in the surrounding countryside, and he liked what he saw—prosperous black farmers. George himself had a plantation employing thirty hands, and local whites tried to discourage his interest in repatriation, assuring him, "*You* are not the kind of man we want to go."

On December 1, 1889, the *Atlanta Constitution* printed an attack on Blyden and Liberia by Charles H. J. Taylor, briefly United States Minister to Liberia. He denounced Liberia as "that black land of snakes, centipedes, fever, miasma, ignorance, superstition and death" and Blyden as a Muslim and fetish-worshipping hypocrite. Blyden counterattacked, dismissing his opponent as a mulatto: "I won't answer him," he told a reporter. "If he were a white man I should reply to him; if he were a Negro I should endeavor to convince him, but he is neither, and is not concerned with the work I have undertaken."

Traveling from Savannah to Florida, Blyden was forced to ride in the "Nigger Car, but it was very comfortable," he reported. "I was very glad for it gave me the opportunity of conversing freely with those sturdy work-

Edward Wilmot Blyden, by an unidentified photographer, 1894.
Nigerian Museum.

It was during his last American tour, one year after this photograph was taken, that Blyden, then sixty-three, finally admitted the infeasibility of colonization. Exponents of repatriation were shocked to hear him declare that black emigration had to be postponed because "Africa is not yet ready for the exiled Negro and he is not ready for it."

ing men who came in at various stations on Africa. I found that they were all anxious to go. They say that they see no chance here for their children and matters are getting worse." The conservative *Florida Times-Union* approvingly wrote that "Dr. Blyden has met no full blooded negro who is not in sympathy with his mission. . . . *The Times-Union* urges no coercive measures of colonization, but the rich field [Liberia] is open to voluntary immigrants, and Dr. Blyden seems to be the heaven-appointed medium for helping to solve the [race] problem."

In Washington, Blyden addressed the American Colonization Society and was present when Senator Butler's bill to appropriate $4,000,000 for black repatriation was considered. Butler quoted liberally from Blyden's *Christianity, Islam and the Negro Race,* but in the end the bill never came to a vote. Blyden had warned the Society that the time was not yet ripe for massive repatriation. The South still needed black labor, and "Europe still thinks she can take and utilize Africa for her own purposes. She does not yet understand that Africa is to be free for the African or for nobody." Yet grass-roots support for emigration continued. Months after Blyden returned to Liberia, the Society found itself embarrassed by an impostor who impersonated Blyden among blacks in Arkansas and collected contributions to fraudulent "Blyden Clubs."

Blyden's last visit to America in 1895 was marked by a reconciliation with the anti-emigration black establishment. Exponents of emigration were shocked to hear him say that repatriation must be postponed because "Africa is not yet ready for the exiled Negro and he is not ready for it." Alexander Crummell, an old colleague at Monrovia College, was now an Episcopal minister in Washington and doyen of the black intelligentsia. He no longer supported repatriation and was delighted with Blyden's change of heart. So also was Francis J. Grimké, pastor of the Fifteenth Street Presbyterian Church (a leading black congregation in Washington), who believed that emigration could never solve the race problem in the United States. There was also, perhaps, further reason why Blyden felt black Americans would, for years to come, be unsuited to African colonization. To Grimké he wrote: "One coming to this country from abroad realizes far more than he could be reading at a distance the unsatisfactory condition, intellectual and spiritual, of the American people, both white and black. One is struck by the almost entire absence of the ideal and spiritual, owing to the overwhelming influence of the material." The writers and philosophers whom Blyden had admired, "the Websters, Sumners, Emersons, Bryants, Longfellows, Holmes, Lowells etc., have given place to the Vanderbilts, Astors and Goulds. The originators of thought and the prophets of the unseen are succeeded or superseded by the Standard Oil and railroad magnates." The movement back to Africa, at heart a spiritual concept, could not survive in an age which had so lost touch with the ideal.

17
Georges Clemenceau
1841-1929

by J. B. Duroselle

The legislative power here has the upper hand. That is the peculiarity of the situation, or rather of this government. Congress may, when it pleases, take the President by the ear and lead him down from his high seat, and he can do nothing about it except to struggle and shout. But that is an extreme measure, and the radicals are limiting themselves, for the present, to binding Andrew Johnson firmly with good brand-new laws. At each session they add a shackle to his bonds, tighten the bit in a different place, file a claw or draw a tooth, and then when he is well bound up, fastened, and caught in an inextricable net of laws and decrees, more or less contradicting each other, they tie him to the stake of the Constitution and take a good look at him, feeling quite sure he cannot move this time.

—*Observations several months before the impeachment trial of*
Andrew Johnson,
Le Temps, September 25, 1867

J. B. DUROSELLE is a Professor at the Sorbonne (University of Paris I), teaching the history of international relations. He has been visiting professor at several American universities and is a foreign member of the American Philosophical Society. He is the author of *Wilson to Roosevelt, American Foreign Policy*.

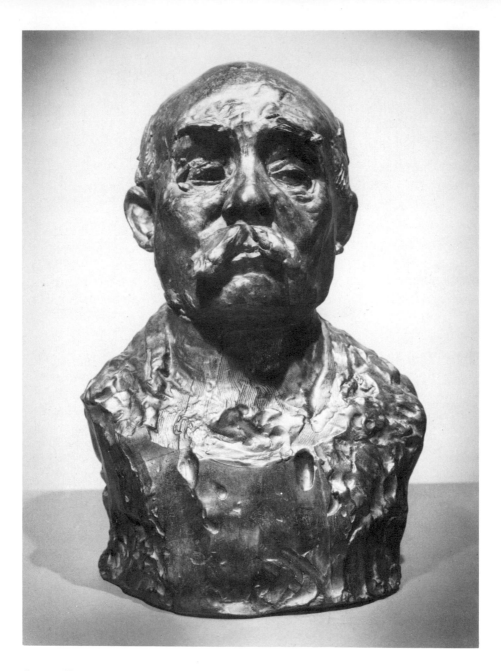

Georges Clemenceau, by Auguste Rodin, bronze, 1911. New Orleans Museum of Art, on extended loan from Mr. and Mrs. Pierre B. Clemenceau.

This bronze bust is considered to be Rodin's greatest portrait of a statesman. Clemenceau, after enduring eighteen sittings, was disappointed; but the artist liked it, comparing it to a clenched fist.

IN 1919, after four years of a most bloody war, the fate of the world was decided by three men: the British Prime Minister, David Lloyd George; the President of the United States, Woodrow Wilson; and the French Prime Minister, Georges Clemenceau, the "Tiger of France." The exchanges between Wilson and Clemenceau were frequently sharp, sometimes dramatic. But it would be very wrong to draw a black-and-white contrast between the Frenchman and the American. John Maynard Keynes, the great British economist, did just this in his analysis of the Versailles Conference. He saw Wilson as a "blind and deaf Quixote," and Clemenceau as a "cynical nationalist," the "French Bismarck." In fact, both men were passionate democrats, ardent believers in justice, eager to promote a "just peace." Despite their disagreements and their different methods, they were friends.

To understand the roots of this friendship, one must remember how deeply the United States had influenced the French statesman. As a young man, he made two trips to the United States, and he returned, an old man, in 1922. He married an American, Mary Plummer, who bore him three children. Although Clemenceau never wrote a book about the United States, he wrote in a dazzling prose numerous powerful and original articles, which demonstrated that he was one of the most interesting and discerning of French travelers.

Georges Clemenceau was born in 1841 in the Vendée, a province of western France. His father, Benjamin Clemenceau, was an ardent republican and, like Georges, was imprisoned during the reign of Napoleon III. Georges, at a very tender age, became a passionate believer in republican ideals. While a student in Paris, he wrote for newspapers of the far-left and, in 1865, he became a medical doctor. But instead of practicing, he determined to travel, very probably because he felt unhappy in the authoritarian atmosphere of Imperial France. He needed, so to speak, physically to visit countries with democratic regimes, and to talk with theorists and practitioners of liberalism. There were other reasons too: he was young, he liked traveling, he wanted to see the world.

Clemenceau went first to England, and then, in the summer of 1865, he sailed for New York on the *Etna,* arriving after the defeat of the South and Lincoln's assassination. His stay would last for five years. In the beginning, he lived off an allowance from his father but, when he discovered that his father wished him to return to France, he decided to stay and earn his own living. He accepted a position as professor of French and riding master at a young ladies' boarding school, Miss Aiken's, in Stamford, Connecticut. He also managed to be named foreign correspondent for the republican newspaper, *Le Temps*—quite a departure for that paper. Clemenceau first found lodgings in a house in Greenwich Village owned by the librarian of the French community; then he lived in a room which had formerly been occupied by his arch-enemy Louis Bonaparte, who was to become Napoleon III. Clemenceau frequented the Union League as well as Tammany Hall, and was a close friend of Horace Greeley, the editor-in-chief of the *New York Tribune.* He went quite frequently to Washington—where he met the future President, General Ulysses S. Grant—and to nearby Virginia. He also went to see the newly pacified South, and spent some time with a Florida planter.

Clemenceau fell in love with one of his pupils, Mary Plummer, and asked her to marry him, but insisted that, he being an atheist, there be no

Georges Clemenceau, by an unidentified photographer, circa 1864, in *Clemenceau— American Reconstruction 1865–1870,* 1928.

After completing his medical studies, Clemenceau left the France of Napoleon III for several years' travel in the Anglo-Saxon world. He settled in Greenwich Village, remarkably enough in a room once occupied by Napoleon III, and began his reports for the Parisian journal *Le Temps* on America's reconstruction after the debacle of civil war.

The Catharine Aiken School in Stamford, Connecticut, by an unidentified photographer, circa 1860. The Stamford Historical Society, Inc.

At Miss Aiken's, a girls' school in Stamford, Connecticut, Clemenceau became a teacher of history, literature, and riding. He fell in love with one of his pupils, Mary Plummer, who later became his wife.

religious ceremony. The family refused, and he returned to France. However, she soon summoned him back; he sailed for New York, married there without a religious ceremony, and brought his bride to France in August of 1870, just as the Franco-Prussian war was breaking out. It must be mentioned that after a few years of happiness, the birth of two girls and one boy, this marriage went awry, and after some infidelities here and there, it ended in a divorce in 1884 (the very year divorce was again made legal in France).

A scrutiny of Clemenceau's articles in *Le Temps* furnishes an interesting study of American politics at the period of the Reconstruction. It would be interesting to know if the topics were assigned by the paper or were Clemenceau's own choices. In any case, his articles were only concerned with the political scene. Unlike his predecessors Tocqueville, Michel Chevalier, Gustave de Beaumont, he did not examine social mores or economic problems. An essay on the instruction of young ladies and Miss Aiken's school in Stamford would have been entertaining, but except for a very few allusions in private letters, Clemenceau never spoke of his experience there.

What were his views on American politics? Above all, he intensely enjoyed living in a free and democratic country. He arrived full of enthusiasm and excited by the North's victory, and was an ardent admirer of Lincoln (he wept when he heard of Lincoln's death). He loathed every kind and form of slavery, although he understood the intricacies of the problem: "Only a very short while ago great liberators like Washington and Jefferson, didn't they have slaves?" Sixty years later, in his *Au soir de la pensée*, (in literal translation, "in the evening of thought"), Clemenceau wrote:

> When I arrived in the United States, after the capture of Richmond, I was surprised to find in the southern states a remarkably cultured society in which a strong pro-slavery bias intermingled with the most genteel and sentimental literary discussions. At night, I would usually find on my bedside table some reading matter which clearly demonstrated that slavery had existed since biblical times.

He felt close to the Republicans who, "having abolished slavery, have managed to write into their platform equal civil and political rights regardless of race or color." The Democrats, however, were dredging up hatred against the black man in an attempt to deprive him of his civil rights:

> Any Democrat who does not cleverly slip into his speech some comment insinuating that a negro is a degenerate gorilla is considered a mealy-mouth. What? Give power to a savage race which can never be civilized, whose intelligence level is barely above that of a beast? This is the theme of all the Democrats' speeches.

Two events fascinated Clemenceau: the impeachment proceedings against Andrew Johnson, who had interfered with the Reconstruction programs, and the presidential election of November 6, 1868. He attended the Senate session on March 13, when the ailing Thaddeus Stevens, leader of the radicals, was carried in:

> His illness has made rapid strides but his energy has grown even more rapidly . . . if it were not for the burning fire of his piercing eyes, one would think that life had already forsaken his motionless body in which still boils all the bile that was Robespierre's. The Sergeant-at-arms stands up and calls three times for Andrew Johnson, President of the United States and summons him to come and answer the charges brought against him by the Congress.

Andrew Johnson and the Donkey,
by Thomas Nast, pastel, date unknown.
National Portrait Gallery, Smithsonian
Institution.

"King Andy," as his Republican opponents called President Andrew Johnson,
was, for Clemenceau, an unsympathetic
figure. Johnson's association with the
Democratic party, then given to hate-
mongering against the freed man, offended
the Frenchman's liberal beliefs. Still
Clemenceau felt that Johnson, although "a
stubborn cuss," had some fine qualities,
and he was "glad the impeachment failed
and that he served out his term."

*Thaddeus Stevens being carried into the
Capitol,* wood engraving from *Frank Leslie's
Illustrated Newspaper,* March 28, 1868. Li-
brary of Congress.

Clemenceau observed Thaddeus Stevens,
passionate leader of the radical Republicans, being carried into the Senate chamber to do battle in the impeachment
proceedings against Andrew Johnson. "If
it were not for the burning fire of his
piercing eyes," Clemenceau wrote, "one
would think that life had already forsaken
his motionless body in which still boils all
the bile that was Robespierre's."

Clemenceau recognized that Stevens was an extremist, and yet he had little liking for Johnson, finding him too partial to the South.

Clemenceau was intensely interested, as well, in the electoral campaign of 1868 and the Chicago convention. The fever and excitement of the politicians, the meetings, the hoopla amused him:

> *The Americans, like all self-controlled people, have their eccentric side. You will find them very harsh toward people from southern regions, willingly accusing them of being too effusive and sometimes wanting in dignity and decorum. And yet these solemn gentlemen, so stiff and displaying rigid Anglo-Saxon restraint, must need at times to relax and free themselves of their shackles, loosen the reins and allow themselves the pleasure of acting foolishly.*

As a European democrat, accustomed to more solemnity and ceremony, Clemenceau was impressed and astonished at the lighthearted approach of the voters : "What should be a serious and considered act is dressed up into a grotesque display," a "debauchery of the minds." On the other hand, all the goings-on seemed rather quaint and attractive to someone who had been a prisoner of the Napoleonic dictatorship:

> *There are countless meetings and endless parades. The most prominent politicians of both parties crisscross the country every which way, following each other rapidly from town to town so the excitement will remain at fever pitch. The speakers exhaust themselves with talk and the crowds with cheers. The streets are all decked out as for a national holiday. There isn't a farm, no matter how remote, where the farmer cannot see from a window the . . . Stars and Stripes waving above the village to announce a town meeting. In New York, there are torchlight parades with floats depicting allegorical scenes, among which is a Goddess of Liberty handsomely garbed and striking a fine pose.*

After reporting Grant's election to the presidency, Clemenceau concluded, "there is finally harmony in the government, the executive and legislative branches are now working together, the radical party has a free field and the revolution is off again on its glorious way." He was carried away by his own optimism: "Everywhere you look, you notice political or social problems. But in the United States there is fortunately a strange ability to bend with the wind, to recognize and profit from mistakes, to change courses, thanks to which pessimistic predictions are almost always quickly proven false."

Clemenceau's political career began in 1870 when he returned home, at the beginning of the Franco-Prussian War. He took part in the *coup d'état* of September 4, 1870, when the Emperor Napoleon III was overthrown and the Third Republic established. After the war, he was elected deputy, became the leader of the extreme left, and was known, in the shaky parliamentary government of the time, as the "destroyer of ministries." From 1893 to 1902, having lost his seat in Parliament, he became a top-ranking journalist and editor of the crusading *l'Aurore*. Elected to the Senate in 1902, he was made a cabinet minister for the first time in 1906, at the age of sixty-five, and then, a few months later, was named Prime Minister. From 1909, when he left office, he was a member of the Opposition until he was called, eight years later, to be Prime Minister during the First World War. However, he was not re-elected in 1920, and he lived on, away from the political

The nomination of General Grant as Republican candidate for president, Crosby's Opera House, Chicago, by an unidentified artist, wood engraving, from *Leslie's,* June 6, 1868. Library of Congress.

The 1868 Republican Convention in Chicago nominated Ulysses S. Grant. Clemenceau was present, and found the political hoopla astonishing in an Anglo-Saxon people: "The American carnival takes place every four years, and lasts about two months. The pretext is the presidential election. . . . When the will of the people has been expressed and asserts itself, order is suddenly reestablished. The victor mounts the steps of the Capitol, and the vanquished retires to meditate vengeance."

scene, making no public pronouncements, until his death on November 24, 1929, at the age of eighty-eight.

Could it be said that Clemenceau was deeply influenced by his transatlantic experience? Certain Americans have thought so, attributing his greatness to his years in the United States; but Clemenceau was rarely influenced by anything and just smiled at such ideas. He liked the drive of American democracy, not its political structure. He opposed the concept of the presidency, and preferred the parliamentary system. In later years, he would chide the United States for its prideful ways, its irritating puritanism, its moralizing ("On any occasion great or small . . . you have to raise your right hand and kiss the Bible").

After many years, when, in his countless articles, there had been virtually no mention of the United States, Clemenceau found himself, in 1919, confronted by the great American, Woodrow Wilson. The big debate between the two men is, of course, famous. It concerned the safety and protection of France. Wilson believed that France would be made secure through the establishment of the League of Nations. Clemenceau would have preferred military guarantees. He believed that Wilson had no conception of European matters. As the representative of an Old Europe, torn to shreds, he was worried by the immoderate optimism of the American people, whose life-history was too short to have known adversity.

Fifty-two years after his first visit, retired from politics, the old Clemenceau returned to the United States in 1922, on a private trip suggested by his friend, the American Ambassador Myron T. Herrick. "While in New York," Clemenceau wrote, "I searched for the little house where I had lived fifty-seven years ago—but in vain. . . . I found the town quite changed." He then went on to Boston, Chicago, and St. Louis. In Washington, he was lavishly received by President Warren G. Harding, who, he decided, had

> no idea of the ways of European thought and opinion. . . . I tried to make him understand, as I had with Wilson, that it was of vital importance to the United States that it should not lose interest in what was happening in Europe and that it should, now more than ever, walk hand-in-hand with its old allies. But I saw clearly I was preaching to the wind.

Finally, he paid Wilson a visit and found him in bed, one arm paralyzed, and heartbroken by the failure of the treaty.

Close to the end of his life, Clemenceau thought of writing a book about Americans but gave up the idea. For the rest of his life, he was to have mixed feelings about the United States. It was a typical French attitude—admiration for the vitality, the youth, and the enthusiasm of the country, but annoyance with its shortcomings, "overweening arrogance," and a "megalomania" which precluded interest in European affairs. "The future will tell the tale, but I greatly fear that America will reap the consequence of her extravagant pride."

Translated by HOPE C. W. PATTERSON

Henryk Sienkiewicz, by Kazimierz Pochwalski, oil on canvas, 1890.
Muzeum Henryka Sienkiewicza.

Troubled by the political climate of Poland in the 1870s, the young writer Sienkiewicz traveled
to California in the year of the American Centennial to establish a Utopian colony.

18
Henryk Sienkiewicz
1846-1916

by Longin Pastusiak

In Europe when two gentlemen are presented to each other, they spring at once from their seats, sweep off their hats and bow, flaunt the tails of their dress coats in great delight, shake hands, make sheep's eyes at each other, utter assurances of their immense pleasure at having the opportunity to meet, and then they toss at each other the most impudent compliments, such as "For a long time I have been looking forward to making your acquaintance," or "I have heard so much about you," or "I feel fortunate to meet you." In other words, they prance about each other like two monkeys in ardent courtship. How ridiculous! . . .

Here when someone introduces two people he simply says: "Mister X, this is Mister Y." Mister X does not rise, does not remove his hat, does not even extend his hand, but simply nods his head and says "Hello." Mr. Y likewise nods and responds "Morning," and thereupon the two men are acquainted. At their next encounter they slap each other on the back with a "How do you do, old fellow?" It's as simple as all that.

—Portrait of America

LONGIN PASTUSIAK is head of the American Studies Department of the Polish Institute of International Affairs. His most recent books on America, published in Warsaw, are *Half a Century of US Diplomacy, 1898–1945* and the forthcoming *Poles at the Birth of the American Republic.*

HENRYK SIENKIEWICZ, winner of the Nobel Prize in 1905 for his novel *Quo Vadis,* was thirty years old when he sailed for America in 1876. At that time, he was already a well-established columnist for a Warsaw newspaper, *Gazeta Polska.* It was a difficult time in Polish history. The uprising of 1863 for Polish independence had failed, and the country was still partitioned among Prussia, Austria, and Russia. In this pessimistic political climate, Sienkiewicz and a group of his fellow intellectuals—among them Count Charles Chalapowski and his wife, the famous actress Helena Modjeska— became interested in America. Intrigued by the approaching Centennial Exposition, they had the idea of founding a Utopian colony modeled on the Brook Farm community of Transcendentalists in New England. Sienkiewicz, who had been reading a romantic account of California by the Polish jour- nalist Julian Horain, was chosen, with Julius Sypniewski, another member of the group, to scout an appropriate location in that state. Many years later, Helena Modjeska remembered their romantic expectations:

Oh, but to cook under the sapphire-blue sky in the land of freedom! What joy! To bleach linen at the brook like the maidens of Homer's 'Iliad'! After the day of toil, to play the guitar and sing by moonlight, to recite poems, or to listen to the mockingbird! And listening to our songs would be charming Indian maidens, our neighbors, making wreaths of luxuriant wild flowers for us! And in exchange we should give them trinkets for their handsome brown necks and wrists! And oh, we should be so far away from every-day gossip and malice, nearer to God, and better.

Sienkiewicz arrived in centennial America in March 1876 and, after a few days' stay in New York, took a transcontinental train to San Francisco. Although not very impressed by American trains—they had, he felt, an un- deserved reputation for speed and comfort—he enjoyed his position as the first Pole to report on the transcontinental route and arrived in California with high hopes. He and Sypniewski selected Anaheim, in Southern Cali- fornia, as the site for their Polish "Brook Farm," because of the excellent weather for agriculture and because they would be able to communicate with the predominantly German-speaking community while learning Eng- lish. The rest of the party of eight arrived in the fall of 1876. Urban idealists with no experience of manual labor, they soon realized how unprepared they were to face the difficult life of pioneer farmers. "We had several cows," Helena Modjeska later wrote, "but there was no one to milk them. . . . We had chickens, but our fine dogs made regular meals of the eggs. . . . The hares continued to be diseased, and our winter crop of barley was fast dis- appearing in the mouths of the neighboring cattle, although I tried myself to shoot at the latter with my revolver. My shooting did not even scare them." So the group decided to disband, Modjeska to recoup her fortune as an actress in San Francisco and Sienkiewicz to continue to write his letters from America, which appeared in the Polish journals *Gazeta Polska, Kurier Codzienny,* and *Przeglad Tygodniowy* until he returned to Warsaw in 1878.

Sienkiewicz's earliest letters from America were not sympathetic to the new country. Making the same mistake which most foreign visitors make today, he judged America at first by what he saw in New York. The city dis- appointed him. There were too many hotels and banks and no historical monuments:

Helena Modjeska, by an unidentified photographer, 1897. Library of Congress.

In her memoirs of life in Warsaw, the actress Helena Modjeska recalled the gathering at which she and her friends decided on an American adventure: "I always consider that evening as a stroke of fate which . . . was to push us into a mightier world than we had been in hitherto. . . . Someone brought news of the coming Centennial Exposition in America. Sienkiewicz . . . described the unknown country in the most attractive terms. Maps were brought out and California discussed. . . . Dr. Karwowski entered just when we were most interested in Sienkiewicz's description of an imaginary storm in the ocean, and said to me jokingly:—

"'You need a change of air, Madame. Why not make a trip to America?'

"'That is a good idea,' my husband answered. 'Why not?' and he looked at me.

"I repeated, smiling, 'Why not?'"

> *You must look for history of the United States in Washington; in New York you will find only merchants. Business, business, business, from morning till night, that is all you see, read, and hear. . . . Wealth is the chief criterion by which men are measured, and even the idiom of the language reflects this sentiment. Here people do not say a man* has *a certain amount of money, but that he is* worth *so many thousands.*

Sienkiewicz was offended, too, by the filth and corruption of the city. No city spent as much as did New York for the maintenance of order and municipal services, yet it was "a hundred times dirtier" than other cities: "I predict at the outset that all the efforts of the Warsaw municipal authorities to compete with New York in untidiness will be of no avail." And so skilled were New York's municipal thieves that "European corruption pales into insignificance."

On his transcontinental journey to California, Sienkiewicz witnessed a yet more unpleasant side of American life. In Ketchum, Iowa, encountering "with joy and surprise" his "first wild Indians," a delegation of Sioux on their way to meeting with American officials, he noted the hostility of the other travelers:

> *It is difficult to comprehend the extent and hatred of the American frontiers-*
> *man for the Indian. . . . According to the philosophy of the frontier, the*
> *white man has the same right to exterminate Indians as he would rattle-*
> *snakes, grizzly bears, and other harmful creatures. While New York curb-*
> *stone philanthropists from time to time arrange charity balls at which*
> *Indians are exhibited, out on the frontier a merciless and dreadful war wages*
> *incessantly.*

This was a short time before General Custer's defeat at the battle of Little Big Horn.

Sienkiewicz's views on America underwent a certain evolution. After his initial bad impression, he gradually became more optimistic: "I can only repeat that while not shutting my eyes to the darker aspects of American society, the longer and more closely I observe it, the brighter it appears to me." He liked his neighbors in California and marveled at their prosperity:

> *One cannot speak here of poverty in the same sense as one does in Europe,*
> *where it is synonymous with hunger. In Anaheim I was told, for example,*
> *that Brown or Harrison or Down was extremely poor. But what does this*
> *mean? . . . Is this person on the point of starvation? Far from it! He eats meat*
> *three times per day and has wine with his meals, for this is the least expensive*

Bird's Eye View of Anaheim, Los Angeles Co., California, by E.S. Glover, lithograph, circa 1875. Bancroft Library, University of California, Berkeley.

Sienkiewicz and his companion Sypniewski chose Anaheim as a place for their experiment because of its gentle climate, and because they could communicate with its German-speaking population. The efforts of these young Polish intellectuals to root themselves in the New World came to nothing—they were hopeless as farmers—but Sienkiewicz later drew upon his Anaheim experiences in writing his short stories.

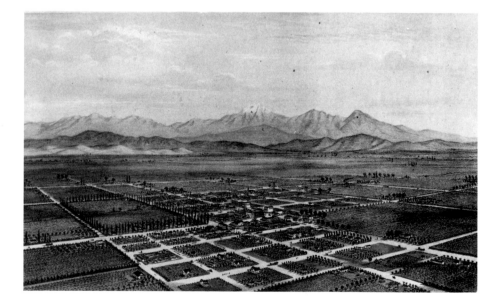

Chicago Fire: view north from about Congress St., between Wabash and Michigan Avenues, by Landy of Cincinnati, 1871.
Chicago Historical Society.

The Great Chicago Fire of 1871 had leveled the heart of the city. But reconstruction had begun immediately, and by the time of Sienkiewicz's visit five years later, Chicago was thriving once again. He saw in its resurrection the vitality of the country: "Within a few years no traces of the fire will remain—and if the town should burn again, it will once more be rebuilt. It will be rebuilt twice or even ten times, for the energy of these people surmounts all misfortunes and all disasters."

> *drink here. Why, then, is he considered poor? Simply because he does not have on hand a hundred dollars in cash! Good heavens! How many literary figures, lawyers, and doctors do I know in Warsaw . . . none of whom has on hand a hundred dollars in cash! But we do not call this poverty, and certainly not destitution. . . . Destitution in Poland makes teeth chatter from cold, blots bodies from hunger; it begs, steals, and murders.*

Coming from a country which not only knew hunger, but had also lost its independence and lacked democratic privileges, Sienkiewicz was acutely sensitive to the benefits of American democracy. "It exists," he wrote, "not only as an institution and a theory, but also in men's relations with one another." He was impressed by the fact that Americans had great respect for every kind of labor. He considered this attitude "the key" to understanding American democracy, "which at first seems to be incomprehensible." He advised Europe that, if it could learn to respect labor, "its people will acquire political and social equality more quickly than through any institutional changes."

Sienkiewicz was somewhat naïve about the American social structure: "Everybody here stands on the same social level, with no one towering above another." Though he was partly right in his belief that social classes in the European sense did not exist in America, it is difficult to understand why he failed to notice any social ladder in the United States. In any case he contradicted himself, describing elsewhere the difficult situation of poor people, Negroes, Indians, and Chinese. For example:

> *I was in San Francisco the night a massacre of the Chinese was expected. By the light streaming from burning buildings along the coast marched huge, menacing crowds of workers, carrying banners bearing such inscriptions as the following: "Self preservation is the first law of nature." . . . Order was at last restored, but only after the railroads, which had provoked the disturbances by reducing the wages of white men, agreed not to reduce wages and to dismiss their Chinese employees.*

The second element of American democracy was the accessibility of education. Sienkiewicz felt that the average American was not a learned person; but he was impressed by the fact that education was more widespread and more evenly distributed in America than in Europe: "The mental development of the people is more uniform, and mutual understanding is therefore more easily achieved." There was, however, a price to pay. He was critical of the intellectual level of Americans and found newspapers in the United States inferior to European ones: "In Poland a newspaper subscription tends to satisfy purely intellectual needs and is regarded as somewhat of a luxury which the majority of the people can heroically forego; in the United States a newspaper is regarded as a basic need of every person, indispensable as bread itself." Sienkiewicz also concluded that the fine arts in the United States were not yet as highly developed as in Europe. He was optimistic, however, and predicted that culture would flourish as soon as American society accumulated wealth, subjugated nature, and began to feel a certain surfeit of life and of the world of reality.

The Chinese Question, by Thomas Nast, engraving, from *Harper's Weekly,* February 8, 1871. National Portrait Gallery, Smithsonian Institution.

To Sienkiewicz, the California Chinese were a "peaceful and timid people" forced to live in squalor. Imported by American companies as cheap labor, they represented competition for the white working class. Sienkiewicz gave his Polish readers an account of one anti-Chinese riot: "I was in San Francisco the night a massacre of the Chinese was expected. By the light streaming from burning buildings along the coast marched huge, menacing crowds of workers, carrying banners bearing such inscriptions as the following: 'Self-preservation is the first law of nature.'"

The third factor of American democracy, according to Sienkiewicz, was "the lack of marked disparity in manners." In Europe, he observed, the upper class differed from the lower not only in wealth and education, but also in manners: "Knowledge may not be so profound nor good manners so refined in the United States as in Europe but both are certainly more widely diffused." And this was the essence of American democracy.

As a reporter, Sienkiewicz knew that his readers back home would be very interested in the social customs of the Americans, and particularly in those which differed from their own. His first impressions were not favorable. He noted "the disgusting custom" of chewing tobacco: "If you glance at any group of people you will notice that majority of the men are moving their jaws rhythmically, as though they were some species of ruminating animals." He was astonished to see men at the dinner table with their hats on. "They do not take off their hats even in private homes, and yet they remove their coats everywhere, even in the presence of ladies or in places where dignity would require otherwise." It shocked him to see Americans reading newspapers with their feet propped up on the table, or leaving the table at the end of a meal without expressing thanks to fellow diners. And he found American eating customs disgraceful:

> According to American custom, numerous porcelain dishes filled with a variety of foods are placed simultaneously before the guest. You have before you all at one time soup, meats, fish, eggs, puddings, tomatoes, potatoes, ice cream, strawberries, apples, almonds, coffee—in a word, a countless variety of dishes in small servings. Begin with whatever dish you please, eat what you like; nobody pays any attention to you. A Negro stands over you like an executioner over a condemned man. He keeps filling your glass with ice water whenever you take a sip and replies invariably, "Yes sir!" to all your requests. As a result of this mode of serving, everything you eat is cold, stale, and unappetizing, even in the best restaurants. American cuisine is the worst on earth. It ignores all consideration for your health and well-being in order to speed you through your meal so that you can return as quickly as possible to business.

He concludes that this lack of graciousness "makes even the most enthusiastic admirers of the Americans admit that in this respect European nations surpass the United States." He admitted, however, that the observation was superficial. Americans possessed many fine qualities, "but these can be appreciated only after closer acquaintance."

Despite the corruption in politics, in the legal system, and elsewhere, Sienkiewicz felt that Americans achieved a high level of morality. With the exception of port cities, where newly arrived immigrants, pressed by poverty, committed crimes, and of the frontier, where society was not yet organized, "I can say that I know of no people who are more law-abiding than the Americans." He was pleasantly surprised to find that public safety was greater in America than anywhere else: "Believing the rumors about the United States which I had heard in Europe, I used to go about at first with a revolver at my belt, brass knuckles in my pocket and a sword concealed in my walking cane. I was armed like some bandit in an opera." Housebreakings or burglaries were less frequent in the United States than in Warsaw, Paris, Berlin, or other European centers—observed Sienkiewicz. "Private property here is so sacred that one might practically leave it on the public highway and yet it would not be disturbed." Sienkiewicz did not try to determine the basis of American morality. Certainly, he felt, it had nothing to do with the practice of religion; Americans possessed only a semblance of deep religious sentiment.

There were many references in Sienkiewicz's letters to American women. It is not surprising. He was an admirer of the fair sex, very sensitive to the beauty of women, and, being very handsome, he was successful in dealing with them. He came to the United States believing that the emancipation of women there had been fully realized. Expecting to find a large number of women doctors, lawyers, scholars, and even clergy, he was disappointed with the reality. "Women here do not take an active part in the industrial public life of the nation." In fact, America lagged behind Europe in this respect. Sienkiewicz noted that men and women in America received the same education, but only in the elementary and secondary schools; women generally did not go on to specialized education. The education of American women was imperfect even in the fine arts: "I have never met a woman who could draw or paint. Knowledge of music is more widespread, but it is, unfortunately, extremely superficial. Americans lack perseverance, musical talent and artistic perception."

Sienkiewicz felt that American women were quite shallow. They were, to him, like spoiled children. (He attributed the excessive attention paid

A Polish ecclesiastical goods store on Milwaukee Avenue, Chicago, by an unidentified photographer, circa 1872.
Polish Roman Catholic Union, Museums and Archives, Chicago.

Stanislaw Slominski stands here, in front of his ecclesiastical goods shop, one of the earliest Polish business ventures in Chicago. Sienkiewicz, interested in the fate of his countrymen who had settled in the New World, found that most of them were not political refugees but "workers who have come in quest of bread." Ignorant of American customs and language, they faced an uncertain future, finding "the road to success as agonizing as the road to the Cross."

them to the fact that the demand for them was far greater than the supply; in some states the ratio was 1 to 5.) Uncultivated culturally, they were even less industrious about household duties and cooking; but they were concerned about their clothes: "Even on the boulevards of Paris, one does not see so many fashionable gowns as on Broadway in New York or on Kearney Street in San Francisco. . . . In all of this there is little taste but much display." He found American women bold and provocative coquettes: "Here the woman is the aggressor." He told of a conversation with "a beautiful girl with a snow-white complexion, blue eyes, and auburn hair":

> *"I regret very much that I do not know your language and therefore cannot speak directly to you."*
>
> *"That doesn't matter," replied the young lady, "If you wish, I shall be your teacher."*
>
> *"You are very kind indeed and I am grateful to you."*
>
> *"But I shall be your teacher only on one condition."*
>
> *"I agree in advance to everything; but pray, what is your condition?"*
>
> *"Well, providing that during the lessons you let me squeeze your hand from time to time."*
>
> *I confess, I was completely flabbergasted!*

Sienkiewicz probably had some success with American women; he reported that foreigners, because of their polish, had great appeal.

These are only a few of Sienkiewicz's thoughts. His letters create a much more detailed and diverse portrait of America. His descriptions of landscapes, for example, are remarkable. He also discussed Polish-American communities in the United States and recorded their attempts to preserve their native culture. In a melancholy mood, he concluded that

> *sooner or later they will forget. They will change everything, even their names, which English teeth find too difficult to chew and which interfere with business. How long this will take is difficult to say. But just as Poland disappeared, so will this same, sad fate inevitably befall her children who, today, are scattered throughout the world.*

But Sienkiewicz felt that his poverty-stricken countrymen had radically improved their lives. For all the costs, and whatever America's shortcomings, the New World was finer than the Old: "If I were asked," Sienkiewicz wrote, "which society has produced the better civilization, I should without hesitation concede superiority to the American." He thought that the main task of civilization was to promote happiness. "We must admit that the opportunity for happiness is incomparably greater in America than anywhere in Europe. American democracy approaches nearest that ideal society for which we have striven through the ages."

Sienkiewicz's two-year visit to the United States had an impact on the development of his further literary career. His American experience can easily be traced in many of his short stories and novels written later in Poland. A number of characters introduced in his famous Trilogy are based upon people he met during his travels in America. Even more important was the psychological benefit of his visit. Seeing a young, energetic, expanding country bolstered his optimism and may well have encouraged him to write the historical novels which would strengthen the hearts of Poles during difficult times in their history.

Charles Boissevain, by Willem Witsen, oil on canvas, 1916. NRC Handelsblad.

Boissevain, a veteran journalist for the Dutch newspaper *Het Algemeen Handelsblad,* was assigned in 1880 to comment on American life. His reports were published in 1881 and 1882 as the two-volume *Van't Noorden naar't Zuiden.*

19

Charles Boissevain
1842-1927

by A. N. J. den Hollander

I prefer our Dutch pigs as the owners of future hams, but their American counterparts as symbols of a young zest for life. Stand in front of a Dutch pigsty and one sees symbols of unashamed ease, of sensual comfort, of cosy, delightful sleepiness. . . . But the quick . . . American pigs are totally different. They are independent, rapid in their movements, not too fat, cheerful and merry. They investigate everything; their snouts are constantly mobile; they insert their noses into everything searching for a grain of wheat in the mud, noticing everything.

—*From the North to the South*

DR. A. N. J. DEN HOLLANDER has been Professor of Sociology and American Studies at the University of Amsterdam since 1946 and is Director of the Amerika Institute there. He is also President of the European Association for American Studies. Since 1930, when he began research for his book on the Southern 'poor whites' he has published a number of books and articles.

WHEN *Het Algemeen Handelsblad,* the leading Dutch newspaper, decided
to send Charles Boissevain to the United States in 1880, he was already a
seasoned and versatile staff journalist, soon to become editor-in-chief. His
assignment to go and look at the United States was an unusual one for any
Dutch newspaper to give in those years, and the initiative of the *Algemeen
Handelsblad* was little less than sensational. Boissevain's reports were soon
published as a two-volume book, *Van't Noorden naar't Zuiden* (translated
"From the North to the South," 1881–1882), in Haarlem.

In the Netherlands, the trip to America seemed to be not without serious risks. "For fifteen years," Boissevain wrote, "I have been carrying life
insurance with a solid, wealthy, dignified insurance company in Amsterdam. By paying an extra premium, I was allowed to cross the Atlantic Ocean,
to use transportation on American rivers and railroads; I was not forbidden
to search for the North Pole; I could visit the Mormons, descend into the
mines of Colorado, search for gold in the plains of Nevada and California . . .
but I was not allowed to travel south of Charleston." Boissevain was no
pathfinder; he traveled in comfort and followed well-beaten tracks. He
stayed in some of the large cities in the Northeast, New York City and Boston especially; he went to see Niagara Falls (in mid-winter); he spent some
time in Chicago; he made an excursion through the prairie states into Iowa;
he went south by Mississippi steamer to New Orleans; and he continued
from there by rail to Atlanta and through the Piedmont region to Richmond.
He then explored Washington, D. C., and left for home from New York City.

An earlier Dutch commentator, the Abbé Corneille de Pauw, described
America in 1770 as a horrible place filled with strange animals and weird
plants, and attacked by a climate which steadily undermined human capa-
bilities. Columbus's discovery, de Pauw concluded, was a tragic and dangerous mistake. But Boissevain was willing to accept the United States as it
was, or at least as it seemed to him to be, without having his perception
directed by *"idées recues";* and this may have been helped by a contributing
circumstance. Although we can conclude, from the amount of published
material, that Dutch readers around 1880 were very interested in the United
States, it also seems that no dominant American image prevailed, either
rose-colored or nightmarish. Boissevain cannot have been much burdened
by preconceived ideas concerning the United States, and this was no mean
advantage.

Almost all Dutch commentators on America showed considerable understanding of the country and a fundamental sympathy with its people.
Certainly it is hazardous to refer to that intangible thing called "national
character." A balanced and impartial judgment cannot be expected from
every Dutch citizen by some sort of *droit de naissance.* Nonetheless, there
are certain Dutch traits which make for easy understanding of America and
for successful communication: our capacity for calm appraisal, our solid determination to fulfill our commitments, our self-discipline, our attention
to detail verging on perfectionism. While perhaps not likely to evoke wild
enthusiasm from other nationalities, these Dutch traits may well have contributed toward fair assessment and mutual respect between Holland and
America.

Boissevain's method for carrying out his adventurous assignment was
not to engage in the systematic gathering of facts through carefully selected

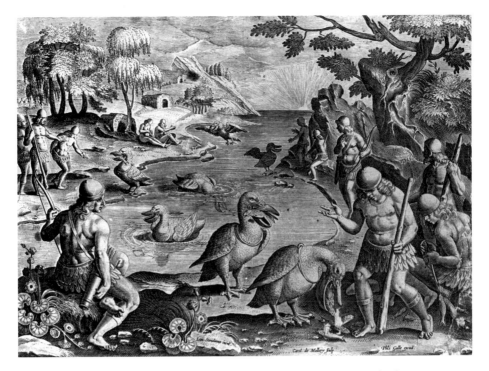

Imaginary view of America, by Karel van Mallery after a drawing by Jan van der Straet, engraving, 17th century. The New-York Historical Society.

The pseudo-scientific contention that the North American climate degenerated all life was popularized in eighteenth-century Europe by the Dutch abbé, Corneille de Pauw. By the late nineteenth century, the Dutch picture of America was no longer nightmarish, but no new image had yet taken its place. Boissevain traveled to the United States in 1880 to satisfy his countrymen's reawakened curiosity about the New World.

informants. He just absorbed what entered his mind, noted down what might interest the readers of his newspaper, and only occasionally pursued more thoroughly what attracted his special attention. The day-to-day registration of observations and comment, especially when written under the influence of some external discipline (as the newspaper correspondent is subject to) has its advantages. Impressions and experiences are recorded when they are fresh; the selective process has not had time to make itself felt; data cannot be cut to measure so easily in order to fit some grand tableau. Boissevain's book distinctly demonstrates this advantage of the traveling journalist. His careful reporting addressed itself less to political institutions than to industrial and social conditions, to social life generally.

Boissevain caught the spirit of the American character. He liked the tonic, optimistic, buoyant, turbulent American life. He was quick to perceive that Americans are always in a hurry (including the undertaker whom he saw rushing through New York's streets on his way to the cemetery). The marvelous resurrection of Chicago, after the great fire of 1871, illustrated for him the unbounded energy, resilience, and vigor of the Americans. Boissevain smiled at the endearing American proclivity to bestow exaggerated titles, and at their penchant for glorification of the trivial in other respects. He was intrigued by the wild speculation going on everywhere, the joy in working hard, the readiness to accept risks, the self-confidence of those he came in contact with, the disarming pride of the self-made man. He commented at large on the blessings of popular education, the spread of the common school, the civilizing influence of the Yankee schoolmarm throughout the country, the religiosity of the people which he defined as "morality touched by emotion." Boissevain noted the high morality in general—aside from politics, business, and an inclination to sudden violence.

He was struck by aspects of social behavior: the non-deferential social intercourse, the informal treatment of persons in high political positions, the ubiquitous handshaking, the brusqueness of demeanor, the lack of gaiety, the abundant hospitality, the general good nature under impositions, obstacles, inconveniences that would have annoyed Europeans no end. He admired the lively, elegant, proud ladies, approved of the absence of unpleasant feminism, thought little of the American stage ("the Americans are not a dramatic people"). He marveled at the number of newspapers and magazines but was shocked by the energetic reporters, whose insolent insistence displeased him. He remarked that an American could endure almost all states except solitude. He was amazed by the tense pursuit of popularity in American life, which he related to the democratic system: one never knew whose vote one might need on some occasion.

Boissevain's speculative mind led him to make some strange predictions and startling hypotheses. Indulging in anthropo-geographical explanations, a fashionable practice in his time, Boissevain considered the American air, "concocted of sunshine and champagne," partly responsible the American's enormous energy and initiative. On the subject of the black population, he stated that they were "moving more and more southward and will, if I am not mistaken, make Texas and Mexico their homeland." He considered the Negroes, together with the Indians and the Irish, the great assimilation problem of the nation, "but perhaps the least indigestible element."

But a number of Boissevain's insights were very shrewd. He was convinced that the need for building ever-higher houses in the cities would bring about an entirely new architectural style. He did not hold (as so many Europeans did, including James Bryce) that American democracy was by its nature prejudicial to the arts. Their development would come, he thought; the country was still too young for one to expect much in this respect. He pointed out that the many small European *rentiers,* who had bought American railway shares and bonds, had thereby helped in promoting the large import of cheap American grain from the Middle West, thus contributing to the lowering of land values in Great Britain and to the curtailment of the power of the British aristocracy. He explained to his readers that American countryfolk differed from their European counterpart: "What is called a *paysan* in France has never existed in the United States as a social type." He justly expected that the civil service reform would soon do away with many abuses of the spoils system. Boissevain commented upon countless other phenomena he thought fascinating, curious, or noteworthy—with unflagging interest and kind sympathy always, with malice never, and with misdirected speculation occasionally.

Boissevain felt that his own country could learn a great deal from the United States; he was immensely impressed by the spectacular difference

Rose's Canal decorated with flags, Amsterdam, by J. M. A. Rieke, watercolor, 1889.
Archives, City of Amsterdam.

In the late nineteenth century, the Netherlands was just emerging from a long period of economic and social stagnation. By contrast, America was dynamic, and Boissevain found it
exhilarating.

between this dynamic country and his sluggish homeland. Studying the
beneficial results of free enterprise, he concluded that confident entrepre-
neurism and untrammeled competition would be useful for his own country: there, after a prolonged period of inertia and stagnation, an economic
renascence had been under way since the seventies, but modernization and
industrialization still had a long way to go. Around 1880, the Netherlands
was still an economic backwater where hundreds of thousands lived in
misery; where the social system, if not completely petrified, was yet solidly
stratified; and where a poor boy's chances of making something of himself
were slight indeed.

Boissevain was one Dutch traveler for whom the settlements of refugees
from the Netherlands, who had fled from their country for religious reasons,
held no special attraction. He weighed opportunities for would be emigrants, and concluded that those who had no special skills or knowledge,
or sufficient capital, would do better to stay at home. He deplored the fact
that the American government had never composed and published an immigrant's guidebook and suggested that the Dutch government should send
an informant to the United States for Dutch emigrants; but he had not come
to America mainly to discover what promise the country offered to poverty-
stricken people.

The Kings of Wall Street, by Buek and Lindner, chromolithograph, published by Root and Tinker, 1882. National Portrait Gallery, Smithsonian Institution.

Syndics of Cloth Hall, by Rembrandt van Rijn, photogravure, 1661, in *Rembrandt, his Life, his Work and his Time,* 1894.

Boissevain saw the American tycoons as masters of their age. Like the burgomasters of the Dutch Golden Century, they exuded a splendid self-confidence: "One finds people like Jacob de Witt, burgomaster of Dordrecht . . . again and again in Chicago, Omaha and elsewhere in the Mississippi Valley and one can compare the vanity of the Americans who are begging Europe to send them portrait painters to the vanity of our forefathers. . . . Those broadshouldered men with their lion faces and determined features . . . inspire confidence and respect.''

Boissevain deliberately chose not to dwell upon the crudities of American life, nor upon its unpleasant features. He had no patience with earlier British authors who had harped on such aspects of the New World. "When one is depicting a foreign people, full light should fall upon the main things. . . . The cuspidor in the South, the revolver in the West, poor municipal government in New York City, gambling in Chicago do not deserve a place in the foreground. They are background shadows which give special splendor to the lighted parts."

Boissevain's benevolent myopia, as a product of his upbringing, is easy to understand. Fundamentally, he thought in the same terms as the Americans to whom he presented his letters of introduction. They must have talked with him, informed him; they must have guided him further to friends; and they must have shaped his perception of the American social scene. The leading classes in both countries shared a spirit of tolerance and belief in human dignity; also they had in common an attractive (though somewhat naïve) conviction that, ultimately, the good things are the simple things, and that a few simple truths underlie all the complexities and perplexities of the modern universe. As a Dutch "Wasp," Boissevain shared with his American hosts the same religious beliefs, love of liberty, spirit of economic enterprise. He was a son of a country that showed many analogies, in its history, with the United States. They were both born from revolt against an overbearing distant political power; and neither country had a tradition of feudalism, a court of any importance, a strong central authority, or clerical domination. There were enormous differences as well, but the two nations were sufficiently alike to understand each other fairly easily when a meeting took place on a common social level. Let us not forget that many so-called typical American traits are simply middle-class traits the world over. Boissevain, as a typical Dutch burgher, must have been sufficiently steeped in bourgeois values and preconceptions to feel intuitively akin to dominant American norms and values. Not only did he accept them without questioning; he admired them sincerely. His mind was, of course, no more a faultless mirror than anyone else's. Because of his social position in the Netherlands, he shared the convictions peculiar to the middle class in America: its acquisitiveness and sentimentality, its queer mixture of high-mindedness and cynicism, its preoccupation with health (and the preservation of human life generally), its exploitation of fellow human beings, and its philanthropy. Like the bourgeois in every country who have newly attained a stable position, he glorified comfort, security, and conformity. Boissevain's class never cherished the harsher facts of life, the sharp impact of reality; neither did he.

Boissevain's own personality led him to a somewhat un-Dutch enthusiasm; for with other Dutch commentators one finds almost always a characteristically European reluctance to separate the good from the evil. For example, John Huizinga wrote in his travel report, *Amerika Levend en Denkend* (translated "America Living and Thinking," 1927): "the observer of the American scene finds himself constantly wavering between enthusiasm and aversion, and even in later reflection it is not possible to resolve all contradictions." Boissevain was little plagued by this sort of ambivalence. His eulogy of the American business tycoon has an antiquarian flavor. He quickly noticed how much the social framework in America differed from the European one. The *nouveaux riches,* he found, were not a popular object for derision in the United States. Boissevain immediately perceived that, in America, education and wealth did not always go hand in hand; and he made the American attitude so much his own—at least during his stay there—that he let himself go in boundless praise and admiration of the robber barons, supermen who he thought a national blessing. As the opinion of an "enlightened liberal," a socially progressive and humane publicist, his veneration of the Hunts and Vanderbilts now makes curious reading. He presented them to his countrymen as a glowing example of what can be achieved by working hard, fearing God, obeying an ethical sense, pushing ahead instead of being content with the status quo. He compared the ebullient tycoons whom he met in Chicago to the lusty Dutch burghers in the large civic portrait group painted in the Dutch Golden Century:

> *One finds people like Jacob de Witt, burgomaster of Dordrecht and father of Jan de Witt, again and again in Chicago, Omaha and elsewhere in the Mississippi Valley and one can compare the vanity of the Americans who are begging Europe to send them portrait painters to the vanity of our forefathers. The pride, the republican pride of the parvenu, in the best sense of the word, of the man who has nothing and nobody but himself to thank for what he has achieved . . . those broadshouldered men with their lion faces and determined features . . . inspire confidence and respect . . . their showing-off, their weapons, their colorful costumes . . . it is vanity but delightful vanity. Long live the self-confidence and the vanity of the American nation!*

As to the influence of Boissevain's book in the Netherlands, little can be said. The author's sagacious, eloquent, and gracious presentation of the Great Experiment as a huge success, appearing in one of the country's most influential newspapers, must have carried conviction. It can hardly have failed to fire the speculations of its readers about the mirage in the West. Perhaps the influence has been mainly a subtly pervasive one, establishing or reinforcing a diffused favorable disposition in the Netherland's middle class towards the great neighbor across the Atlantic.

20
Bjørnstjerne Bjørnson
1832-1910
and
Halvdan Koht
1873-1965

by Sigmund Skard

To see a Norwegian peasant again as an American citizen and a member of the county board—I saw them by the hundreds—, that's a beautiful sight; but to see his grandson as an American gentleman . . . that is bound to silence all defamation; because here you have in front of you the finished result, that which in America is the idea and aim of all endeavor through its institutions.

—Verdens Gang, August 25, 1881

I was happy in America. Not because I felt happy about conditions as they are. But the people inspired me with confidence. The very air in America seemed to be filled with vigor and willpower. It did not occur to anybody that anything might be impossible. One just went ahead and did whatever seemed to be right and useful. And the people demanded that everything be done fairly and properly. You hear much about rottenness and lawlessness and misuse. In spite of this, there is in the people a determination that justice be done. I do not doubt that carried by this determination the people will be able to correct everything that is still imperfect.

—Capital and Labor in America

SIGMUND SKARD was Professor of American Literature at the University of Oslo from 1946 to 1973. He has written many scholarly works, translations, and seven volumes of poetry. His most recent book is *The United States in Norwegian History*.

Bjørnstjerne Bjørnson, by Erik Theodor Werenskiold, oil on canvas, 1885.
Nasjonalgalleriet, Oslo.

This portrait was done by Werenskiold, the pioneer of modern painting in Norway, five years after Bjørnson's return from the United States—where, in New England, he had found his second home.

IN SPITE OF its small population, Norway has long-standing connections with America. Norse vikings were the first Europeans to set foot on American soil. In the eighteenth century, Norwegians were encouraged by the American Revolution to break away from their Danish masters across the sea. When that happened, in 1814, the free Norwegians looked to the American Constitution in creating their own. All through the nineteenth century the Norwegians, in a new union with the conservative Swedish monarchy, struggled to fulfill the promises of their own Constitution. The great Norwegian poet, Henrik Wergeland, pointed to America as "the cradle of our own liberty." And from the 1830s onward, the letters from the many Norwegian emigrants to the States strengthened the image of America as "the Utopia of the Common Man."

A number of important Norwegians visited the United States. Two are of special importance: Bjørnstjerne Bjørnson, the dominant literary figure in late nineteenth-century Norwegian history, and Halvdan Koht, Norway's leading historian in the first half of the twentieth century.

Bjørnson's boundless vitality was matched by his moral strength and unselfish concern for his fellow beings. He was a great poet, novelist, and playwright, and in 1903 he was awarded the Nobel Prize for Literature. But he was equally active in politics, and in the public discussion of religious, social, and literary questions. From his pen came books, articles, pamphlets, and letters which brought home to his fellow-countrymen—sometimes even to the rest of Europe—what moved his mind and warmed his heart.

America played a part in this ceaseless activity. In his public role, Bjørnson saw himself as Wergeland's heir and successor. He shared Wergeland's devotion to America, and in a similar way used the country as a spiritual ally. Like his contemporaries, he was upset by the American Civil War and its aftermath of political decay and corruption. But he believed in the basic health of American society and its power of resilience. He found this optimism confirmed in Walt Whitman's poetry, which moved him like a sight, on the ocean, of "drifting icebergs that announce the arrival of spring." When, in the fall of 1880, he was offered an opportunity to visit the United States, he happily accepted, and spent eight months there.

Bjørnson went "for his own personal development," not in order to produce a book; but he attracted much attention in the United States, and many interviews and reports were reprinted in the press at home. In addition, he wrote for his wife a series of extensive travel accounts. They were promptly published in Norwegian newspapers—such as *Verdens Gang*, published in Christiania (now Oslo)—and often caused heated debates.

He came with a serious purpose, but also with the hope of having a grand experience. And he was not disappointed. Most of his travel letters still make good reading because of their originality and objectivity. He reported to his wife almost daily about everything happening to him, because he had to share his boyish exultation about the wonders of the New World. And his receptivity had no limits. He wrote with the same enthusiasm about the industrial methods of producing felt, the perfect ventilation system at Wellesley College, the "matchless" American kitchen stoves and rat traps, and his own dizzy balancing act between the sky and the East River across the half-finished Brooklyn Bridge. But for all this feverish tourist activity, Bjørnson did not forget why he had come. He wanted to

Cartoon of Bjørnson's American experience, by an unidentified Norwegian artist, published in *Krydseren,* September 1880. Universitetsbiblioteket, Oslo.

As an opponent of monarchy, Bjørnson traveled, in the fall of 1880, to the capital of liberalism. Here he is depicted, fist upraised, on his way to America and then, on his return, being hailed as Indian chief by figures representing Republicanism.

confirm his image of an ideal America, which he used in his battles with conservative writers at home. But he also harbored doubts and wanted to measure his image against American realities.

Bjørnson limited his travels. The New England states provided him with most of his impressions of America. Feeling that the Norwegian newcomers, still largely unassimilated, could tell him little about America in general, he spent only three winter months in the Middle West, where he lectured in Norwegian settlements. He did not go to the West Coast, nor to the South. He spent some time in New York, but only after his main impressions were clear in his mind.

He made his headquarters in Cambridge, Massachusetts, at Elmwood, the home of James Russell Lowell (who was then serving as United States Ambassador in London). Surrounded by cultivated upper-class society, he was received by the Governor of Massachusetts and by ex-President Ulysses Grant and met personally, or exchanged letters with, the literary worthies of the time, including Ralph Waldo Emerson, Walt Whitman, Henry Wadsworth Longfellow, and William Dean Howells. From this cultural stronghold, he also made excursions into the New England countryside. He visited historic shrines and factory districts, studied local institutions, and attended public functions.

Bjørnson hastened to tell his readers at home that, for the most part, his high hopes about America had not been frustrated. In New England, he had found a truly democratic society, where the political system functioned well, where universal suffrage proved a blessing, where there appeared to be little class discrimination, and where everyone enjoyed a sense of prosperity and well-being. To Bjørnson, this democratic liberty was symbolized in the free position of women. He wrote back from a feminist meeting in Boston that this gathering was not marked by cheap enthusiasm, as one might have feared, but by quiet and mature self-respect. "I could hardly master my emotions. I felt that I was sitting in the future."

Critics at home pounced upon these rosy descriptions right away. They pointed out that New England was a small and not typical part of the United States. They made fun of Bjørnson's touch of naïveté, and ridiculed his incessant use of superlatives. Bjørnson surely was enthusiastic about America, but he was no sentimental dreamer. New England at the time still remained outside the deluge of immigration, and still kept much of its stability and tradition. A good many of Bjørnson's positive observations were founded on reality. Nor was he blind to the seamy side of American life. He found that American tolerance had its limits. He noticed an icy greed behind the friendly social relations, and a touch of craze in American idealism. But he tried to balance one against the other: "Both bad and good are larger here than at home." The American political machine was frightening in many

Norwegian settlers in Minnesota in the 1880s, by an unidentified photographer, date unknown. Minnesota Historical Society.

Known as a religious free thinker, Bjørnson shocked his conservative Lutheran countrymen in the American West—"that hive of preachers," as he called it. During a tour through Minnesota and Wisconsin, he berated his audiences for their superstition and crude provincialism.

View of Worcester, Massachusetts, by R. Cooke after the Norwegian painter, P. Anderson, lithograph, circa 1837.
I. N. Phelps Stokes Collection, Prints Division, The New York Public Library, Astor, Lenox and Tilden Foundations.

In Worcester, Bjørnson spent "some of the loveliest and most serious days I have ever lived." The homes were clean, the gardens carefully cultivated, and the workers, unlike "those bent-down, shy, worn-out poor creatures which you see so often on our side of the Atlantic," radiated strength and health.

ways, but served its purpose of activating the masses. There was corruption enough; but "no other nation exposes and castigates its culprits more mercilessly at the whipping post of public opinion."

Bjørnson was fully aware that his experience of America had been limited. But he firmly believed New England to be "the spiritual center" of the Union. When, upon his return, he was attacked for his biased image of America, he answered in an article called "Endless Slander of an Entire Nation." There he maintained that, in studying America, it was wise "to begin with the most advanced states, and in those with the most advanced individuals." Thereafter, one may "look for the exceptions, mistakes, shortcomings, and . . . search eagerly for their reasons."

At the heart of Bjørnson's optimism were his impressions of the Americans as human beings. The main achievement of the United States, he wrote, was that it had taken "all the human slag from the mines of monarchical Europe," and extracted precious metals from it. He discussed the transformation: "In America it is changed, it sparkles, is forged, and through school, work, public spirit, political and religious battles, in the second or third generation acquires that human value that is the highest achievement and the most beautiful adornment of liberty." He saw in America a daring and a fullness of life lacking in Europe, which brought out the best in the newcomers and made them confident, frank, and unafraid.

He was struck by these qualities just after his arrival, when he was invited to a political gathering in Boston. Americans, he observed, compared very favorably with European royalty. He was amazed by "the strength and health of these Americans, these rich eyes, these manly features, this violent, but always controlled willpower." The sight filled Bjørnson himself with a new zest for life. And he had the experience again and again.

During his visit to the labor district of Worcester, "some of the loveliest and most serious days I have ever lived," every person he talked to seemed happy. He visited the homes of the workers; they showed a cleanly comfort, rare at that time in the homes of the laboring class in Norway. But above all, he saw the faces of these people, on their Sunday excursions in the country. He noticed, in the American woman, "a free, independent look"; she was "not one of those bent-down, shy, worn-out poor creatures which you see so often on our side of the Atlantic."

Bjørnson's image of America was a vision, born out of one great experience. He never again tried to recreate it. But it was not just a poet's dream. The image played its part in the victorious battles at home for a full democracy, in which Bjørnson was one of the main protagonists. And the impressions continued to live in his own writing. Time and again, in his novels and plays, America was made to stand for free thinking, an open mind, and a willingness to build the world in accordance with real needs rather than dead traditions. For Bjørnson, the Brooklyn Bridge was a symbol of the America he loved. It was, he wrote, the embodiment of "the bold spirit, the tremendous abilities, the grand vision of the future of that nation."

Halvdan Koht, by Henrik Ingvar Sørensen, oil on canvas, 1952.
Aase Gruda and Sigmund Skard.

Editor of Bjørnstjerne Bjørnson's letters and a leading Norwegian Socialist, the historian Halvdan Koht came to America in 1908. He later wrote of his visit: "It seemed to me that I was looking into the future."

IN THE 1880s, Norway was becoming swiftly industrialized. The conflict-
ing forces of capital and labor were soon to prove more important than the
forms of government; and social democracy became the catchword of the
day. The conservatives closed their ranks as defenders of business interests;
the liberals turned into a party of social reform; and the socialists demanded
a structural change of society itself. In 1903, the socialists won their first
seats in the Storting (Norway's legislature). Thirty years later, they were to
take over the government of Norway, and to hold it for another thirty years.

Here again, America came into the picture, because similar forces were
dividing its society, only more violently. Norwegians followed with anxiety
the conflicts within the idolized republic. The hanging of the Haymarket
anarchists in Chicago shocked the Norwegian nation, as it did the world.
And other American news was no less disturbing.

Norwegian liberals sought comfort in the writings of new social thinkers
in America, from Edward Bellamy to Henry George, and in political reform figures, from Grover Cleveland to Woodrow Wilson. The socialists
followed the progress of organized labor with interest and hope. They were
even more encouraged by a growing sense of social responsibility among
ordinary American citizens. And, in their eyes, Theodore Roosevelt, the
"trust-buster," seemed at times to be talking pure socialism.

A leading spokesman of this newborn radical interest in America was
the scholar and statesman Halvdan Koht. He was a man of amazing vigor,
physical and intellectual. His literary output ran to almost two hundred
books and more than thirty-six hundred articles. He was one of the leading
historians of his generation, not only in Norway, but in Europe. He was
also a brilliant literary historian. Among his works in that field is the standard biography of Henrik Ibsen and a six-volume edition of Bjørnstjerne
Bjørnson's letters. He was active in many areas of Norwegian life, political
and cultural, a leading figure in the labor movement, and, from 1935 to
1941, the country's Minister of Foreign Affairs.

From his student days, Koht wrote in the newspapers about American
foreign policy from a socialist point of view. The details of history concerned him less than the general trends. He was equally interested in the
economic, social, and spiritual forces (literature, art, and religion). The
interplay of those forces, he felt, was bound to appear with particular clarity
in the United States, a country that was newly settled and unhampered by
the burden of tradition. Deep down, he may also have recognized in the
American character that spontaneous vitality that was so strong in himself.

Koht went to the States in 1908, and stayed for almost a year. In Norwegian university circles at the time, visiting America to study history was
regarded as sheer folly; nobody had done such a thing before. He crossed
the ocean in a spirit of expectancy. On his first stroll up the streets of Manhattan, walking until his legs would carry him no longer, he was overwhelmed by his impressions. "The earth seemed to rise beneath my feet.
The vigor in everything I saw, pressed me hard. It seemed to me that I was
looking into the future."

Like Bjørnson before him, he paid little attention to the Scandinavian
sector of America. But, unlike Bjørnson, he made a point of seeing as much
as possible of the entire Union—metropolitan, suburban, and rural areas.
Traveling in more than half of the states, he went to legislative sessions, saw

Eugene Debs addressing a meeting in a railroad yard, by an unidentified photographer, circa 1908. Brown Brothers.

At the time of Koht's visit in 1908, Debs was running as the Socialist Party's candidate for President, campaigning across the country in a train known as the "Red Special" and attracting enormous crowds. Koht felt that America's great liberal tradition was embodied in the labor leaders who struggled to curtail the overweening influence of the barons of industry.

local bosses, and heard simple stump speakers. He visited institutions of education on all levels, from Harvard University and Booker T. Washington's Tuskegee Institute to experimental "children's republics" and ordinary grade schools. He saw the best society and the worst, visited factories and farms, city slums and Negro shacks, Beacon Hill and Coney Island.

He was no less thrilled by the American landscape. There are delighted descriptions of his hike to the bottom of Grand Canyon, and of California: ". . . a rich and beautiful paradise. I had never seen so wealthy a land, and the feeling that I was part of a fairy tale reasserted itself." He eagerly studied American literature, theatre, and art—which in Europe were then regarded with condescension. He met important Americans, the historian Frederick Jackson Turner, the economist Thorstein Veblen, Jane Addams at Hull-House in Chicago, and President Theodore Roosevelt; and he was particularly impressed by Supreme Court Justice Oliver Wendell Holmes, "a free-born aristocrat who understood the new times." Everywhere, he "only had to open his senses, receive, and learn, absorbing life through all the pores of body and soul." When he left the country, "revived and rejuvenated," he felt that he knew the United States better than he did his own Norway.

Koht was later to use this extensive and solid knowledge of America in his scholarship. But, at the time, he also judged the United States with the eye of a political activist. Here, of course, his viewpoint was bound to differ with that of Bjørnson. Koht saw the economic and social powers at work beneath the American surface, even in New England. He spent a good deal of time in the deep South, analyzing race relations. And he followed, with a critical eye, the day-to-day workings of politics, both at the top level and the grass roots.

Above all he studied the capitalist system—the all-pervading influence of big finance and the domination by the trusts. He had no illusions about the strength of the trusts, or about the social ills created and tolerated by them. But he also met the spokesmen of public reform and the heads of the labor movement. He saw, in these men, the spirit of the great American tradition, and tried to gauge the strength of the various forces that were working for improvement.

Booker T. Washington and President Theodore Roosevelt at Tuskegee, by an unknown photographer, date unknown. Tuskegee Institute.

Booker T. Washington and Theodore Roosevelt (standing together to the left) were, for Koht, pivotal American figures. Roosevelt's attempts to elevate the national sense of responsibility impressed him immensely, and he saw a similar spirit at work in Washington's efforts to create "in his people a new determination." Koht attended a meeting of black farmers in Tuskegee: "Booker T. Washington was in the chair. If any speaker got lost in abstractions or platitudes, he interrupted right away: What have you *done*?"

By necessity, his judgment often was harsh. But it did not affect his basic optimism. Time and again, he returned to the idea that the United States was "unfinished." Everywhere Koht saw change and growth, a state of daring experimentation: "The very air . . . seemed to be filled with vigor and willpower." The study of America to him was "a study in youth": the country was not at the end of its development, but at the beginning. Later Koht was asked to compare England and America. "'Well,' I responded quickly, 'the difference is that England lives on its past, America on its future.'"

In particular, he was struck by the American style of radicalism. Without using emotionally loaded terms, Americans were imperceptibly adopting many socialist ideas about equality and justice, government regulation and public ownership. Behind this re-thinking Koht saw "the strong sense in this nation of right and wrong." Theodore Roosevelt, he felt, embodied this style. Koht did not by any means admire everything he did, and was particularly opposed to his imperialistic foreign policy. Two years before, as consultant to the Nobel Prize Committee, Koht had tried in vain to prevent having the President nominated for the Peace Prize. But Roosevelt had finer qualities. Above all, to Koht, he was powerful "like a mountain . . . firm and tight from internal strength." Koht saw in him a personal emanation unequalled in any other human being except Bjørnstjerne Bjørnson. And this strength he saw as typical of the nation: "an immense underground spring of vigor, courage, and faith."

Halvdan Koht's visit to the United States, from 1908 to 1909, was the first among many. He became the founder of American studies in Norway and wrote a number of articles and books on the development of American civilization. As a scholar, he kept in touch with his colleagues in the United States and brought his positive image of their country to the wider reading public.

In his political activity, Koht also looked to America. The strongest force in American life was, to him, its practical idealism. In the 1930s, he saw that idealism in President Franklin D. Roosevelt who, he felt, was "making the sense of social responsibility a living part of American political life even within the private capitalist system." Here Koht believed that America and Norway were trying to accomplish the same ends. In 1937, at the approach of the Second World War, Koht visited the United States in his official capacity as Minister of Foreign Affairs. He emphasized Norway's position within the democratic front against the rising tide of totalitarianism.

When war came to Norway in April 1940, Koht, as Foreign Minister, was the first to receive, and the first to reject, Hitler's ultimatum, and to choose resistance. After serving with the Free Norwegian Government in London, he spent the remaining war years in the United States. There, in a book called *The Voice of Norway* (1944), he explained to American readers the spiritual traditions of his own people. After the war, in *The American Spirit in Europe* (1949), he tried to measure the historic impact of the United States—that nation which had captivated him in his youth, which in his own words had become "his second home," and which still, in his old age, embodied so many of his hopes for the future.

21
James Bryce
1838-1922

by Edmund Ions

Europeans think that the legislature ought to consist of the best men in the country, Americans that it should be a fair average sample of the country. Europeans think that it ought to lead the nation, Americans that it ought to follow the nation.

—American Commonwealth

EDMUND IONS is Reader in Government at the University of York, England. He was a Harkness Commonwealth Fellow at Harvard University from 1958 to 1960 and has held visiting fellowships at Columbia and Stanford Universities. His books include *James Bryce and American Democracy, 1870–1922* and *Political and Social Thought in America, 1870–1970*.

James Bryce, by Sir William Orpen, oil on canvas, date unknown.
Aberdeen Art Gallery, Scotland.

A frequent visitor to the United States in the late nineteenth century, the Scotsman James Bryce earned his reputation as Tocqueville's successor with the publication of *The American Commonwealth,* a classic study of constitutional government.

IN THE 1860s and 1870s, with the rising tide of republicanism in Europe, Great Britain was engaged in a far-reaching debate on representative government. In these debates, the American Republic provided an ideal canvas for observing the working of new institutions founded on fresh principles. The basic question, as Tocqueville had warned in his writings, was how to reconcile the leveling tendencies of democracy with the need for public order and for some form of authority in government.

Among the many young men interested in these questions was a Scot named James Bryce, who won a scholarship to Oxford University from Glasgow in 1857. Bryce's father, a schoolmaster at Glasgow High School and a classical scholar and mathematician, had had a distinguished career as a student at Glasgow University, but it hardly matched the extraordinary career of his son James at Oxford. Not only did the hard-working young Scot take first class honours in Literae Humaniores (classics), as well as in History and Law, but he took almost every university prize available in these fields. Bryce's abilities brought him naturally into the company of a gifted set of contemporaries, including one who was three years his senior, Albert Venn Dicey, the future author of scholarly works on history and constitutional law. After Oxford, the two friends studied for the Bar and went into practice; they also took an interest in Liberal politics during the period of great rivalry between Gladstone and Disraeli.

In August 1870, Bryce and Dicey decided to visit the United States to study its constitutional government. Dicey's family connections guaranteed that the two friends would not lack invitations and contacts when they arrived in New York. His elder brother Edward, a journalist, had spent six months in the United States during the Civil War, and his cousin Leslie Stephen, the Victorian man of letters, was friendly with many American literary figures. James Bryce was thirty-two, Dicey thirty-five when they set out. Bryce had a robust physique, toughened by strenuous walking tours in the Alps and in his native Scotland. The journal he kept of his trip to America recorded many early morning baths in cold mountain streams and lakes as he traveled through the White Mountains in New Hampshire, to the Midwest, and up the Mississippi to Minneapolis.

The two friends planned separate itineraries for parts of their trip, meeting up occasionally to compare notes and to travel together. From New York, where they called on E. L. Godkin, editor of *The Nation,* they traveled to Boston where they met, among others, Henry Wadsworth Longfellow and Oliver Wendell Holmes, Jr., who became one of Bryce's lifelong friends. To get the feeling of a different America, Bryce made plans to go by railroad to Chicago. There he planned to study the coeducational system and the use of women teachers in mixed classes. It was an article of faith in England at the time that the sexes should be rigidly separated, as in the English Public Schools, which were exclusively for boys. Bryce's discovery that coeducation was highly successful in Chicago encouraged him to work for the education of women in Britain. Also, he was able to add a knowledge of legal practices in the Midwest to what he had learned in Boston. But his journey to the Midwest was not exclusively one of intellectual enquiry. He wanted to see the sights, and went up the Mississippi to Minneapolis to see the Falls of St. Anthony, a favorite attraction for nineteenth-century travelers in America. As he traveled, Bryce noted that the railroad cars were full of

The Trial of Queen Caroline in the House of Lords, by Sir George Hayter,
oil on canvas, 1823. National Portrait Gallery, London.

Splendid with "its fretted roof and windows rich with the figures of departed kings, its
majestic throne, its Lord Chancellor in his wig on the woolsack, its benches of lawnsleeved
bishops," the English House of Lords stood in dramatic contrast to the spare American Senate.
Therein, Bryce felt, lay the essential difference between a traditional society proud of its "air
of listless vacuity and superannuated indolence," and the energy and spontaneity of a new and
practical society.

Scandinavian immigrants going "up country" to the frontier regions of the
Northwest. Returning to Chicago, he met with Dicey once more, and together they compared impressions. They both agreed, as Bryce wrote, that
"Chicago is the handsomest city we have seen in America. You feel that
those who have built the city have felt it was becoming great, and have been
inspired by this spirit to do their best."

 This sense of optimism was a dominant impression in Bryce's mind.
Nevertheless he wanted to see all sides of America. He had already gleaned
that political life in the cities could show a much less attractive side. This
he saw for himself in Rochester, New York, on his journey back to the East.
The Democratic Party of New York State was assembling there to prepare
for the fall elections for state and local offices, including the New York Gov-
ernorship. The party was at that time dominated by Tammany Hall, the corrupt political machine based in New York City, which was already in-
famous for its plunder of the city treasuries. At Rochester, the forces of
reform, headed by the aging Samuel J. Tilden, were routed by the Tammany
forces, controlled by "Boss" William Marcy Tweed, who would soon be
exposed by the *New York Times* for graft, embezzlement, and outright
plunder on a mammoth scale. Bryce observed Tweed at the podium at the
Rochester convention, "a fat, largish man, with an air of self-satisfied good

humor and a great deal of shrewd knavery in eye and mouth." And, reflecting on the whole proceedings, Bryce noted: "The whole thing helps one to realise more vividly the working of their system. . . . Hardly anyone seems to think any principle is at stake in this context; it is simply [a struggle] for place and power."

When Bryce prepared to return to England with Dicey in November 1870, his impressions of America were mixed, yet on the whole favorable. Above all, he was impressed by the easy social relationships. The stiffness of Victorian society at home, the barriers between the social classes, and the sense of rigid hierarchies where people accepted their allotted "station in life" were distinctly absent in America. Bryce agreed with an observation Oliver Wendell Holmes, Sr., had made in Boston: "Holmes thought American manners much lighter and easier than English, of whose stiffness and awkwardness he remarked in a way we admitted to be just." So readily did Bryce take to American informality and self-confidence, that he wrote to his sister in Scotland: "Were it not for all of you at [home] I really think I would emigrate hither: there is a sort of freedom and spirit about the place and people which one doesn't get in England."

With such an impression, it could only be a matter of time before Bryce returned to America. His appointment as Professor of Jurisprudence at Oxford delayed his next trip to 1881, when he finally managed to put aside professional duties for another extended visit. By 1881, the network of railroads spanning America from east to west and north to south had advanced remarkably. Bryce traveled west through Kansas to Colorado and Utah, through Salt Lake City to San Francisco, up to Oregon, then south again to St. Louis, on through Kentucky and Tennessee to Georgia and so up to

The Tammany King-dom, by Thomas Nast, engraving, in Harper's Weekly, October, 1870. National Portrait Gallery, Smithsonian Institution.

New York's Tammany Society was organized originally as a social and charitable group, but by the middle of the nineteenth century, "Tammany Hall" had been transformed into the fulcrum of the Irish political "Ring" which ran the city's Democratic machine. William Marcy Tweed, born in New York in 1823, had become its leader by the time of Bryce's first American visit. "Boss" Tweed was described by Bryce as "a fat, largish man, with an air of self-satisfied good humor and a great deal of shrewd knavery in eye and mouth."

The main street of Hastings, Nebraska, by F. J. Bandholts, photograph, circa 1909.
Library of Congress.

In American life, Bryce found a serious drawback: its uniformity. Towns separated by vast
distances were barely distinguishable from one another. "Their monotony haunts one like a
nightmare."

Washington. With some marked exceptions, he found very little to differen-
tiate one American city from another.

> *In all the same wide streets, crossing at right angles, ill-paved, but planted
> along the sidewalks with maple trees whose autumnal scarlet surpasses the
> brilliance of any European foliage. In all the same shops, arranged on the
> same plan, the same Chinese laundries, with Li Kow visible through the win-
> dow, the same ice-cream stores, the same large hotels with seedy men hover-
> ing about in the cheerless entrance hall, the same street cars passing to and
> fro with passengers clinging to the door-step, the same locomotives ringing
> their great bells as they clank slowly down the middle of the street. . . . Their
> monotony haunts one like a nightmare.*

Unlike a number of other travelers, Bryce did not allow his distaste for
the charmlessness of American life to affect his view of its real value: its
vigor and its institutions. Contrasting the splendor of the House of Lords,
"its fretted roof and windows rich with the figures of departed kings, its
majestic throne, its Lord Chancellor in his wig on the woolsack, its benches
of lawn-sleeved bishops," with the "severe and practical" Senate chamber,
devoid of any historical charm, he concluded that there was, nevertheless,
an advantage to the American style: "The Senate seldom wears that air of
listless vacuity and superannuated indolence which the House of Lords
presents on all but a few nights of every session. The faces are keen and
forcible, as of men who have learned to know the world, and have much to
do in it; the place seems consecrated to great affairs."

An idea was beginning to form in Bryce's mind for a major work on
American democracy. He had already written articles on American life in
English journals, but he now planned a detailed treatise exploring every

aspect of the political and social framework of the American Republic. In the next few years, the form of the book evolved. Another trip to America in 1883 gave Bryce further opportunities to collect material and to talk with scholars and educators, lawyers, editors, and state and federal government officials. In 1888, the first edition of Bryce's *American Commonwealth* came off the presses. It was a prodigious work, the first (and now comparatively rare) edition running to three volumes; subsequent editions were compressed to two volumes. Reviewers on both sides of the Atlantic hailed a masterpiece (Woodrow Wilson, then a young professor at Wesleyan University, called it "a noble work"), and it quickly became a classic.

The two volumes ranged over every aspect of American society. Sections were devoted to the historical and constitutional background, together with the legal and social framework of institutions. "The State is not to them," Bryce wrote, "as to Germans or Frenchmen, and even to some English thinkers, an ideal moral power, charged with the duty of forming the characters and guiding the lives of its subjects. It is more like a commercial company, or perhaps a huge municipality created for the management of certain business in which all who reside within its bounds are interested." In such a society, it was not surprising that great power and prestige resided in the titans of industry:

> These railway kings are among the greatest men, perhaps I may say are the greatest men in America. . . . They have power, more power . . . than perhaps any one in political life, except the President and the Speaker, who after all hold theirs only for four years and two years, while the railroad monarch may keep his for life. When the master of one of the greatest Western lines travels towards the Pacific on his palace car, his journey is like a royal progress. Governors of States bow before him; legislatures receive him in solemn session; cities seek to propitiate him, for has he not the means for making or marring a city's fortunes? . . . They receive that tribute of admiration which the American gladly pays to whoever had done best what every one desires to do.

Bryce was struck by how little the government acted in concert to dominate and shape the commercial and social forces in the nation. This was, he felt, because its branches were "unconnected; their efforts are not directed to one aim." As a result,

> Parties are formed and dissolved, compromises are settled and assailed and violated, wars break out and are fought through and forgotten, new problems begin to show themselves, and the civil powers, Presidents, and Cabinets, and State governments, and Houses of Congress, seem to have as little to do with all these changes, as little ability to foresee or avert or resist them, as the farmer, who sees approaching the tornado which will uproot his crop, has power to stay its devastating course.

Bryce also commented on the spirit of the society as a whole. He marveled at the American love of bigness: "Beyond the Atlantic, the sense of immensity, the sense that the same thought and purpose are animating millions of other men in sympathy with himself, lifts a man out of himself, and sends him into transports of eagerness and zeal about things intrinsically small, but great through the volume of human feeling they have attracted." American society, Bryce observed elsewhere in his book, with its

Union Pacific Railroad officials meeting in a railroad car at Echo City, Utah,
by Andrew J. Russell, photograph, 1868. The Oakland Museum.

"These railway kings are among the greatest men, perhaps I may say are the greatest men in America," Bryce observed. "When the master of one of the Western lines travels towards the Pacific on his palace car, his journey is like a royal progress."

An imaginary encounter between Ambassador Bryce and the athletic President Roosevelt,
by John T. McCutcheon, drawing, date unknown. Edmund S. Ions.

Bryce's success as British Ambassador to the United States between 1907 and 1913 was enhanced by his great friendship with Theodore Roosevelt. Bryce, who was president of the British Alpine Club, would delight friends with his accounts of a jersey-clad Roosevelt jogging around Washington in a blizzard or climbing a two-hundred-foot cliff in Rock Creek Park.

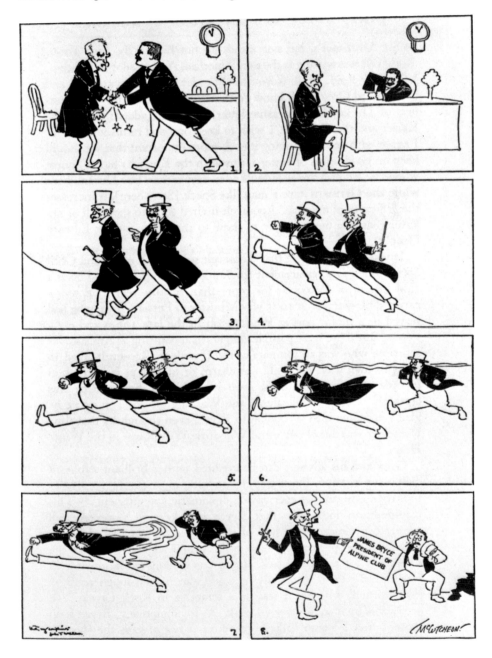

tendency "to seek truth only in the voice of the majority, to mistake prosperity for greatness," needed

> a succession of men like the prophets of Israel to rouse the people out of
> their self-complacency, to refresh their moral ideals, to remind them that
> the life is more than meat, and the body more than raiment, and that to whom
> much is given of them shall much also be required. If America has no prophets
> of this order, she fortunately possesses two classes of men who maintain
> a wholesome irritation. . . . These are the instructed critics who exert
> a growing influence on opinion through the higher newspapers, and by
> literature generally, and the philanthropic reformers who tell more directly
> upon the multitude.

Bryce criticized those aspects of American democracy which he thought were unseemly or which fell short of the aspirations of the Founding Fathers. His sharpest criticism was reserved for the political bosses and machine politicians who had taken control of so many city administrations in America. In a much-quoted passage, Bryce remarked: "There is no denying that the government of cities is the one conspicuous failure of the United States. . . . The faults of the State governments are insignificant compared with the extravagance, corruption, and mismanagement which mark the administrations of most of the great cities." Of course, Bryce was writing at the high tide of political corruption. He was to revise some of his opinions later, when the reform movements of the Progressive era brought fundamental changes to the pattern of machine domination. At the time he wrote, however, the observation was accurate, its truth underlined by a letter he received in 1889 from a former Police Commissioner in New York City: Theodore Roosevelt wrote to Bryce, "No one can help admiring the depth of your insight into our peculiar conditions."

Bryce continued to comment on American democracy and institutions for the rest of his life. He had by now left his Oxford chair and entered Liberal politics to serve in Gladstone's Cabinet. The life of politics never really suited him, however, and when, in 1906, he was offered the post of British Ambassador in Washington, he accepted. Together with his wife Marion, he made his home in America from 1907 to 1913. In an important period for relations between the United States, Britain, and Europe, Bryce was a highly successful, peripatetic ambassador, who gave an extraordinary number of lectures and addresses to audiences in all parts of the Union.

By now Bryce had earned the nickname *"Anima naturaliter Americana"* (a truly American spirit) among educators. He also proved to be a skilled diplomat, his mission greatly assisted by personal friendships with three successive Presidents in office, Theodore Roosevelt, William Howard Taft, and Woodrow Wilson. Bryce returned to England in 1913, and was created a Viscount in recognition of his services. When war came to Europe in 1914, Woodrow Wilson continued to seek the counsels of his old teacher and friend. His personal emissary, Colonel Edward House, visited Bryce in London in 1915 and 1916. Those counsels continued throughout Woodrow Wilson's struggle to establish the League of Nations. When the United States Senate voted against membership, Bryce prophesied that the League could not last. As one who had followed in the closest detail the emergence of the United States to a position of world power in the half-century from 1870 to 1920, he felt that twentieth-century America had to accept the responsibilities which came with power. The New World could not ignore the fortunes of the Old by retreating into isolationism; indeed, in the twentieth century, more than in any other, the wealth and power of the New World would be needed to redress the powers of the Old. In this, as in other respects, Bryce brought to his long commentary on the fortunes of the United States the broad vision of a statesman, and the candor of a trusted friend.

José Marti, by Herman Norrman, oil on canvas, circa 1891, in *Iconografiá del Apóstol Marti,* 1925. Library of Congress.

Marti's only life portrait was painted in New York by Norrman, a Swedish painter who lived there from 1887 to 1890. The Cuban poet and revolutionary is shown in his office where he wrote his reports on the United States for newspapers throughout Latin America.

22
José Martí
1853-1895

by José de Onís

*Human annals record nothing comparable to the marvelous pros-
perity of the United States. Do its roots go deep? Are the ties of common sacrifice and pain that hold other nations together more enduring
than those of common interest? Does that colossal nation contain
savage, uncontrollable forces? Does the absence of the feminine spirit,
the source of artistic sense and the complement of the national spirit,
harden and corrupt the heart of that astounding country? These are
questions which only time will answer. What is apparent today is that
there has never been a happier, more spirited, more comfortable, more
integrated, more jovial and light-hearted people engaged in such useful
pursuits in any land on earth, nor any that created and enjoyed greater
wealth, covering its oceans and rivers with a greater number of gaily
decorated steamers, or turning out with more bristling order and in-
genuous happiness on sandy beaches, gigantic boardwalks, and brilliant
fantastic midways.*

—*"Coney Island," La Pluma, Bogotá, December 3, 1881*

José de Onís is Professor of Modern Languages at the University of
Colorado at Boulder. As a Guggenheim fellow he traveled in Cuba during
1955 and 1956. He is the author of *The United States as seen by Spanish
American Writers.*

WHEN JOSÉ MARTÍ wrote these words back in 1881, he was still a newcomer to the United States, and the final stages in his struggle for the Independence of Cuba had not yet begun. He was all illusion, all faith, all optimism about the whole spirit of the age. He saw in this continent unlimited possibilities of success, of invention, of Democracy; he saw in it a new era for humanity. In all of his travels, this was the only country where he had felt a real surprise. At last he had found a nation where freedom was a reality. In New York, he was dazzled by the spectacle before him, and he wondered when similar scenes would be possible in his native Cuba and in the rest of Latin America. In the United States, a country he learned to love, he found refuge during the fifteen most critical years of his life. Yet, as one can sense in this early quotation, his attitude never did achieve the tone of unconditional admiration expressed by Domingo Faustino Sarmiento, his distinguished Latin American predecessor.

Upon his arrival in New York on January 1, 1880, he found a number of Venezuelan and Cuban families who had resolved most of the difficulties of immigration and had begun to play an important role in the cultural life of the city. Among the most distinguished of these families was that of Juan J. Peoli, whose home near Columbus Circle became a meeting place for the finest artists and writers of both Americas. José Martí became a close friend of the entire family. He was bound to them not only by cultural ties, but by values and ideologies as well; for the Peoli family tradition was imbued with the spirit of many generations of European, South American and Cuban revolutionaries. The relationship between Martí and Carmita Miyares, one of the cousins, was by no means a simple love affair; there existed between them artistic and political affinities, very deep and difficult to define.

In this home, where on the walls hung the portraits Peoli had painted of José Páez, the Venezuelan hero of the battle of Carabobo, and of General Sickles (who, as Martí said, "won the battle of Gettysburg with an overwhelming assault"), the nineteenth-century ideals of the Liberal Revolution still burned strongly. Martí had spent most of his life outside Cuba and was therefore unable to meet personally many of the Cuban heroes of the previous generation. Juan J. Peoli, on the other hand, had known them all; and through him, Martí became acquainted with their ideas. The Peoli home was the point of confluence between Venezuelans and Cubans. Among the most frequent guests were the colorful José Páez and his circle of admirers. It was often the meeting place for the Hispanic Literary Society of which Martí, for a time, was president.

One day Tomás Callazo, a friend of the Peolis, proposed that Martí write articles on art and culture for a weekly newspaper, *The Hour,* published in New York. It was in this publication that some of Martí's first impressions of the United States appeared. About this time he was also writing for several reviews in Latin America, where many of the same ideas were expressed more extensively in Spanish. Martí was, without doubt, the first Latin American who knew the United States in all its aspects. He disseminated this knowledge through the articles he contributed regularly to *La Nación* of Buenos Aires—which, in the edition of his complete works, occupy fourteen volumes entitled *Escenas norte Americanas* and three entitled *Norte Americanos.* Through these articles, Martí came to the attention

José Martí with the Peoli family, by an unidentified photographer, 1888. José de Onís.

Martí was a frequent companion of the Peolis, a distinguished Cuban family whose home in New York City was a meeting-place for artists and writers of both Americas. Here, he is pictured (second from the left) with the Peoli family on an outing at Sandy Hill, on the Hudson River.

of Charles A. Dana, editor of the New York *Sun,* who asked him to write art criticism for his newspaper. The two men became friends, and their mutual admiration lasted until Martí's death in 1895.

In his late years, Sarmiento read, in *La Nación,* the articles of the young Martí and sensed, before anyone else, the unique personality of the man. "There is nothing in Spanish to compare with Martí's bellows, and after Victor Hugo, France can offer nothing like his mental resonance," he wrote. Despite his admiration for Martí's qualities, Sarmiento profoundly disagreed with him about the United States:

> *I would wish that Martí give us less Martí, less of the Latin, less of the Spanish in race, and less of the South American, and a little more of the Yankee, the new type of modern man. . . . He should be our eye viewing the movement of mankind where it is swiftest, most intellectual, freest, best directed toward society's high purposes in order that he might communicate this to us, to correct our missteps and show us the right road.*

There was always present in Sarmiento the disposition (which had prevailed throughout the nineteenth century in the progressive and liberal spirits of Latin America) to regard the United States as the model, guide, and elder brother in the great family of American nations. To be sure, there had coexisted another attitude, of those who saw in the United States a future threat to their weaker, disorganized nations. Martí's attitude—which was to be that of the epoch which began with him—was new: it was neither the one nor the other, but rather both together. Martí summed up in a

The Unveiling of the Statue of Liberty Enlightening the World, by Edward Moran, oil on canvas, 1886. Katherine Hellman. Photograph from Frick Art Reference Library.

"Thou art like the poet's dream, as great as space, spanning heaven and earth." The unveiling of the Statue of Liberty was, for Martí, a moving event: "In her presence eyes once again know what tears are. She seemed alive, wrapped in clouds of smoke, crowned by a vague brightness, truly like an altar with steamers kneeling at her feet!"

phrase, written in 1889, this union of love and fear: "We love the land of Lincoln, but [referring to the leader of a group interested in the annexation of Northern Mexico] we fear the land of Cutting."

In 1884, he had already voiced, though with reservations, the fear that the United States might become an imperialist nation: "The nation which has been the home of liberty must not—God forbid—become the dragon on which conquest mounts, nor the new tomb of mankind, in the manner of those despotic corrupt nations which have degraded or dominated the world." Underlying this attitude of Martí was his conviction that a deep, radical difference existed between the two Americas:

> There are two nations in America, and only two, whose souls differ greatly by reason of their origins, antecedents and habits, and whose only resemblance is their fundamental human identity. On the one hand is our America . . . on the other the America which is not ours, whose enmity is neither prudent nor practical to encourage, and whose friendship, maintaining a firm decorum and wise independence, it is useful and not impossible to win.

His fear of the United States was to grow and be confirmed in later years, until he became convinced that its internal development would create a superabundance of strength and lead to a new phase of expansion beyond its frontiers into Latin America. His prophetic words were quickly followed by events which bore them out.

Martí's criticism of the intentions of the United States toward Latin America was at times so harsh that some editors suppressed entire passages. Bartolomé Mitre, the director of *La Nación* of Buenos Aires, himself an expert on the United States, explained to Martí that they did not want the readers to believe they were launching a deliberate campaign against the United States, a nation so meritorious and worthy of emulation in all aspects, "which you know and interpret so well." And in 1882, Fausto Teódoro de Aldrey, of *La Opinión Nacional* of Caracas, wrote to him: "Try in your articles not to criticize too severely the vices and customs of that nation, because it is not liked here and would injure my reputation."

Martí was always afraid that the Latin Americans would imitate the faults and not the virtues of North America. He advocated the development of a new culture, but he believed that it was not wise, or even possible, for Cuba to adopt wholesale the traditions of a completely foreign culture. He understood that the United States had to be imitated in principle, but he also knew that the great North American republic had realized its effective and original form of government by adhering to conditions peculiar to its own primarily Anglo-Saxon culture. Latin America must also develop along original lines. Concerning the annexation of Cuba to the United States, a widely discussed topic in those days in both Cuban and American circles, Martí wrote, in 1886, that only someone who was ignorant of the differences between the two Americas, "or one who loved the United States more than he loved Cuba," could honestly consider this.

His reporting of the American scene reached its highest poetic expression in articles such as "Dedication of the Statue of Liberty," "Oklahoma Land Rush," "The Charleston Earthquake," "Coney Island," and "General Páez' Funeral." These represented moments when enthusiasm and wonder overwhelmed his ambivalence about this country. On October 29, 1886, in an essay later published in *La Nación* of Buenos Aires, he wrote about the

James Gillespie Blaine, by George P. A. Healy, oil on canvas, 1884. Newberry Library.

Of the "master politician" Blaine, America's Secretary of State, Martí wrote: "Such astounding capacity for survival, such ardent, indomitable faith in himself and in his fortune, win him the admiration and control of the great mass of a country made up of men who see in life itself a challenge for conquest."

dedication of the Statue of Liberty. People came to it, as if to an altar, to contemplate their own "goddess guarding the gates of America, greater than all those the ancients worshipped."

> *Liberty, it is thine hour of arrival! . . . Flags are reflected on faces, heartstrings are plucked by a sweet love, a superior sense of sovereignty brings to countenances a look of peace, nay of beauty. And all these luckless Irishmen, Poles, Italians, Bohemians, Germans redeemed from oppression or misery, hail the monument to Liberty because they feel that through it they themselves are uplifted and restored. . . . In her presence eyes once again know what tears are. She seemed alive, wrapped in clouds of smoke, crowned by a vague brightness, truly like an altar with steamers kneeling at her feet!*

Like Sarmiento, Martí considered the open door policy toward immigration an excellent practice, "the secret of the prosperity of the United States," but he sensed that the immigrants had a tendency to embrace the national defects rather than the virtues. "Those elements which are responsible for the annihilation of the Indian, the maintenance of slavery, and the attack and plunder of neighboring countries, instead of becoming absorbed, were intensified by the continuous introduction of European immigrants." And since the immigrants represented innumerable votes, they adversely influenced American politics. When a series of strikes besieged the United States, Martí blamed their excesses on the immigrants. "It would be more prudent if [Americans] did not allow the most unfortunate and irate elements of Europe to pour their dregs of hate into their midst." After the Chicago incident, in November 1887, when the police fired into a crowd of strikers, killing six of them, his attitude changed strongly to sympathy for the workers. All forms of coercion that might in any way curtail man's freedom, whether exercised by an individual or by the masses, were abhorrent to him.

Many of Martí's essays were devoted to the arts and literature. He was particularly partial to those authors who had a social consciousness. To him, style was merely a vehicle; the important thing was ideas. He was drawn to Ralph Waldo Emerson, because he felt that this New England writer was interested in the creation of an American literature that was an expression of the New World, not only of the United States but also of Latin America. In America, there was being forged a new national religion, stripped of ceremony and form, and based on human reason; the pantheistic poetry of William Jennings Bryant, and the natural philosophy of Emerson, were a monument to Christian faith being raised in the name of freedom.

Political figures and events make up a large part of Martí's communications to Latin America. On the eve of Grover Cleveland's election in 1884, Martí had seen this liberal Democrat "on the road to becoming the leader of the freest, greatest people on earth." But after Benjamin Harrison's victory of 1888, the entire scene changed. "Behind him, casting the yellow glaze of his wary eye on his silenced adversaries was Blaine," the master politician. Martí both feared and admired Secretary of State James G. Blaine. "There is a Latin sparkle in the acts and feelings of this eloquent North American." He possessed a frightening vitality: "even when lying, his lips never lose their eloquence." His ruthless tactics were admired by the great masses who "saw in life itself a challenge for conquest." In an article published in *La Nación* on November 7, 1886, Martí states:

> *His exceptional aggressiveness dazzles and wins even his enemies in this aggressive, fighting country. . . . Blaine's very defects: the gravest proven accusations, his stubborn determination to place himself by every means over and above whomever stands in his way, his apparent lack of scruples or shame in committing and hiding public faults are as mirrors in which masses of people see themselves reflected and pardoned, for they see in the public sinner who triumphs the sanction of the country's boundless love of success.*

Coney Island Beach at Sea Beach Walk (West 10th Street) as seen from the old iron pier, by an unidentified photographer, 1885. Francis K. Moore Collection of Coney Island.

As "an immense valve of pleasure," Coney Island suggested, to Martí, "the majesty of the country that supports it." Still he viewed the charm and dazzle with "a melancholy sadness," masking, as it did, America's spiritual emptiness.

The Opening of the Cherokee Outlet, September 16, 1893, by an unidentified photographer.
Oklahoma Historical Society.

In his account of the first Oklahoma Land Rush, Martí was at his most exuberant: "Miles of
wagons; a welter of horsemen; random shots fired in the air; songs and sermons; taverns and
sporting houses; a coffin, followed by a woman and child; from the four corners of that land
besieged by settlers one cry goes up 'Oklahoma! Oklahoma!' "

Because of his interest in Latin America, Blaine figures prominently in
Martí's writings. At first, during President Garfield's administration, the
Cuban was very favorably impressed with Blaine. Here was a friend, a man
who hoped to increase commercial relations by reciprocal tariff treaties. But
only three months later, in December 1881, Blaine's policy toward Latin
America frightened Martí. He saw him as the brilliant leader of those Republicans who, conscious of the power of their country and wanting to
turn it to their advantage, tried to divert the nation from the peaceful program of the Democrats and initiate a turbulent international policy of expansion and aggression.

Later, as Secretary of State for President Harrison, Blaine presided
over the First Pan American Congress, and it was during this conference
that Martí's distrust of Blaine's program became strengthened and clarified.
Martí judged the United States to be, in this period, "a nation that is beginning to regard liberty as its sole privilege and invoke it to deprive other
nations of theirs." And, in 1892, he stated: "Beyond doubt the hour has
come for this country, egged on by protectionism, to bring into the open its
latent spirit of aggression." The motive that led him to fight and die for the
independence of Cuba was that of "preventing in time the United States
from extending its power over the Antilles, and falling, with this added
strength, upon our lands of America."

Martí died in 1895 on the battlefield, fighting at the outbreak of the Cuban Revolution. He did not live to see the war of the United States with Spain in 1898, the first of the series of its armed interventions in Latin America. From 1898 on, Latin American writers, almost without exception, have taken Martí's prophetic words to heart and have expanded upon them to interpret the events in their own time, using phrases which have since become stereotypes, such as *"el peligro yanki"* (the Yankee threat) and *"el imperialismo del dólar."*

José Martí was the initiator and creator of the Modernist epoch in Hispanic culture, which would come to represent the line of demarcation between the nineteenth and twentieth centuries. He had become the channel through which much of the contemporary idealism of the late nineteenth century found its way into modern Latin America; and his death, as Rubén Darío stated in *Los Raros*, was a loss not only for the Cubans, but for the entire American continent. Charles Dana wrote in an obituary, published in the New York *Sun* on May 23, 1895:

> *Of such heroes there are not too many in the world, and his warlike grave testifies that, even in a positive and material age, there are spirits that can give all for their principles without thinking of any selfish return for themselves.*
>
> *Honor to the memory of José Martí, and peace to his manly and generous soul.*

"Well, I hardly know which to take first!" by "Boz" (pseudonym for Morgan J. Sweeney), in *Boston Globe*, May 28, 1898. Library of Congress.

Martí's sentiments toward America became a mixture of love and fear. He realized that once the United States had achieved internal integration, its superabundance of strength would inevitably lead to expansion beyond the limits of its own frontiers. "The nation which has been the home of liberty," he wrote in 1884, "must not . . . God forbid . . . become the dragon on which conquest mounts."

Antonín Dvořák, by Max Švabinský, drawing, date unknown.
Muzeum Antonína Dvořáka.

Through his composing, conducting, and teaching during a three-year stay in the United
States, Antonín Dvořák brought to Americans a new sense of the possibilities in their folk
music.

23
Antonín Dvořák
1841-1904

by Ludmila Bradová

The Americans expect great things of me and the main thing is, so they say, to show them to the promised land and kingdom of a new and independent art, in short, to create a national music. If the small Czech nation can have such musicians, they say, why could not they, too, when their country and people is so immense. . . . It is certainly both a great and splendid task for me and I hope that with God's help I shall accomplish it.

—Letter written from Boston, November 1892

LUDMILA BRADOVÁ, the Director of the Museum Antonína Dvořáka, studied organ and piano in the Prague Conservatory and received her doctorate in 1957. She takes part in the ''Prague Spring'' international music festivals and is, at present, making a study of Dvořák's correspondence.

IN THE FALL OF 1892, Antonín Dvořák, the great Czech composer, arrived from Prague to take up his duties as Director of the National Conservatory of Music in New York. Dvořák was welcomed enthusiastically to America amid great hopes that he would have a profound effect on the development of an original national music. As an acknowledged Master, he was expected to give shape to a symphonic tradition which could express the landscape, the folklore, the ideals of a new world, and to awaken a generation of American composers to the possibilities of their heritage.

The idea of living in America, of investing his creative forces in a young and newly developing country, was suggested to Dvořák by the American composer Dudley Buck when they met in London in 1886. Only after six years of struggling for original and vigorous expression and for material security under the Austro-Hungarian monarchy, which had no inclination to support Czech artists, did Dvořák finally realize his ambition. The Master was invited to New York by Mrs. Jeanette M. Thurber, founder and President of the National Conservatory of Music, in a telegram which she sent from Paris in June 1891. During the following year, he negotiated his contract with the Conservatory. He spent the summer before his departure with his family at their summer retreat in Vysoká, where he wrote the *Te Deum* and *American Flag* cantatas, the latter set to a poem by the American poet Joseph Rodman Drake, which Mrs. Thurber had sent. These were going to be performed in the fall for the fourth centennial of Columbus's discovery of America. In the middle of September 1892, Dvořák left Czechoslovakia, accompanied by his wife, two of their children, and his friend Josef Jan Kovařík (an American of Czech origin who was to live with the Dvořáks during their stay).

Dvořák liked America, and liked his situation there. "And why shouldn't we," he wrote back to a friend in Prague, "when it is all so lovely and free here and one can live so much more peacefully—and that is what I need." He was satisfied with his family's domestic arrangements: "We live in 17th street East, 327 (only 4 mins. from the school) and are very satisfied with the flat. Mr. Steinway sent me a piano immediately—a lovely one and, of course, free of charge, so that we have one nice piece of furniture in our sitting-room." About musical conditions in the new country, he wrote enthusiastically:

> *Just imagine how the Americans work in the interests of art and for the people!* . . . *The concert on December 1st will be for only the* wealthy and the intelligentzia, *but the preceding day my work will also be performed for poor workers who earn 18 dollars a week, the purpose being to give the poor and uneducated people the opportunity to hear musical works of all times and all nations!! That's something, isn't it?*

American composers, he found, were "all much the same as at home—brought up in the German School, but here and there another spirit, other thoughts, another colouring flashes forth, in short, something Indian (something à la Bret Harte). I am very curious how things will develop."

The Master spent his life in New York "very quietly," according to his companion and chronicler Kovařík. His teaching schedule at the Conservatory was not very demanding. He had only eight pupils, some "from as far away as San Francisco. They are mostly poor people, but at our Institute teaching is free of charge, anybody who is really talented—pays no fees!"

The Dvořák family, by an unidentified photographer,
in *Antonín Dvořák the Composer's Life and Work in Pictures,* 1955.

Invited to be the Director of the National Conservatory of Music, Dvořák (standing at the right) arrived in New York with his family and his friend Josef Jan Kovařík in the fall of 1892. America pleased him: "It is all so lovely and free here," he wrote home, "and one can live so much more peacefully—and that is what I need."

Harry Thacker Burleigh, by Laura Wheeler Waring, oil on canvas, date unknown. National Portrait Gallery, Smithsonian Institution.

One of Dvořák's outstanding American pupils, Harry T. Burleigh, helped select spirituals for the *Symphony "From the New World."* Dvořák believed that American music had to be founded on the "beautiful and varied themes" of Negro melodies.

Spillville, Iowa, Church and School, by an unidentified photographer,
in *Antonín Dvořák: Letters and Reminiscences,* 1954.

"How grand it will be," Dvořák wrote about his plans to spend the summer of 1893 in Spill-
ville, Iowa, a Czech settlement. It would, he hoped, be like Vysoká, his retreat in Bohemia:
"The priest has two pairs of ponies and we shall ride to Protvín, a little town near Spillville.
Here in America there are *names of towns and villages of all nations under the sun!!*"

He was also required to judge music submitted for competitions. Dvořák
seldom went out "into society," although he did attend some concerts;
otherwise he would spend his evenings playing "darda," a card game he
was fond of, at home.

At the beginning of January 1893, Dvořák began to envision a work of
far greater extent than the two earlier cantatas, but he concealed his project
from others for a long time. On February 9, he wrote, on the title page,
"Symphony No. 8 in E minor": this, his first composition originating on
American soil, was to become the famous *Symphony "From the New World"*
("*Z nového světa*"). The title, according to Kovařík, caused some confusion:

> *There were and are many people who thought and think that the title is to be
> understood as meaning the "American" symphony, i.e. a symphony with
> American music. Quite a wrong idea! This title means nothing more than
> "Impressions and Greetings from the New World"—as the Master himself
> more than once explained.*

It is an important distinction, for although the musical content shows American influences, the style is Czech. Dvořák's memory of Bohemia was an
important source of emotional and ideological inspiration. His impressions
of New York provided much of the raw material for his work. There are
other sources too: the second movement, originally entitled "Legend," was
inspired by the burial scene in *Hiawatha*; and another scene in Longfellow's

poem, of Indian festivity and dancing in the woods, prompted the final movement. Dvořák reacted strongly to a critic's suggestion that he had borrowed Indian and Negro motifs: "It is a lie, I only sought to write in the spirit of these American folk-melodies." Although not the first to draw upon this musical material, his manner of processing it, of fusing it anew, made *"From the New World"* an explosive force in the development of America's symphonic tradition.

Always governed by a strong sense of his mission, "to discover what young Americans had in them and to help them express it," Dvořák became convinced that Negro melodies should be "the real foundation of any serious and original school of composition to be developed in the United States." He expressed his opinion in the *New York Herald* on May 21, 1893, just at the time that *"From the New World"* was being completed. Dvořák felt that the "beautiful and varied themes" of Negro melodies "are the product of the soil. They are American." And, furthermore, "they are pathetic, tender, passionate, melancholy, solemn, religious, bold, merry, gay or what you will." Here indeed was "music that suits itself to any mood or any purpose." Throughout his stay in America, the Master strove, in his own compositions and many other ways, to show American composers the infinite possibilities of their folk music. Among the important composers, both black and white, to be influenced by Dvořák were his pupils, Harry T. Burleigh (arranger of Negro spirituals), and William Arms Fisher (editor of folk song collections), and the later composers William Grant Still (*Afro-*

Antonin Dvořák conducting at the Chicago World's Fair, by E. V. Nadherný, medium unknown, 1893. Muzeum Antonína Dvořáka.

Dvořák's style of conducting was tightly controlled rather than histrionic. When he directed his own works on "Czech Day" at the Chicago World's Fair, reviewers described him as "not perhaps in any way charming, but his every movement has significance."

American Symphony), John Powell (*Rhapsodie nègre*), Louis Gruenberg (*Emperor Jones*), David Guion (*Arkansas Traveler*), Robert Nathaniel Dett (*Chariot Jubilee*), and Thurlow Lieurance (*Medicine Dance*).

In early June, Dvořák, with his wife and six children (the four who had been left behind in Prague came to America in May), set out for their summer vacation in Spillville, a Czech settlement. The Master looked forward to it as "*our summer Vysoká in the State of Iowa.*" On their arrival, which Kovařík described, "everything was in readiness—except a piano." For the Master, Spillville was a return to the bucolic: "After eight months I heard again the singing of birds! And here the birds are different from ours, they have much brighter colours and they sing differently, too." Here, the Master's typical day, described by Kovařík, was most unlike a day in New York.

> He got up about four o'clock and went for a walk—to the stream or the river —and returned at five. After his walk he worked, at seven he was sitting at the organ in church, then he chatted a little, went home, worked again . . . and then went for a walk. . . . Almost every afternoon he spent in the company of some of the older settlers. He got them to tell him about their bitter and difficult beginnings in America.

In a letter, Dvořák gave his impression of the Iowa countryside:

> It is very strange here. Few people and a great deal of empty space. A farmer's nearest neighbour is often 4 miles off, especially in the prairies (I call them the Sahara) there are only endless acres of field and meadow and that is all you see. You don't meet a soul (here they only ride on horseback) and you are glad to see in the woods and meadows the huge herds of cattle which, summer and winter, are out at pasture in the broad fields. Men go to the woods and meadows where the cows graze to milk them. And so it is very "wild" here and sometimes very sad—sad to despair.

Dvořák's particular sense of this countryside can be seen in both the compositions he produced there, the *"American" String Quartet in F major op. 96,* and the *String Quintet in E flat major for two violas op. 97.* Writing to a friend, he declared, "I should never have written these works 'just so' if I hadn't seen America." In the *"American" Quartet,* the Master seems to be striving for an economical and concise, although in no way impoverished, means of expression: a possible American influence, and a new departure for Dvořák. The musical content, emotionally simple, and the moods in the last two movements, first light and playful and then idylically calm, are surely the effect of his pastoral surroundings. Dvořák's other composition, the *String Quintet for two violas,* is another kind of response to Spillville. It has a less intimate quality; serenity is the prevailing mood, interrupted occasionally by tones of melancholy contemplation. Reflecting the composer's impressions of his wanderings in the woods and prairies, it has, in its melodies, echoes of folk songs and spirituals; and, in its characteristic drum rhythms, echoes of the song-and-dance productions of nomadic Indians which he witnessed. Writing to a friend, the Master said, "I can, without hesitation, count these . . . works as my best and most original."

Dvořák returned to New York by way of Chicago, in order to participate in the Chicago World Exhibition; and on "Czech Day," celebrated there on August 12, he conducted some of his own works. He had an impressive influence as a conductor during his stay in America. He had made his debut in Carnegie Hall on October 21, 1892, performing his three overtures—*In Nature, Carnival,* and *Othello*—as well as the *Te Deum* Cantata. After that, he was always in great demand, conducting mainly his own compositions. The *Chicago Tribune* described him, in this role, as "not perhaps in any way charming, but his every movement has significance." He conducted modestly, according to his observers, with those involuntary movements of the body that showed he was re-living, in the performance, the process of composition; and his inner concentration manifested itself in a rigidly upright stance, a sharply etched expression, and a clear and penetrating gaze.

Dvořák's second year in America, when, as Kovařík writes, "he had his whole family round him, was, I am firmly convinced, the happiest year of his life." The Master composed a number of minor pieces during the autumn, the most significant of which was the *Sonatina in G major for violin and piano op. 100.* To commemorate having reached this stage in his work, he wrote the sonatina for two of his children, Toník and Otilka, taking their performing abilities into account. In a letter, he said, "It is intended for the young dedicated to my two children, but let grown-ups also amuse themselves with it as they will." The themes are light-hearted, although there are some introspective passages; this alternating between moods is typical of Dvořák's American compositions. The introductory melody in the second movement has a quality of boiling emotions; and it is said to have been written by the Master as he watched the churning, dynamic movement of the Minnehaha Waterfall in Minnesota, which he had visited on his way back from Spillville. Indeed, this melody became so popular in its own right that Dvořák's publisher had it printed by itself—without the composer's knowledge—and sold it under titles such as "Indian Canzonetta," "Indian Lament," and "Indian Lullaby."

Dvořák was also occupied, during the fall, with strenuous preparations for the first performance of his *Symphony "From the New World."* On December 15, 1893, it had its world première at the concert of the Philharmonic Society in Carnegie Hall. It was conducted by the German conductor Anton Seidl. The Master did not attend the first performance on a Friday afternoon but went, with his family, on Saturday evening. The *New York Herald* gave an account of Dvořák's triumph:

> *After the second movement he was given an enthusiastic ovation. Storms of applause resounded from all sides. Everyone present turned to look in the direction in which the conductor, Anton Seidl, was looking. . . . At last a sturdily built man of medium height, straight as a fir-tree from the forest, whose music he so splendidly interprets, was discovered by the audience. From all over the hall there are cries of: "Dvořák! Dvořák!"*

There is perhaps no orchestra in the world which has not played this symphony, and no conductor who has not conducted it.

A chance incident at about this time brought Dvořák into contact with that most famous composer of Negro songs and spirituals, Stephen Foster. The Master happened, one day, to overhear the local church choir in the street serenading the pastor with songs by Foster, whose talents were at the time unrecognized. Dvořák was immediately struck by this music, and he arranged "Swanee River" as a small cantata, which was performed, and well received, at a National Conservatory concert in the Madison Square Garden Hall in January 1894.

Title page of original manuscript of the *Symphony "From the New World."*
Heirs of Antonín Dvořák.

Dvořák wrote the *Piano Suite in A major op. 98* in February. It was the last composition to exhibit his characteristic American style: light, coordinated, and practical. But his sister-in-law observed, during this period, that "in spite of his splendid position and material prosperity," he was "terribly homesick for his country. . . . On my departure from New York, when they all accompanied me on board, Dvořák broke into tears and said: 'If I could, I should go with you and it were only between-decks!' " His letters began to have enthusiastic accounts of his musical triumphs in America, strangely side by side with poignant signs of yearning for home. In March, Dvořák produced *Biblical Songs op. 99.* It is a somber work, undoubtedly influenced by unhappy news from his homeland of the serious illness of his father (he died two days after the conclusion of the *Songs*, on March 28), and the deaths of the composers Tchaikovsky, Gounod, and later von Bülow. Dvořák wrote the ten songs in rapid succession. The text was taken from David's Psalms in the Czech version of the Royal Bible, and the verses were selected to create a poetical cycle which would complement the musical one. The profound emotional content of this music is expressed with absolute simplicity, and the work is a supreme expression both of the composer's vocal creativity and of his religious feeling.

In the next month, Dvořák and his family sailed back to Europe to spend the summer in Vysoká. During the summer, he completed a cycle of piano compositions, *Humoresques op. 101*, which he had outlined the summer before in Spillville. The temperament of this work embraces both light and the shadows of grief and pain; it alternates quickly between gay and melancholy ideas. As a gift of thanksgiving for his family's safe return to Bohemia, Dvořák donated a new organ to a church near Vysoká, and played it at its dedication on September 8th. He returned to the United States in October, bringing his wife and only the youngest of their six children; the other five remained in Prague. This was to be Dvořák's last year in America, and it was not as happy as the previous one: "We were used to the children and now we haven't them and are sad at having to be without them. . . . And when a letter does come from the children, you can imagine with what impatience we seize it and read it." At the beginning of November 1894, more and more overcome with longing for his native Bohemia, Dvořák began to outline his famous *Concerto for Violoncello and Orchestra in B minor op. 104*. Next to the *Symphony "From the New World,"* this is his most famous work. The style is romantic in the extreme, and the mood of rich lyricism is conveyed perfectly in the choice of the violoncello as the solo instrument. One may say that in this composition Dvořák has made a break with America, for the piece is devoid of those American elements found in earlier works; and instead one has a strong impression of introversion and longing for Czechoslovakia. Before leaving America for good, Dvořák began work on the *String Quartet in A flat major op. 105*; but he only wrote part of the first movement in New York, and finished the rest in Czechoslovakia.

Whatever the expectations of his hosts, Dvořák never did become an American, either as an individual or as an artist. His fully original and basically Slavic personality and style of musical expression remained essentially unchanged throughout his three-year stay in New York. Nevertheless, his effect on American music was to be profound. Responding to the stimuli around him, he integrated American elements, particularly folk music, into his own work and, in doing so, opened a path for the development of American composition. When he returned to Czechoslovakia, he intended, in his own words, "to go on working for the good and development of our national art . . . [I] shall, with God's help, fulfil what I have dedicated my life to and what I have dreamt of." A profoundly patriotic Czech, Dvořák had sought to instill in American composers a sense of their own patriotism.

SWAMI VIVEKANANDA
·The Hindoo Monk of India·

Swami Vivekananda, by Goes Lithographic Co., Chicago, lithographic poster, 1893.
Vedanta Society of Northern California and Vedanta Society, Berkeley.

Traveling in the early 1890s through the "Yankee land," as he called it, Swami Vivekananda
passed a mystic's judgment on a materialist society and captured the imagination of his
American audience.

24
Swami Vivekananda
1863-1902

by C. B. Tripathi

Asia laid the germs of civilization, Europe developed man, and America is developing women and the masses. . . . The Americans are fast becoming liberal . . . and this great nation is progressing fast towards that spirituality which was the standard boast of the Hindus.

—Letter written from Chicago, November 1893

C. B. TRIPATHI, Professor of History at the University of Allahabad in India, is currently in the United States on a Senior Fulbright Hays Award. He was a founder of the Indian Congress of American History and has served as its President. He is now working on a study of *India and the United States: Early Contacts (1784–1833 A.D.)*.

AMONG the international delegates to the Parliament of Religions which convened at the Chicago World's Fair in 1893 was a Hindu monk, Swami Vivekananda, from India. At this exposition, the Swami charmed audiences with his magical oratory, and left an indelible mark on America's spiritual development. He remained in the United States for about three years, moving from one part of the country to the other with his message of universal love, and won a number of disciples. Completely engrossed in his mission, he never cared to write any consistent account of his experiences; but he did write a number of letters to his friends and disciples in India, in which he freely expressed his views on American society.

This saint-philosopher was born Narendranatha Dutta, in 1863, to an aristocratic family. His father, an attorney at Calcutta High Court, directed him to study both Oriental and Western cultures. A voracious reader with a prodigious memory, Narendra (as the young man was called) excelled in his studies at Presidency College, and at the General Assembly's Institution which had been founded by the Scottish General Missionary Board. Calcutta was then passing through strong tides of social change, reflecting the impact of Western ideas. Narendra could not ignore the problems created by British rule, which disturbed many thoughtful Indians, and he accepted membership in Brahmo-samaj—a society which was then the spearhead of the social reform movement in Bengal. During this period of questioning, he developed an intense desire to reconcile faith and intellect. Coming into contact with Sri Ramakrishna, a renowned saint, he gradually became, under this famous teacher's hypnotic influence, a favorite disciple. At the age of twenty-one, when Narendra passed his B.A. examination, his father suddenly died, leaving the family in deep debt. Frustrations in material ventures and a heightening spiritual consciousness ultimately turned Narendra's mind away from this mundane life. After the death of his master Ramakrishna in 1886, he renounced the world, assumed the saintly name of Swami Vivekananda, and organized his brother disciples into a new institution, called the Ramakrishna Mission. From 1888 to 1892, he wandered throughout India among the poor, and became convinced that he should devote his life to educating the multitude.

At about this time, in late 1892, Swami Vivekananda heard about the Parliament of Religions to be held in Chicago. His followers urged him to attend it as a representative of Hinduism. The Swami agreed that he should go, having long felt a need to see America, and he hoped also to obtain financial help there for his mission. He set sail by way of China and Japan, and reached Chicago in July 1893, two months before the Parliament was scheduled to open. Coming from a warmer climate, with the meager provisions of a monk, he soon found that the £187 he had brought with him was insufficient to pay for all the clothing, travel, and board and lodging that he needed. As he wrote to a friend in India:

> You cannot hire a cab for less than three rupees [one dollar], nor get a cigar for less than four annas [eight cents]. . . . The Americans are so rich that they spend money like water, and by forced legislation keep up the price of every thing so high that no other nation on earth can approach it. . . . Not even in Europe is there a country like this in luxury.

Hoping to minimize his expenses, he left Chicago for Boston, where, he had heard, the prices were lower. On the train he met an elderly lady,

Vivekananda as a delegate to the Parliament of Religions, by an unidentified photographer, in *Swami Vivekananda in America,* 1958.

On the opening day of the Parliament of Religions at the Chicago World's Fair, the Swami electrified his audience. "When that young man got up and said, 'Sisters and Brothers of America,'" a disciple later recalled, "seven thousand people rose to their feet as a tribute to something they knew not what; and when it was over and I saw the scores of women walking over the benches to get near him, I said to myself, 'Well, my lad, if you can resist that onslaught, you are indeed a god.'"

Miss Katherine Abbott Sanborn, who invited him to live at her farm, "Breezy Meadows," in Metcalf, Massachusetts. Miss Sanborn, a lecturer and author, was a gregarious person by nature, and provided the Swami with many introductions. Through her, he met Professor John Henry Wright of Harvard, who, profoundly impressed, made the necessary arrangements for him to attend the Parliament of Religions. During the few weeks that the Swami spent in and around Massachusetts, he delivered lectures on social and cultural life in India and attracted good audiences in Boston, Annisquam, Salem, Lynn, and Saratoga Springs. Then he went on to the Chicago World's Fair to attend the Parliament. Seated among the representatives of religions from around the world, Swami Vivekananda, dressed in saffron and orange robes and a turban, immediately commanded attention. He made, on the opening day, an electrifying speech, ending with these words:

*Sectarianism, bigotry and its horrible descendant, fanaticism . . . have filled
the earth with violence, drenched it often and often with human blood, destroyed civilisation and sent whole nations to despair. . . . I fervently hope
that the bell that tolled this morning in honour of this convention may be the
death knell of all fanaticism, of all persecutions with the sword or with the
pen and of all uncharitable feelings between persons.*

Invitations to lecture started pouring in from around the country.
Wherever he went, Swami Vivekananda was asked to live with American
families, and he was impressed by their open-hearted manner: "An American meets you for five minutes on board a train and you are his friend, and
the next moment he invites you as a guest to his home, and opens the secret
of his whole living there." American homes, in the Swami's opinion, were
in no way inferior to those anywhere else in the world:

*I have heard many stories about the American home: of liberty running into
licence, of unwomanly women smashing under their feet all the peace and
happiness of home-life in their mad liberty-dance, and much nonsense of that
type. . . . American women! A hundred lives would not be sufficient to pay
my deep gratitude to you! . . . "The Oriental hyperbole" alone expresses
the depth of Oriental gratitude—if the Indian Ocean were an inkstand, the
highest mountain of the Himalaya the pen, the earth the scroll and time itself the writer, still it would not express my gratitude to you.*

To Swami Vivekananda, the American woman was the central pillar,
not only of the home, but of the society as a whole: "It is the women who
are the life and soul of this country. All learning and culture are centered
in them." Coming from Bengal, where the Goddess Durga, the Divine
Mother, has been worshiped through the ages as the manifestation of the

Durga Mahishasuramardini, Mysore, India,
grey-black pot stone, 12th century A.D.
Los Angeles County Museum of Art.

Swami Vivekananda saw in America's
intellectual women the force of the Goddess
Durga, worshipped in Bengal as the Divine
Mother whose power rules the world. "If I
can raise a thousand such Madonnas—
incarnations of the Divine Mother—in
our country before I die, I shall die in
peace."

"If you want to be a yogi," in the New York *Herald,* March 27, 1898.

So lasting was the impression that the fashionable community had taken up Swami Vive-kananda and his yoga lessons that an Iowa newspaper referred to him, years later, as "the Hindoo monk and philosopher who preached himself into New York's exclusive Society." A satire on this lionizing of the Swami, the "Farce-Comedy Success" *My Friend from India,* played throughout America in 1896.

power and energy which controls and directs the world, the Swami believed that American women represented that same force in their society:

> They are Lakshmi, the Goddess of Fortune, in beauty, and Sarasvati, the
> Goddess of Learning, in virtues—they are the Divine Mother incarnate. If
> I can raise a thousand such Madonnas—incarnations of the Divine Mother
> —in our country before I die, I shall die in peace.

The Swami, however, could not accept America's own sense of its women, and found some social customs unpardonable. He told a women's group: "When I . . . see what you call gallantry, my soul is filled with disgust." Women were treated as nothing more than sexual playthings:

> Your men . . . say, "Oh madam, how beautiful are your eyes!" What right
> have they to do this? How dare a man venture so far? And how can you per-
> mit it? Such things develop the less noble side of humanity.

As a result, Vivekananda argued, American women paid undue attention to their physical beauty: "To them, ministering to their body is a great thing. . . . A thousand instruments for paring nails, ten thousand for hair-cutting, and who can count the varieties of dress and toilet and perfumery? . . . Their enjoyment is their God." Himself a monk, and coming from a society in which a very high standard of purity and chastity was demanded from unmarried girls, he lamented moral laxity. "I should very much like our women to have your intellectuality," he said, addressing a gathering of ladies in New York, "but not if it must be at the cost of purity. I admire

The Vivekananda Cottage, by an unidentified photographer, date unknown.
Ramakrishna-Vivekananda Center.

In the summer of 1895, the Swami established a permanent base for his work in America in a
house on Thousand Island Park, an island in the St. Lawrence River. There, twelve students
sat at the feet of their guru, and he initiated two of them into the final vows of monasticism.
The island is still a center of Vedanta teachings.

you for all that you know, but I dislike the way that you cover what is bad
with roses and call it good. Intellectuality is not the highest good. Morality
and spirituality are the things for which we strive.''

Between American and Indian marriage customs the Swami saw enormous differences. For instance, in India, most of the family relationships
were through sons, because the daughter, after being married, would go to
live with her husband's family. But in America,

> *the relationship is through girls. The son marries and no longer belongs to
> the family, but the daughter's husband pays frequent visits to his father-in-
> law's house. They say:*
>> *Son is son till he gets a wife*
>> *Daughter is daughter all her life.*

In the Swami's own society, a girl's marriage was settled, in her early childhood, by her father; but an American girl would select her own husband. He
had to be a man after her own heart and, furthermore, he had to be a
moneyed man or one of great social prominence. One husband-hunting
scenario was, to the Swami, particularly astonishing:

Here near my lodgings is the Waldorf Hotel, the rendezvous of lots of titled
but penniless Europeans on show for "yankee" heiress to buy. You may have
any selection here, the stock is so full and varied. There is the man who talks
no English; there are others who lisp a few words which no one can under-
stand; and others are there who talk nice English, but their chance is not so
great as that of the dumb ones—the girls do not think them enough foreign
who talk plain English fluently.

As a religious reformer, Swami Vivekananda lamented the absence in
America of a real understanding of God: "Nowhere have I heard so much
about love, life and liberty as in this country, but nowhere is it less understood. Here God is either a terror or a healing power." He was critical of
women who, having failed to find a husband, became "very churchy":
"Between them and the priests they make a hell of earth and make a hell of
religion." He found the American clergy too much involved in material
pleasure and, moreover, ill-equipped for the work assigned to them. A pervasive materialism, he felt, hindered the development of American religion.
"The people of this christian land will recognise religion only if you can
cure diseases, work miracles, and open up avenues to money." Americans
were still much too young to understand renunciation.

The Swami, however, did feel that some spiritual benefit could arise
from American materialism: only through material progress could the misery of the poor be reduced. To this extent, America, with its message of
hope and promise of dignity, fulfilled the precepts of his own Vedanta religion. He later recalled:

Aye, you may be astonished to hear that as practical Vedantists the Ameri-
cans are better than we are. I used to stand at sea-shore at New York, and look
at the immigrants coming from different countries, crushed, down-trodden,
hopeless, unable to look a man in the face. . . . And, mark you, in six months
those very men were walking erect, well-clothed, looking every body in the
face; and what made this wonderful difference? Say, this man comes from
Armenia, or somewhere else where he was crushed down beyond all recogni-
tion. . . . Even the air murmured around him as it were, "There is no hope for
you, hopeless and a slave you must remain"; while the strong man crushed
the life out of him. And when he landed in the streets of New York, he found
a gentleman, well-dressed, shaking him by the hand; it made no difference
that the one was in rags and the other well-clad. . . . He went about, and
found a new life, that there was a place where he was a man among men. Per-
haps he went to Washington, shook hands with the President of the United
States, and perhaps there he saw men coming from distant villages, peasants,
and ill-clad, and all shaking hands with the President.

"I love the Yankee land," the Swami later wrote to a friend. "I like to
see new things. I do not care a fig to loaf about old ruins and mope a life out
about old histories and keep sighing about the ancients." He marveled at
what America had to offer—"the place, the people, the opportunity for
everything new." His stay transformed his attitudes about India; he became
"horribly radical." He wanted to infuse some of the American spirit into
his homeland, "that awful mass of conservative jelly-fish," where an accumulation of traditions, which had outlived their usefulness, had put a stop
to progress. "Caste," he wrote, "is simply a crystallized social institution,
which after doing its service is now filling the atmosphere of India with its

stench, and it can only be removed by giving back to the people their lost social individuality." Freedom was at the heart of what America could teach India; it was "the only condition of growth; take that off, the result is degeneration." Yet, in the end, each nation had something to teach the other: "As regards spirituality, the Americans are far inferior to us, but their society is far superior to ours. We will teach them our spirituality, and assimilate what is best in their society."

Having found a very receptive audience in the United States for the propagation of his religious ideas, Swami Vivekananda remained there for about three years. He had succeeded in winning many friends, admirers, and some disciples; he had even been lionized, for a time, by New York's Four Hundred, who flocked to his yoga classes. The Swami went back to India in April 1896, to return only once more in 1900. He spent most of this time, about a year, on the West Coast in San Francisco and Los Angeles; and ultimately he founded a center in the San Antonio Valley, southeast of San Francisco, called "Shanti Ashram." After his return to India, he devoted all his time and energy to the development of his mission—to ameliorate the condition of the masses. His failing health did not allow him to continue for very long, and he left this world in 1902. The Vedanta Society, which he established in America, now serves thousands of people who seek spiritual solace in this mad race for power and money.

25

Giuseppe Giacosa
1847-1906

and

Giacomo Puccini
1858-1924

by Ben Lawton

The European artist . . . begins to feel an undefinable intellectual malaise which at first he can't define. . . . He perceives that something is missing . . . the testimony of the past. . . . Americans in the boldness of their youth are insensitive to this void.

— Impressions of America

Everywhere in the world
the roving Yankee
takes his pleasure and profit
indifferent to all risks. . . .
He's not satisfied with life
unless he makes his own
the flowers of every shore . . .

— Madame Butterfly

BEN LAWTON is instructor of Modern Languages and Literature (Italian) and Interdisciplinary Film Studies at Purdue University. He has contributed articles on Italian cinema and literature to journals in Italy and the United States, and has compiled a text for Italian cinema courses: *Literary and Socio-Political Trends in Italian Cinema*.

Giuseppe Giacosa in his studio, by ''P. T.'', medium unknown, 1900. Photograph courtesy of Museo Teatrale alla Scala.

Chiefly known as librettist for three of Puccini's best-loved operas—*La Bohème, Madame Butterfly,* and *Tosca*—Giacosa traveled to the United States in the fall of 1891. His *Impressioni d'America,* published in 1898, is a vivid account of Italian life in America in the late nineteenth century.

AT 10:00 A.M. on a clear October morning in 1891, the luxury liner *Le Bretagne* left Le Havre and headed for the United States. Suddenly, the unreliable North Atlantic weather changed. The passengers, terrified of the stormy seas and incapacitated by seasickness, took refuge in their cabins. Only one man continued to appear on deck and eat regularly at the Captain's table. His considerable girth and long flowing beard gave him an air of benevolent solemnity. But his dark, shining eyes missed nothing. Giuseppe Giacosa was already hard at work on *Impressioni d'America* (translated "Impressions of America"), a little-known book which is the most important record of the Italian perception of America towards the end of the last century. Almost exactly twenty years later, in 1911, another far more famous Italian, Giacomo Puccini, set sail for New York. As he relaxed in the imperial suite of the *George Washington,* he recalled his first triumphal visit to America in 1907. The handsome, moody composer hoped for an even greater success. But not even this idol of opera lovers the world over was prepared for the unprecedented welcome his *Girl of the Golden West* was to receive.

Why did these two Italians come to America? Why did two of the most important Italian artists of the period write almost exclusively about the United States during this twenty-year time span? How typically *Italian* was their response to this country?

GIUSEPPE GIACOSA was born near Ivrea, at the foothills of the Aosta Valley Alps, on October 21, 1847. He studied law at the University of Turin, but quickly turned to literature after his first disastrous appearance in court. By 1891 he was a well-known dramatist. An early exponent of naturalism in Italy, he wrote several collections of short stories and sketches of his native Val d'Aosta, and numerous articles for newspapers and magazines. In the United States, he is almost exclusively remembered as the co-writer of the librettos of Giacomo Puccini's *La Bohème, Tosca,* and *Madame Butterfly.* Strangely, his *Impressioni d'America* (1898), which is one of only a few such works by Italians in that time, has never been translated into English and is virtually forgotten even in Italy.

The book is singularly devoid of the information we would normally expect to find in the autobiographical description of such a journey. It contains virtually no dates, and only a few cities are named. From Giacosa himself, we guess that he must have traveled extensively, since he casually refers to incidents which occurred in Cincinnati, the Deep South, New York, Chicago, Detroit, Boston, and Niagara Falls. From other sources, we know that he came to this country for the production of *La Dame de Challant,* which he had written in French for Sarah Bernhardt.

Giacosa's attention was immediately drawn to the self-assurance and handsome good looks of the Americans he met. He was particularly struck by American young women, and compared them favorably with the more inhibited Italian women. In fact, this was his initial impression of America. He was the first in line to disembark, his beard bristling with impatience, when a "beautiful girl of about twenty years of age" asked to be the first to descend. His Italian gallantry was touched, he offered her his arm, and together they descended the ramp. "And so it happened that I was the first to touch the soil of America holding the arm of a young, beautiful American

The Bowery at Night, by William Louis Sonntag, Jr., watercolor, circa 1895.
Museum of the City of New York.

The churning quality of American life fascinated Giacosa. Everywhere he found a "proud awareness of physical energy." But he recognized, too, a dangerous undercurrent: "In the not too distant past [the Americans] must have been unrestrained and extremely violent."

girl whom I had never seen before nor would I ever see again, but whose company of a minute seemed a gentle welcome and an excellent promise of things to come."

In his book, Giacosa discusses both the promise and failure of American life. Overlooking New York's harbor, he is overwhelmed by the city's power and energy; "no other body of water is so completely surrounded by factories, is so noisy . . . so full of life, so different in all its aspects and movements, so strongly strikes the imagination and the mind." And yet, he cannot fail to notice that "all the neighborhoods by the sea seem in incurable decay. . . . [They] are dark, filthy, poorly paved . . . virtually nobody sleeps there." As he explores the city, from the exclusive suburbs to the Bowery, he perceives an American phenomenon: the separation of working and residential environments. Whereas in Italy the two are identical, in America one must travel some distance between them. He asks himself whether this does not "exacerbate the formidable American individualism." He judges that the absence of the "mitigating influence of the home . . . accustoms the American to an almost complete doubling of his nature . . . to a separation of his emotions from his will and his intellect." This causes him to "leave his loving, helpful humanity at home and to arm himself for business with a harsh, thankless selfishness." Nothing seems to have any permanence; nothing stands as "witness to the past." And yet,

Giacosa observes that a product of this way of life, "the proud awareness of physical energy," is at the root of a new "social aesthetic" which can contribute to "the progressive development of the human race."

Giacosa perceives that both the good and the bad in Americans derive from their optimism. Freed from the shackles of tradition which hobble Europeans, they are more progressive, more creative, and better able to cope with a reality which they perceive to be ever-changing. American energy has, however, its less desirable corollary effects. Giacosa observes that the people are prone to incredible excesses: "Americans drink in silence because they enjoy being drunk more than drinking." He observes the same intemperance in men who pay lip service to what he defines as the traditional European aesthetic. In describing the home of one millionaire, he writes: "The random collection of so many masterpieces produces a visual sensation identical to that of a strong fist in the eye." And while he is astonished, at first, by the many laws regulating social behavior, he eventually comes to realize that they, too, are a result of the American temperament: "In the not too distant past [the Americans] must have been unrestrained and extremely violent." It is, therefore, "comprehensible that . . . good manners be enforced by the policeman." Americans, however, refuse to be easily pigeonholed. With candor surprising in a man of his nationalistic and artistic pride, Giacosa confesses that "anyone who has lived here for any length of time must acknowledge that the [American] people behave in a more civilized and more dignified fashion than ours," and that he found "among the many men of . . . varied culture . . . a great originality in judging art and life."

Chicago, in Giacosa's opinion, expresses the American paradox better than any other city. His admiration for its quintessentially American energy does not blind him to the ultimate physical, social, and psychological consequences:

> American life blossomed more naturally in Chicago: enormous factories, endless streets, fantastic stores. . . . At first sight [it] seemed abominable; upon further reflection I recognized that it was admirable beyond words . . . [and yet] the people are anxious and frowning. . . . The chief characteristic of the city life of Chicago is violence. . . . I wouldn't want to live there for anything on Earth; but I believe that those who ignore it do not completely understand our century, of which it is the ultimate expression.

Almost half of Giacosa's book is dedicated to the activities and treatment of Italians in the United States. When he learns what confronts the newly arrived immigrant, he is upset by it; here he sees most clearly the two faces of America. With righteous indignation, he writes that even though the "chief of police of New York has stated publicly that of all the immigrant groups the Italian is that which produces the least number of assassins, thieves and trouble makers of all kinds . . . only the Chinese and the Blacks . . . are under them in the public opinion."

What Giacosa cannot at first understand is why Americans, who admire hard work, ostracize Italian immigrants, for they are industrious and they willingly accept the most humiliating and dangerous jobs. But then he sees that Italians do not live up to the ideal of prosperity. People who earn no more than Italian immigrants live in "nice, comfortable, solid homes, similar to those in which . . . almost only lawyers, doctors, and judges live in

Immigrant workmen, by an unidentified photographer, circa 1900. Brown Brothers.

Giacosa hoped that his compatriots in the United States would learn to overcome their history of privation. Unlike the native Americans, who shared a "vigorous feeling of social equality and personal dignity," the immigrants, Giacosa concluded, did not think beyond survival.

Italian towns." He begins to perceive that while, for the Italian laborer, it is sufficient not to die, the American worker "considers prosperity to be an indispensable condition of life." All Americans, regardless of social condition, share the "same vigorous feeling of social equality and personal dignity." He is particularly impressed by the gore-splattered butchers of the notorious Chicago slaughterhouses. He describes these people at length, covered with blood at work; and then, as they leave in their clean new clothes, "a crowd of 'gentlemen' which our dandies could take as an example of elegance." These men do economize, he says, but their economies begin after they are well off, not at the poverty level. The privations and humiliations which the Italian immigrants accept are to them "the mark of an inferior, decadent race."

Giacosa realizes that Americans do not and cannot understand the urgent needs which push the Italian immigrant to "heroic" extremes of self-sacrifice. He states that "it is we, who know our domestic conditions, who must judge our compatriots in an entirely different light . . . [and acknowledge] that the greatest part of their suffering is a manifestation of great . . . valor." He has finally understood that the root cause for the tragic misunderstanding between the two peoples is, ironically, to be found in each nationality's best inherent qualities. How can a people "which is now writing its history" understand or be understood by one with a history of a thousand years of foreign oppression?

What is Giacosa's final appraisal of America? He judges it by its effect on the Italian immigrant, more than by its technological wonders and great riches. While he is thrilled to find Italo-Americans who remember the *"bella Italia,"* he also recommends that the immigrants become Americanized. His hope is that the traditional Italian class barriers and social inhibitions which kept the poor spiritually enslaved will be broken. This attitude, which was shared by many at the time, is best expressed in the words of Rosa, an Italian peasant who came to the United States in 1884 at the age of fifteen: "They [the upper-class Italians] wouldn't dare hurt me now I come from America. Me, that's why I love America. That's what I learned in America: not to be afraid."

GIACOMO PUCCINI, for whom Giacosa had co-written the librettos of several operas, was close to the American ideal of the romantic Italian artist: slender, handsome, with an elegant mustache, he was among the most popular opera composers of his time. The heir to a long line of composers of ecclesiastical music, Puccini was born in Lucca, Tuscany, on December 22, 1858. He grew up in abject poverty after the death of his father. When he was eighteen, after having heard Verdi's *Aïda,* he decided to break with family tradition and become an opera composer.

Puccini's economic situation was desperate during his years as a student at the Milan Conservatory, and the idea of America as a land of economic opportunity was often present in his mind. In one fairly typical letter, written in 1890 to his brother Michele, who had emigrated to South America, we read: "I pile up debts every month. Soon the climax will come, and then God help me! If I could find a way of making money I'd come where you are. Is there any opening for me? I'd leave everything and go."

In time he was to succumb to the lure of the American dollar, but with mixed emotions. In the fall of 1906, he accepted an invitation to come to New York during January and February of the following year. For the then considerable sum of eight thousand dollars he was to supervise the production of several of his operas at the Metropolitan, including *Manon Lescaut* and *Madame Butterfly.* On January 18, at 6 P.M., Puccini disembarked from the S. S. *Kaiserin Auguste Victoria.* By 8 P.M., he was at the Metropolitan, attending the première of *Manon,* which he described in a letter dated the following day: "New York is extraordinary! *Manon's* first night was almost beyond description! Enthusiastic reception by a theater filled to overflowing." However, the enthusiastic response of the American public to his works ("It's my operas that draw the biggest crowds") and the sights and sounds of the new city did not sustain him for long. The pace of life in New York was rapidly overwhelming the Maestro. By January 25 he writes, "I'm well, but I'm badly in need of a little peace and quiet," and in a letter dated February 18 he allows his complete exhaustion to show: "I've had all I want of America." And yet, he had already announced that his next production would be a still nameless "American" opera, set in California. He promised Gatti-Casazza, the Director of the Metropolitan, the right to present the world première.

The composer wrote two "American" operas—*Madame Butterfly* should also be considered such. He controlled all aspects of his operas, but it is difficult to determine exactly what part his various collaborators had in choos-

Giacomo Puccini, by Arturo Rietti, oil on canvas, 1906.
Museo Teatrale alla Scala.

Two hours after disembarking in New York, in the fall of 1906, Puccini was at the Metropolitan Opera House attending the première of his *Manon Lescaut*. Soon thereafter he resolved to compose an American opera set in California, which became *The Girl of the Golden West*.

ing the source material. Puccini first saw *Madame Butterfly* as a play in London in 1900, where it was being produced by David Belasco, an important figure of the American stage. It traces an American naval officer's love affair with a Japanese geisha, whom he eventually abandons. The exotic setting of the play and its inchoate tragic elements fascinated Puccini, who immediately demanded the rights to opera production. Belasco is said to have consented at once to the request of the "impulsive Italian [with] tears in his eyes and both arms around [my] neck," but it was not until fourteen months later that the agreement was finally signed. Giacosa and his co-writer, Illica, were finally able to begin work on the libretto.

In Belasco's play, the American lieutenant is callous and arrogant, but this portrait of him is offset by the ludicrous caricature of the Japanese. In the opera, he is set against the purity and simplicity of the geisha, Cio-Cio-San, whose suicide lends the work the nobility of a classical tragedy. Lieutenant Pinkerton would seem to characterize the worst aspects of the Americans described in Giacosa's book. In his first aria, which is introduced by the opening strains of the "Star-Spangled Banner," Pinkerton defines himself, the "roving Yankee":

> *He's not satisfied with life*
> *unless he makes his own*
> *the flowers of every shore . . .*
> *So I'm marrying*
> *in Japanese fashion*
> *for nine hundred and*
> *ninety-nine years. With the right*
> *to be freed every month:*
> *America forever!*

Pinkerton personifies the most negative aspects of American individualism. And yet the portrayal is not completely negative. Those qualities of civility which Giacosa had observed in Americans are found here in Sharpless, the American Consul to Nagasaki, and in Kate, Pinkerton's "real American bride," who both do their utmost to mitigate the effects of Pinkerton's conscienceless actions. Their efforts, however, are in vain. With Cio-Cio-San's death, Pinkerton is compelled to face the consequences of his unthinking individualism:

> *. . . an easy going creed*
> *that makes life delightful*
> *but saddens the heart.*

On December 10, 1910, an absolutely unprecedented event took place. The Metropolitan presented the world première of a grand opera set in the gold-mining camps of California: *La Fanciulla del West (The Girl of the Golden West)*. The great Arturo Toscanini directed a brilliant cast which included Enrico Caruso, Emmy Destinn, and Pasquale Amato. The response of the New York public was overwhelming. According to his biographer, Mosco Carner, Puccini took "no less than fifty-two curtain calls," and "on behalf of the management Gatti-Casazza placed on his head a massive silver crown adorned with ribbons in the national colours of Italy and the United States."

Why did Puccini choose so unlikely a setting for a grand opera? In

Geraldine Farrar in the role of Cio-Cio-San with her child, Trouble, by Aimée Dupont, photograph, 1908. Library of Congress.

Seven years before he visited the United States, Puccini saw a London production of David Belasco's play, *Madame Butterfly,* and was enthralled by the story of the love affair between a young Japanese geisha and an American naval officer. Only Cio-Cio-San's suicide leads the officer, Pinkerton, to regret, in the words of Puccini's 1910 opera,

> *an easy going creed*
> *that makes life delightful*
> *but saddens the heart.*

Italy, at the age of twenty-two, he described a spectacle that has become a legend there in its own right, and which helped form the Italian image of the Wild West: "Buffalo Bill has been here. I enjoyed the show. They are a company of North Americans with some Red Indians and buffaloes." In February of 1907, while in New York for the production of *Madame Butterfly,* he wrote to a friend: "Here too I have been on the lookout for subjects, but there is nothing possible, or rather, complete enough. I have found good ideas in Belasco, but nothing definite, solid, or complete. The 'West' attracts me as a background, but in all the plays which I have seen, I have found only some scenes here and there that are good." Soon thereafter, he saw Belasco's *Girl of the Golden West,* but not until July did he finally decide that this was to be the opera he would do next.

With his usual thoroughness, Puccini researched all aspects of America. He was particularly interested in authenticity of dialogue and in finding suitable American tunes to weave into the operatic fabric. Snatches of Zuñi Indian melodies and of ragtime—"Old Dog Tray," "Belle of the Barber's Ball," "Dear Old House," and "Dooda Day"—caught the fancy of the public. The success of some of his arrangements was such that in 1922 he sued an American ragtime composer for plagiarism, and won!

When Giuseppe Giacosa died in 1906, Puccini hired Carlo Zangarini to write the adaptation of the play, principally because his mother came from Colorado and because he supposedly spoke English. Puccini, however, as usual wanted a "libretto which can move the world." Since it was not forthcoming, according to Zangarini himself, the composer became the real author of the libretto. More than ever before, therefore, he is responsible for every aspect of this opera.

The plot is standard western fare. Minnie, the beautiful, pistol-packing hostess of the "Polka," a mining camp saloon, is the miners' Bible-quoting schoolmarm. The miners, a motley, whiskey-guzzling crowd, never quite dare threaten her virtue. They spend their time feeling homesick, worrying about their gold, preparing to lynch random strangers, and dancing with each other. Jack Rance, the sheriff, is a gambler who desires Minnie. In a twist of the plot, he loses a crooked card game against her and so must free her lover, the notorious bandit Ramerrez (also known as Dick Johnson). Ramerrez is tall, handsome, dresses fashionably, "robs you like a gentle-man," and says he has never killed anyone. When the miners finally capture him, Minnie boldly rides up at the last moment and, clenching a pistol between her teeth, orders, begs, and pleads with them not to hang him. The miners, touched by her love for the bandit, set him free, and the two lovers exit singing: "Good bye, beloved country: good-bye, my California."

It has been suggested that this opera exploits, to the point of parody, trite Western themes, and that Puccini was pandering to his public in order to tap the lucrative American market. While it was certainly true that Puccini hoped for commercial success, his attachment to the opera—"the best . . . I have written," he wrote on August 10, 1910—suggests a deep commitment to the themes it portrays. The "Wild West" setting provided a vehicle for enlarging upon the attitudes toward America expressed in *Madame Butterfly*.

The Girl of the Golden West can be seen as a metaphor for the Italian encounter with America. Minnie, the paragon of virtue, stands for the American dream. She is the object of desire who, in the midst of "curses and quarrels," shares the "worries and the wants" of the miners. Even though she contradicts herself often, her essential message is

   . . . there is no sinner
   for whom there is no possibility of redemption.

It is this promise which beckons immigrants to America. In the opera, all persons are defined in terms of their relationships to her and to the ideal she represents.

But the dream is set against a dark background. In a world in which money rules, Minnie is also a commodity exploited by the bartender, Nick, who says to her "in low tones":

   please walk around
   every one of your words, every smile
   is a sale.

Racism, too, is found in the opera: favorite insults are "yellow face" and "Chinese face." And the miners, in their propensity for violence and exces-sive drinking, represent the archetypal America described by Giacosa.

The finale of Puccini's *The Girl of the Golden West* performed at the Metropolitan Opera House in 1910, by the Mishkin Studio, photograph. Museum of the City of New York.

For the December 1910 world première of Puccini's *La Fanciulla del West,* the Metropolitan assembled a dazzling cast headed by Enrico Caruso, Emmy Destinn (both in the center), and Pasquale Amato (at the right), under the direction of Arturo Toscanini. Set in the gold mining camps of California, *Fanciulla* was based, like *Madame Butterfly,* on a Belasco play.

But they also reveal a not particularly American sentimentality. In one outburst which counterpoints the ongoing poker game, one of them sings:

> *I've had enough . . .*
> *I'm sick*
> *ah, send me away!*

Furthermore, their search for gold is not characterized by heartless energy and adventurousness. The miners, several of whom are immigrants from Cornwall, Australia, and Mexico, curse "this golden west" where "the gold poisons the blood of those who look at it."

The opera's plot turns on the relationship between Ramerrez, the outsider, and Minnie. Like the immigrants described by Giacosa, Ramerrez has fatalistically accepted his destiny. Suddenly he perceives Minnie, *the dream.* But what can he do? If she learns the truth about him, she must certainly reject him. Everything seems to conspire against him:

> *Let me say just one word,*
> *but not in self-defense:*
> *I am accursed. I know! I know!*

But I would not have robbed you!
I am Ramerrez, I was born a vagabond:
my name was thief
from the day I was born.
But while my father lived
I didn't know it. . . .
My only riches, my only bread
for my mother and my brothers, for the future,
my inheritance from father:
a gang of highwaymen! I accepted it.
That was my destiny!
But one day
I met you . . . I dreamt
to go far away with you,
to redeem myself completely in life
of work and love . . . And my lips whispered
a prayer: Oh God!
Let her never know my shame!
The dream was in vain!

Yet somehow the miracle takes place. Even though he has merely been spared, not accepted, by the miners (representing the common man), the dream itself not only accepts him in the end; it prefers him above all others.

Why Nick and the miners agree to free Ramerrez becomes clear in the last scene of the opera. In their eyes, not the least of the bandit's crimes is the "theft of [Minnie's] love." And yet, when she reminds them of her many kindnesses towards them, they are moved. Puccini would seem to be saying that each immigrant group fears the competition of the next arrivals. It is only when the former immigrants realize that a universal welcome is the basis of the American dream that they can overcome their fear of the most recent "foreigner."

The Girl of the Golden West contains the two major components of the American myth. Hope and brutality are seen in their extreme manifestations: the Golden West, and the lynch mob. And yet, for Puccini, the dream, the often flawed message of hope, does exist for those who perceive its essence.

John Butler Yeats, self-portrait, pencil, possibly 1919.
Professor William M. Murphy.

The artist Yeats, father of the poet, sailed to New York from Dublin in 1907. Always intending to return to Ireland, he lingered in Greenwich Village throughout the remainder of his life, a model for America of what he called "the art of living."

26
John Butler Yeats
1839-1922

by Denis Donoghue

You must not think I do not admire and really adore this American character, which is now growing up, even while it is so easy to laugh at and even sometimes hate. A sort of European old-maidishness gets between me and them. Depend upon it it is a mistake sometimes to have been too well brought up, it prevents you realising that in America everything hitherto respected including your politeness and reticence is quite out of date. *Every day of my life, I meet with some fresh surprise. People will do and say anything, and except a few things like the multiplication table, nothing is sacred.*

—*Letter written from New York, July 3, 1912*

DENIS DONOGHUE is Professor of Modern English and American Literature at University College, Dublin. He is the author of *Connoisseurs of Chaos, Yeats,* and, most recently, *Thieves of Fire.*

IN DECEMBER 1907, John Butler Yeats set out from Dublin to Liverpool and thence to New York for a visit which, as it turned out, lasted fifteen years. He never went back to Dublin, never left the United States, and died in New York City at a small hotel, at 317 West 29th Street, on February 3, 1922. The expenses of the visit were paid, to begin with, by Andrew Jameson, Hugh Lane, and other Dublin friends. Thereafter, Yeats lived from hand to mouth, from brush to canvas, from fee to fee, gift to gift.

He was born in 1839 at Tullylish, County Down, Ireland, where his father was the local Protestant rector. Educated privately for some time, he eventually turned his mind to the profession of law, qualified as a barrister, and was called to the Bar in 1866. In fact he never practiced law, though he did a little apprentice work. He sensed that his true vocation was art, in the widest meaning of a term which included poetry, good taste, excellent manners, lively conversation, and the instinct of a gentleman. On September 10, 1863, he married Susan Pollexfen, a delicate, melancholy woman who bore him five children and died in 1900. The children were William Butler Yeats the poet, Robert Yeats who died at the age of three, Jack Yeats the painter, Elizabeth Corbet Yeats (known as Lolly), and Susan Mary Yeats (known as Lily). In 1867 Yeats moved to London, where he tried to establish himself as a portrait painter and merely established himself as a personality. He acquired experience and some artistic training, but few commissions. He moved back to Dublin in 1881, but his fortunes did not improve; he did not charge enough for his portraits, labored too long over his canvases, and acquired too easily the fame of a good talker. In 1887 he tried London again, but returned to Dublin in 1900 after his wife's death. There, in 1902, Yeats met the American lawyer and connoisseur John Quinn.

This meeting was the crucial event of Yeats's later life, and it virtually determined the course of that life for twenty years. Quinn in 1902 was in his Irish phase, a mood of enthusiasm for everything Irish in literature, drama, and art. The mood did not last forever; Quinn dealt with his moods by allowing one to supersede another. But his dealings with Irish artists for a few years after 1902 resulted in certain obligations to which he remained faithful. John Butler Yeats was one of these artists. When Yeats went to New York in the winter of 1907, Quinn received him, gave him commissions, money, introductions. Without that patronage, Yeats could not have survived. A week before his death, Yeats received from Quinn the last of many services: "Many thanks for the $30, I have been badly wanting underwear and socks."

Yeats never intended staying in America; he was always promising to go home. "I have sworn a deep oath that I will not spend another Xmas in New York—a powerful home-returning instinct possesses me. It has always been there, and at Xmas it gets terrible," he wrote in December 1910. The noise of New York City irritated him, "noisy trains, noisy tongues, noisy streets," and he yearned to "wander once more under those trees at Churchtown, along that lane going towards the mountains . . ." But one year led to another, and he stayed. Even when Quinn was planning a holiday in Ireland and offered to pay Yeats's fare and expenses in return for the pleasure of his company, the painter dithered, offered excuses, and in the end Quinn sailed without him. After a few years, Yeats's friends in Ireland knew that he would not come back, and they received his promises with an ironic

John Quinn, by John Butler Yeats, oil on canvas, *1908.* National Portrait Gallery, Smithsonian Institution.

The American lawyer John Quinn, Yeats's principal patron, commissioned his own portrait soon after the artist's arrival. Exasperated after "eight solid Sundays" had gone into sittings, Quinn demanded that Yeats talk less and paint more. The finished product satisfied neither of them. Contrite, Quinn then asked his friend to do a self-portrait, taking as much time as he wished, and Yeats worked on it for the rest of his life.

smile. A Dublin wit remarked that Yeats was an old man who ran away from home and made good.

There were many reasons for staying in New York. Yeats was incorrigibly hopeful, his buoyancy kept him alive, every defeat made success still more probable. So he responded to the vitality of America, which he sensed even in the noise of New York. "Hope, the great divinity, is domiciled in America, as the Pope lives in Rome," he told Oliver Elton. He was nostalgic when he thought about Dublin, but on the other hand Dublin was one of the two cities where he had failed, London being the other, and there was no point in repeating a doomed experiment. Ireland was always ready to welcome him, but not to give him a living. In America he could give lectures, write articles for newspapers and magazines, and find a few commissions, if not enough to satisfy him. On April 7, 1910, he wrote to his son William:

> *I am now busy with two lectures, one for an Irish Club which will pay me 25 dollars, the other for the Church of the Ascension, 5th. Avenue, for which I will get nothing, but it means fame, and my subject is 'The human side of the Catholic Church by an ultra-Protestant.' The title is, you will see, a* stroke of genius—*to be delivered May 1st. I am of course very anxious.*
>
> *I have also to write an article on the Women's Suffrage for the* Harper's Weekly. *It will be my fourth article for them. My portrait of John O'Leary is now exhibiting at 'The Independent Artist,' a sort of rival body just launched in antagonism to the Academy here.*

Yeats's letters to his son report every occasion of success, while they evade the necessity of mentioning disappointments or failures. The father was anxious to assure his son that he was doing well, making a name for himself, in the New World. Indeed, a minor reason for staying in New York rather than returning to Dublin was that it was agreeable to place a gap of three thousand miles between father and son, especially when the son's fame vastly exceeded his father's. They could communicate well enough by letter, and in any event the son made occasional visits to New York: it was

Yeats at Petitpas, by John Sloan, oil on canvas, 1910.
The Corcoran Gallery of Art.

Yeats, remembered as the "best conversationalist in New York," frequently presided at the restaurant in the Petitpas boardinghouse in Greenwich Village. John Sloan appears at the extreme right. The others are Van Wyck Brooks (extreme left), Alan Seeger (at Yeats's left), and next to him Dolly Sloan. Mlle Celestine Petitpas, one of the three French sisters who owned the restaurant, is serving fruit. Next to her is Robert Sneddon, a writer. The lady to his left is Eulabee Dix, an American miniaturist. Fred King is on Sloan's left and and lady in the foreground is Mrs. Charles Johnson, wife of an Irish scholar.

enough. The father's influence was already a major element in the son's intellectual and poetic life, the correspondence between them was tolerable to both, and perhaps convenient to the father. Meanwhile the father courted fame.

Yeats delighted in general thoughts. Nothing gratified him more than to reflect upon differences between the Irish and other people, contrasts between Englishmen and Americans, the nature of "the modern woman," the distinctions between character and personality, materialism and idealism. His mind was not intense or complex; it was too easily satisfied by ostensibly grand comparisons and contrasts. Famous as an after-dinner speaker, he favored the mental habits appropriate to that medium, the immediate effect, the touches of ingratiation, the scintillating contrast:

> *I am lecturing this week at Philadelphia, 25 dollars and all expenses and a luncheon paid for. I mean to take as my subject that Ireland is now an example to the world (at least as it is among the peasants in the West) in that it is more occupied with the question* how to live *than it is with the question* how to make a living.

Yeats told his son William, "When I was young, the definition of a gentleman was a man not wholly occupied in getting on." When William thought of accepting a job on the *Manchester Courier,* at the age of twenty-five and in dire need of earning a living, he eventually decided to decline the offer; and his father said, "You have taken a great weight off my mind." When John Butler Yeats let his mind run upon the distinction between living and making a living, he thought of living as the prerogative of artists, Catholics, women, especially American women beautiful with gaiety and nonchalance; and of making a living as the prerogative of men of the world, Protestants, men given to dullness and accumulation. He himself made a living in Protestant America by capitalizing upon the same distinction. It was necessary to avoid starving to death, but he took the harm out of this necessity by showing that he was barely committed to it; he kept himself a free man by adding charm and irony to what was otherwise the most pressing burden.

As an artist, Yeats favored effects congenial to the orator. It is true that he labored over his canvases, painting and re-painting; he was never satisfied. But it is also true that he could never interest himself sufficiently in those parts of a portrait which he considered merely instrumental. His portraits often concentrate his sense of the sitter in the eyes and face, and the painting in these respects is often magnificent; but when he moved from the eyes and face to the arms, hands, and shoulders, he lost interest. Many of his portraits, as a result, are all life in the face, and death everywhere else. When he treated a subject, either in paint or words, he maintained his interest in it only to the point at which it yielded up a memorable contrast or resemblance. His drawings and sketches are more successful than his paintings because they catch the gist of the matter, they encourage speed and nonchalance, and the artist is not under oath to fill up all the spaces. In the official canvases, Yeats was under contract to fill space and delineate the body, two laborious requirements in an artist who always remained more amateur than professional, more a gentleman than a craftsman. It was easier to please the Irish Club and the Church of the Ascension, *Harper's Weekly* and *The Seven Arts*.

America gave Yeats what Ireland and England denied: opportunity. He made new friends in New York, "the friendliest place in the world." Quinn opened many doors for him, and soon his range of friends included the literary critic Van Wyck Brooks, the poet Alan Seeger, and above all, John Sloan, a fellow painter. He was welcomed everywhere, whether on his own behalf or in recognition of his son's fame. Sloan's painting, *Petitpas,* shows Yeats in a characteristic posture of success at the head of his table in the Petitpas boardinghouse in Greenwich Village, sketchbook in hand, smoking a cheroot, holding forth to his friends. On May 9, 1908, he wrote to William:

> She [Lily, his daughter] sees that I am making a success (it is not altogether made, since I am only getting 15 dollars—£3—for each sketch) yet wants me to go back [to Ireland] with her. I think I ought to stay, but that she ought to be with me. . . . To leave New York is to leave a huge fair where any moment I might meet with some huge bit of luck. Everybody says why not go to Newport whither all fashion is now wending. Some nights I sleep like a top dreaming of luck.

Dolly and John Sloan, by John Butler Yeats, pencil, July 1910.
Delaware Art Museum, on permanent loan from Mrs. John Sloan.

Close friends of Yeats, Dolly and John Sloan helped him, in his words, *"so materially in New York.* They have worked for me as if I was a brother—or a father—really worked." He thought Sloan's paintings and etchings of New York, most of which depicted the "war of the poor against the rich," well done—"and tho' a Socialist he keeps his paintings pure art."

He wrote to Ruth Hart, a friend in Ireland, about his life at Petitpas, where he found the good luck of company:

Here I dine every night at a queer French restaurant where a large party gather, mostly foreign, and dine without either coat or waistcoat—in a garden d'été, which is a backyard. Three good-looking young Breton women who used to be servants run the place, all three with pleasing personalities, hospitable and gay. Such quantities of talk, all smoking and drinking claret at 5^d a bottle. The ladies are as talkative as the men, the talk sometimes, only sometimes, in English—but I am an artist, and am there to see.

On the whole, Yeats loved America because he loved Americans; he was far more interested in the people than in the landscapes, buildings, vistas, or settings. "They don't understand art and have no manners, but there runs through all ranks a goodness and kindness, and their humor is all based on this kindness." The Americans, he reported to his son Jack, "are the most human, that is the most affectionate, sympathetic, and helpful people that ever lived under the wide sky." He was struck by the American ideal of service, the citizen's moral sense, but he did not profess to understand it. He did not concern himself with politics in any practical sense; he was not much interested in the administrative aspects of society, but only in its variety and color. American Suffragettes were preferable to their glum English companions, because they pursued their cause without losing their native charm and ease. He was interested in American ideas, often to the extent of deploring them. The idea, which he ascribed to Ralph Waldo Emerson, that every man is a genius if he only knew it, was, to Yeats, "Protestantism gone mad." Sometimes he thought the famous American energy mere restlessness, extroverted and boisterous. "The American can-

Manuscript letter from John Butler Yeats to John Quinn, 1 November 1908, including a sketch of Yeats and Isadora Duncan walking down Broadway. Professor William M Murphy.

The daring but surprisingly "demure"—as Yeats described her—Isadora Duncan was a controversial figure even among the experimentalists of Greenwich Village. "I saw her," Yeats wrote, "dancing on the biggest stage in New York—a figure dancing all alone on this immense stage.... Several people said: Is it not like watching a kitten playing for itself? We watched her as if we were each of us hidden in ambush. I don't wonder that at first New York rejected her—she stood still, she lay down, she walked about, she danced, she leaped, she disappeared, and re-appeared—all in curious sympathy with a great piece of classical music, and I did not sometimes know which I most enjoyed, her or the music."

not possess himself in peace and so his poetry and literature are all for the newspapers, and the poetry he has is whistled down the wind. His whole talk is of joy and happiness—talk, as I tell him, only fit for athletes and football-players—a shallow vulgar paradise easily come at by anyone except the true artist and poet who seek a something quite different." Yeats explained to the scholar and critic Oliver Elton what the something quite different was, and the difficulty of pursuing it in America:

> *What America needs to rescue it from its unrest and its delirious collectivism is* poets *and* solitaries, *men who turn aside and live to themselves and enjoy the luxury of their own feelings and thoughts. Poets here are orators—have to be so, since the public is their paymaster and ready to pay them handsomely if only they will desert their caves of solitary personal feeling and come out and work for their generous and affectionate masters.*

But Yeats himself could not have borne that solitude, even if he had been free to choose it; he was too gregarious to live by his own aesthetic creed.

So he enjoyed America, a place of chances and choices. He went to see Buffalo Bill at Madison Square Garden; he insisted upon seeing the peculiar

William Butler Yeats, by John Butler Yeats, oil on canvas, 1907. Professor William M. Murphy.

The elder Yeats was forever haunted by his son's success and judgment. After he died, "Willie" said of him: "He had his hopes and ambitions to the last, constantly writing that he was painting his masterpiece."

spectacle of baseball; he went to Coney Island with Quinn, Sloan, and Ezra Pound, a trip recalled in Pound's *Canto LXXX:*

> *or his, William's, old 'da' at Coney Island*
> *perched on an elephant beaming like the prophet*
> *Isaiah*
>   *and J. Q. as it were aged 8 (Mr. John Quinn)*
> *at the target.*

America was promises. "Anything may turn up here—a lecture, an article, a portrait. It is a high gaming table where the poorest has a welcome and a chance." Above all, Yeats was grateful to America for giving him, after Dublin and London, a third chance. America, he found, was tender to those who asked for a fresh start: naturally, since that was what the Americans had asked for themselves. While Yeats recognized that America often cut itself off from the past, including its own past, and acted as though the world were born yesterday, if not today, he was able to take the harm out of this amnesia by making a new morality from it. At least America did not indulge itself in recrimination, scolding the poor soul for every crime or misdemeanor ever committed. If the people had a short memory, at least it meant that they were quick to forgive as well as to forget. That suited Yeats. His own past was a place he had no wish to revisit.

In the end he was reluctant to go back to Dublin. "I wrote to Willie some time ago that I was afraid to return to Dublin, afraid as a child dreads the fire. And I may add that New York saved my life, all of which is a dark saying which, however, I could elucidate." In the summer of 1921 he fell ill. By September he was telling his friends that he was going home. He fell ill again, and postponed his departure till December. He took up the unfinished self-portrait on which he had been working, off and on, for years. "I now see that it is the making of a masterpiece," he told Quinn, having seen and despised some portraits by the portrait painter Laszlo. "To know good you must have seen evil. I have seen Laszlo and now I appreciate Yeats." But oratory intervened again:

> *Last night at the MacDowell Club I was one of ten poets, including Amy Lowell; all of them quite as illustrious as myself; and we read from our works. I read my poem 'Autumn'; it begins*
>   *'Great lady of the darkening skies'*
> *and I forgot to mention that the subject was 'Autumn.' So what they made of it I don't know or who they thought the great lady was.*

A few days later he died. He was buried in Chestertown, a village in the lower Adirondacks, where one of his friends owned a vacant lot. His headstone bears the inscription: "In Memory of John Butler Yeats of Dublin, Ireland. Painter and Writer." William Butler Yeats wrote to his sister Lolly on the day after their father's death:

> *If he had lived longer, he would have grown helpless and known that he was helpless. He had his hopes and ambitions to the last, constantly writing that he was painting his masterpiece. . . . An American publisher who came to see me a few weeks ago had promised to sit for him on his return to New York. He lived in hope and I think the past hardly existed for him, and his hopes filled his life.*

In fact the past did exist for John Butler Yeats, but chiefly as something to be circumvented, outlived, cajoled into peace.

Sholom Aleichem, by Numa Patlazhan, bronze, 1912.
Marie Waife-Goldberg, daughter of Sholom Aleichem.

This bust was made in 1912, two years before Sholom Aleichem's second and final visit to the United States. The "Jewish Mark Twain," as one of his publishers called him, articulated the immigrant's predicament in the New World.

27
Sholom Aleichem
1859-1916

by Bel Kaufman

Since Columbus discovered America in 1492, the same land has been discovered over and over by every new immigrant.

—Wandering Star

BEL KAUFMAN, Sholom Aleichem's granddaughter, is the author of the long-time best seller, *Up the Down Staircase.* She has taught English in New York high schools and colleges and is a popular public speaker, alternating between writing and addressing Jewish audiences and state-wide education conventions.

SAY "Sholom Aleichem" to a Jew anyplace in the civilized world, and his face will light up. Not only is it a familiar greeting, meaning literally: "Peace be with you," and colloquially: "Hello!," but it's the pen name of the great Jewish humorist, who so completely identified with his people that he became their most loved and cherished writer. His stories are read in thousands of homes to the sound of laughter, but his own life—especially towards the end, in this country, where he died, burned out at fifty-seven—was one of struggle and disappointments. At the time of his death, he was describing America through the eyes of characters he created, new immigrants—the boy Mottel and his family—whose comments reflect the exuberance, the eye for absurdity, the rueful irony, and the compassion of Sholom Aleichem himself.

He was born Sholom Rabinowitz on March 2, 1859, in the town of Pereyaslov in the Ukraine, the third of a dozen children. His mother died in the cholera epidemic when he was twelve; his sharp-tongued stepmother inspired his first literary effort: *Glossary of Stepmother's Curses*. He was a brilliant student; at seventeen he was engaged as a tutor to fifteen-year-old Olga Loyeva, who eventually became his wife. They had six children, one of whom was my mother. Impractical, generous, and trusting, he twice lost a fortune on the Kiev stock exchange; for the rest of his life, he was beset by financial worries. He worked prodigiously, writing in Yiddish—a language he raised to the status of literature—stories, novels, monologues, and plays, and giving public readings of his works to enthusiastic audiences, for he was a consummate actor.

Wandering from country to country in search of a home, he visited the United States twice; first briefly, in 1906, with hopes of establishing himself in the New World. These hopes soon turned to disillusionment. Two of his plays opened on the same night in two rival Yiddish theaters in New York; both failed. His work was vulgarized by the competing producers accustomed to the low taste of the time. "They even buy their jokes for money," he wrote in a letter, "or borrow them from each other." But he was confident that one day the Yiddish theater in New York would come into its own and that his plays would succeed: "My eyes won't see it," he wrote to his son-in-law, "but yours will."

He did not return to this country until the outbreak of the First World War; this visit, in December of 1914, was his last. He died a year and a half later.

In a photograph with both of his grandchildren, taken before he left for America, he looks happy. His arms enfold us: me, chubby and beribboned on his right knee, my cousin Tamara on his left. Not too long after, sensing that his days were numbered, he wrote to my parents in Odessa, Russia, where we were living: "I have won great honors in my lifetime . . . but Tamara and Belochka won't remember me."

Sholom Aleichem's final year was a difficult one: plagued by sickness, he made desperate efforts to support his large family here. His European royalties were cut off by the war, his writings for the Jewish papers and his public readings yielded but little money, yet he remained hopeful and optimistic. When the *New York World*, then the newspaper with the largest circulation in New York, undertook to print some of his stories in English in its Sunday Magazine, he wrote jubilantly to my parents that in all the stations on the elevated train, large posters proclaimed: "Read Sholom Alei-chem, the Jewish Mark Twain! . . . Original! New! Humoristic!" But the death of his eldest son, Misha, who had been expected daily to arrive in New York and who died suddenly abroad at the age of twenty-five, was a tragedy that shortened his own life. "A mistake," he wrote to my parents; "instead of the son saying the prayer for the dead for his father, the father has to do this for his son."

Sholom Aleichem died on May 13, 1916, in a house on Kelly Street in the Bronx. For three days and nights thousands of mourners filed past his coffin in the shabby living room for a last look at their Sholom Aleichem. Some 150,000 people, according to the *New York Times*, lined the streets at his funeral. In Odessa, a cable arrived with the words: "Papa very sick." We understood what they meant.

Sholom Aleichem lies buried in Mt. Carmel Cemetery in Brooklyn, among the workers, as he requested in his will:

> *Wherever I may die, let me be buried not among the rich and famous, but among plain Jewish people, the workers, the common folk, so that my grave may honor the simple graves around me, and their simple graves honor mine, even as the plain people honored their folk writer in his lifetime.*

This remarkable document was read into the *Congressional Record* and published in the *New York Times*, which called it "one of the great ethical wills in history." In it, he asks to be remembered on the anniversary of his death with laughter, by having family and friends gather together to read one of his merriest stories aloud in whatever language was best understood.

Sholom Aleichem with granddaughters Belochka and Tamara, by an un-identified photographer, 1912. Bel Kaufman.

This has been an inviolable tradition in our family; most frequently read are his hilarious stories of America.

"WE DO what all Jews do," says one of Sholom Aleichem's characters, "we emigrate to America." America was the land of freedom, equality, and limitless opportunity to the Jews of Eastern Europe eager to escape the poverty and pogroms in their "*shtetls*," or townlets. Such a "*shtetl*" was Sholom Aleichem's fictional Kasrilevka, "a town no bigger than a yawn," peopled by paupers who knew how to laugh at themselves and their hardships. In one of his stories, a Jew promises Rothschild the secret of eternal life: "Move to my shtetl," he says, "for in the history of our town, no millionaire has ever died there." America was the land of milk and honey, of "gold rolling the streets, yours for the picking." It was a tale of many marvels, told and retold by the downtrodden. It was a dream, a folk fantasy.

The fantasy soon faded, if not in the ship's steerage, then on Ellis Island, "The Isle of Tears," where families were herded together like cattle, or tragically separated. And it was quite dispelled in the cities, to which they

Immigrants at Ellis Island, by Ilya Schor, wood block print, circa 1953. Resia Schor.

Aleichem's lyrics captured his peoples' dream of the New World:
> *This America, they say,*
> *Brings great fortunes, joy to all.*
> *And to Jews it's Paradise,*
> *Incomparable.*

But the immigrant experience generally began with a rigorous induction at Ellis Island, where families were often separated. In the shadow of the Statue of Liberty, Ellis Island gained quick notoriety among the immigrants as the "Isle of Tears."

Hester Street on the Lower East Side of New York, by Warren Dickerson, photograph, circa 1905. History Division, Natural History Museum of Los Angeles County.

At the time of Sholom Aleichem's visits, the American Jewish community was dismissed, in the centers of Jewish learning abroad, as a community of peddlers. Sholom Aleichem attacked this point of view, and prophesied for American Jewry "a new and glorious epoch. . . . Those who have changed the verse of 'From Zion will come forth the Law and the word of the Lord from Jerusalem' to read 'From Kiev will come forth the Law and the word of the Lord from Amsterdam,' will now have to change it once again to read: 'From America will come forth the Law and the word of the Lord from New York.' . . . I, who often indulge in jest, mean this very seriously."

brought their own culture and in which they founded their own *"shtetls,"* where they continued to struggle for existence. "All Kasrilevka is here!" cries the boy Mottel when he finds himself on New York's Lower East Side. "Velvel" has turned into "Willy" here, "Mendel" into "Mike," the butcher from the old country has become a rabbi, the doctor pushes a pushcart, but the sights and sounds and smells are those of home. Men trading, women chattering on the stoops, babies dozing, children playing. "He who has not seen a New York street has never seen anything beautiful," says Mottel. Yet in a letter to a friend, Sholom Aleichem confides: "You know well the ghetto of this hell they call New York."

Uniquely the voice of his people, he understood their frustration at the discrepancy between their dream of America and the reality, and he exorcised it by making them laugh. He describes America through the innocent eyes of his characters; much of the humor and the bite lies in the artful naïveté of Mottel, in the greenhorn ignorance of his older brother Eli, in the boundless enthusiasm of Eli's friend Pinney. "A mere mortal should wash

Sholom Aleichem, by Lola (pseudonym for Leon Israel), in *Der Kundes,* December 18, 1914. Photograph courtesy of Bel Kaufman.

Sholom Aleichem's arrival in New York's Lower East Side prompted this cartoon. The Yiddish caption reads: "Where am I? Logically I should be in New York, but the smells are the smells of Kasrilevka."

his hands before pronouncing the name of America!" Pinney exclaims. He envisions a classless society, where a tailor may be sitting right next to the President of the United States, where "the lowly may become great and the dead almost come to life." He is sure that every great American began by working at the most menial tasks: "Didn't Carnegie, Rockefeller, Vanderbilt sweep the streets, sell newspapers, shine shoes for a nickel? And wasn't Mr. Ford, the king of automobiles, once a taxi driver? Were Washington and Lincoln born great? . . . Or take our President today, Mr. Wilson, how did he start out? Begging your pardon—as a mere teacher!"

"Everything is possible in America," explains a character from another story, Berel Isaac: "You can do whatever you please. Want a factory?—You can set up a factory. Feel like opening a little store?—You can do that too. Want a pushcart?—That's also permitted. Or you can become a peddler, or work in a shop. It's a free country. You can bloat up from hunger, drop dead on the street—no one will stop you."

This was laughter through tears, humor squeezed out of adversity. "You may as well laugh," Sholom Aleichem wrote. "Even if you don't see the joke, laugh on credit. You may see the joke later, and if not, you're that much to the good." There is a resilient resignation in this, the resilience of survival. The Jews who streamed into this country on a wave of immigration early in the century could laugh with recognition at the problems confronting characters even greener, even poorer than they.

"In America people don't walk—they run. They write fast, talk fast, speed underground." They even eat on one foot. And in the subways and elevated trains "such crowds and shoving and crushing together . . . One goes out, two get in. With God's help, one seat is free—but there are a dozen customers for it!" Eli's wife hates being lifted up in the elevated railway and plunged down under the earth. "America," she declares, "should have its two feet on the ground."

But Mottel delights in everything: the marvels of hot and cold water coming out of the wall through taps, the iron box with holes for a stove, the joys of the moving pictures. He has learned that "on the fourth of July the United States conquered its enemies"; that "all right" means "don't worry"; and that in America it's a custom to move. "That is if you don't pay rent, you go to court, and they throw you out on the street." He explains that every salesman here is permitted to extol his own goods; this is called advertising. "You may be well aware that my work isn't worth a cent, but I can price it at a million. That's America—a free country!" As for children, America was made for them. In the old country Jewish children could not get into schools; here they are dragged to school; besides, books and supplies are free. Best of all, teachers are not allowed to hit children. "Try not to love such a country!"

Like his Mottel, Sholom Aleichem was full of youthful enthusiasm. He was fascinated by American fountain pens, door chains, desk ornaments, and he was thrilled by a new invention: the phonograph. Too poor to buy one, he used to ride long distances by elevated railway and subway to the home of an affluent friend who possessed one—to listen and to marvel. He even made a recording, the only one of his voice, but it was erased by mistake in the recording studio.

"You've got to stay alive even if it kills you," Sholom Aleichem wrote; and his characters do just that. Yet for all their struggles, they know that they can sleep without fear of pogroms or arrest. "We sweat and toil till we're blue in the face, but we're free." They know that they can become citizens and vote. And they know that "everybody suffers and makes a living." Except perhaps the millionaires on Fifth Avenue: they are happy, for they can have anything they want. "The rich are even welcome into the next world!"

Everything is possible in America, even working in a sweatshop, where you must punch a peculiar clock that tells the exact hour and minute you came in, and where you're docked a half day's pay if you're a few minutes late or leave a few minutes early. "If you faint from the gas fumes, you're docked a whole day's pay." The workers in the shop strike, the strikers get hurt, and Pinney the idealist is forced to cry: "Shame on you, Columbus! Shame on you, Washington! Shame on you, Lincoln!"

There is nothing a man cannot learn to do in America, so they try their hands at many jobs. Eli works as a tailor, as a waiter in a delicatessen, he is even ready to shovel snow—but not on the street. "Do you want your portion of snow brought to you into the house?" asks Pinney. He hasn't been napping either: he is, in turn, a pants presser and an insurance collector of nickels and quarters each week. Everybody in America gets insured. And everybody in America buys on the installment plan. "For a dollar a week you can furnish a princely apartment!" Eli's job is to try to collect money for a furniture company, but people keep complaining to him: "Why don't the drawers open? Why do I see two faces in the mirror?" The family decide to set up a newsstand. All seven pitch in selling candy and cigarettes—one for a penny; if you want something cheaper, then two for a penny. Unfortunately, customers are scared away by so many people behind the counter.

"There is a saying here, a harsh saying: 'Time is money,'" Sholom Aleichem wrote. Although he was critical of American materialism and emphasis on business, his feeling about this country was positive and optimistic. "Very soon American Jewry will begin a new and glorious epoch in our history," he wrote. He saw America as the land of the future; he appreciated its scope; and he loved its energy and vitality.

It was one of his ardent wishes to have his books translated into English and his plays produced in New York, but he never lived to see his hopes realized. In the *New York World* on December 26, 1915 appeared this notice: "One of the world's greatest writers lives in New York. His fame is international, for his stories and sketches and dramas are read and quoted and laughed at and wept over in Russia, in Poland, in Austria and Germany . . . a genius of whom we know little or nothing . . . because the writing on which his reputation is founded is unknown to the great majority who can not read Jewish papers." Three months before his death, he wrote to my parents that there was no publisher in America willing to publish his books, or even a section of them, in English.

"The saddest beginning is better than the happiest ending," he once said. Today his plays are produced in repertory companies all over the world, and are hits in New York, both in Yiddish and in English. *Fiddler on the Roof*, based on his Tevye stories, introduced him to a wide English-speaking audience, though he himself would be amused to find Tevye, the humble milkman, transformed into a musical extravaganza. His books, which have appeared on best-seller lists, are translated into sixty-three languages. His name is known even to those who do not read Yiddish. Pity he can not know this.

By this time he has become part of the cultural heritage of this country, and Belochka, long since off his knee, is writing, in English, these very words.

Everything is possible in America!

28
Liang Ch'i-ch'ao
1873-1929

and

Hu Shih
1891-1962

by Jerome B. Grieder

The American political system is a wonder of the world. Why? Because in America there are two forms of government [state and federal], and the American people feel two different kinds of patriotism. In essence, America is forty-four republics which together constitute a Republic. . . . Other nations are created out of a people. The American nation is constituted out of a people and *the smaller nations created by that people.*

                              —Travel Notes from the New World

It is common knowledge that America is a free country . . . but it is not generally acknowledged that America is the country which loves freedom least. . . . America has won its freedom; its people take freedom for granted, no longer perceiving it as an invaluable possession.

                              —Hu Shih's Diary While Studying Abroad

JEROME B. GRIEDER is Professor of Asian History at Brown University, and the author of *Hu Shih and the Chinese Renaissance.*

Liang Ch'i-ch'ao, by an unidentified photographer, circa 1913.
Hoover Institution on War, Revolution, and Peace.

An outspoken reformer, Liang Ch'i-ch'ao sailed to the New World in 1903, from his Japanese
exile, to promote his cause among the American Chinese.

IN REMARKABLE CONTRAST to the Japanese of the late Tokugawa and early Meiji times, the Chinese in the nineteenth century were indifferent tourists. Complacent in their sense of material and cultural self-sufficiency, lethargic in their response to forces that prompted political reform, the Chinese remained, in the receding tide of their great tradition, more securely insular than their island neighbors—until, at the end of the century, a tidal wave of political catastrophe swept away every vestige of self-assurance. Then, in the aftermath of defeat by Japan in 1895, the abortive reform movement of 1898, and the humiliation of the Boxer Rebellion and its politically disastrous consequences, Chinese advocates of radical reform looked abroad for inspiration and traveled abroad in search of support.

For most, Japan was the limit of experiment. It offered, close at hand, the advantages gained by a half-century head start along the road to intellectual and political modernity. Refracted through the lens of Japanese enthusiasm and aspiration, the West was more Prussian than American, reflecting more of Bismarck than of Jefferson. The Chinese, themselves searching for the sources of political direction and national purpose, were by no means immune to the force of such an example. Yet America was appealing, too: because of its revolution, the great symbolic act of emancipation that had "turned slaves into masters" (in the words of one turn-of-the-century revolutionary tract); and because of its burgeoning power and self-confidence at the end of the great century of transcontinental expansion—a fascinating phenomenon, albeit ambiguous in its implications for Chinese reformers.

In America, moreover, there were many Chinese—more than eighty thousand in 1900—who had emigrated not as travelers but as laborers, and who congregated in scattered enclaves all across the land, in the crowded Chinatowns of San Francisco and New York, in smaller cities along the new railroads that Chinese labor had helped to build, or in the sparsely populated mining towns of the Rockies. It was natural that Chinese political radicals in exile, denied direct access to their countrymen at home, should address themselves to these *émigré* Chinese, seeking from them political support and financial backing: as did Sun Yat-sen, the indefatigable spokesman for anti-Manchu revolution; and as did Liang Ch'i-ch'ao, the most influential advocate of constitutional monarchy.

LIANG CH'I-CH'AO was born in Kwangtung province in 1873. Nothing in his traditional scholar-gentry lineage, or in his early education, foreshadowed the enormous authority he was to wield in the early years of the twentieth century as a critic of the venerable institutions of Confucian monarchy. From 1890 onward, Liang was wedded to the reformist cause; in the course of the ensuing two decades, he became its most prolific and impassioned propagandist. After the brief excitement of imperial sponsorship during the Hundred Day Reform in the summer of 1898, he faced, with his mentor K'ang Yu-wei, the swift reaction and the bitterness of flight to Japan in the autumn, pursued by the maledictions of the aging and reactionary Empress Dowager. In Japan, Liang threw open the doors of his mind to every intellectual opportunity that exile afforded. He remained a monarchist, but he spoke with a fervor that inclined more and more to a revolutionary declaration. In an outpouring of essays and polemical tracts, Liang labored, with remarkable effect, to popularize for Chinese audiences

The Empress Dowager of China, Tze-Hsi, by Katharine Augusta Carl, oil on canvas, 1903. National Collection of Fine Arts, Smithsonian Institution.

As protectress of orthodoxy in the last years of China's Manchu dynasty, the Empress Dowager thwarted the forces of constitutional reform allied to the Emperor. Liang, a leader of the reformers, was forced into exile when the Empress successfully instituted a coup in 1898 against her nephew.

the principal traditions of modern Western thought and politics. By the time he sailed for the New World in February 1903, he had become, at thirty, the unrivaled architect of progressive Chinese opinion, the persuasive champion of freedom, of liberated individualism, of public-spirited democracy.

Liang's American tour had two purposes, the first of which dictated his itinerary and provided the focus for his experience. He traveled as the representative of the *Pao-huang hui* (the Society for the Protection of the Emperor) to promote, among Chinese in the United States, the cause of constitutional reform in general, and in particular the interests of the young emperor against the vindictive machinations of the dowager Empress. But he came also to see for himself the machinery of modernity, the engines of democracy, at work in all their startling complexity. He spent two months in Canada, five in the United States, and in this time, as one old friend wistfully conceded "he saw more than I did in my three years there."

Liang's travel account is partly straightforward narrative and partly, in the style typical with him, discursive commentary on sundry matters of interest: the history of immigration to the United States; the Monroe Doctrine; the workings of financial trusts; the social position of American women. Liang was an enterprising tourist, a man of vast curiosity sometimes rather randomly employed, with a quick sense of place and mood, and a discerning eye for revealing detail. He saw some things which appalled him. Of the tenement districts in New York City, he wrote:

> *In summer, along the streets where live the Italians and the Jews the pavements are blocked by old women and youngsters, youths and young girls, squatting on stools outside their doorways, dressed in rags, their faces pinched and sullen. The trolley tracks do not reach these districts, and even carriages are few. . . . Jumbled one atop another they live, tens of families to a building, the better part without light or air, and the kerosene lamps burning day and night. The stench assaults the nose.*

He was ready to praise as well; far more to his liking than the crowded cities of the Northeast was the nation's capital in May:

> *After the grimy turmoil of such places as New York, Boston, or Philadelphia, suddenly to arrive here indeed moves one, as does sweet, sad music, the sound of the stringless lute . . . the taste of sea-perch and lily-root, with inexpressible delight. The city is built entirely in accordance with artistic inspiration and plan. No other city has escaped the vicissitudes of history, or its remains; but Washington springs full-blown from human creativity.*

Central Park—Winter, by William Glackens, oil on canvas, date unknown.
The Metropolitan Museum of Art, George A. Hearn Fund, 1921.

"The main object and justification," wrote Frederick Law Olmsted of his creation, Central Park, "is simply to produce a certain influence in the minds of people and through this to make life in the city healthier and happier. The character of this influence is a poetic one." To Liang Ch'i-ch'ao, Olmsted's notion was frivolous: "If this land were given over to commercial use, the rents would come to three or four times the annual revenues of the Chinese government. From a Chinese point of view, such waste is lamentable, lamentable!"

Liang's approach to America was open-minded, candid, and not without a saving sense of irony. He found it "surpassing strange," on visiting Grant's Tomb, that a nation which had allowed the former president to endure the poverty of his last years would lavish vast sums upon his final resting place. Central Park astonished Liang for a different reason: a tract larger than the French and International Concessions of Shanghai taken together, lying profitless in the very heart of the city. "If this land were given over to commercial use, the rents would come to three or four times the annual revenues of the Chinese government. From a Chinese point of view, such waste is lamentable, lamentable!"

On several occasions, Liang was sought out by American socialists: his reputation as a reformist leader had preceded him, and sympathetic Americans were anxious to furnish him with radical prescriptions for China's future. All their advice he received with faint amusement and some misgiving. "The socialists whom I have encountered inspire respect by their sincerity and their social concern. They never leave off preaching. . . . They revere and believe in the writings of Marx, no less than the Christians believe in the New Testament. . . . Socialism is a kind of superstition, and since no power in the world is stronger than that of superstition, it is evident that socialism must overspread it." Liang hoped that China might be spared; however radical his political views might appear in the context of decadent imperial autocracy, he remained conservative in respect to social revolution, and confident that Chinese problems necessitated no such agonizing solutions.

Liang found much to engage his interest. His itinerary—first across Canada, then from New England to New York, south as far as New Orleans, thence through the Midwestern heartland to Chicago, and finally across the northern plains to the Pacific coast—provided ample opportunities for detailed accounts of railroads, factories, and public libraries. Great men fascinated him, too. In New York, J.P. Morgan granted him an audience that lasted only long enough for the great financier to deliver a brief homily on enterprise ("the success or failure of any venture is determined before the work itself begins") before Liang excused himself, uncharacteristically awed and speechless in the presence of this "King of the Trusts." With John Hay, the Secretary of State, he was less diffident. Hay impressed him as "sober and reticent, an austerely incorruptible man—one knows at a glance that he's an old hand at foreign affairs." Liang exploited his two-hour visit with Hay in the latter's Washington residence to instruct as well as to learn. "I told him of the present circumstances in which the imperial dynasty finds itself, and of the intellectual trends of the last year or two. Mr. Hay, it seemed, could hardly contain his astonishment. He urged me to publish such an account." Liang's meeting with President Theodore Roosevelt, the following morning, was shorter and much less flattering. "Nothing of consequence was said," Liang reported; Roosevelt had merely wished him success in his enterprise, and gone on to express the somewhat daunting opinion that the sense of civic responsibility which Liang sought to inspire in his countrymen could usefully begin with Chinese living in America.

Intended or not, this was a thrust which must have cut close to the bone. Everywhere Liang went, he counted Chinese heads: laundrymen in New

York; students, a mere handful, at Columbia, Yale, Harvard, Berkeley; restauranteurs in Butte, Montana. And everywhere he assessed the temper of his countrymen and the nature of their experience. He was painfully sensitive, more on their account than on his own, to the overt insults and subtle humiliations of discrimination. But Chinese attitudes distressed him as much, and had, in the end, an even more telling effect on his opinions. In the populous Chinatowns of New York and, especially, San Francisco, Liang found something he could not have found at home. Here were Chinese communities, moderately prosperous, moderately literate, served by a modern press (six Chinese-language newspapers were then publishing in San Francisco), open to political organization—yet they were torn by private political feuds, and given more to selfish enterprise than to the pursuit of common purposes or the public good.

By October, when Liang boarded the *Empress of China* (a nice irony for the man on whose head the old woman had placed a tempting bounty) to return to Yokohama, he had come to a despairing conclusion. The Chinese, he wrote, are too clannish, too provincial, to act as citizens of the city or nation, too servile in their acceptance of tradition to bear the responsibilities or enjoy the advantages of liberty, too lacking in distant vision to promote progressive change:

> *Freedom, constitutionalism, republicanism—these are but the general terms which describe majority rule. But China's majority, the great, the vast majority of Chinese, are as I have described them here. Were I now to advocate rule by this majority, it would be no different from advocating national suicide. . . . At present, the Chinese must accept authoritarian rule. . . . Those born in the thundering tempests of today, forged and molded by iron and fire—they will be my citizens twenty or thirty, nay, fifty years hence. Then we will give them Rousseau to read, and speak to them of Washington.*

"Joe" Ming's Cook, by J. P. Ball and Son, photograph, 1893. Montana Historical Society.

In Montana, Liang found some of his countrymen working as cooks. Elsewhere they were laundrymen, students, and purveyors to their own communities; but everywhere, Liang was disappointed to observe, they lacked public spirit. Divided among themselves, they were unable to see beyond their private concerns.

Liang Ch'i-ch'ao had seen much that intrigued him in America, from the streetlights of New York City to the bears and geysers of Yellowstone Park. One suspects, in the end, that he had discovered little that he really *liked,* but he found much to admire, from the entrepreneurial miracle of the great trusts to the cultural glorification of manual labor. And certainly he had found much to perplex and trouble him, much that he deemed unworkable or unworthy. Why were politicians, as a rule, such mediocre sorts? What did the corruption of city government imply for democracy? How could one justify the tyranny of the political parties? Why was the American presidency a weak office, except in times of emergency? To whom, in this political system, might one look for purposeful leadership? To these questions, and others just as pertinent and ominous, Liang returned pessimistic responses. Liang's American tour confirmed in him an inclination, based on cultural inheritance, education, political experience, and very likely temperament, to take an elitist view of social leadership and responsibility. He returned to Japan to argue, with all the great eloquence at his command, for reform under the guidance of an enlightened—and well-counselled—monarch. His valedictory salute to America was penned a short time later:

> Woe is me! Republicanism! For ten years I have been drunk on it, I have dreamed of it, I have sung its praises. Now finally we must part. . . . Republicanism! Republicanism! I love thee, but not so much as I love my fatherland! . . . I cannot bear again to defile thy sweet name . . . We take leave of each other forever. . . . I return from America to dream of Russia.

Hu Shih arrived in the United States in the autumn of 1910. In the seven years since Liang's visit, the Wright brothers had taken to the air at Kitty Hawk, and Henry Ford had announced the birth of the Model T; Taft had come to the White House; dollar diplomacy had come to the State Department; and the world had moved, step by unmindful step, closer to the Great War. In China, these had been years of unremitting and hastening crisis. The dissolution of the old order was symbolized, perhaps insured, by the abolition in 1905 of the examination system, the cornerstone of Confucian privilege and responsibility. At the same time, the dynasty's faltering attempts at political Westernization foreshadowed the overwhelming difficulties that would encumber the creation of a new order to replace the old.

Under these inauspicious conditions, a new generation of students had matured, buffeted by political uncertainty, filled with reformist or revolutionary zeal. Hu Shih was one of this generation. Born in 1891, the son of an inconspicuous Ch'ing official who died in 1895, Hu had received an education neither conventionally traditional nor thoroughly modern. In his early teens he had left his native Anhwei, drawn like so many others to Shanghai, where at least the rudiments of Western knowledge might be acquired. There, amidst the political turmoil that swept through the radical "new schools," Hu laid in random fashion the groundwork of an education sufficiently "modern" to qualify him, in 1910, for a Boxer Indemnity scholarship. He was not yet nineteen years old when he embarked for America.

When the Revolution came in 1911—predictable, yet in the event itself unexpected—Hu was a second-year student at Cornell University. Some months later, reading the news of Liang Ch'i-ch'ao's return from exile, he commented in his student diary: "Whatever our people has learned of

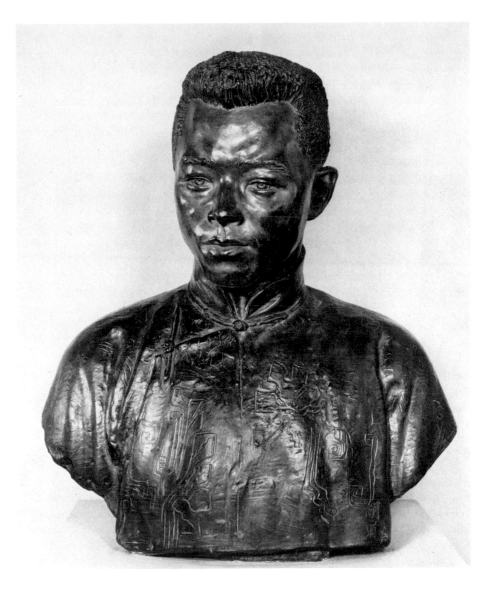

Hu Shih, by Malvina Hoffman, bronze, 1932. Field Museum of Natural History.

In the fall of 1910, seven years after Liang's visit, Hu Shih arrived in the United States. Hu had been educated in one of the "new schools" in Shanghai, where he had acquired an elementary knowledge of Western thought. Not yet nineteen, he sailed for America to begin his studies at Cornell University.

nationalism, or of world affairs, in the last fifteen years, is entirely due to him. . . . Without Liang's pen, a thousand Sun Yat-sens . . . could not have achieved such quick success." It was an appropriate compliment: Hu was to disagree with Liang deeply and enduringly on many issues in later years, but the two were much alike in political disposition: wary of revolutionary impetuosity, committed to moderate solutions, and certain that the enlightened minority must bear the responsibility for setting the direction of progressive change. It is interesting, therefore, that the example of America offered such contrary lessons to each. Liang had been intrigued, but he departed more skeptical than he had come; he was not won over. Hu Shih was captivated. It is, indeed, no great exaggeration to say that, in his case, the experience made the man.

Granted, Hu Shih's American experience was very different from Liang's. He stayed not seven months, but seven years, and returned to China at last with a bachelor's degree from Cornell, a Ph.D. from Columbia, and a well-informed acquaintance with many aspects of American life which Liang had glimpsed, if at all, only in passing. Even afterwards, the America of Progressivism and Wilsonian idealism remained for Hu an inspiration and a promise. When, in the rancorous intellectual debates of the 1920s and 1930s, Hu defended "the West" against charges of materialism and spiritual impoverishment, or argued the case for democracy against proponents of disciplined dictatorship, it was not the West in general, but the America of his student years, to which he looked.

Title page from Hu Shih's Diary as a student (1911–1917). Photograph courtesy of Department of Manuscripts and University Archives, Cornell University.

At Cornell, Hu Shih enrolled in the College of Agriculture. "When I first arrived in this country," he explained in his student diary, "plowing and sowing were my ambition. Literature was an insignificant skill, useless to the cause of national salvation." In time, however, Hu's interests shifted, and he transferred to the College of Arts and Sciences to study philosophy.

John Dewey, by Joseph Margulies, watercolor, 1946. National Portrait Gallery, Smithsonian Institution.

After reading the works of the American philosopher John Dewey, in 1915, Hu Shih made pragmatism "a guiding principle of my life and thought and the foundation of my own philosophy." Hu took his doctorate at Columbia under Dewey and went on to become a leading exponent, in Peking, of an experimental approach to social and intellectual problems.

In accordance with the prevalent assumption that a Chinese student should learn something useful, Hu Shih began his studies in the College of Agriculture at Cornell. It was not a productive choice, and before long he transferred to the College of Arts and Sciences and to a major of philosophy that led him, eventually, to Columbia for graduate study under John Dewey's tutelage. Pragmatism has been called a distinctly American philosophy, and Hu Shih's reputation as its leading exponent in China in the twenties and thirties certainly reinforced his image as a thoroughly Americanized thinker. His debt to Dewey was, in fact, considerable; but his commonsense aversion to abstruse doctrines was already evident before he came under Dewey's influence. The mark of Hu's American experience was less an attachment to any specific philosophical point of view than an acceptance of the impalpable possibilities in American life.

Hu's last years in Shanghai had reflected the frustrations and the sense of drift common to students in that time and place. The first, and in some respects the most enduringly visible, influence of American life on him was its infectious optimism. In America, he later recalled, "there seemed to be nothing which could not be achieved by human intelligence and effort." Such cheerful conviction may account for the energy with which Hu devoted himself to his studies, although he felt he had a tendency to spread himself too thin. Hu maintained a steady interest in, among many other things, the history of ideas, but he never became a proper philosopher. He became, rather, one of China's first modern intellectuals: detached from the passions of immediate political causes, and utterly persuaded of the self-evident validity of certain general values of the mind—clarity, skepticism, and tolerance.

Hu Shih's American education proceeded outside of, as well as within, the structure of his formal studies. He was greatly inspired by the theater of social realism; he read, or read about, Imagist poetry; and he attended exhibitions of modern art. He became, in other words, thoroughly cosmopolitan in intellect and taste. So, too, with his political opinions. He was active in the international student movement, which was then, against the somber backdrop of the European war, a rallying ground for idealistic young pacifists. He thus came into contact with a number of the most celebrated progressive reformers of the day: Norman Angell, Lyman Abbott, Oswald Garrison Villard, Washington Gladden—and in the summer of 1913, he met President Wilson himself, in his eyes "the supreme product of Western civilization." The motto of the Cornell Cosmopolitan Club— "Above All Nations Is Humanity!"—became for Hu an enduring article of faith.

At a less exalted level, the example of American institutions was decisive in shaping Hu's appreciation of democratic political processes. Witnessing democracy in practice, he came not only to esteem it in its American setting, but to believe that democracy is of all political systems the most elementary, and therefore the most easily transportable from one social milieu to another. Hu Shih's courses in American politics at Cornell were conducted without benefit of textbooks; students were required instead to read the newspapers regularly, to study in detail various kinds of state legislation, and to attend local political functions. "To this day," Hu wrote twenty years later, "I despise men who have gained their understanding of politics from textbooks." On election night in 1912 (sporting the Bull Moose button he had worn throughout the campaign), Hu joined the crowds milling around the newspaper offices in downtown Ithaca, "cheering like mad" as the election returns were posted throughout the night. "Such enthusiasm for politics is memorable indeed," he commented. No less impressive was a session of the Ithaca Town Council:

> Deliberative assemblies of this kind can be extremely instructive; no visitor should let the opportunity slip. Last year in Washington, I took advantage of every spare moment to visit the Congress, especially the House of Representatives, but what I saw and heard there cannot compare to this in genuine interest. One of the councilmen is a teacher at the university; the others are all local merchants: one, I am told, owns a cigar store, another runs a dairy; one is a clerk in a department store, one a coal merchant, one a construction engineer. . . . The former mayor is a friend of mine; he once worked in a laundry, and now owns it. Their spirit of republican equality is truly inspiring.

Out of such experiences grew an unfaltering confidence in democratic processes at the grass-roots level, coupled with the conviction that democracy in principle is essentially no more than democracy in practice. In July 1914, Hu, a recent convert to Wilsonianism, summarized the Independence Day oratory in terms which anticipated the argument he would use, after his return to China, against the advocates of political tutelage:

> The pivotal issue which those who discuss freedom must consider is this: Mr. Wilson contends that the government's responsibility is to reduce constraints on freedom, to enable all men to live free lives. . . . Mr. Roosevelt, on the other hand, would have the government serve as the people's guardian, sustaining and assisting it as one nurtures a child. I follow Mr. Wilson.

In China, two decades later, when many of his friends had come to the view that the survival of a nation beset by civil war and foreign aggression could only be secured under the forceful guidance of a "modern" dictatorship, Hu pressed the case for democracy with undiminished confidence and vigor:

> Look at American democracy—is it not a very elementary political system? I witnessed two national elections in America, and a number of local elections, and saw a great many citizens of limited competence putting their right to vote to good use. . . . My views are not a joke, but [are] the conclusion drawn from seven years' assiduous observation of constitutional democracy in actual practice, which awakened me to the realization that this is not an unattainable ideal, but simply a commonsense system of politics.

Hu Shih left America in the summer of 1917 with a deep sense of personal regret. He wrote, "Leaving this home of my own making, to return to the land of my forefathers, I cannot easily decide whether my feelings are of sorrow or joy." He arrived in China, nevertheless, full of confidence. "If hopes are dupes, fears are liars," he had written in his diary, borrowing the sentiment from Arthur Clough's *Say Not the Struggle Nought Availeth.* "This is the great prescription for the world's present ills. The pity is that none dare try it."

For a few years, events in China seemed to justify Hu's optimism. The collapse of an established political orthodoxy, the revival of intellectual *esprit* after the bitter disappointments of the early republican years, the influx of new ideas—all combined to generate an environment of intellectual innovation and daring unprecedented in China's revolutionary history. In this congenial setting, Hu Shih was at his active best: promoting the new vernacular literature, urging upon his audiences the purposeful individualism and the critical habits of mind that would undergird a new cultural and political order, inveighing against immoderate or precipitate solutions to complex problems. Within a decade of his return, however—as the anarchy of warlordism plunged China deeper into crisis, as cultural radicalism merged with revolutionary political ideologies—increasingly it came to seem that Hu Shih's years in America had estranged him from the temperament of his times. His cosmopolitanism was ill-suited to the mood of a nationalistic student generation; his belief in intellectual freedom seemed irrelevant in conditions of social bondage; his faith in the slow educative potential of democratic institutions did not serve the urgent tasks of nation-building.

LIANG CH'I-CH'AO, after 1911 a republican *malgré lui,* died in 1929. Several unsuccessful attempts to enlighten the policies of the warlord regimes of the teens had diminished his reputation. The spectacle of Western self-destruction in the Great War of 1914–1918, and its revolutionary aftermath, had confirmed his earlier doubts. His last years were spent in culturally introspective scholarship as, more and more, he came to prize the distance, historical more than physical, which he hoped would safeguard China from such disaster. Hu Shih was disappointed. Liang had been a man born before his time, Hu observed after attending the funeral in Peking; fame had been thrust upon him too early. His influence had been enormous, but his accomplishments, in the end, insubstantial. It was a judgment that many had rendered against Hu himself before his death in Taiwan in 1962, though to the end of his life his own sense of public purposefulness was stout armor against private despair.

In a certain light China's twentieth-century history may be read as a vindication of Liang Ch'i-ch'ao's rejection of the American example. However different in form China's present government may be from Liang's idea of enlightened autocracy, its nationalistic vision is informed by a similar concern for forceful leadership in control of the processes of modernization. Hu Shih's cosmopolitanism, his faith in the values of intellectual and political liberty, remained in the Chinese context no more than abstractions. But in another way, what Hu Shih had to say—and it was a message drawn directly from his American experience—touched upon the very essence of the great liberation of popular energies that has transformed China in the last half-century. Hu sought tirelessly to persuade his countrymen that the capacity to make the decisions which gave shape to political experience is the natural possession of every man, a power which need only be exercised to become real. "Young China believes in democracy," he wrote in 1915; "it believes *that the only way to have democracy is to have democracy*. Government is an art, and as such needs practice. . . . The Anglo-Saxon people would never have had democracy had they never practiced democracy." Before we dismiss this credo as irrelevant to the revolution that unfolded in China in the ensuing decades, we would do well to listen to another voice. In the late 1940s, as the civil war reached its climax, a Communist political leader in the liberated areas of North China told an American reporter: "It is utterly useless to train people for democracy beforehand. If the people lead a democratic life, their habits will naturally be transformed. Only through the practice of democracy can you learn democracy."

29
H. G. Wells
1866-1946

by George Shepperson

So in its broad features, as a conflict between the birth strength of a splendid civilization and a hampering commercialism, I see America.

—*The Future in America*

GEORGE SHEPPERSON is Professor of Commonwealth and American History at the University of Edinburgh. His major work, *Independent African,* is in the field of Afro-American and African history. Recently, however, he has turned his attention to British writers with an international reputation, such as Rudyard Kipling and H. G. Wells.

H. G. Wells, by Jane Wells, photograph, 1895.
University of Illinois Library, Urbana-Champaign. Courtesy of Estate of H. G. Wells.

In the spring of 1906, Wells went to America to question not only its people "but the mute, expressive presences of house and appliance, of statue, flag and public building, and the large collective visages of crowds, what it is all up to, what it thinks it is all after, how far it means to escape or improve upon its purely material destinies." He sought America's common purpose.

When Herbert George Wells made his first visit to the United States, in April and May 1906, he was nearly forty. Yet Wells had been familiar with the problems and the promise of American life from an early age. His father, a restless romantic who trudged from one dead-end job to another, thought at one time of trying his luck in the American goldfields, and Wells realized how close his family had been to becoming American citizens. The Wells's home at Bromley in Kent, England, poor though it was, had some books which the young Wells read, by American authors such as James Fenimore Cooper and Washington Irving; and when his mother went back to domestic service as housekeeper to Up Park mansion in Sussex, he was permitted to read the books in its library, amongst which was Thomas Paine's *Common Sense*. Wells's start in journalism was made in 1893 on a London paper owned by the American millionaire, W. W. Astor. And by the turn of the century when Wells, as author of the futuristic romances such as *The Time Machine, The Island of Dr. Moreau,* and *The War of the Worlds,* was a famous figure, he had little difficulty moving in those sections of English society which were frequented by rich and clever Americans abroad.

But aspects of America, other than its entrepreneurship and affluence, were known to Wells at this time. Like many British intellectuals, his socialist views had been influenced by Henry George's critique of the American experience, *Progress and Poverty;* and he was familiar with the criticisms of the American way of life by the novelists of his day. One of them, Stephen Crane, came to England at the end of the century, and he and Wells were friends. Crane was enthusiastic about what he called Wells's "genius for writing of underclass people"; and Wells called Crane "one of those stark American writers" who, like himself, "broke away from the genteel literary traditions of Victorian England."

H. G. Wells's speculations about the future were influenced by American writers. Perhaps he caught the American habit of looking into the future as a boy, when he may well have read Washington Irving's *Rip Van Winkle.* Certainly, Wells's crystal-gazing tendency was strengthened by his reading of Edward Bellamy's *Looking Backward, or 2000–1887*, which is a clear influence on Wells's *When the Sleeper Awakes* (1899); and both Bellamy's book and William Dean Howells's Utopian story, *A Traveller from Altruria,* are part of the genesis of H. G. Wells's *A Modern Utopia,* which was published the year before he paid his first visit to the United States.

On this occasion, it was natural for H. G. Wells to seek the advice of his most notable American friend, Henry James. James and Wells had first met in 1898, and they lived near each other in the south of England for some years. The relationship of the two men was one of mingled admiration and annoyance with each other's writings and attitudes to culture. Wells, in his novel, *Boon* (1915), made cruel criticisms of James; and the break between the two of them inevitably ensued. Its origins, perhaps, may be seen as far back as Wells's visit in 1906 to Boston, James's former home. Wells later wrote:

> My main thesis is that culture, as it is conceived in Boston, is no contribution to the future of America. It matters little in the mind of the world whether any one is concentrated upon medieval poetry, Florentine pictures, or propagation of pills. The common significant fact in all of these cases is

this, a blindness to the crude splendor of the possibilities of America now,
to the tragic greatness of the unheeded issues that blunder towards solution.
Frankly, I grieve over Boston—Boston throughout the world—as a great
waste of leisure and energy, as a frittering away of moral and intellectual
possibilities. We give too much to the past. New York is not simply more
interesting than Rome, but more significant, more stimulating, and far more
beautiful, and the idea that to be concerned about the latter in preference to
the latter in preference to the former is a mark of a finer mental quality is
one of the most mischievous and foolish ideas that ever invaded the mind
of man.

As a foremost exponent of that "mischievous idea," James, the American in Europe, stood at what Wells would later call "an opposite pole" to his own perspective: that of a European drawn to the newness, the raw promise of American life.

Thus, in the spring of 1906, Wells crossed the Atlantic "full of curiosity about America." He was interested not so much in "the United States for what they are" but in "how they will shape up presently, what they will lead to, what seeds they will sow and how they will wear." He came armed with many introductions from James, who could not, however, rise to the challenge of easing Wells's way through the more exotic parts of the country. "I suppose you know no one in Salt Lake City?" Wells wrote to James on 25 January 1906. "If I could get any insight into the social life of that place I would brave that extra long journey from Chicago very willingly." And if Wells had any intention of going to San Francisco, the great earthquake and fire of 18 April 1906 made that impossible. He was in New York when the disaster occurred, and he noted that no one seemed in the least dismayed. A new San Francisco—indeed, a fresh New York, were that city to become a blazing ruin—could be built. That spirit was at the heart of the

Henry James in New York at the studio of
Alice Boughton, by Alice Boughton,
photograph, 1906, in *Henry James,*
1975. Harry T. Moore.

Men of opposing sensibilities, Henry James and H. G. Wells found in America the touchstone for their differences. James provided his friend with introductions throughout the United States but it was, in the end, the Englishman who felt more at home there. Well's *The Future in America* was, James thought, a "loud" book about "a yelling country."

Maxim Gorky with Maria Andreyeva, by the Mishkin Studio, New York, photograph, 1906. Library of Congress.

Maxim Gorky and his common-law wife were in America during Wells's visit, to raise funds for the victims of the 1905 revolution in Russia. They were hounded by American prudery, and Wells was enraged. The country, he wrote, couldn't "stand Gorky's morals," but found it easy to accept the corruption of its own cities.

country he was eager to explore. The Americans, he observed, had no sense of finality but only "of inexhaustible supply, of an ultra-human force behind it all."

H. G. Wells had to be content with visiting New York, Boston, Chicago, and Washington. His works had been published in the United States since 1896; and, although he had complained before he crossed the Atlantic that " 'English Jules Verne' is my utmost glory, reviews of my book appear among the dentifrice advertisements," he found his reception on the spot both enthusiastic and serious. He lectured in what he termed "the embattled universities of America," for which he then had considerable admiration. Furthermore, he met representatives of the unsensational, socially conscious America, such as Jane Addams and her staff at Hull-House, Chicago, with whom he discussed the Fabian Society (the British reformist socialist group of which, with George Bernard Shaw, Wells was a leading member). This was the America which appreciated H. G. Wells, not as the writer of "wild pseudo-scientific extravaganzas," but as, in the words of Jack London, "a sociological seer, sane and normal as well as warm and human."

As a socialist and a sociologist, Wells was quick to note the anomalies in the American dream. In *The Future in America,* his book about this transatlantic trip, he wondered at the blindness and cruelty possible in a society whose democratic promise was so ripe. Saddest, perhaps, was America's "Tragedy of Colour," as he entitled one of his chapters. Trapped within it were black leaders of such stature as Booker T. Washington and W. E. B. Du Bois, whom he met during his visit. Sad, too, and bizarre was the treatment accorded the Russian writer Maxim Gorky, who had come to America while Wells was there in 1906 to raise funds for the victims of the revolution of 1905 in Russia. Because Gorky's common-law wife, the actress Maria

Andreyeva, was not his wife in the eyes of the Russian Orthodox Church, he was hounded out of the United States. The two writers met both before and after the Russian's deportation. Wells was enraged by America's puritanical treatment of Maxim Gorky and by the insult accorded Maria Andreyeva. He saw in it the difficult position of women in America.

For Wells the socialist, America's greatest problem, and Europe's, was the pervasiveness of private ownership. Until "her land, her public services, and the whole of her great economic processes" could be rescued from the "irresponsible control of private owners," injustice was institutionalized. Wells cited the case of a working man, William MacQueen, imprisoned on false charges of anarchist activity in Paterson, New Jersey:

> I have very clearly in my memory the figure of young MacQueen, in his gray prison clothes in Trenton jail, and how I talked with him. He and Mr. Booker T. Washington and Maxim Gorky stand for me as figures in the shadow—symbolical men. I think of America as pride and promise, as large growth and large courage, all set with beautiful fluttering bunting, and then my vision of these three men comes back to me; they return presences inseparable from my American effect, unlit and uncomplaining on the sunless side of her, implying rather than voicing certain accusations. America can be hasty, can be obstinately thoughtless and unjust.

In spite of all Wells's reservations about the United States, he saw, during his first visit of 1906, what he called "the birth strength of a splendid civilization." He wrote:

> I see it, the vast rich various continent, the gigantic energetic process of development, the acquisitive successes, the striving failures, the multitudes of those rising and falling who come between, all set in a texture of spacious countryside, animate with pleasant timber homes, of clangorous towns that bristle to the skies, of great exploitation districts and crowded factories, of wide deserts and mine-torn mountains, and huge half-tamed rivers.

But if Wells was impressed by America's "growth invincible," he was not prepared to accept the constant claim that the United States was a young country. "America," he wrote, "is an older country than any European one, for she has not rejuvenesced for a hundred and thirty years. In endless ways America fails to be contemporary."

The intensity of Wells's book matched the intensity of the society he had come to explore and inspire. Henry James offered one criticism of *The Future in America,* written to Wells on November 8, 1906, which conveys its essence admirably: it was "too *loud,* as if the country shouted at you, hurrying past, every hint it has to give and you yelled back your comment on it; but also, frankly I think the right and only way to utter many of the things you are delivered of is to yell them—it's a yelling country, and the voice must pierce or dominate."

Central to H. G. Wells's view of America was his perception that "the typical American has no 'sense of state.' I do not mean that he is not passionately and vigorously patriotic. But I mean that he has no perception that his business activities, his private employments, are constituents in a large collective process; that they affect other people and the world forever, and cannot, as he imagines, begin and end with him." It was an American failing which Wells also explored in his frighteningly prophetic novel *The War in the Air* (1908). The remarkable chapter on the aerial invasion of New York

Aerial Attack on New York, by an unidentified artist, in *The War in the Air,* 1908.
University of Illinois Library.

Wells used New York City as a symbol for both the creative and destructive power of America.
In his novel, *The War in the Air,* which included an imaginary aerial invasion of the city, Wells
described "the inhuman force of it all."

obviously drew upon Wells's impressions of the great city in 1906: "the unprecedented multitudinousness of the thing, the inhuman force of it all."
"And over all the torrential confusion of men and purposes," he wrote in
his novel, "fluttered that strange flag, the stars and stripes, that meant at
once the noblest thing in life and the least noble, that is to say Liberty on
the one hand and on the other the base jealousy the individual selfseeker
feels towards the common purpose of the State."

That contradiction between the possibilities and limitations of American life struck Wells most forcefully when he was invited to the White
House to lunch with President Theodore Roosevelt, whom he had long
wanted to see:

> *As I talked with President Roosevelt, there came back to me quite forcibly
> that undertone of doubt that has haunted me throughout this journey. After
> all, does this magnificent appearance of beginnings, which is America,
> convey any clear and certain promise of permanence and fulfillment what-
> ever? . . . Is America a giant childhood or a gigantic futility, a mere latest
> phase of that long succession of experiments which has been and may be for
> interminable years—may be, indeed, altogether until the end—man's social
> history?*

Wells had struck a "familiar vein of thought in the President's mind. He
hadn't, he said, an effectual disproof of a pessimistic interpretation of
the future." And then, with a reference to the conclusion of Wells's *The
Time Machine,* Theodore Roosevelt declared slowly, "Suppose, after all . . .
that should prove to be right, and that it all ends in butterflies and morlocks
[a reference to the latter days of the world and the underground race, the

Theodore Roosevelt, by an unidentified photographer, circa 1912. Division of Political History, Photograph courtesy of the National Museum of History and Technology, Smithsonian Institution.

"I can see him now," Wells wrote of Theodore Roosevelt, "and hear his unmusical voice saying 'The effort—the effort's worth it,' and see the gesture of his clinched hand and the—how can I describe it? the friendly peering snarl of his face, like a man with the sun in his eyes. He sticks in my mind as that, as a very symbol of the creative will in man."

Morlocks, who, in Wells's story, preyed upon mankind]. *That doesn't matter now.* The effort's real. It's worth going on with. It's worth it. It's worth it— even so . . ." To H. G. Wells, Teddy Roosevelt was "a very symbol of the creative will in man, in its limitations, its doubtful adequacy, its valiant persistence amid perplexities and confusions. In his undisciplined hasti-ness, his limitations, his prejudices, his unfairness, his frequent errors, just as much as in his force, his sustained courage, his integrity, his open intelli-gence, he stands for his people and his kind."

America's contradiction continued to challenge H. G. Wells for the rest of his life. At the end of *The Future in America,* he wrote, "It seems to me that in America, by sheer virtue of its size, its free traditions, and the habit of initiative in its people, the leadership of progress must ultimately rest." For the remainder of his days, Wells kept an eye on America, watching particularly for any lapses from this responsible role which he had assigned to it.

Thus, although Wells did not visit the United States again until after the First World War, American issues were never far from his mind. When the War broke out in 1914, he wrote, at the suggestion of the British Chancellor of the Exchequer, David Lloyd George, an appeal to the American people, and he did all that he could to bring the United States into the conflict on the side of the Allies. When the war ended in 1918, Wells urged the United States to take a positive and constructive role in the peace settlement. In November 1917, in a letter which he sent through Bainbridge Colby for the attention of President Wilson, he had called upon the United States to become the "advocate of the new order" in the world. Similar thoughts were in Wells's mind when he visited the United States for short periods in 1921, 1934, 1935, 1937, and 1940. In spite of all of Wells's criticisms of America in the 1920s and 1930s for not assuming its responsibilities of world leadership, it was to the United States that he went, when the Second World War had broken out, on a coast-to-coast lecturing crusade with the theme "Two Hemispheres or One World," in search of support for his Declaration of Human Rights.

It was to the English-speaking peoples, especially the United States and Britain, that Wells had assigned a major role in the emergence of the World State as far back as the beginning of the twentieth century when he had published his *Anticipations*. At the end of *The Future in America*, however, Wells showed that he was by no means certain that America could play this part in the achievement of an international government. And yet, from the time of his first visit to the United States in 1906, he never gave up the hope; and he never lost interest in America or ceased to question its destiny. With memories of this visit in mind, H. G. Wells expressed his American credo when he wrote "Some Plain Words to Americans" in *The Way The World is Going* (1928): "America is part of my spiritual home and Old Glory one of my quarterings. I have a loyal feeling for the American eagle. It is so loyal a feeling that I cannot bear to think of that bird as anything but aquiline."

H. G. Wells, by Theodore Spicer-Simson, medallion, 1921. National Portrait Gallery, London.

301   *H. G. Wells*

Bibliography

A great many of the sources used in writing these essays are available only in their original languages. The following is offered for the convenience of the English-speaking reader.

Marquis de Chastellux

CHASTELLUX, FRANÇOIS-JEAN MARQUIS DE. *Travels in North America* (edited and translated by Howard C. Rice, Jr.). Chapel Hill, 1963.

Pavel Svin'in

DAVIDSON, MARSHALL B. "Voyage Pittoresque aux États-Unis de l'Amérique," *American Heritage,* Vol. IX, No. 2, February 1964.

JEFFREY, MARGARET. "As the Russians Saw Us in 1812," *Metropolitan Museum of Art Bulletin,* Vol. I, No. 3, 1942.

YARMOLINSKY, AVRAHM. *Picturesque United States of America, 1811, 1812, 1813.* New York, 1930

Charles Sealsfield

JORDAN, E. L. *America: Glorious and Chaotic Land; Charles Sealsfield Discovers The Young United States.* Englewood Cliffs, New Jersey, 1969.

SEALSFIELD, CHARLES. *The Americans as They Are.* London, 1828.
—*The Cabin Book.* New York, 1844.

Frances Trollope

FRAZEE, MONIQUE PARENT. *Mrs. Trollope and America.* Publications de la Faculté des Lettres et Sciences Humaines de l'Université de Caen, France, 1969.

GERBI, ANTONELLO. *The Dispute of the New World: The History of a Polemic, 1750–1900* (translated by Jeremy Moyle). Pittsburgh, 1973.

TROLLOPE, FRANCES. *Domestic Manners of the Americans* (with illustrations by Auguste Hervieu). London, 1832.
—*Domestic Manners of the Americans With a History of Mrs. Trollope's Adventures in America* (edited by Donald Smalley). New York, 1960.
—*The Refugee in America: A Novel.* London, 1832.
—*The Life and Adventures of Jonathan Jefferson Whitlaw; or Scenes on the Mississippi.* London, 1836.
—*The Barnabys in America; or the Adventures of the Widow Wedded.* London, 1843.

Sándor Farkas Bölöni and Ágoston Mokcsai Haraszthy

GASPAR, STEVEN. *Four Nineteenth-Century Hungarian Travelers in America.* Unpublished dissertation, University of Southern California, 1967.

KATONA, ANNA. "Hungarian Travelogues on the Pre-Civil-War United States," *Hungarian Studies in English,* 1971.

LUKINICH, IMRE. "American Democracy as Seen by Hungarians of the Age of Reform," *Journal of Central European Affairs,* Vol. 3, 1948.

WAGNER, FRANCIS S. "The Start of Cultural Exchange Between the Hungarian Academy of Sciences and the American Philosophical Society," *The Hungarian Quarterly,* April–June, 1965.

Alexis de Tocqueville

LIVELY, JACK. *The Social and Political Thought of Alexis de Tocqueville.* Oxford, 1965.

PIERSON, GEORGE W. *Tocqueville and Beaumont in America.* New York, 1938.

RICHTER, MELVIN. "The Uses of Theory: Tocqueville's Adaptation of Montesquieu," *Essays in Theory and History, An Approach to the Social Sciences* (edited by M. Richter). Cambridge, 1970.

TOCQUEVILLE, ALEXIS DE. *Democracy in America* (edited by J. P. Mayer and Max Lerner; translated by George Lawrence). New York, 1966.

Harriet Martineau

MARTINEAU, HARRIET. *Society in America.* London, 1837.
—*How to Observe.* Philadelphia, 1838.
—*Retrospect of Western Travel.* London, 1838.
—*Autobiography* (edited by Maria Weston Chapman; 2 volumes). Boston, 1877.

MILLER, MRS. F. FENWICK. *Harriet Martineau.* London, 1844.

WEBB, R. K. *Harriet Martineau; A radical Victorian.* New York, 1960.

Fanny Kemble

KEMBLE, FRANCES ANNE. *Journal (August 1, 1832–July 17, 1834).* Philadelphia, 1835.
—*Journal of a Residence on a Georgian Plantation in 1838–1839.* New York, 1960.

LOMBARD, MILDRED E. "Contemporary Opinions of Mrs. Kemble's *Journal of a Residence on a Georgian Plantation," Georgia Historical Quarterly,* December, 1950.

RUSHMORE, ROBERT. *Fanny Kemble.* New York, 1970.

WRIGHT, CONSTANCE. *Fanny Kemble and the Lovely Land.* New York, 1972.

Charles Dickens

DICKENS, CHARLES. *American Notes.* New York, 1842.
—*Martin Chuzzlewit.* New York, 1844.
—*Letters* (edited by Walter Dexter; 3 volumes). Bloomsbury, 1937.
—*Speeches* (edited by K. J. Fielding). Oxford, 1960.
—*Letters* (edited by Madeline House, Graham Storey, *et al.;* 3 volumes). Oxford, 1965.

FORESTER, JOHN. *The Life of Charles Dickens* (edited by J. W. T. Ley). New York, 1928.

JOHNSON, EDGAR. *Charles Dickens: his Tragedy and Triumph* (2 volumes). New York, 1952.

WILKINS, WILLIAM CLYDE (ed.). *Charles Dickens in America.* London, 1911.

John Manjirō

KANEKO, HISAKAZU. *Manjirō, the man who discovered America.* Tokyo, 1956.

SAKAMAKI, SHUNZŌ. *Japan and the United States, 1790–1853,* The Transactions of the Asiatic Society of Japan, Second Series, Vol. XVIII, Tokyo, 1939.

WARRINER, EMILY V. *Voyager to Destiny.* New York, 1956.

Domingo Faustino Sarmiento

BUNKLEY, ALLISON WILLIAMS. *The Life of Sarmiento.* Princeton, 1952.

LEONARD, IRVING A. "Sarmiento's Visits to North America: A Famous Argentine in the United States of the 1840s," *Michigan Alumnus Quarterly,* Vol. XIIX, August 1943.

ONÍS, JOSÉ DE. *The United States as seen by Spanish American writers, 1776–1890.* New York, 1952.

SARMIENTO, DOMINGO FAUSTINO. *Life in the Argentine Republic in the Days of the Tyrants; or, Civilization and Barbarism* (translated by Mary Mann). New York, 1868.
—*A Sarmiento Anthology* (translated by Stuart Edgar Grummon, edited by Allison Williams Bunkley). Princeton, 1948.
—*Sarmiento's Travels in the United States in 1847* (edited and translated by Michael Aaron Rockland). Princeton, 1970.

Fredrika Bremer

BREMER, FREDRIKA. *America of the Fifties: Letters of Fredrika Bremer* (edited by Adolph B. Benson). New York, 1924.
—*The Homes of the New World; Impressions of America* (translated by Mary Howitt). New York, 1853.

ROOTH, SIGNE ALICE. *Seeress of the Northland: Fredrika Bremer's American Journey, 1849–1851.* Philadelphia, 1955. Includes complete bibliography.

Louis Kossuth

KOSSUTH, LOUIS. *Select speeches of Kossuth* (edited by Francis W. Newman). London, 1853.

PULSZKY, FRANCIS and THERESA. *White, red and black.* London, 1853.

SEBESTYEN, ENDRE. *Kossuth, a Magyar apostle of world democracy.* Pittsburgh, 1950.

TEFFT, BENJAMIN F. *Hungary and Kossuth: or, an American exposition of the Hungarian Revolution.* Philadelphia, 1852.

The First Japanese Mission to the United States

DULLES, FOSTER RHEA. *Yankees and Samurai: America's role in the Emergence of Modern Japan: 1791–1900.* New York, 1965.

FUKUZAWA, YUKICHI. *The Autobiography of Yukichi Fukuzawa* (translated by Eiichi Kiyooka). New York, 1966.

HARRIS, TOWNSEND. *The Complete Journal of Townsend Harris* (edited by Mario Emilio Cosenza). Tokyo and Rutland, Vermont, 1959.

JOHNSTON, JAMES D. *China and Japan, being a Narrative of the Cruise of the U.S. Steam Frigate Powhatan, in the Years 1857, '58, '59 and '60, including an account of the Japanese Embassy to the United States.* Philadelphia, 1861.

MURAGAKI, NORIMASA, AWAJI-NO-KAMI. *Kokai Nikki, the Diary of the First Japanese Embassy to the United States of America* (translated by Helen Masu Uno). Tokyo, 1958.

TREAT, PAYSON JACKSON. *Diplomatic Relations between the United States and Japan, 1853–1895.* Stanford, 1932.

William Howard Russell and Edward Dicey

DICEY, EDWARD. *Six Months in the Federal States.* London, 1863.

NEVINS, ALLAN (ed.). *America Through British Eyes.* London, 1948.

RAPSON, RICHARD L. *Britons View America, Travel Commentary 1860–1935.* Seattle, 1971.

RUSSELL, WILLIAM H. *My Diary North and South.* London, 1863.

Edward Wilmot Blyden

BLYDEN, EDWARD WILMOT. *A Voice From Bleeding Africa.* Monrovia, 1856.
—*Christianity, Islam and the Negro Race.* London, 1887.

HOLDEN, EDITH. *Blyden of Liberia.* New York, 1966.

LYNCH, HOLLIS R. *Edward Wilmot Blyden, Pan-Negro Patriot.* London, 1967.

WILSON, HENRY S. (ed.). *Origins of West African Nationalism.* London, 1969.

Georges Clemenceau

CLEMENCEAU, GEORGES. *American Reconstruction 1865–1870* (edited with an introduction by Fernand Baldensperger, translated by Margaret MacVeagh). New York, 1928.

WATSON, DAVID R. *Georges Clemenceau*. London, 1974.

WILLIAMS, WYTHE. *The Tiger of France, Conversations with Clemenceau*. New York, 1949.

Henryk Sienkiewicz

HASKINS, JANINA W. "The Image of America in Accounts of Polish Travelers of the Eighteenth and Nineteenth Centuries," *The Quarterly Journal of The Library of Congress,* Vol. 22, No. 3, July 1965.

MODJESKA, HELENA. *Memories and impressions of Helena Modjeska, an autobiography*. New York, 1910.

NOBILIS, SISTER M. "Sienkiewicz and the Poles in America," *Polish–American Studies,* Vol. II, Nos. 1–2, January–June 1945.

SIENKIEWICZ, HENRY. *Portrait of America, Letters of Henry Sienkiewicz* (edited and translated by Charles Morley). New York, 1954.

"Sienkiewicz and America," *Polish-American Studies* (St. Mary's College Symposium), Vol. XV, Nos. 3–4, July–December 1958.

Charles Boissevain

HANDLIN, OSCAR (ed.). "An Amsterdam Journalist: Charles Boissevain," *This Was America*. Cambridge, Massachusetts, 1969.

ROWEN, HERBERT H. *America: A Dutch Historian's Vision, from Afar and Near*. New York, 1972.

Bjørnstjerne Bjørnson and Halvdan Koht

KOHT, HALVDAN. *The Voice of Norway*. New York, 1944. Includes a brief biography of Bjørnson by Sigmund Skard.
—*Education of an Historian*. New York, 1957.
—*The American Spirit in Europe*. Philadelphia, 1949.

LARSON, HAROLD, and HAUGEN, EINAR. "Bjørnson and America—A Critical Review," *Scandinavian Studies and Notes*, 13, 1933–1935.

James Bryce

BRYCE, JAMES. *The American Commonwealth* (3 volumes). New York, 1888. (Subsequent editions in 2 volumes.)
—"America Revisited: The Changes of a Quarter-Century," *Outlook,* March 25, 1905, pp. 733–740; and April 1, 1905, pp. 846–855.
—*University and Historical Addresses Delivered During a Residence in the United States as Ambassador of Great Britain*. New York, 1913.
—*Modern Democracies* (2 volumes). New York, 1921.
—*International Relations* (eight lectures delivered in the United States in August 1921). New York, 1922.

FISHER, HERBERT A. L. *James Bryce* (2 volumes). New York, 1927.

IONS, EDMUND. *James Bryce and American Democracy*. London, 1968.

José Martí

LIZASO, FELIX. *Martí, Martyr of Cuban Independence*. Albuquerque, 1953.

MANACH, JORGE. *Martí, Apostol of Freedom*. New York, 1960.

MARTÍ, JOSÉ. *The America of José Martí* (translated by Juan de Onís with an introduction by Federico de Onís). New York, 1953.

Antonín Dvořák

LOWENBACH, JAN. *Music in America*. Prague, 1948.
—*Josef Jan Kovařík, Dvořák's American Secretary*. Prague, 1947.

SOUREK, OTAKAR, *The Life and Work of Antonín Dvořák* (4 volumes). Prague, 1954–57.

Swami Vivekananda

BURKE, MARIE LOUISE. *Swami Vivekananda in America, New Discoveries*. Calcutta, 1958.
—*Swami Vivekananda, His Second Visit to the West, New Discoveries*. Calcutta, 1973.

VIVEKANANDA, SWAMI. *The East and the West*. Almora, India, 1944.
—*Letters of Swami Vivekananda*. Almora, India, 1964.
—*The Complete Works of Swami Vivekananda*. Almora, India, 1964.

Giuseppe Giacosa and Giacomo Puccini

CARNER, MOSCO. *Puccini: A Critical Biography*. New York, 1959.

PUCCINI, GIACOMO. *La Fanciulla del West*. New York, 1910.
—*Letters of Giacomo Puccini* (edited by Giuseppe Adami; translated and edited in English version by Ena Makin). Philadelphia, 1931.
—*Madame Butterfly*. New York, 1905.

TORRIELLI, ANDREW J. *Italian Opinion of America as Revealed by Italian Travelers, 1850–1900*. Cambridge, Massachusetts, 1941.

John Butler Yeats

REID, B. L. *The Man from New York: John Quinn and His Friends*. New York, 1968.

YEATS, JOHN BUTLER. *Essays Irish and American*. Dublin and London, 1918.
— *Early Memories: Some Chapters of Autobiography* (with Preface by William Butler Yeats). Churchtown, Dundrum, 1923.
—*Letters to His Son W. B. Yeats and Others 1869–1922* (edited with a Memoir by Joseph Hone, and a Preface by Oliver Elton). London, 1944.

YEATS, WILLIAM BUTLER. *Autobiographies*. London, 1955.

Sholom Aleichem

ALEICHEM, SHOLOM. *Wandering Star*. New York, 1952.
—*Adventures of Mottel the Cantor's Son* (translated by Tamara Kahana). New York, 1953.
—*Stories and Satires* (translated by Curt Leviant). New York, 1959.
—*Some Laughter, Some Tears* (translated by Curt Leviant). New York, 1969.

GRAFSTEIN, M. W. (ed.). *Sholom Aleichem Panorama*. Ontario, Canada, 1948.

SAMUEL, MAURICE. *The World of Sholom Aleichem*. New York, 1963.

WAIFE-GOLDBERG, MARIE. *My Father Sholom Aleichem*. New York, 1968.

Liang Ch'i-ch'ao and Hu Shih

CHANG, HAO. *Liang Ch'i-ch'ao and Intellectual Transition in China, 1890–1907*. Cambridge, Massachusetts, 1971.

GRIEDER, JEROME B. *Hu Shih and the Chinese Renaissance: Liberalism in the Chinese Revolution, 1917–1937*. Cambridge, Massachusetts, 1970.

Hu, Shih. *The Chinese Renaissance*. Chicago, 1934.

HUANG, PHILIP C. *Liang Ch'i Ch'ao and Modern Chinese Liberalism*. Seattle, 1972.

LEVENSON, JOSEPH R. *Liang Ch'i-ch'ao and the Mind of Modern China*. Cambridge, Massachusetts, 1953.

H. G. Wells

BERGONZI, BERNARD. *The Early H. G. Wells*. Manchester, 1961.

DICKSON, LOVAT. *H. G. Wells: His Turbulent Life and Times*. London, 1969.

MACKENZIE, NORMAN and JEANNE. *The Time Traveller. The Life of H. G. Wells*. London, 1973.

WELLS, H. G. *The Future in America. A Search after Realities*. London, 1906.
—*The War in The Air*. London, 1908.
—*H. G. Wells: Journalism and Prophecy, 1893–1946* (edited by W. Warren Wagar). London, 1964.
—and JAMES, HENRY. *Henry James and H. G. Wells. A Record of their Friendship, their Debate on the Art of Fiction, and their Quarrel* (edited by Leon Edel and Gordon N. Ray). London, 1958.

National Portrait Gallery

Supplement to *Abroad in America: Visitors to the New Nation 1776–1914*

The following items, not in the Checklist, have been included in the exhibition:

Giacomo Costantino Beltrami, 1779–1855

ENRICO SCURI, 1805–1884

Oil on canvas, date unknown
87 × 59

○ Accademia Carrara di Belle Arti

H. G. Wells, 1866–1946

SIR WILLIAM ROTHENSTEIN, 1872–1945

Black chalk on paper, 1912
15⁷/₈ × 12¹/₄

✓ National Portrait Gallery, London

The First State Election in Detroit, Michigan

THOMAS MICKELL BURNHAM, 1818–1866

Oil on canvas, 1837
21¹/₂ × 30³/₄

✓ The Detroit Institute of Arts, Gift of Mrs. Samuel T. Carson

Mrs. Anthony Wayne Rollins [Sarah (Sallie) Harris Rodes]

GEORGE CALEB BINGHAM, 1811–1879

Oil on panel, 1834
28 × 23

○ Mrs. Ellsworth A. MacLeod

Battle of the Little Big Horn

Unidentified Indian artist

Chromolithograph, ca. 1866
Gordon Hendricks

Pictograph, natural dye on cotton
69 × 87

○ Mrs. Andrew Wyeth

Poster, Adler Thomashefsky National Theatre, September 26, 1913 for play by Abraham Goldfaden

Printer: Lipshitz Press, New York
44 × 27

✓ American Jewish Historical Society, Waltham, Massachusetts

European Notions of American Manners and Customs

FREDERICK BURR OPPER, 1857–1937

Chromolithograph, in *Puck*, November 16, 1881

✓ Enoch Pratt Free Library, Baltimore, Maryland

The Playfair Papers, or: Brother Jonathan, the Smartest Nation in all Creation

Hugo Playfair, London, 1841, 2 vols.
✓ Princeton University Library, Richard Waln Meirs Collection of Cruikshankia

Including: "Liberty Hall Dining Parlor," aquatint by Robert Cruikshank, 1789–1856, and "House of Representatives During a High Debate on Denouncing the Anti Slavery Petitions," etching by Robert Cruikshank

OAS

Checklist entries 32, 107, 110, 112, 113, and 121 were not included in the exhibition.

Storm in the Rocky Mountains
Unidentified artist after the undated original by Albert Bierstadt, 1830–1902

Lenders
to the Exhibition

Aberdeen Art Gallery,
Scotland

Albany Institute of History and Art

Beth-Sholom Aleichem,
Tel-Aviv, Israel

American Antiquarian Society

American Philosophical Society

American Swedish Historical Museum,
Philadelphia

The Art Institute of Chicago Library

Bodleian Library, Oxford University

Boston Public Library

Bowers Museum,
Santa Ana, California

Fredrika-Bremer-Association,
Stockholm, Sweden

George Mercer Brooke, Jr.

Anne S. K. Brown Military Collection,
Brown University Library

Amon Carter Museum of Western Art,
Fort Worth, Texas

Sarah Chambers

Le Comte Louis de Chastellux

Chicago Historical Society

The Cincinnati Historical Society

Columbia University Libraries

The Corning Museum of Glass,
Corning, New York

Delaware Art Museum

Detroit Public Library, Burton
Historical Collection

Duke University Library

Heirs of Antonín Dvořák

Essex Institute,
Salem, Massachusetts

Town of Fairhaven,
Massachusetts

Field Museum of Natural History,
Chicago

Gemeentearchief,
Amsterdam

Jean and Kahlil Gibran

Harvard Business School

Harvard-Yenching Library, Harvard
University

Einar Haugen

David W. Hazel

Katherine Hellman

Hirschl & Adler Galleries,
New York

The Historic New Orleans Collection

The Historical Society of Pennsylvania

Hoover Institution on War, Revolution
and Peace, Stanford University

Lee Houchins

Houghton Library, Harvard University

Hudson's Bay Company,
Winnipeg, Canada

The Hungarian Reformed Federation of
America, Washington, D.C.

University of Illinois Library,
Urbana-Champaign

Edmund S. Ions

Mrs. E. M. Jacobsen

Victor Jacobs

Keio University Library and Information
Center, Tokyo, Japan

Kochi Castle Office,
Tokyo

Ledlie I. Laughlin, Jr.

The Library Company of Philadelphia

Library of Congress

William S. Lieberman

Lilly Library, Indiana University

Andrew Longacre

Los Angeles County Museum of Art

Louisiana State Museum,
New Orleans

Lowell Historical Society,
Lowell, Massachusetts

Mrs. Ellsworth A. MacLeod

Tracy W. McGregor Library, University
of Virginia, Charlottesville

The Mansell Collection,
London

The Mariners Museum,
Newport News, Virginia

Maritime Safety Agency,
Tokyo, Japan

Maryland Historical Society

Massachusetts Historical Society

The Metropolitan Museum of Art

Metropolitan Opera Archives

The Millicent Library,
Fairhaven, Massachusetts

Montana Historical Society,
Helena

Moorland-Spingarn Research Center,
Howard University

Kiyoshi Morita

The Mount Vernon Ladies' Association of
the Union

William M. Murphy

Musée National du Château de
Versailles

Múséo Historico Sarmiento,
Buenos Aires, Argentina

Museum of Fine Arts, Boston

Museum of the City of New York

Muzeum Antonína Dvořáka,
Prague, Czechoslovakia

Muzeum Henryka Sienkiewicza,
Oblegorku, Poland

NRC Handelsblad,
Rotterdam, Holland

Nasjonalgalleriet,
Oslo, Norway

National Archives and Records Service,
Washington, D.C.

National Collection of Fine Arts,
Smithsonian Institution

National Gallery of Art,
Washington, D.C.

National Museum,
Warsaw, Poland

The National Museum of History and
Technology, Smithsonian Institution

National Portrait Gallery,
London

Prince Charles Philippe d'Orléans
Bourbon, Duc de Nemours

New Bedford Whaling Museum

The New Jersey Historical Society

The New York Public Library

The Newberry Library,
Chicago

Ada Nisbet

Vesterheim, Norwegian-American
Museum, Decorah, Iowa

Östermalm's High School,
Stockholm

Walter Hines Page Library, Randolph-
Macon College

The Pennsylvania Academy of the Fine
Arts

Philadelphia Museum of Art

Enoch Pratt Free Library,
Baltimore

Presbyterian Historical Society,
Philadelphia

Museum of Art,
Rhode Island School of Design

Duchesse Edmée de la
Rochefoucauld

Abby Aldrich Rockefeller Folk Art
Collection, Williamsburg, Virginia

Philip H. & A. S. W. Rosenbach
Foundation, Philadelphia

Resia Schor

Sealsfied-Sammlung Kresse, Charles
Sealsfield-Gesellschaft, Stuttgart

Sigmund and Aase Gruda Skard

Sophia Smith Collection, Smith College
Library

Sophienburg Museum,
New Braunfels, Texas

Ira Spanierman, Inc.,
New York

THE STAMFORD HISTORICAL SOCIETY, INC.,
Stamford, Connecticut

RUTH CHAMBERS STEWART

UNIVERSITETSBIBLIOTEKET I OSLO,
Oslo, Norway

UNIVERSITY OF CHICAGO LIBRARY

VASSAR COLLEGE ART GALLERY

VEDANTA SOCIETY OF NORTHERN CALIFORNIA
AND VEDANTA SOCIETY, *Berkeley*

DR. AND MRS. RICHARD VOGLER

MARIE WAIFE-GOLDBERG

WILLARD D. WHITFIELD

MRS. ANDREW WYETH

YALE UNIVERSITY LIBRARY

YIVO INSTITUTE FOR JEWISH RESEARCH, INC.,
New York

Checklist
of the Exhibition

Items are listed in the order of their appearance in the exhibition. Dimensions are in inches, height preceding width.

---

1 (page 2)
Marquis de Chastellux, 1734–1788
Attributed to MADAME MARIE LOUISE
ELISABETH VIGÉE-LE BRUN, 1755–1842
Oil on canvas, 1789
Size not available
Le Comte Louis de Chastellux
Posthumous portrait painted from memory, prior to October 5, 1789, when Madame Le Brun, the favorite painter of Queen Marie Antoinette, fell under suspicion of the Revolutionary government and fled to Italy.

2 (page 5)
Washington and his Generals at Yorktown
Attributed to CHARLES WILLSON PEALE,
1741–1827
Oil on canvas, circa 1786
$29\frac{9}{16}$ x $21\frac{3}{8}$
Maryland Historical Society
Washington is the central figure of the group of six officers standing in the foreground. He is extending his arm across the figure of the Marquis de Lafayette. Standing between Lafayette and Washington is General Benjamin Lincoln. To Washington's left is the Comte de Rochambeau. The Marquis de Chastellux stands to Rochambeau's left. Lieutenant Tench Tilghman is the figure at the far right.

3
Reddition de l'Armée Angloises Commandée par Mylord Comte de Cornwallis aux Armees Combinées des Etats Unis de l'Amérique et de la France aux ordres des Generaux Washington et de Rochambeau à Yorktown et Glocester dans la Virginie, le 19 Octobre 1781.
Imaginary view published by Mondhare, Paris
Engraving, date unknown
$15\frac{5}{8}$ x 22

Anne S. K. Brown Military Collection,
Brown University Library

4 (page 9)
Samuel Adams, 1722–1803
SAMUEL OKEY, active in America 1773–1780,
after JOHN MITCHELL, after the 1770–1772
oil by JOHN SINGLETON COPLEY, 1738–1815
Mezzotint, 1775
$13\frac{1}{2}$ x $9\frac{1}{2}$
Inscribed: *"Mr. Samuel Adams/J. Mitchell pinx!/Sam!. Okey Fecit./When haughty NORTH impress'd with proud Disdain,/ Spurn'd at the Virtue which rejects his Chain;/ Hear with a Tyrant Scorn our Rights implor'd,/ And when we su'd for Justice sent the Sword:/ Let ADAMS rest in Warfare nobly try'd,/ His Country's Saviour: Father, Shield, and Guide,/Urg'd by her Wrongs he wag'd y^e glorious Strife/Nor paus'd to waste a Coward Thought on Life./Printed by and for Chas Reak & Sam!. Okey/New port Rhode Island. April.1775."*
Massachusetts Historical Society

5
Old Lutheran Church, in Fifth Street, Philadelphia
WILLIAM BIRCH, 1755–1834
Engraving and etching, 1800
$9\frac{1}{8}$ x $11\frac{1}{8}$
Inscribed: *"Old LUTHERAN CHURCH, in Fifth Street PHILADELPHIA/Drawn & Engraved & Published by W. Birch & Son./Sold by R. Campbell & Co. N° 50 Chestnut Street, Philad^a 1800."*
The Library Company of Philadelphia

6 (page 7)
Voyage de Newport à Philadephie, Albany, &c.
Marquis de Chastellux, Newport,
Rhode Island, 1781
(Printed by the Royal French Navy)
Houghton Library, Harvard University

7
Voyages de M. Le Marquis de Chastellux Dans L'Amérique.
Marquis de Chastellux, Paris, 1786
(two volumes)

Victor Jacobs
These volumes were a gift to George Washington, and the title page of the second volume bears his signature.

8
Examen Critique Des Voyages Dans L'Amérique Septentrionale, De M. Le Marquis De Chastellux
J. P. Brissot de Warville, London, 1786
The Newberry Library, Chicago

---

9   (page 12)
Pavel Petrovich Svin'in, 1787–1839
D. KOCH, dates unknown, after an unlocated portrait by WASSILIJ ANDREJEWITCH TROPININ, 1776–1857
Engraving, in *Sketches of Russia,* Moscow, 1839
$6 \times 4\frac{7}{16}$
Library of Congress, Rare Book Division
Tropinin's portrait of Svin'in was painted sometime after the latter's return from the United States in 1813. The background is a view of Niagara Falls, presumably from a sketch by Svin'in.

---

10   (page 16)
A View of the Summer Garden in St. Petersburgh
WILLIAM KNEASS, 1780–1840, after a drawing by PAVEL SVIN'IN
Aquatint, 1813
$4\frac{3}{4} \times 7\frac{3}{8}$
The Library Company of Philadelphia

11
Pantheon of Russian Authors
Karamsin, Moscow, 1801, presented to the American Philosophical Society by Pavel Svin'in
American Philosophical Society

12
Letter, Pavel Svin'in to Dr. James Mease, October 18, 1812, presenting Pantheon of Russian Authors *to the American Philosophical Society*
American Philosophical Society

13   (page 17)
Deck Life on the Paragon, *one of [Robert] Fulton's steamboats, with Fort Putnam and West Point in the background*
PAVEL SVIN'IN, 1787–1839
Watercolor on paper, circa 1812
$9\frac{7}{8} \times 14\frac{5}{16}$
The Metropolitan Museum of Art, Rogers Fund, 1942

14
Travel by stagecoach near Trenton, New Jersey
PAVEL SVIN'IN, 1787–1839
Watercolor on paper, circa 1812
$6\frac{7}{8} \times 9\frac{3}{4}$
The Metropolitan Museum of Art, Rogers Fund, 1942

15   (page 19)
The Pennsylvania Hospital, Philadelphia
PAVEL SVIN'IN, 1787–1839
Watercolor on paper, circa 1812
$5\frac{3}{8} \times 8\frac{1}{2}$
The Metropolitan Museum of Art, Rogers Fund, 1942

16
Two Indians and a white man, probably the artist
PAVEL SVIN'IN, 1787–1839
Watercolor on paper, circa 1812
$5\frac{7}{8} \times 8\frac{5}{8}$
The Metropolitan Museum of Art, Rogers Fund, 1942

17
Mourning Piece for George Washington
ENOCH G. GRIDLEY, active 1803–1919, after JOHN COALES, JUNIOR, 1776/80–1854
Engraving, 1810
$14 \times 10\frac{1}{8}$
Anne S. K. Brown Military Collection, Brown University Library

18   (page 20)
John Bill Ricketts with his horse Cornplanter
GILBERT STUART, 1755–1838
Oil on canvas, circa 1793–1799
$29\frac{5}{8} \times 24\frac{1}{4}$
National Gallery of Art, Washington, D.C., Gift of Mrs. Robert B. Noyes in memory of Elisha Riggs, 1943

19
"Observations of a Russian in America," by Pavel Svin'in, in *Syn Otechestra,* Russia, 1814
Library of Congress

---

20   (page 22)
Charles Sealsfield, 1793–1864
C. RUST, dates unknown
Photograph, Solothurn, Switzerland, 1864
Sealsfield-Sammlung Kresse, Charles Sealsfield-Gesellschaft, Stuttgart, Germany

---

21
Die Vereinigten Staaten von Nordamerika
C. Sidons [Sealsfield], Stuttgart, 1827
Sealsfield-Sammlung Kresse, Charles Sealsfield-Gesellschaft, Stuttgart, Germany

22 (page 24)
Kreuzherren Monastery, Prague
Photograph, date unknown
From original in Charles Sealsfield-Gesell-
schaft, Stuttgart, Germany

23 (page 25)
John Quincy Adams, 1767–1848
HORATIO GREENOUGH, 1805–1852
White marble, 1828 or 1829
Height $12\frac{5}{8}$
Museum of Fine Arts, Boston

24
General Andrew Jackson
Unidentified artist
Watercolor, 1819
$9\frac{3}{4} \times 7\frac{7}{8}$
Ledlie I. Laughlin, Jr.

25
Letter, Charles Sealsfield to Brantz Mayer,
4 November 1837
Boston Public Library

26
Der Libanoner Morgenstern, July 23, 1830
Published by Jacob Stover, Lebanon,
Pennsylvania
Private collection

27
Market Square, Germantown
WILLIAM BRITTON, dates unknown
Oil on canvas, circa 1820
$12\frac{1}{4} \times 19\frac{7}{8}$
Philadelphia Museum of Art

28 (page 28)
The Olivier Plantation, Alexandria, Louisiana
MARIE ADRIAN PERSAC, active Louisiana
1857–1872
Watercolor and collage on paper, 1861
16 x 22
Louisiana State Museum

29
The Presidents of the United States
JOHN WILLIAM CASILEAR, 1811–1893, after
ROBERT WALTER WEIR, 1803–1889
Engraving, 1834
Inscribed: *"Designed by Robert W. Weir./*
Engraved by J. W. Casilear/The Presidents of
the United States./From Original and Accurate
Portraits./Painted & Engraved expressly for the
New York Mirror."
Division of Graphic Arts, The National
Museum of History and Technology,
Smithsonian Institution
Clockwise from top center: George Washington,
Thomas Jefferson, James Monroe, Andrew
Jackson, John Quincy Adams, James Madison,
John Adams.

30
Trial by Jury [formerly known as *Trial in a*
Country Court]
A. WIGHE, dates unknown
Oil on canvas, 1849
$34\frac{3}{4} \times 47\frac{3}{4}$
Museum of Art, Rhode Island School of
Design

31
Das Cajütenbuch oder nationale
Charakteristiken
Charles Sealsfield, Elberfeld, 1844
Sealsfield-Sammlung Kresse, Charles
Scalsfield-Gesellschaft, Stuttgart, Germany

32
Saengerhalle, Meeting Place of Germania
Singing Society
JULIUS PLOETZE, dates unknown
Oil on canvas, 1862
35 x 29 (approximate)
Sophienburg Museum, New Braunfels,
Texas

33 (page 32)
Frances Milton Trollope, 1780–1863
AUGUSTE HERVIEU, 1794–post 1858
Oil on canvas, circa 1832
$4\frac{7}{8} \times 3\frac{7}{8}$
National Portrait Gallery, London

34
The Matthew-orama for 1824, or Pretty
Considerable D-D Particular Tid-Bits from
America, — Being 'All Well at Natchitoches.'
GEORGE CRUIKSHANK, 1792–1878
Hand-colored broadside cartoon, 1824
Size not available
Dr. and Mrs. Robert Vogler

35
Original manuscript of Frances Trollope's
Domestic Manners of the Americans
Lilly Library, Indiana University, Bloom-
ington

36 (page 35)
Cincinnati: The Public Landing
JOHN CASPER WILD, circa 1804–1846
Gouache on paper, 1835
$19\frac{7}{8} \times 25\frac{3}{4}$
The Cincinnati Historical Society

37 (page 36)
Mrs. Trollope's Bazaar
Unidentified artist
Engraving, date unknown
$9\frac{1}{2}$ x 6
Inscribed: *"The Bazaar. Erected By Mrs.*

Trollope, 1828–9; Demolished in March, 1881"
The Cincinnati Historical Society

38
Henry E. Spencer, ?–1882
AUGUSTE HERVIEU, 1794–post 1858
Watercolor on paper, 1830
$5\frac{1}{4}$ × 4
Andrew Longacre
Spencer was the editor of the Cincinnati
Daily Whig *and mayor of Cincinnati from
1843 to 1851.*

39
Electra Spencer, dates unknown
AUGUSTE HERVIEU, 1794–post 1858
Watercolor on paper, 1830
$5\frac{1}{4}$ × 4
Andrew Longacre

40
Oliver M. Spencer, 1781–1838
AUGUSTE HERVIEU, 1794–post 1858
Watercolor on paper, 1830
$5\frac{1}{4}$ × 4
Andrew Longacre
*Spencer, a Cincinnati merchant, was the author
of* Indian Captivity, a True Narrative of the
Reverend O. M. Spencer by the Indians in
the Neighbourhood of Cincinnati.

41
Thomas Jefferson, 1743–1826
MICHEL SOKOLNICKI, 1760–1816, after
TADEUSZ ANDRZEJ BONAWENTURA
KOSCIUSZKO, 1746–1817
Aquatint, 1798/99
$9\frac{7}{8}$ × $8\frac{5}{16}$
National Portrait Gallery, Smithsonian
Institution

42
Frances Trollope's "Notebook #1"
Lilly Library, Indiana University,
Bloomington

43
Scene in a Fashionable Boarding House
JOHN H. BUFFORD, active 1835–1871
Lithograph, colored, circa 1840
$11\frac{1}{4}$ × $9\frac{3}{4}$
Museum of the City of New York

44 (page 39)
The Trollope Family
CEPHAS GRIER CHILDS, 1793–1871, and
HENRY INMAN, 1801–1846
Lithograph, circa 1832
$10\frac{3}{4}$ × $12\frac{3}{4}$
Inscribed: *"Published by Childs & Inman
Lithographers, 122 Walnut Street, Philadel-
phia./From a sketch taken from life, made in
Cincinnati in 1829/Entered according to act
of Congress in the year 1832 by Childs & Inman

*in the Clerks office of the District Court of the
Eastern District of Pennsylvania."*
The Cincinnati Historical Society

45
Domestic Manners of the Americans
FRANCES TROLLOPE, New York, 1832
Walter Hines Page Library, Randolph-
Macon College, Ashland, Virginia
*First American edition, with marginal notes
by irate readers such as "Liar . . . She is a
fool . . . You old bitch, you don't know what
refinement is . . . Hell is too good a place for
you, you insane wretch . . ."*

46 (page 40)
Box at the Theatre
JOHN B. PENDLETON, 1798–1866 after
AUGUSTE HERVIEU, 1794–post 1858
Lithograph, 1832, from *Domestic Manners of
the Americans,* New York, 1832, facing page
116
Photograph courtesy Harvard University
Library

47
*"Trollopania; Being A Series Of Sketches To
Be Referred To In Perusing The Domestic
Manners of the Americans, By Mrs. Trollope."*
In David Claypoole Johnston's *Scraps
No. 4,* 1833
American Antiquarian Society

48
*Trollopiad, or Travelling Gentlemen in
America*
NIL ADMIRARI, ESQ. (pseudonym for Fred-
erick William Shelton), New York, 1837
Library of Congress

---

49 (page 44)
Sándor Farkas Bölöni, 1795–1842
Unidentified artist
Engraving, in Bölöni's *West European Diary,*
1943
Photograph courtesy Dr. Alfred Reisch

---

50 (page 47)
Mount Vernon, Tomb of Washington, 1832
GEORGE LEHMAN, ?–1870, after JOHN
RUBENS SMITH, 1775–1849
Lithograph, 1832
Size not available
The Mount Vernon Ladies' Association of
the Union

---

51 (page 44)
Ágoston Mokcsai Haraszthy, 1812–1869
Photograph by R. H. Furman, San Francisco,
of an unlocated daguerreotype
Portage Free Library, Portage, Wisconsin

52
Indian Council at Tallequah
JOHN MIX STANLEY, 1814–1872
Oil on canvas, 1843
31 x 40
National Collection of Fine Arts, on loan
from the Department of Ethnology, the
National Museum of Natural History,
Smithsonian Institution

53   (page 52)
Alexis de Tocqueville, 1805–1859
THÉODORE CHASSÉRIAU, 1819–1856
Oil on canvas
$64\frac{1}{4}$ x $52\frac{3}{8}$
Musée National du Château de Versailles

54
De la Démocratie en Amérique
ALEXIS DE TOCQUEVILLE, Brussels, 1835
Library of Congress

55   (page 55)
Gustave de Beaumont de la Bonninière, 1802–1866
Unidentified artist [signature illegible]
Drawing, 1837
Original unlocated; reproduced in G. W.
Pierson, *Tocqueville and Beaumont in America*, New York, 1938, facing page 22

56
Marie, ou l'Esclavage aux Etats-Unis, Tableau de moeurs américaines
Gustave de Beaumont, Brussels, 1835
Tracy W. McGregor Library, University of
Virginia.

57   (page 56)
Vue de la prison d'Auburn prise du Belveder d'American hotel
GUSTAVE DE BEAUMONT, 1802–1866
Ink and wash drawing, July 14, 1831
$4\frac{1}{4}$ x $6\frac{1}{4}$
Photograph courtesy The Beinecke Rare
Book and Manuscript Library, Yale University
From the unlocated "Romanet" album of Beaumont's sketches of the United States.

58
Du système pénitentiaire aux Etats-Unis, et de son application en France
Gustave Auguste de Beaumont de la
Bonninière, Paris, 1833
Library of Congress

59   (page 57)
Forêt de Saginaw, Tocqueville and Beaumont with their Indian guide

GUSTAVE DE BEAUMONT, 1802–1866
Ink and wash drawing, 25 July 1831
$4\frac{1}{4}$ x $6\frac{1}{4}$
Photograph courtesy The Beinecke Rare
Book and Manuscript Library, Yale University
From the unlocated "Romanet" album of Beaumont's sketches of the United States.

60
City of Detroit, Michigan
WILLIAM J. BENNETT, 1787–1844, after
FREDERICK GRAIN, active 1833–1857
Aquatint, 1837
$15\frac{5}{8}$ x $24\frac{3}{4}$
Inscribed: *"Painted by W. J. Bennett from sketch by Fred^k. Grain/Eng^d. by W.J. Bennett/ New York. Henry I. Megarey,/City of Detroit, Michigan./Taken from the Canada shore near the Ferry."*
Burton Historical Collection, Detroit Public
Library.

61
American Log-House. Snake Fence, &c. &c.
JOHN HALKETT, dates unknown
Watercolor, circa 1822
12 x $18\frac{1}{2}$
Hudson's Bay Company, Winnipeg, Canada

62   (page 62)
Harriet Martineau, 1802–1877
CHARLES OSGOOD, 1809–1890
Oil on canvas, 1836
36 x 29
Essex Institute, Salem, Massachusetts
Harriet Martineau was visiting the Stephen C. Phillips family in Salem, Massachusetts, when her host commissioned Osgood—a native Salem artist—to paint this portrait.

63
Society in America
Harriet Martineau, London, 1837
Library of Congress

64
Retrospect of Western Travel
Harriet Martineau, London, 1838
Library of Congress

65
The Abolition Garrison in Danger, & the Narrow Escape of the Scotch Ambassador
Unidentified artist
Lithograph, 1835
Size not available
Inscribed: *"The Abolition Garrison in Danger, & the Narrow Escape of the Scotch Ambassador. Boston, Oct. 21st, 1835."*

The New York Public Library
Photo reproduction of the original in The New-York Historical Society

66
Anti-slavery Banner "The Almighty/Has No Attribute/That Can Take Sides/With The Slave Holder."
Massachusetts Historical Society

67　(page 65)
Fifth Anniversary of the Massachusetts Anti-Slavery Society, Wednesday, January 25, 1837
Broadside, 1837
Sophia Smith Collection, Smith College Library

68　(page 66)
Margaret Fuller, 1810–1850
HENRY BRYAN HALL, SENIOR, 1808–1884
Stipple engraving, date unknown
$9\frac{1}{4} \times 6$
National Portrait Gallery, Smithsonian Institution

69
Solitude
MARY S. CHAPIN, dates unknown
Watercolor, date unknown
$15\frac{1}{4} \times 13\frac{5}{8}$
M. & M. Karolik Collection, Museum of Fine Arts, Boston

70
John and Abigail Montgomery
JOSEPH H. DAVIS, active 1832–1837
Watercolor on paper, 1836
$8\frac{7}{8} \times 14$ (sight)
National Gallery of Art, Edgar William and Bernice Chrysler Garbisch Collection

71
Letter, Harriet Martineau to Charles Brooks, January 25, 1835, describing her experiences in Washington, D.C.
Library of Congress, Manuscript Division

72　(page 70)
United States Senate Chamber
THOMAS DONEY, active in New York City, 1844–1852, after JAMES A. WHITEHORNE, 1803–1888
Engraving, probably 1846
Inscribed: *"Designed by J. Whitehorne, N.A./ Engraved by T. Doney/United States Senate Chamber./Engraved from Daguerreotype Likenesses in the National Miniature Gallery of Anthony, Clark & Co. (Late Anthony, Edwards & Co)/Published by Edward Anthony, 247 Broadway, N. York./Proof/Printed w Powell & Co."*
National Portrait Gallery, Smithsonian Institution

73　(page 72)
Frances Anne Kemble, 1809–1893
THOMAS SULLY, 1783–1872
Oil on canvas, 1833
$30 \times 25\frac{1}{8}$
The Pennsylvania Academy of the Fine Arts, Bequest of Henry C. Carey, 1879
Kemble is portrayed in the role of "Beatrice."

74
Fanny Kemble's annotated journal
Fanny Kemble, Philadelphia, 1835
(2 volumes)
Brander Matthews Collection, Columbia University Libraries

75　(page 75)
Pierce Butler, 1807–1867
Photograph of a lost daguerreotype, probably made around 1840
From the original in The Historical Society of Pennsylvania

76　(page 76)
House lived in by Fanny and Pierce Butler on the Georgia plantation, 1838–1839
Photograph, in Fanny Kemble Wister's *Fanny, The American Kemble*, Tallahassee, 1972

77
Georgia plantation scene in 19th century
From original photograph at the Historical Society of Pennsylvania

78
On To Liberty
THEODOR KAUFMANN, 1814–post 1887
Oil on canvas, 1867
$36\frac{1}{16} \times 56$
Hirschl & Adler Galleries, New York

79　(page 78)
A Planter's Lady
AUGUSTE HERVIEU, 1794–post 1858
Engraving, frontispiece in Frances Trollope's *The Life and Adventures of Jonathan Jefferson Whitlaw or Scenes in the Mississippi*, London, 1836, Vol. II

80　(page 79)
Woodcutter's Cabin on the Mississippi
ENDICOTT and SWETT, engravers active in Baltimore and New York, 1831–1836, after AUGUSTE HERVIEU, 1794–post 1858
Lithograph, in Frances Trollope's *Domestic Manners of the Americans*, New York, 1832

81
The Sedgwick Mansion, Stockbridge, Massachusetts

COATS and COSINE, after an original sketch
by JOHN KIRK, circa 1823–circa 1862
Steel engraving, date unknown
$8\frac{3}{8}$ x 6
Inscribed: *"From an original sketch/J. Kirk/
The Sedgwick Mansion, Stockbridge, Mass./
Birthplace of C. M. Sedgwick/G. P. Putnam &
Co. N. Y./Printed by Coats & Cosine."*
National Portrait Gallery, Smithsonian
Institution

82
Catharine Maria Sedgwick, 1789–1867
ASHER BROWN DURAND, 1796–1886, after
an unlocated portrait by CHARLES
CROMWELL INGHAM, 1796–1863
Line engraving, 1832
$4\frac{5}{16}$ x $3\frac{7}{16}$
Inscribed: *"Painted by Chas. Ingham & Eng.
by A. B. Durand/Catharine M. Sedgwick/
[sign]/Entered according to act of Congress
in the year 1832 by James Herring in the clerk's
office of the District Court of the Southern
District of New York."*
National Portrait Gallery, Smithsonian
Institution

---

83   (page 82)
Charles Dickens, 1812–1870
FRANCIS ALEXANDER, 1800–1881
Oil on canvas, 1842
44 x $35\frac{1}{2}$
Museum of Fine Arts, Boston, Gift of the
Estate of Mrs. James T. Fields

84
*Synopsis of Phrenology; and the Phrenological
Developements. Together with The Character
and Talents, of C. Dickens Esq. As Given By
L. N. Fowler Feb. 5 1842.*
Inscribed at bottom of pamphlet: *"Taken by
L. N. Fowler at the Residence of the Hon. John
Davis, in Worcester, while Mr. Dickens was
visiting there."*
American Antiquarian Society

85
Streets of Boston Tremont Street
EPHRAIM BOUVÉ, 1817–1897 and WILLIAM
SHARP, c. 1802–?, after PHILIP HARRY
(active in Boston, 1843–1847)
Lithograph, 1843
$11\frac{15}{16}$ x $13\frac{3}{16}$
Inscribed: *"P. Harry delt./Entered according
to act of congress in the Year 1843 by P. Harry
in the clerk's office of the district court of Mas-
sachusetts/THE STREETS OF BOSTON TRE-
MONT STREET./Bouvé & Sharp, Liths. 221
Washington St. Boston."*
The Boston Public Library, Print Department

86
*Yankee Notes for English Circulation, Or Boz
in A-Merry-Key. "A Comic Song . . . arranged
to an American Air"*
James Burton and George Loder, London
Sheet music, date unknown
Professor Ada Nisbet, University of Cali-
fornia, Los Angeles

87   (page 87)
*Lowell Offerings, November, 1845. A Reposi-
tory of Original Articles Written by "Factory
Girl."*
Lowell and Boston, 1845
Massachusetts Historical Society

88
Mill Pond and Mills, Lowell, Massachusetts
THOMAS DOUGHTY, 1793–1856
Oil on canvas, circa 1833
26 x $35\frac{1}{2}$
Harvard Business School

89
*General View of Lowell. From House of Elisha
Fuller, Esquire*
E. A. BARRAR, dates unknown
Lithograph, 1834
Size not available
Lowell Historical Society

90
The Book Bindery
Unidentified artist
Pencil and watercolor, 1852
$5\frac{1}{8}$ x $9\frac{7}{8}$
M. & M. Karolik Collection, Museum of
Fine Arts, Boston

91
Niagara Falls
Unidentified artist
Oil on panel, circa 1850
24 x 34
Abby Aldrich Rockefeller Folk Art Collec-
tion, Williamsburg, Virginia

92
Snapping Turtle (Peter Pitchlyn) 1806–1881
GEORGE CATLIN, 1796–1872
Oil on canvas, 1836
29 x 24
National Collection of Fine Arts, Smith-
sonian Institution

93   (page 88)
Five Points, New York, Park and Worth Streets
Unidentified artist
Lithograph, in Valentine's *Manual of the
Corporation of the City of New York*, 1855
7 x $11\frac{3}{4}$

Inscribed: "*McSpedeon & Baker, Lith./For Valentine's Manual/Five Points, 1827.*"
National Portrait Gallery, Smithsonian Institution

94
View of the Terrific Explosion at the Great Fire in New York
NATHANIEL CURRIER, 1813–1888
Lithograph, New York, 1845
$8\frac{7}{8}$ x $12\frac{1}{8}$
Inscribed: "*Lith. & Pub. by N. Currier, 2 Spruce St., N.Y., View of the Terrific Explosion At The Great Fire in New York./From Broad St. – July 19th 1845./Engine No. 22 destroyed, and several lives lost./17 stores blown up./ Entered according to Act of Congress in the year 1845 by N. Currier, in the Clerk's Office of the District Court of the Southern District of New York.*"
The Metropolitan Museum of Art, Bequest of Adele S. Colgate, 1963.

95
Eastern State Penitentiary
CEPHAS CHILDS, 1793–1871, after JOHN HAVILAND, 1792–1853
Lithograph, hand-colored, date unknown
$12\frac{1}{4}$ x $16\frac{1}{2}$
Inscribed: "*J. Haviland Architect Del./C.G. Childs Sc./Bird's Eye View of The New State Penitentiary, Now Erecting Near Philadelphia.*"
The Historical Society of Pennsylvania

96
Letter, Charles Dickens to Frances Trollope, 16 December 1842
Henry W. and Albert A. Berg Collection, The New York Public Library, Astor, Lenox and Tilden Foundations

97
Martin Chuzzlewit
CHARLES DICKENS, London, 1844
Professor Ada Nisbet, University of California, Los Angeles

98   (page 91)
The British Lion in America
Unidentified artist
Woodcut, 1868, reproduced in *Dickens in Cartoon and Caricature*, 1924
This is based on one of the well-known photographs of Dickens by Jeremiah Gurney of New York.

99
Manjirō, 1827–1898
Probably KAWADA SHŌRYŌ working under the instruction of Manjirō
Sumi and watercolor on Japanese paper in

John Mung's (Manjirō's) *The Story Five of Japanese; A Very Handsome Tails*, October 26, 1852 (four volumes)
The Philip H. and A. S. W. Rosenbach Foundation Museum
The Millicent Library, Fairhaven, Massachusetts
Also used in the exhibition were the following illustrations from these volumes:
Map of Manjirō's whaling voyages, probably by Kawada Shōryō, diptych, $8\frac{3}{4}$ x $11\frac{1}{2}$
Halcain Island, by John Mung, $10\frac{1}{4}$ x $6\frac{1}{2}$
Crew keep their wives portraits, $10\frac{1}{4}$ x $6\frac{3}{8}$
Stern of John Howland, probably by Kawada Shōryō, diptych, $10\frac{1}{4}$ x 13
View of Hawaii, by John Mung, diptych, $10\frac{1}{4}$ x 13
New Bedford Harbor, $10\frac{1}{2}$ x $6\frac{3}{8}$
View of Boston Harbor, probably Kawada Shōryō, after Manjirō's original crayon drawing of 1846, $10\frac{1}{2}$ x $6\frac{3}{8}$

100
Ship John Howland *of New Bedford*
Unidentified artist
Oil on canvas, circa 1845
$24\frac{3}{8}$ x $29\frac{5}{8}$
New Bedford Whaling Museum; Gift of John H. Ricketson

101
Logbook of the whaler John Howland
Willard D. Whitfield

102
Captain William H. Whitfield
Photograph, date unknown
Town of Fairhaven, Massachusetts

103
Letter, Manjirō to Captain William H. Whitfield, Honolulu, October 30, 1848, thanking Whitfield for his "fatherly treatment."
Willard D. Whitfield

104
Mrs. Higgins
Daguerreotype, Philadelphia, date unknown
$3\frac{3}{4}$ x $3\frac{1}{4}$
Mrs. Ruth Chambers Stewart and Miss Sara Chambers

105
Manjirō's translation of the navigational tables of Nathaniel Bowditch's The New American Practical Navigator, *14th edition, 1844. Translated by order of the Japanese Government, 1855–1857.*
Hydrographic Department, Maritime Safety Agency, Tokyo

106
*Kakemono, scroll of the English alphabet
lettered by Manjirō*
Kochi Castle Office, Tokyo

---

107 (page 104)
Domingo Faustino Sarmiento, 1811–1888
FRANKLIN RAWSON, dates unknown
Oil on canvas, Chile, 1845
Size not available
Muséo Historico Sarmiento, Buenos Aires

108
Viajes en Europa, Africa y America
DOMINGO SARMIENTO, Santiago, Vol. II,
1851
Library of Congress

109   (page 107)
An Argentine gaucho
Photograph, tipped into *Recuerdos del Peru*,
1868
From original in Library of Congress, Division of Prints and Photographs

110   (page 108)
Horace Mann, 1796–1859
Attributed to WILLIAM RIMMER, 1816–1879
Marble, date unknown
Size not available
Muséo Historico Sarmiento, Buenos Aires

111
Mary Peabody Mann, 1806–1887
Daguerreotype, made soon after her marriage in 1843
Massachusetts Historical Society

112
*Dictionary of the Spanish and English
Languages*
Boston, 1847
Muséo Historico Sarmiento, Buenos Aires
*Used by Sarmiento during his United States
visit*

113
Diario de Gastos, *Sarmiento's diary of expenses of his visit to Europe and America,
beginning in Valparaiso, 28 October, 1845*
Muséo Historico Sarmiento, Buenos Aires

114
The Low Pressure Steamboat "Isaac Newton"
NATHANIEL CURRIER, 1813–1888, after
CHARLES PARSONS, 1821–1910
Lithograph, colored, 1855
$20\frac{1}{4}$ x $30\frac{11}{32}$
Inscribed: *"Ch. Parsons Del./Lith. N. Currier/
Entered according to Act of Congress in the
year 1855 by N. Currier in the Clerk's Office
of the District Court of the Southern District
of N.Y./The Low Pressure Steamboat "Isaac
Newton."/Passing The Palisades On The
Hudson River New York"*
Library of Congress, Division of Prints and
Photographs

115
Advertisement for the steamship "Bristol"
ENDICOTT & CO., after CHARLES PARSONS,
1821–1910
Lithograph, colored, date unknown
$22\frac{1}{4}$ x 26
Inscribed: *"Grand Saloon Of The World
Renowned Steamers,/Bristol and Providence./
Commander A. G. Simmons. Commander B.
M. Simmons./Forming the Fall River Line in
connection with the others of the Fleet, namely,
the Newport, Old Colony, Metropolis and
Empire State, making/ in connection with the
Old Colony Rail Road the Great U. S. Mail
Route between New York and Boston via
Newport and Fall River./ A. P. Bacon Superintendent/ Jay Gould President./ Parsons &
Atwater del./ Lithographed and Painted in
Color by Endicott & Co. 39 Beekman St. New
York. . . ."*
The Mariners Museum, Newport News,
Virginia

116
New Orleans
SCHWABE, dates unknown
Lithograph, date unknown
Size not available
Inscribed: *"Lith. v. Schwabe/New-Orleans/
Lith Anst von W. Hagelberg. Berlin"*
The Historic New Orleans Collection

117
Comfort
AUGUSTO FERRAN, dates unknown
Lithograph, hand colored, circa 1850
$10\frac{3}{16}$ x $8\frac{1}{8}$
Inscribed: *"TIPOS CALIFORNIANOS/2/
Augusto Ferran to Litografió./Augusto Ferran/
Litogra. de L. Marquier Ce. de Lamparilla
No. 96"*
Amon Carter Museum of Western Art, Fort
Worth, Texas

118
The Wedding Day
NATHANIEL CURRIER, 1813–1888 and
JAMES MERRITT IVES, 1824–1895
Lithograph, date unknown
Size not available
Library of Congress, Division of Prints and
Photographs

119
*Annual Affair of American Institute at Niblo's
Garden*
B. J. Harrison, active in New York in the
1840s
Watercolor drawing, 1845
$20\frac{1}{4}$ x $27\frac{1}{2}$
Museum of the City of New York
*The American Institute held annual fairs to
publicize and market American products.*

120　(page 113)
The Argentine Legation to the United States
Photograph, 1865
Muséo Historico Sarmiento, Buenos Aires

121
*Sarmiento's doctorate from the University of
Michigan, 1868*
Muséo Historico Sarmiento, Buenos Aires

122　(page 114)
Fredrika Bremer, 1801–1865
Olof Johan Södermark, 1790–1848
Oil on canvas, 1843
$33\frac{1}{2}$ x 25
Östermalm's High School, Stockholm

123
Hemmen i nya verlden
Fredrika Bremer, Stockholm, 1853
American Swedish Historical Museum,
Philadelphia

124　(page 117)
Fredrika Bremer
Attributed to Mathew B. Brady, circa
1822–1896
Photograph, circa 1849, from glass plate
negative
National Archives and Records Service,
Washington, D. C.

125
Poem, *To Fredrika Bremer*
James Greenleaf Whittier
In *National Era,* Washington, D.C., Novem-
ber 15, 1849, page 2
Library of Congress

126　(pages 118 and 120)
*Fredrika Bremer's sketchbook with drawings
made in Denmark and America (including
portraits of Ralph Waldo Emerson and Julia
Ward Howe)*
Fredrika-Bremer-Association, Stockholm,
Sweden

127
Revival Meeting
Jeremiah Paul, ?–1820

Oil on panel, date unknown
19 x 24
Ira Spanierman Inc., New York

128
Fredrika Bremer's copy of A. Wiborg's
Carta Ofver, *1824 edition*
American Swedish Historical Museum,
Philadelphia

129
*Fredrika Bremer's carpetbag used during her
American visit*
American Swedish Historical Museum,
Philadelphia

130　(page 124)
Louis Kossuth, 1802–1894
Walter G. Gould, 1829–1893
Oil on canvas, 1851
$31\frac{7}{8}$ x $25\frac{1}{4}$
The Hungarian Reformed Federation of
America, Washington, D.C.; on long-term
loan from The Historical Society of
Pennsylvania

131　(page 127)
*Kossuth Attended By The Spirits of Freedom
and History and the Guardian Genius of
Hungary, with his Own Good Angel Calmly
Bearing him Through Space to America*
Unidentified artist
Wood engraving, in *Gleason's Pictorial
Drawing Room Companion,* December 27,
1851
9 x $8\frac{3}{4}$
The Hungarian Reformed Federation of
America, Washington, D.C.

132
Grand Reception of Kossuth
Nathaniel Currier, 1813–1888
Lithograph, 1851
$8\frac{1}{8}$ x $12\frac{1}{8}$
Inscribed: *"Lith. & Pub. by N. Currier, 152
Nassau St. Cor. of Spruce N. Y./Entered Ac-
cording to Act of Congress in the year 1851 by
N. Currier, in the Clerk's Office of the District
Court of the Southern District of N. Y./
GRAND RECEPTION OF KOSSUTH,/"The
Champion of Hungarian Independence" At
The City Hall, New York, December 6th 1851./
GROSSER EMPFANG KOSSUTH'S, "Der
Kæmpfer Für Ungarn's Unabhængigkeit"
Bey Dem Stadt Haus, New York, December 6
ten 1851."*
Museum of the City of New York

133　(page 131)
Governor Kossuth Welcome to Massachusetts
Unidentified artist

Wood engraving, *Gleason's Pictorial Drawing Room Companion*, May 15, 1852
$8\frac{1}{4} \times 9\frac{1}{4}$
The Hungarian Reformed Federation of America, Washington, D. C.

134 (page 130)
Hungarian Fund Dollar, New York, 2 February 1852
The Hungarian Reformed Federation of America, Washington, D.C.
"Kossuth Fund dollars," printed in 1, 5, 10, 20, and 100-dollar denominations, were bonds issued to generate financial support for Hungary's cause.

135
Louis Kossuth
FREDERICK DE BOURG RICHARDS, active in New York 1844–1845 and in Philadelphia 1848–1866
Daguerreotype, circa 1851–1852
Chicago Historical Society, Charles F. Gunther Collection

136
Kossuth Calabash-type flask
The Corning Museum of Glass, Corning, New York

137
Kossuth's March in Hungary or Remembrance of the Years, 1848 and 1849
Arranged for the piano by Gustave Blessner
Sheet music, published by Gouenhoven, Swill & Co., 1852
American Antiquarian Society

---

138 (page 134)
The Japanese Ambassadors at the Washington Navy Yard
Attributed to MATHEW B. BRADY, 1823–1896
Photograph, 24 May 1860
National Archives and Records Service, Washington, D.C.

139
The Japanese Embassy And Their Attendants
Wood engraving after photograph by MATHEW BRADY, in *Harper's Weekly*, June 23, 1860
$8\frac{3}{4} \times 13\frac{1}{2}$
National Portrait Gallery, Smithsonian Institution

140
United States–Japanese treaty of 1858 (Exchange Copy)
Records of the Department of State, National Archives, Washington, D.C.

141 (page 158)
America's first ruler, George Washington
Unidentified artist
Wood block in a nineteenth-century Japanese history book
$6\frac{3}{16} \times 4\frac{1}{8}$
Lee Houchins

142
An American Family
YOSHI FUJI
Woodblock print
$14\frac{3}{8} \times 9\frac{3}{4}$
William S. Lieberman

143
Kanrin Maru, the ship which escorted some members of the Japanese Delegation to the United States
YUJIRO SUZUDO, dates unknown
Watercolor on paper
18 x 24 (approximate)
George Mercer Brooke, Jr.

144
Ma'en Gannen Kenbei Shisetsu Zuroku, album of the First Japanese Mission's visit to the United States
Keio University Library and Information Center, Tokyo

145
The Landing of the Japanese Embassy, with the treaty in a box, at the Navy Yard, Washington
Wood engraving, in *Harper's Weekly*, May 26, 1860
$9 \times 13\frac{3}{4}$
National Portrait Gallery, Smithsonian Institution

146
Our Japanese Visitor "Tommy" Among the Ladies of Washington
Wood engraving, in *Harper's Weekly*, June 2, 1860
5 x 7
National Portrait Gallery, Smithsonian Institution

147 (page 142)
Ball given by the City of New York to the Japanese Embassy at the Metropolitan Hotel, June 25, 1860
Wood engraving, in *Harper's Weekly*, June 30, 1860
$14 \times 20\frac{1}{4}$
National Portrait Gallery, Smithsonian Institution

148
Harriet Lane Johnston, 1833–1903
JOHN HENRY BROWN, 1818–1891

Watercolor on ivory, 1878
$4\frac{3}{4} \times 3\frac{1}{2}$
National Collection of Fine Arts, Smithsonian Institution

149
*Fan with waka (short Japanese poem) written
by Masaoki Shimmi, member of the First
Japanese Mission, while in the United States*
KIYOSHI MORITA

150   (page 144)
*Yukichi Fukuzawa photographed with an
American girl (thought to be the photographer's
daughter) in San Francisco*
Reproduced from *The Autobiography of
Yukichi Fukuzawa*, New York and London,
1966, facing page 120

151
*The coming and going of steam trains in
America (scene of an American steam boat with
men and women in front)*
YOSHIKAZU
Woodblock print, date unknown
$14\frac{5}{8} \times 9\frac{3}{4}$ (three panels)
William S. Lieberman

152   (page 146)
William Howard Russell, 1820–1907
Unidentified artist, after unlocated drawing
by Theodore Russell Davis, 1840–1894
Wood engraving, in *Harper's Weekly,* June
22, 1861
$9\frac{3}{8} \times 5\frac{7}{8}$
National Portrait Gallery, Smithsonian
Institution

153
My Diary North and South
WILLIAM H. RUSSELL, London, 1863
Library of Congress
*This book was first published in Boston in
1861 as* The Civil War in America.

154   (page 150)
*The first Flag of Independence raised in the
South, by the Citizens of Savannah, Georgia,
November 8th, 1860*
R. H. HOWELL, dates unknown, after a
drawing by HENRY CLEENEWERCK, active
in Paris 1869–1878
Lithograph, 1860
Inscribed: "*Drawn by Henry Cleenewerck,
Savannah, Ga/Lithographed by R.H. Howell
Savannah, Ga/The first Flag of Independence
raised/in the South, by the citizens of Savannah,
Ga. November 8th 1860./Dedicated to the
Morning News.*" Signed: "*Presented by Jos
Prendergast/to John Devereux Jr Nov 1860/*

*J.P. helped to make the above/Banner and
himself painted/the lettering thereon.*"
Library of Congress, Division of Prints and
Photographs

155
Worship Of The North
ADALBERT JOHN VOLCK, 1828–1912
Pen over pencil, date unknown
$7\frac{3}{4} \times 10\frac{3}{16}$
M. & M. Karolik Collection, Museum of
Fine Arts, Boston

156   (page 151)
Jefferson Davis, 1808–1889
MATHEW B. BRADY, circa 1823–1896
Photograph, circa 1861
From original in Library of Congress, Brady-
Handy Collection

157
*Fancy Portrait of the Virginia Gentleman who
Objected to the Occupation of Alexandria by
Ellsworth's Zouaves, Because They are not
"First Families."*
Wood engraving, in *The New York Illustrated
News*, June 15, 1861
The University of Chicago Library

158
*Panic On The Road Between Bull Run and
Centreville*
Unidentified artist
Pencil, probably July 21, 1861
$9\frac{7}{8} \times 13\frac{1}{4}$ (sheet)
M. & M. Karolik Collection, Museum of
Fine Arts, Boston

159
15 Miles to Bull Run
Wood engraving, in *New York Illustrated
News*, Sept. 2, 1861
Reproduced in *American Heritage*, June 1962

160   (page 153)
Edward Dicey, 1832–1911
Carte-de-visite of an unlocated drawing by
DÉSIRÉ-FRANÇOIS LAUGÉE, 1823–1896;
inscribed to Madame Dicey and signed D.
Laugée
The Mansell Collection

161   (page 152)
Abraham Lincoln, 1809–1864
ALEXANDER GARDINER, 1821–1882
Photograph, February 24, 1861
From original in Library of Congress

162
Six Months in the Federal States
by EDWARD DICEY, London, 1863
Library of Congress

163
Southern Chivalry—Argument vs. Clubs
JOHN L. MAGEE, active in New York 1844–
1847 and in Philadelphia 1850–1867
Lithograph, 1856
$14\frac{1}{2}$ x $21\frac{1}{2}$
Prints Division, The New York Public
Library, Astor, Lenox and Tilden Found-
ations

164   (page 155)
Federal Encampment on the Pamunkey River,
Virginia
J. F. GIBSON
Photograph, May 1862
From original in Library of Congress, Divi-
sion of Prints and Photographs

165   (page 156)
Washington, D.C. in April, 1865
Photograph
Library of Congress, Division of Prints and
Photographs
The view is toward the Capitol from the
southwest.

166   (page 158)
Edward Wilmot Blyden, 1832–1912
RUFUS ANSON, active 1851–1867
Daguerreotype, New York, circa 1852
$3\frac{1}{8}$ x $2\frac{3}{4}$
Library of Congress, Division of Prints and
Photographs

167
Rutgers College in New Brunswick, N. Jersey
NAPOLEON SARONY, 1821–1896 and HENRY
B. MAJOR, active 1844–1854
Lithograph, New York, 1849
$14\frac{3}{4}$ x $23\frac{3}{4}$
Published by the General Synod's Sabbath
School Union of the Reformed Protestant
Dutch Church, 1849
The New Jersey Historical Society

168   (page 160)
Mansion-House of President Roberts, Mon-
rovia, Liberia
AUGUST HOEN, circa 1825–?
Lithograph, 1847
$8\frac{3}{4}$ x $12\frac{5}{8}$
Library of Congress, Division of Prints and
Photographs

169
A Voice From Bleeding Africa, On Behalf of
Her Exiled Children
EDWARD W. BLYDEN, Liberia, 1856
Presbyterian Historical Society, Philadelphia

170   (page 161)
Certificate of freedom for Benjamin Hasell,
Wilmington, North Carolina, October 6, 1853
David W. Hazel

171
Alabama Hall, the first dormitory for women
to be built on the grounds of Tuskegee State
Normal School, Alabama
Photograph, 1883
From the original in Tuskegee Institute,
Alabama

172
Students on the campus of Howard University,
Washington. D.C.
J. W. & J. S. MOULTON
Stereograph, circa 1870
Moorland-Spingarn Research Center,
Howard University

173
Hampton Institute, Richmond
Photograph, circa 1880s
$7\frac{1}{4}$ x $9\frac{3}{8}$
Library of Congress, Division of Prints and
Photographs

174
Letter, Edward W. Blyden to James C. Braman,
December 27, 1882, from the Colonization
Society Office, Washington, D. C., listing the
southern schools he had visited
Massachusetts Historical Society; Papers of
the Trustees of Donations for Liberian
Education

175   (page 163)
Old Potter Palmer Mansion, living room, show-
ing paintings
Photograph, circa 1895
The Art Institute of Chicago Library

176   (page 165)
Edward Wilmot Blyden
Photograph, 1894, reproduced in Sir Hany
Johnston's *Liberia*
Photograph courtesy Nigerian Museum

177   (page 168)
Georges Clemenceau, 1841–1919
AUGUSTE RODIN, 1840–1917
Bronze, 1911
Height $19\frac{1}{2}$
Mr. and Mrs. Pierre B. Clemenceau, on ex-
tended loan to New Orleans Museum of Art

178   (page 170)
*Georges Clemenceau about the time he came to
the United States*
Photograph in *Clemenceau-American Reconstruction 1865 -1870, 1928*

179
*Broadway and Duane Streets, Greenwich
Village*
Photograph, circa 1870
From original in The New-York Historical
Society

180   (page 170)
*The Catharine Aiken School in Stamford,
Connecticut*
Photograph, circa 1860
$11\frac{1}{4} \times 15\frac{1}{2}$
The Stamford Historical Society, Inc.

181
Mary Plummer Clemenceau
Photograph, date unknown, in *The Mentor*,
October 1928, page 17

182   (page 172)
Andrew Johnson with the Donkey
THOMAS NAST, 1840–1902
Pastel on paper, date unknown
$51\frac{1}{2} \times 40\frac{1}{2}$
National Portrait Gallery, Smithsonian
Institution
*"King Andy" is confronted here with the
whimsical donkey scarecrow, which Nast
used to symbolize President Grant's alleged
"Caesarism."*

183   (page 172)
Thaddeus Stevens being carried into the Capitol
Unidentified artist
Wood engraving, in *Frank Leslie's Illustrated
Newspaper*, March 28, 1868
From the original in Library of Congress

184
Thaddeus Stevens, 1792–1868
Carte-de-visite, date unknown, autographed
by Stevens
$3\frac{3}{8} \times 2\frac{1}{8}$
National Portrait Gallery, Smithsonian
Institution

185
The Lost Bet
WINTERS ART COMPANY after a painting by
JOSEPH KLIR, dates unknown
Lithograph, 1892
$19\frac{3}{4} \times 29\frac{3}{8}$
Chicago Historical Society
*A scene in Chicago after the Grover Cleveland
victory over Benjamin Harrison in 1892.
Having lost his bet, a Republican pulls his
Democratic friend through the city in a cart.*

186
Taking the Oath and Drawing Rations
JOHN ROGERS, 1829–1904
Plaster, painted, 1865
Height 23
Albany Institute of History and Art, Ben-
jamin Walworth Arnold Collection
*A southern woman swears an oath of allegiance
to the United States in order to draw food for
her family.*

187
*The "Big Four" at the Paris Peace Conference:
David Lloyd George of Great Britain, Vittorio E.
Orlando of Italy, Georges Clemenceau of
France, and Woodrow Wilson of the United
States*
Photograph, 1919
From the original in National Archives and
Records Service, Washington, D.C.

---

188   (page 176)
Henryk Sienkiewicz, 1846–1916
KAZIMIERZ POCHWALSKI, 1855–1940
Oil on canvas, Krakow, 1890
$47\frac{1}{4} \times 31\frac{1}{2}$
Muzeum Henryka Sienkiewicza, Oblegorku,
Poland

---

189   (page 179)
Helena Modjeska, 1840–1909
Photograph, 1897
From original in Library of Congress, Divi-
sion of Prints and Photographs

190
Bird's Eye View of Anaheim
E. S. GLOVER, dates unknown
Lithograph, circa 1878
$13\frac{1}{2} \times 24$
Inscribed: *"Drawn by E. S. Glover, Los Angeles,
Cal./A.L. Bancroft & Co., Lith., San Francisco./
Bird's Eye View of ANAHEIM, Los Angeles
Co., Cal./Looking North to The Sierra Madre
Mountains."* [*plus locations*]
Bowers Museum, Santa Ana, California

191
Ten Minutes for Refreshment
Unidentified artist
Chromolithograph, 1886, published by The
Great American Tea Co., New York
$21\frac{3}{4} \times 31\frac{7}{8}$
Chicago Historical Society
*This is a sardonic view of the railway age and
the "quick lunch."*

192   (page 181)
*Chicago Fire, view north from about Congress
Street between Wabash Avenue and Michigan,
of the ruins*

Landy of Cincinnati
Photograph, 1871
$14\frac{3}{4}$ x $18\frac{1}{2}$
Chicago Historical Society

193
State Street, Looking North from Madison, Chicago
Photograph, circa 1888
From original in the Chicago Historical Society
The corner of Madison and State Streets in Chicago was publicized as the world's busiest corner.

194 (page 182)
The Chinese Question
THOMAS NAST, 1840–1902
Wood engraving in *Harper's Weekly*, February 18, 1871
13 x 9
National Portrait Gallery, Smithsonian Institution

195
Poles in the streets of Stevens Point, Wisconsin
Photograph, circa 1890
From original in State Historical Society of Wisconsin, Madison

196 (page 184)
A Polish ecclesiastical goods store on Milwaukee Avenue, Chicago
Photograph, circa 1872
From original in Polish Roman Catholic Union, Museums and Archives, Chicago
Owner Stanislaw Slominski stands in front of his store, one of the earliest Polish business ventures in Chicago.

197
Charles Boissevain, 1842–1927
WILLEM WITSEN, 1860–1923
Oil on canvas, 1916
$25\frac{1}{2}$ x $22\frac{1}{2}$
NRC Handelsblad, Rotterdam, The Netherlands

198
Van't Noorden naar't Zuiden, Schetsen en Indrukken van de Vereenigde Staten Van Noord-Amerika
CHARLES BOISSEVAIN, Haarlem, 1882
Yale University Library

199
Recherches Philosophiques sur les Américains ou Mémoires intéressants pour servir à l'histoire de l'espèce humaine . . .
CORNELIUS DE PAUW, Berlin, 1770
Duke University Library

200 (page 191)
The Rozengract decorated with flags, Amsterdam, 17 October 1889
J. M. A. RIEKE, 1851–1899
Watercolor, October 1889
Size not available
Gemeentearchief, Amsterdam

201
Suggestions For The Public Supply of Steam For Heating, For Power, Cooking, Extinguishing Fires, Melting Snow & c.
EDWARD A. SARGENT, active in New York, 1872–1887
Watercolor, heightened with white, circa 1872
11 x $14\frac{9}{16}$
M. & M. Karolik Collection, Museum of Fine Arts, Boston

202
John Pierpont Morgan, 1837–1913
ADRIAN LAMB, 1901– , after the 1888 portrait by FRANK HOLL, 1845–1888
Oil on canvas, 1966
50 x $40\frac{1}{4}$
National Portrait Gallery, Smithsonian Institution

203 (page 192)
The Kings of Wall Street
BUEK and LINDNER
Chromolithograph, 1882, published by Root and Tinker
15 x 21
National Portrait Gallery, Smithsonian Institution
The subjects are: Cyrus W. Field, Russell Sage, Rufus Hatch, Jay Gould, Sidney Dillon, D.O. Mills, William A. Vanderbilt, August Belmont, George W. Ballou, and James R. Keene. Cornelius Vanderbilt's portrait hangs over the mantel.

204 (page 196)
Bjørnstjerne Bjørnson, 1832–1910
ERIK THEODOR WERENSKIOLD, 1855–1938
Oil on canvas, 1885
$57\frac{1}{2}$ x 45
Nasjonalgalleriet, Oslo, Norway

205 (page 198)
Bjørnson in America
Unidentified artist
Cartoon, in *Krydseren*, September 1880
Reproduced in *Aftenposten*, December 3, 1832

206 (page 200)
View of Worcester, Mass.
ROBERT COOK(E), active in Boston in the

1830s and 1840s, after PETER ANDERSON, dates unknown
Lithograph, hand colored, circa 1837–1839
$17\frac{7}{8} \times 27\frac{1}{8}$
Inscribed: "P. Anderson del./On stone by R. Cooke./T. Moore's Lithography Boston./View of Worcester, Mass./Taken From Union Hill."
American Antiquarian Society

207
Bird's Eye View Of The Great New York And Brooklyn Bridge
A. MAJOR, Publisher, New York
Lithograph, colored, 1883
$15\frac{1}{4} \times 24\frac{1}{2}$
Inscribed: "A. Major, Publisher, 330 Pearl St., N.Y./Bird's Eye View Of The Great New York And Brooklyn Bridge,/And Grand Display Of Fire Works On Opening Night./[Pyrotechnics Furnished By Detwiller & Street, New York.]/Commenced January 3, 1870 Finished May 24, 1883."
Museum of the City of New York, The J. Clarence Davies Collection

208
Representative Women
L. SCHAMER, dates unknown
Lithograph, Boston, date unknown
$19\frac{5}{8} \times 16\frac{3}{4}$
American Antiquarian Society

209
Advertisement for a lecture by Bjørnson at McVickers Theater, Milwaukee, Wisconsin, in Norden, a Norwegian-language newspaper, December 8, 1880
From original in Luther College, Decorah, Iowa

210
I. Ellefson's early home, Hendricks, Minnesota
Photograph, circa 1880
From original in Bygdelag Collection, Minnesota Historical Society, St. Paul

211
"Norsk Hotel," the Decorah, Iowa, home of a Norwegian settler which served as a hotel for fellow Norwegians going west.
Photograph, circa 1870
$4\frac{5}{8} \times 7\frac{1}{2}$
Vesterheim, Norwegian-American Museum, Decorah, Iowa

212
Address signed by 132 Norwegians welcoming Bjørnson to Albert Lea, Minnesota, in 1880
Universitetsbiblioteket i Oslo, The Royal University Library, Oslo, Norway

213
Letter, Bjørnson to the Norwegian newspaper Dagbladet, November 2, 1880
Universitetsbiblioteket i Oslo, The Royal University Library, Oslo, Norway

214
Bjørnstjerne Bjørnson
NOTMAN PHOTOGRAPHIC COMPANY, Boston
Photograph, 1880
$5\frac{1}{2} \times 4\frac{1}{8}$
Einar Haugen
This publicity photograph was dedicated to Professor R. B. Anderson, manager of his lecture tour in the United States. It is inscribed on reverse "Dit mishandlede objeket B.B." "your mistreated object B.B."

---

215 (page 208)
James Bryce, 1838–1922
SIR WILLIAM ORPEN, 1878–1931
Oil on canvas, date unknown
36 x 34
Aberdeen Art Gallery, Scotland

216
Excerpt from the manuscript of American Commonwealth by James Bryce, 1888
Department of Western Manuscripts, Bodleian Library, Oxford University

217 (page 211)
The Tammany King-dom/The Power Behind the Throne. He Cannot Call His Soul His Own.
THOMAS NAST, 1840–1902
Wood engraving in Harper's Weekly, October 29, 1870
Size not available
National Portrait Gallery, Smithsonian Institution

218 (page 212)
The main streets of Hastings, Nebraska, and of Atchison and Ottawa, Kansas
F. J. BANDHOLTS
Photographs, circa 1909
Library of Congress, Division of Prints and Photographs

219 (page 214)
Railroad car conference of Union Pacific Officials
ANDREW J. RUSSELL, dates unknown
Photograph, from glass plate negative, 1868
The Oakland Museum, California

220 (page 215)
A Possible Encounter Between Ambassador Bryce and President Theodore Roosevelt
JOHN T. McCUTCHEON, dates unknown
Pen drawing, date unknown
20 x $14\frac{1}{2}$
Edmund S. Ions

221 (page 218)
José Martí, 1833–1895
HERMAN NORRMAN, 1864–1906
Oil on canvas, 1890/91, New York
$16\frac{5}{16} \times 15\frac{3}{8}$
From original in Museo Nacional "José
Martí," Havana, Cuba
Reproduced in Arturo R. de Carricarte's
Iconografiá del Apostol Martí, *1925*

222
Norteamericanos
Gonzalo de Quesada, Editor, Havana, 1909
Library of Congress

223 (page 221)
*José Martí with the Juan Peoli family on an
outing at Sandy Hill on the Hudson River*
Photograph, 1888
From the original in the collection of José de
Onís

224 (page 222)
*The Unveiling of the Statue of Liberty En-
lightening the World*
EDWARD MORAN, 1829–1901
Oil on canvas, 1886
88 x 72
Katherine Hellman

225 (page 225)
*Coney Island Beach at Sea Beach Walk (W. 10th
street) as seen from the old iron pier*
Photograph, 1885
From the original in the Francis K. Moore
Collection of Coney Island

226 (page 226)
*The opening of the Cherokee Outlet, Oklahoma
territory, September 16, 1893*
Photograph, 1893
From the original in Oklahoma Historical
Society, Oklahoma City

227 (page 224)
James G. Blaine, 1830–1893
GEORGE P. A. HEALY, 1813–1894
Oil on canvas, 1884
$30 \times 25\frac{1}{2}$
The Newberry Library, Chicago

228 (page 227)
"Well, I Hardly Know Which To Take First!"
"BOZ" (MORGAN J. SWEENEY), dates
unknown
Cartoon, In Boston *Globe*, May 28, 1898
Library of Congress, Division of Prints and
Photographs
*McKinley is the waiter in a restaurant whose
bill of fare is "Cuba Steak," "Porto Rico Pig,"
and "Sandwich Islands."*

229 (page 228)
Antonín Dvořák, 1841–1904
MAX ŠVABINSKÝ, 1873–1962
Drawing, date unknown
$34\frac{5}{8} \times 27\frac{3}{16}$
Muzeum Antonína Dvořáka, Prague,
Czechoslovakia

230 (page 231)
*Dvořák family shortly after their arrival in the
United States*
Photograph, circa 1892
Muzeum Antonína Dvořáka, Prague,
Czechoslovakia

231 (page 232)
Spillville, Iowa, church and school
Photograph, in OTAKAR ŠOUREK'S *Antonín
Dvořák: Letters and Reminiscences,* Prague,
1954

232 (page 233)
*Antonín Dvořák conducting at the Chicago
World Fair*
E. V. NADHERNÝ, dates unknown
Watercolor on paper, 1893
Muzeum Antonína Dvořáka, Prague,
Czechoslovakia

233 (page 236)
Manuscript of "From the New World"
Symphony No. 9 in E Minor, Opus 95
Heirs of Antonín Dvořák

234
*Silver wreath presented to Dvořák by the
Czech citizens of New York City*
Muzeum Antonína Dvořáka, Prague,
Czechoslovakia

235 (page 238)
*Swami Vivekananda (Narendranatha Dutta),
1863–1902*
Goes Lithographic Co.
Lithographic poster, Chicago, September,
1893
28 x 20
Inscribed: *Swami Vivekananda/The Hindoo
Monk of India [autograph]*
Vedanta Society of Northern California and
Vedanta Society, Berkeley, California

236
*Swami Vivekananda as a delegate to the Par-
liament of Religions*
Photograph, in *Neely's History of the Parliament of Religions and Religious Congresses
at the World's Columbian Exposition,* Chicago,
1893
Library of Congress

237
*Swami Vivekananda picnicing with friends,
South Pasadena, California*
Photograph, 1900
Courtesy Vedanta Society of Southern
California

238   (page 242)
Durga Mahishasuramardini
Unidentified artist
Gray-black pot stone, 12th century A.D.,
Mysore, India, possibly Halebid
Height 34
Los Angeles County Museum of Art

239
Religious Vanity Fair
JOSEPH KEPPLER, 1838–1894
Chromolithograph, *Puck,* October 22, 1879
12 x 18$\frac{1}{2}$
Enoch Pratt Free Library, Baltimore

240   (page 243)
If You Want To Be A Yogi . . .
Cartoon, in New York *Herald,* March 17,
1898
From original in The New-York Historical
Society

241
Playbill for a performance of My Friend from
India *at Hoyt's Theatre, New York, March
1897*
8 x 6
Theatre and Music Collection of the Museum
of the City of New York

242   (page 244)
*The "Vivekananda Cottage" at Thousand
Island Park, New York, where Swami Vive-
kananda lived and taught in the summer of
1895.*
Photograph, date unknown
Ramakrishna-Vivekananda Center, New
York

243   (page 248)
Giuseppe Giacosa, 1847–1906
Unidentified artist, "P.T."
Unlocated portrait, reproduced in *L'Illustra-
zione Italia,* Vol. XXVII, No. 6, 11 February
1900

244
Impressioni d'America
GIUSEPPE GIACOSA, Milano, 1908
Library of Congress

245   (page 250)
The Bowery at Night
W. LOUIS SONNTAG, JR. 1822–1900

Watercolor drawing, circa 1895
13 x 17$\frac{15}{16}$
Museum of the City of New York

246
*Italian Bread Peddlers on Mulberry Street,
New York*
Photograph
7$\frac{1}{4}$ x 9$\frac{1}{8}$
Detroit Collection, Library of Congress,
Division of Prints and Photographs

247   (page 252)
Immigrant workers
Photograph, circa 1900
Brown Brothers

248
Giacomo Puccini, 1858–1924
AIMÉE DUPONT, dates unknown
Photograph, New York, 1908
From original in Library of Congress,
Division of Prints and Photographs

249
Puccini with Giuseppe Giacosa and Luigi Illica
Photograph, date unknown
From original in Archivio Storico Ricordio,
Milan, Italy

250   (page 256)
*Geraldine Farrar 1882–1967 in the role of
Cio-Cio-San in Puccini's* Madame Butterfly,
with her child, Trouble
AIMÉE DUPONT, dates unknown
Photograph, 1908
4 x 5$\frac{7}{16}$
Library of Congress, Division of Prints and
Photographs

251
Libretto for The Girl of the Golden West
Printed by Ricordi & Co., 1910, and personally inscribed by Puccini and all members of
the cast, the conductor, and the director on
opening night.
Theatre and Music Collection of the Museum
of the City of New York

252
Hat worn by Caruso in the role of Dick Johnson
Metropolitan Opera Archives

253
Black wool bag thought to have been used in
The Girl of the Golden West
Metropolitan Opera Archives

254
*Enrico Caruso as Dick Johnson in the premiere
of Puccini's* The Girl of the Golden West
Photograph, 1911
8 x 5$\frac{3}{4}$

Library of Congress, Division of Prints and Photographs

255
The finale of Puccini's The Girl of the Golden West *as performed at the Metropolitan Opera House, 1910*
Mishkin Studio
Photograph, 1910
7 x 9
Theatre and Music Collection of the Museum of the City of New York
Enrico Caruso and Emmy Destinn are at right center. Pasquale Amato is at far right.

256   (page 260)
John Butler Yeats, 1839–1922
Self-portrait
Pencil on paper, 1919
Size not available
Inscribed: *"myself/seen through a/glass darkly/by J. B. Yeats/Oct. 1919"*
Professor William M. Murphy

257   (page 263)
John Quinn, 1870–1924
JOHN BUTLER YEATS, 1839–1922
Oil on canvas, 1908
$27\frac{7}{8}$ x $21\frac{7}{8}$
National Portrait Gallery, Smithsonian Institution

258
Artists' Evening
GEORGE BELLOWS, 1882–1924
Lithograph, 1916
19 x 15
Vassar College Art Gallery
Interior scene of Petitpas restaurant with John Butler Yeats among the assemblage

259   (page 266)
Dolly and John Sloan
JOHN BUTLER YEATS, 1839–1922
Pencil on paper, July 1910
$18\frac{3}{4}$ x $14\frac{1}{4}$
Delaware Art Museum, on permanent loan from Mrs. John Sloan

260
"The American Girl: An Irish View" by John Butler Yeats, in Harpers Weekly, *April 23, 1910*
Library of Congress

261   (page 267)
Letter, John Butler Yeats to John Quinn, 1 November 1908, with sketch of Yeats and Isadora Duncan walking down Broadway
Professor William M. Murphy

262
Isadora Duncan, 1878–1927
JOHN SLOAN, 1871–1951

Etching, 1951
National Portrait Gallery, Smithsonian Institution, Gift of Mrs. John Sloan

263   (page 268)
William Butler Yeats
JOHN BUTLER YEATS, 1839–1922
Oil on canvas, 1907
30 x 25
Professor William M. Murphy

264   (page 270)
Sholom Aleichem, 1859–1916
NUMA PATLAZHAN, 1888–?
Bronze, 1912
Height 19
Marie Waife-Goldberg (Sholom Aleichem's daughter)

265   (page 276)
Sholom Aleichem upon his arrival in New York's East Side
Lola [Leon Israel], dates unknown
Caricature, reproduced in *Der Kundes*, December 18, 1914

266
Excerpts from the manuscript of Sholom Aleichem's Mottel
Beth-Sholom Aleichem, Tel-Aviv, Israel

267   (page 274)
Four illustrations for Mottel
ILYA SCHOR, 1904–1961
Wood block prints, circa 1953
5 x 4
Resia Schor

268
Street scene in Satanov in the Ukraine
Photograph, circa 1910
Yivo Institute for Jewish Research, Inc., New York

269
Street in Zabludow, Belorussia
Photograph, 1916
Yivo Institute for Jewish Research, Inc., New York

270
Tenants on the steps of a tenement in New York's Lower East Side
Photograph, circa 1908
14 x 17
Library of Congress

271
Market Day on Hester Street
Photograph, date unknown
9 x 7
Library of Congress, Division of Prints and Photographs

272
Advertisement for Thomashefsky's People's
Theatre, New York, for the week of April 17,
1911
Yivo Institute for Jewish Research, Inc.,
New York

273 (page 280)
Liang Ch'i-ch'ao, 1873–1929
Photograph, circa 1913
$8\frac{5}{8} \times 7$
Hoover Institution on War, Revolution and
Peace, Stanford, California

274
Hsin ta lu yu chi
Liang Chi'i-ch'ao, 1917
Harvard-Yenching Library, Cambridge
First edition was in 1903

275
The Dowager Empress, Tz'u-hsi
Photograph, twentieth century
From the glass plate negative in the Freer
Gallery of Art, Washington, D. C.
The Dowager Empress is shown here with her
eunuchs, her ladies-in-waiting, and her dog,
Hai Lung ("sea otter").

276 (page 283)
Central Park—Winter
WILLIAM GLACKENS, 1870–1938
Oil on canvas, date unknown
25 x 30
The Metropolitan Museum of Art, George
A. Hearn Fund, 1921

277 (page 285)
"Joe" Ming's cook
J. P. BALL and SON
Photograph, Helena, Montana, 1893
$6\frac{1}{2} \times 4\frac{1}{4}$
Montana Historical Society, Helena

278
New York City Chinatown
Photograph, circa 1912
From original in Library of Congress,
Division of Prints and Photographs

279
Chinese parade, Los Angeles
Photograph, circa 1900
From glass plate negative in History Divi-
sion, Natural History Museum of Los
Angeles County

280
"Big Chinaman Comes," in Walla Walla Daily
Union, *29 August 1903, page 3, column 1*
From original in Penrose Memorial Library,
Whitman College, Walla Walla, Washington

281 (page 294)
H. G. Wells, 1866–1946
JANE WELLS (his wife)
Photograph, 1895
From original in the University of Illinois
Library, Urbana-Champaign. Photograph
courtesy of the estate of H. G. Wells.

282
The Future in America
H. G. Wells, London, 1906
Library of Congress

283 (page 296)
Henry James in the New York studio of Alice
Boughton
ALICE BOUGHTON, (?–1943)
Photograph, 1906, reproduced in Harry T.
Moore's *Henry James,* New York, 1974

284
Copley Square, Boston
ARTHUR CLIFTON GOODWIN, 1866–1947
Oil on canvas, 1908
30 x 36
Museum of Fine Arts, Boston

285
Letter, Henry James to H. G. Wells, 8 November,
1906
Department of Western Manuscripts,
Bodleian Library, Oxford University

286 (page 299)
The War in the Air (illustration)
H. G. Wells, London, 1908
Wells Collection, University of Illinois
Library, Urbana-Champaign

287 (page 297)
Maxim Gorky, 1868–1936, with Maria
Federovna Andreyeva
Mishkin Studio
Photograph, New York, April 27, 1906
$5\frac{9}{16} \times 3\frac{7}{8}$
Library of Congress

288
Booker T. Washington, 1856–1915
Photograph, 1902
$13 \times 9\frac{1}{2}$
Library of Congress

289 (page 300)
Theodore Roosevelt, 1858–1919
Photograph, circa 1912
Courtesy of The National Museum of His-
tory and Technology, Smithsonian Institu-
tion, Division of Political History

291

Julian Ursyn Niemcewicz, 1758–1841
ANTONI BRODOWSKI, 1784–1832
Oil on linen, 1820
$30\frac{1}{4} \times 25\frac{1}{2}$
National Museum, Warsaw, Poland

292

Louis Philippe, 1773–1850
JAMES SHARPLES, circa 1751–1811
Pastel on paper, 1797
$9 \times 7\frac{1}{4}$ (sight)
Prince Charles Philippe d'Orléans Bourbon,
Duc de Nemours
*Louis Philippe was in exile in the United
States from 1797 to 1800.*

290

*François Alexandre Frederic duc de la
Rochefoucauld-Liancourt, 1747–1827*
ANTOINE-JEAN BARON GROS, 1771–1835
Oil on canvas, date unknown
Size not available
Duchesse Edmée de la Rochefoucauld

293

José Francisco, Abbé Correia de Serra, 1750–1823
REMBRANDT PEALE, 1778–1860
Oil on canvas, date unknown
$28\frac{1}{2}$ x $23\frac{3}{8}$
The Historical Society of Pennsylvania
Correia wears the ribbon and medal of the Portuguese Military Order of Christ, the principal diplomatic order of Portugal.

294

Michel Chevalier, 1806–1879
LÉON COGNIET, 1794–1880
Oil on canvas, hexagonal, date unknown
$31\frac{1}{2}$ x $31\frac{1}{8}$
Musée National du Château de Versailles

295   (page 202)
Halvdan Koht, 1873–1965
HENRIK INGVAR SØRENSON, 1882–1962
Oil on canvas, 1951–1952
$39\frac{3}{16}$ x $35\frac{7}{16}$
Sigmund and Aase Gruda Skard

296
Johannes V. Jensen, 1873–1950
VALDEMAR ANDERSEN, 1875–1928
Gouache, 1905
$23\frac{3}{4}$ x $19\frac{3}{8}$
Mrs. Ellen M. Jacobsen

297
Kahlil Gibran, 1883–1931, with Mary Haskell in the background
Self-portrait
Oil on canvas, 1911
22 x $18\frac{1}{4}$
Jean and Kahlil Gibran

298   (page 287)
Hu Shih, 1891–1962
MALVINA HOFFMAN, 1887–1966
Bronze, 1932
Height $22\frac{1}{4}$
Field Museum of Natural History, Chicago

Index of Artists

Following the artist's name, a number in roman type indicates the page where a work is illustrated. An entry number for the Checklist of the Exhibition appears in bold type.

Index

marriage, 7, 101, 109, 121–123, 244–245

Martí, José, 218–227; *portrait*, 218

Escenas norte Americanas and *Norte Americanos* (including articles on North America), 220, 223

Martineau, Harriet, xvi, xvii, 62–71, 80; *portrait*, 62

Autobiography, 66, 69

Demerara, 64

How to Observe, 67

Retrospect of Western Travel, 67

Society in America, 63, 67, 69

Massachusetts, 79–80, 131, 132

materialism, 16, 28, 43, 80, 145, 163, 166, 179, 245, 278, 288, 294

men, 36

Metropolitan Opera House, 253, 254, 255, 258

Gatti-Casazza, 255

Metternich, Prince, 25, 26, 126

Michigan

Saginaw Woods, 57

Michigan, University of, 111–112

Midwest, 198, 199, 209

Minnesota, 120, 199

Falls of St. Anthony, 209

Mississippi, 151–152

Mitre, Bartolomé, 223

Miyares, Carmita, 220

model, America as, 106, 126, 127, 129, 221, 285, 286, 291, 292, 300–301

Modjeska, Helena, 178; *portrait*, 179

Monta, Kiyoyuki, 142

Montana, 285

Montgomery, Alabama, 151

moral sense, 183–184, 190, 195, 206, 216, 267

Morgan, J. P., 284

Motley, John Lothrop, 147

Mount Vernon, 46, 132

Tomb of Washington, 47

Muragaki, Norimasa, Awaji-no-kami, 137, 139, 140

music, 36, 101, 228–237, 249, 253–259

N

La Nación, 220, 221, 223

The Nation, 209

National Conservatory of Music, 230, 231, 235

navigation, 96, 97

Nebraska

The main street of Hastings, Nebraska, 212

Netherlands compared with America, 187, 188, 190–191, 192, 193, 194

New Bedford, 94, 99

New England, 8–9, 79–80, 86, 94, 112, 117, 196, 198, 199, 201

New Jersey, 9

newness, 245, 247, 250–251, 269, 296

New Orleans, 110

St. Charles Exchange Hotel, 110

newspapers, 47, 86, 87, 91, 182, 190, 216

New York City, 15, 55, 87, 88, 91, 117, 127–129, 139, 141, 142, 155, 171, 178–179, 210, 220, 230, 232, 243, 250, 253, 262, 265, 266, 272–278, 282–283, 296, 298–299. *See also* Greenwich Village

Central Park—Winter, 283, 284

Grant's Tomb, 284

Hester Street, 276

New York, Park and Worth Streets, 88

Sholom Aleichem, 274

New York Herald, 129, 233, 235

New York State, 9, 210

Thousand Island Park, 244

New York *Sun*, 221, 227

New York Times, 210, 273

New York World, 272–273, 278

Norrman, Herman, 218

North, 147, 148, 151, 152, 154–155

Norway compared with America, 198, 203

Norwegian attitudes toward America, 197, 198

Norwegian immigrants, 195, 198

Norwegian settlers in Minnesota, 199

O

Oguri, Tadamasa, Bungo-no-Kami, 137, 143

Ohio, 28, 130–131, 132

Oklahoma

The Opening of the Cherokee Outlet, 226

Olmsted, Frederick Law, 283

opera, 249, 253–259

La Opinión Nacional, 223

opportunity, 263, 265, 269, 276

optimism, 181, 189, 193, 195, 210, 251, 263, 289

Oregon, 112

ostentation, 163, 185

Old Potter Palmer Mansion, 163

overstatement. *See* excess

P

Páez, José, 220

Pan American Congress, First, 226

Paterson, New Jersey, 298

de Pauw, Abbé Corneille, 188, 189

Peale, Rembrandt, 21

penal system, 18, 49, 54, 56, 65, 86, 101, 298

Vue de la Prison d'Auburn, 56

Pennsylvania, 9, 26

Peoli, Juan J., 220, 221

José Martí with the Peoli family, 221

perceptions of America, basis for, 117, 193, 201

Perry, Commodore, 102, 134

Petitpas boardinghouse, 265, 267

Yeats at Petitpas, 264

Philadelphia, xviii, 8, 15

Philadelphia Mint, 138

physical features, 249